TALES FROM THE RIVERBANK

TALES FROM THE RIVERBANK

The match by match story of
FULHAM FOOTBALL CLUB

Part 3
Seasons 1969–70 and 1970–71

MARTIN PLUMB

ASHWATER
PRESS

*Author **Martin Plumb** was born in Hammersmith and has been a regular at Craven Cottage since 1963. He was trained in accountancy, but subsequently spent over thirty years in I.T. consultancy, working with many leading software houses. He is a teacher of mathematics and a professional guitarist and keyboards player with a long career in music. He is a respected author and a devotee of heritage railways. He has been with his partner Jean for over 40 years, has three daughters, and lives in Ascot in Berkshire.*

© **Copyright Martin Plumb 2012**

First published in October 2012

The right of Martin Plumb to be identified as the author of this work has been asserted by him in accordance with the Copyright, Designs and Patent Act 1988.

Designed and published by Ashwater Press
68 Tranmere Road, Whitton, Twickenham, Middlesex, TW2 7JB

www.ashwaterpress.co.uk.

Printed and bound by Berforts Information Press, Eynsham, Oxfordshire, England

ISBN 978-0-9548938-5-9

Acknowledgments

So here we are in Riverbank 3, with the team flowing on like the Thames and rolling into the Seventies. Who would have thought it!

Thanks are given to the usual tight-knit crew who have seen this work come to fruition. As usual, to my wife Jean. I thank her for her understanding and patience whilst I disappeared for evenings on end writing.

Again, I would like to sincerely thank Bill Frith and his late wife Betty for the car trips home and away. The times in this book were at the heart of their assistance to me. Maybe none of this would have been written if it hadn't been for them.

A big thank you again to the representatives of all the major national newspaper groups who raised no objection to me extracting sentences from their match reports to be included in the book: Solo Syndication Limited, Express Syndication, NI Syndication Limited, Mirror Syndication International, IPC Media and the Fulham Chronicle.

Many thanks again to members of the British Library Newspapers in Colindale, especially to Vic and others at the library who took an interest in the work.

Similarly many thanks again must go to Anne and the helpful staff at the Hammersmith and Fulham archives. Thanks too must go to Fulham Football Club for permitting me to use extracts from the club's official programmes and handbooks.

Thank you again to David Lloyd and all at TOOFIF for actively supporting the *Riverbank* books. Also to the Fulham Supporters' Trust, and to the 'Friends of Fulham' and 'Hammy End' websites and all other websites who publicise and encourage the books.

Thank you indeed to all supporters who took the time to call, email or comment on the two previous books. I am grateful to them all. Following their suggestions, we have included more unusual, general and anecdotal pictures and words in this volume, which show what supporting Fulham is all about. I am always keen to be contacted by Fulham supporters with material, ideas or any errata. I am contactable via: *Martin_Plumb@talk21.com*.

Lastly thanks go to the 'master lensman', Ken Coton, for all of his hard work, his undying enthusiasm for the project and his all-round know-how in getting books like this published. Thanks to Ken also for access to his collection of Fulham pictures and for the usage of much new material. I still owe him a great deal, for all of his on and off the field support.

Every year we lose Fulham players and fans and celebrities, and it is important to have Fulham's history documented for those who come after us.

Martin Plumb
Ascot, September 2012

Picture Credits

Introduction

There have been many excellent books written about Fulham Football Club, most of them statistical or at a summary level, but the *Riverbank* series drills down to the lowest level. You know from the summaries, for example, that Fulham drew a match 3–3, but this will tell you nothing of the game's character. Did Fulham throw away a three-goal lead? Did they roar back from being three behind? Did they have the lead three times, each time to be pegged back? Or did the lead change hands several times throughout the game? The recollections in this third book will tell you.

The highs and the lows are charted, as well as the in-betweens. They focus on the incidents that changed the direction of matches and Fulham's future: the controversial penalties, the major injuries, the bizarre refereeing decisions, the woodwork, the dismissals and even the weather! It's a 'warts and all' account of the day-to-day life of Fulham Football Club, its players, managers, directors and supporters. It is a blow-by-blow account: the laughter and the tears, the joy and the sadness. Over one hundred Fulham matches are covered in this third book.

Although the writing is predominantly focussed on Fulham FC, it is just as much a statement about the 'soccer scene' of the late Sixties and early Seventies. The text pays particular attention to the Third Division table, and the fluctuating changes in fortune of the clubs that inhabited that division throughout those two seasons. It is written in a style taken from the Seventies, *exactly* as the national and local media saw and recorded it.

The book also utilises, where possible, terminology relevant to that time. All references to the *Second Division* are equivalent to the current (2012–13) *npower Championship,* and references to the *Third Division* are equivalent to the *npower League One.* The book refers to a time when just two points were awarded for a win instead of three. There were then, as now, still twenty-four teams in the Third Division. League positions were decided by goal average rather than goal difference. At this time only two teams were promoted from the Third Division, and only two teams were relegated from the Second Division each season. There were also no 'play off' matches; the champions and the runners-up from the Third Division were automatically promoted. Fulham's score is given first in each report. There are references to full backs, centre forwards and wingers, but very few references to the 'lone' striker, wingback, sweeper or the defensive midfielder sitting just in front of the back four!

The start of the Seventies saw more changes. A white ball was nearly always used, and television was increasingly widening the sport's appeal. Kits changed more frequently, but association football was essentially still a working man's game. Players tended to have long sideburns, long hair and moustaches.

Certainly football was still as physical in the Seventies as in the Sixties. Bookings and dismissals were on the increase, and the professional foul to prevent the other team scoring was accepted as the norm. As the game became increasingly professional, not losing became more important. Due to this, the game declined a little as a spectacle. Teams learned how to frustrate opponents and stifle attacking football. Passing back to the goalkeeper, playing the ball around the defence and time-wasting were also commonplace. Teams came to pack their defences away from home, hoping to grab a goal in just one or two break-outs during a game. Unfortunately it was frequently successful.

This book covers two seasons and begins in August 1969. Fulham, at seemingly rock bottom after two successive relegations, sell a couple of players and buy a couple, but with little cash available manager Bill Dodgin has little manoeuvring space. The team start fairly indifferently, and goals are again hard to come by. Frank Large and Joe Gilroy depart fairly quickly whilst Cliff Jones produces little form.

To counteract this, Fulham place Jimmy Conway on the right wing and fit-again Steve Earle into more of a central role. Les Barrett starts to regain his form, and the Conway-Earle-Barrett era is born. Fulham begin to score goals with ease, even though the defence is still rather shaky.

Things suddenly take off with a massive and totally unexpected eight-goal win at Halifax, and Fulham blast in sixteen goals in three games; then it seems to go wrong. Opposition teams begin to kick lumps out of the forwards and the goals dry up. Fulham slip down the league culminating in a humiliating first round FA Cup defeat by Fourth Division Exeter City. The fans begin to protest and chairman Tommy Trinder is under pressure.

After the New Year in 1970, Fulham reach a rock bottom stage with just two wins in eighteen games and they sit just a couple of places above the Third Division relegation zone. Even the great Johnny Haynes can't turn the tide and he plays his final ever match for Fulham in January. Could it actually be an unprecedented third successive relegation?

However, Vic Halom recovers from injury and returns to the side. It begins a momentum and Fulham's form and goalscoring returns. Win follows win, and the Whites shoot up the table. They produce a run of fifteen games unbeaten scoring freely, and close in on promotion only for 'reject' Malcolm Macdonald to return to the Cottage and score the Luton goal that ends the dream. Fulham, however, finish a creditable fourth. Earle and Conway top the goalscoring charts with just under fifty between them.

Even with this success, Fulham make just one close season signing, central defender Jimmy Dunne; it proves to be the missing link. In the 1970–71 season Fulham start another great run in the league, losing just one of their opening fifteen games. Also in this run, Fulham dispose of three higher division teams in the League Cup – Orient, Queens Park Rangers in front of over 30,000 and cup fighters Swindon Town. By mid-November they have lost just four of their last thirty-nine league games, and are runaway leaders. This is despite having Jimmy Conway missing with a nasty knee injury.

However, nothing is straightforward with Fulham. They produce a mid-season wobble and in seven days are knocked out of the League Cup and then the FA Cup, again in the first round; at one stage they suffer five successive league and cup defeats in a row. By the end of January, Fulham have dropped out of the promotion slots, and are lying a disappointing fourth.

From this point however, Conway returns and so does the sparkle. The goals begin to flow again, and Fulham lose just three of the next eighteen league games, which culminate in an historic win at Bradford City and promotion back to the Second Division. Fulham then need just a draw to secure the championship in their final game against rivals Preston in front of their own fans, but as usual their nerves get the better of them in the 'big one' and Preston sneak the win; a massively disappointing end to a great season. However, the major objective has been achieved, and a new youthful Fulham has been born.

This was the start of the Seventies – the true ***Tales from the Riverbank***. Those of you who witnessed the goals and the thrills, even though it was in the Third Division, would probably not need to debate chairman Tommy Trinder's interpretation of the time, 'You *lucky* people'!

READ ALL ABOUT IT!

Season 1969–70

- ☐ *The arrival of Terry Medwin.*
- ☐ *The shock departures of Malcolm Macdonald and John Ryan.*
- ☐ *Leeds United sending in their second team in the League Cup.*
- ☐ *The arrival of John Richardson.*
- ☐ *The Fulham goalkeeper walking out to become a security guard.*
- ☐ *Fulham down with a stomach bug at Bristol Rovers.*
- ☐ *It's Bill Dodgin (senior) versus Bill Dodgin (junior) at Eastville.*
- ☐ *Fulham go crazy with eight goals at Halifax Town.*
- ☐ *Sixteen goals in three league games.*
- ☐ *Fulham contemplating signing Alex Ferguson (Sir).*
- ☐ *Steve Earle hitting nine in four games – all away from home.*
- ☐ *Jimmy Conway – the penalty king.*
- ☐ *Vic Halom's knee injury.*
- ☐ *The Doncaster Rovers thugs come to town.*
- ☐ *Johnny Haynes getting the Fulham goalscoring record.*
- ☐ *The Luton Town floodlight failure.*
- ☐ *The Luton Town snowstorm farce.*
- ☐ *Supermac's revenge on Fulham at Kenilworth Road.*
- ☐ *Match abandoned at Rochdale.*
- ☐ *George Cohen's testimonial match.*
- ☐ *The first round FA Cup knock-out at Fourth Division Exeter City.*
- ☐ *The arrival of sergeant-major Malcolm Webster.*
- ☐ *George Cohen taking charge of the kids.*
- ☐ *The Bristol Rovers leaflet protest.*
- ☐ *Fulham scoring one of the goals of the season in a rare TV appearance.*
- ☐ *Stockport County turning up in luminous orange.*
- ☐ *Johnny Haynes' final Fulham game.*
- ☐ *Fulham's two wins in eighteen games, and morale at rock bottom.*
- ☐ *Vic Halom's goalscoring return.*
- ☐ *Fulham being hit by a second-half hat trick at Barnsley.*
- ☐ *Reading being hit for four at Elm Park.*
- ☐ *League leaders Brighton thrashed on the Cottage lake.*
- ☐ *Fifteen league games unbeaten.*
- ☐ *Luton Town and Supermac ending the Fulham promotion dreams.*
- ☐ *Fulham Youth victorious in Düsseldorf.*
- ☐ *Jimmy Conway and Steve Earle heading the goalscoring charts.*
- ☐ *Qualification for the forthcoming Watney Cup.*

READ ALL ABOUT IT!

Season 1970–71

- ☐ *The departure of Johnny Haynes and Cliff Jones.*
- ☐ *The arrival of Jimmy Dunne.*
- ☐ *Barry Lloyd being made captain at twenty-one.*
- ☐ *The Watney Cup thriller with Derby County.*
- ☐ *The kids' San Remo 'experience'.*
- ☐ *All five forwards scoring against Bradford City.*
- ☐ *Jimmy Conway's long-term injury.*
- ☐ *Rodney Marsh's first return to the Cottage.*
- ☐ *Queens Park Rangers being rattled out of the League Cup.*
- ☐ *Steve Earle targeting Halifax town again.*
- ☐ *Cup specialists Swindon Town becoming Fulham's next League Cup victims.*
- ☐ *The arrival of George Johnston.*
- ☐ *The fifteen game unbeaten run.*
- ☐ *Being blown off course at Torquay United.*
- ☐ *Stan Brown's testimonial match.*
- ☐ *Dad winning the FA Cup duel of the Dodgins.*
- ☐ *League Cup quarter-final heartache at Ashton Gate.*
- ☐ *Five defeats in a row, and the nerves begin to show.*
- ☐ *The Gillingham pantomime on ice.*
- ☐ *The controversial penalty defeat in the Villa Park cauldron.*
- ☐ *The departure of Dave Roberts.*
- ☐ *Rotherham United bruisers come to town.*
- ☐ *Floodlight flickering against Wrexham.*
- ☐ *Three goals in eight minutes at Gillingham.*
- ☐ *A champagne promotion party at Bradford City.*
- ☐ *The Preston North End letdown.*
- ☐ *The Riverside stand getting the go-ahead.*

SUBSCRIBERS

Grateful thanks are extended to the following who subscribed to this book in advance of publication. Their commitment and support is much appreciated by Martin and Ken.

Riccardo Rossi	Dennis Turner	Mike Lownsbrough
Chris Cox	John Ringrose	Tim Bronock
Barry Sklan	Alfred Bath	Trevor Elias
Keith Ridley	Derek Hicks	Alex, Andrea and Doug Martin
Allan Ross	Melvin Tenner	Richard Cunningham
James Goldthorpe	Michael Brame	Dave Wilson
Martin Goldthorpe	Gary Lewis	Michael John Brooks
R C Shore	Eric Mckenzie	Stephen Alambritis
Mick Roots	Paul Cooper	Graham McDermott
Carlo Roberto	Gary See	Derek Brewer
Martin Stern	Adrian Main	Jonathan Brewer
John Friend	Robert Fennell	Eric Sheppard
Graham Cook	Ralph Leech	Tim Rowley
David Wallis	Stephen Reisbach	Tony Camilleri
Anthony Ramos	Martyn White	David Sweiry
Nick Wood	Michael Craig	Christopher Wheeler
Alan Burge	Timothy Craig	Dr Neil Springate
David Hamilton	Julian Payne	Ed Holford
Pete and Gareth Mackay	Russell Potter	Diana Showan
Chris Newbold	Ted Cann and Ethan Cann	Clive Collard
Peter O'Donovan	Sue Maida	Ian Lee-Dolphin
Si and Harry Magee	John Mills	David Wyman
Alan & Liese Lawrence	Peter King	Lol Peacock
Dave Bird	Martin Chalet	John Clarke
Peter Jacobs	Mike Neale	Dave Roberts
P F Brown	Chris Shailer	Roy Searle
Norman Reynolds	David Pearce	Bill Frith
Harry Aidan Hance	Jim, Joe & Siobhan Dwyer	Barry Searle
Steve Pound MP	David Elliott	David Lloyd
Chris Conti	Peter L Smith	Bill Plummer
Keith Dumas	Liam Gain	Christoph Schmidt
Peter Donnison	David Daly	Frank Roche
Herbert Robinson	Joanna Plumb	Christopher McBrien
Bob Langford	David Page	Dominic McBrien
Tony Gilroy	John Worley	Kevin McBrien
John Thompsett	Keith Smith	Gerry Plumb
Peter Woodman	Barry Lloyd	Geoff Hill
Michael Wontner-Riches	Dave Bell	Alex Petrovic
John Page	Ian Taylor	John Walters
John C Evans	Dave Gale	Dave and Viv Salisbury

SUBSCRIBERS

Grateful thanks are extended to the following who subscribed to this book in advance of publication. Their commitment and support is much appreciated by Martin and Ken.

The Hale/O'Brady family
Eric Holman
Martin Beasley
Bob Sulatycki
Ms Rowena Jane Tompkins
Michael Heatley
Les Barrett
Donald Cook
Christopher Simon Payne
Clive Page
Malcolm Steel
Peter F Harris
Anthony Speed
Edward Bennett
John Galea
Chris Finn
Robert Heath
Valerie English
Mike Lawrence
Harold William Speed
Mark Wooding
Dave Gardner
Dominic Lang
Graham Hortop
Yvonne Haines
Steve Earle
Nick Boswood

John Shirley
John Ellison
Edward Bennett
Stan Brown
Roger Tye
Mick Petrovic
Fred Callaghan
Phil Cowan
Nick Johnson
Derek Jeffery
Vivien Hildrey
Lee Manning
Stella Fenwick
Jason Bowyer
Jim Woolley
David N Millard
Reg Houlton
Neddy, Kubi, Nadia, Rae & Vint
David John Lye
Roy Brown
Gerard Benedict Lyons
Philip Hayes
Mick Meyer
Steve Murrell
Alan Charles Faulkner
Les Strong
David MacDonald

Joe Orr
Teresa Catt
Geoff Brailey
Antony Collins
Greg Collins
Ray Kemp
James and Johnny Cook
George Phillips / Lance Phillips
Keith Evemy
Desmond Matthew Lynch
Peter Wilhelmsson, Sweden
Richard Codd
Chris Scott
John Hatton
Paul Hatton
Matthew Hatton
Dave Fitzwater
Joe Murchan
Ken Place
Peter Grinham
John Went
Alan Phelps
Brian Williams
Mark Newman
Stephen Kettle

The coat of arms of the former Borough of Fulham carried the motto PRO CIVIBUS ET CIVITATE *– For Citizen and State – and appeared on the front of Fulham FC programmes during the 1950s and part of the 60s. Over subsequent years it was changed and adapted, but retained the feature of the River Thames, which formed the boundary of the borough for approximately 3½ miles. The crossed swords and mitre were taken from the arms of the See of London, the borough's most ancient association with history. The ship represents the wintering of the Danes on Thames side in 879 (who thus missed the founding of Fulham Football Club by precisely 1,000 years!).*

IN REMEMBRANCE

John Norman Haynes
(The Maestro)
(1934 – 2005)

John Gilchrist
(1939 – 1991)

Frank Large
(1940 – 2003)

Alan Mansley
(1946 – 2001)

Re-setting the Scene

A council estate at the start of the Seventies

Following the stringent and prudent living of the mid-Sixties, things had changed. The era saw a new dawn and at last it seemed that the end of post-war austerity had finally arrived. There seemed to have been a major shift. Families appeared to have some disposable income for once in the new era of love and peace.

Families were offered the opportunity to buy their homes from the council, and for a number that meant a mortgage for the first time, even though many parents were approaching fifty. A number accepted, and all those identikit houses began to take on a character of their own with new porches, windows and doors.

Tiled and lino floors began to disappear and some children saw carpet in their home for the first time. Some houses had carpet upstairs as well, and it was pure luxury to draw your legs over the side of the bed in winter to feel something warm beneath your feet.

The coalman and chimney sweep began to go the way of the dinosaurs, as gas fires very quickly replaced coal, leaving the empty, black bunkers to the cobwebs and spiders. There was also an end to the choking paraffin heaters, as gas fires were now installed in halls as well, and the unthinkable – warmth upstairs – was almost possible. One or two houses actually had the ultimate – central heating.

To complement this new found luxury were the first 'gadgets': electric blankets, a Goblin Teasmaid for the morning cuppa, an electric toaster for instant breakfast, and a hostess trolley for those special party occasions. Adults no longer had radiograms but hi-fi systems with separate speakers, because stereo had arrived. Better furniture was available and affordable and G-Plan and teak were highly fashionable. It was a time when orange, brown and beige were fashionable colours. Also in vogue was beech Habitat furniture.

The disappearance of coal was felt on the railways as well; nearly all of the remaining steam locomotives were piled up in a scrap-yard in Barry in Wales awaiting the cutters. Beeching's work was almost done, and a huge percentage of the rail network had been dismantled and demolished, leaving many areas without stations. Steam had disappeared leaving the network with diesel and electric power.

Main lines and branch lines were all targeted, none being spared the axe, and even Brunel's beautiful designs and architecture were not immune from the diggers and bulldozers. Many ornate and sumptuous stations were destroyed, disappearing in clouds of rubble before disbelieving eyes. The 'manual' semaphore method of railway signalling was also being phased out, and as many went to MAS (Multiple Aspect Signalling) or coloured lights, along with electric points, this spelt the end of many Edwardian signal boxes that also crumbled in the dust. Also gone were the snaking freight trains, as much more haulage was being delivered by road instead, and many rail goods yards were left abandoned for nature to reclaim.

Car numbers began to rise rapidly; many of the estate's homes and gardens were modified where possible to include a garage, and where this was not possible, green areas on the estates were replaced with more garages. Cars were now not just the domain of the adult either; young people in their late teens and early twenties were taking tests, unthinkable a decade earlier, and were mobile for the first time. Popular models targeted were an ageing Morris Traveller, Ford Anglia, Ford Prefect or a Mk1 Cortina. Those who couldn't afford cars bought a Honda 50 moped, although these weren't allowed on motorways. Some bought old motor cycles – a Norton Dominator perhaps or a Norton 650 SS (Super Sport). Bicycles were starting to be left to rust leaning against flowery garden walls. In some ways it was good that people could drive as despite the demise of the rail network, public transport by bus was often uncomfortable, very unreliable and still expensive. The Routemaster bus never seemed to arrive, and then literally three arrived at once.

After the opening of the M1 to the north in 1959–60 and a decade of relative inaction, the explosion of motorways began in the early Seventies with the M4 to the west and Wales followed by the M3 south-west to the prettier parts of England. The unstoppable era of the motor car was here to stay.

Then there were the aircraft. In the early Seventies came the talk of a merger between British Overseas Airways Corporation (BOAC) and British European Airways (BEA), which ultimately materialised in the colours of British Airways. Even the first jets, the Boeing 707 and VC10 were now dated, and alongside the deafening roar of the Air France Caravelle came the arrival of a new aircraft – the stretch Boeing 747, the first Jumbo Jet, a long-haul, wide-body aircraft of significant capacity. Such were the advances that the initial Concorde airliners were also under construction. In a way it was a shame that the reassuring and peaceful droning of propeller aircraft you were lulled to sleep by was slowly vanishing: the Brittania, Viscount, Constellation and Stratocruiser. With the new found wealth some families were travelling abroad for the first time for 'exotic' holidays to places such as Majorca, Crete, Greece, Malta and Cyprus.

Even for students the world seemed to open up, and many would do up an old minibus and travel freely over to Corfu via Italy, sleeping rough on the warm sand at night. Others would hitch rides across to various locations in Europe, whilst others followed the 'hippy trail' to Iran, Pakistan and Afghanistan.

Sport had changed and England were world champions at football, and special stamps had been produced to commemorate them as winners. Hopes were high that they could retain the trophy in South America, and many considered that England had an ever better team this time around. In the 1970 World Cup there was actually analysis and debate during the matches for the first time. There was a panel chaired by Jimmy Hill, of course, with conflicting personalities such as flamboyant Manchester City coach Malcolm Allison, an eloquent Irish foil in Wolves' Derek Dougan, abrasive Scot Paddy Crerand of Manchester United and a younger footballer, Arsenal full back Bob McNab. These lively encounters were the forerunners of the Hansen and Lineker era that we have today. Even the cricket had improved. In 1971 Yorkshire's Ray Illingworth took a side to Australia which would result in a controversial marathon series and England regaining the Ashes.

Many other familiar sights and sounds were also disappearing alongside the chimney sweep such as the rag and bone man and the road sweeper, who was replaced by an automated council vehicle. The only timely reminder of home deliveries was the milkman and perhaps the Pools collector; a full perm 'eight from ten' treble chance (22½p stake for 45 lines) was still the nearest people were to winning a fortune before the National Lottery. Even the groceries were now rarely delivered; certainly not 'open all hours' and no longer a Granville on a bike. Alongside tinned food, most homes now had a refrigerator instead of just a cool larder and some were experiencing frozen food for the first time. Arising out of the earth following the expansion of Tesco came the first local supermarkets like Fine Fare. It was a revolution.

The first packet meals appeared as well, and the country began an attempt to experiment away from the British 'meat, spuds and two veg' diet of the Sixties towards exotic 'foreign' food like *Vesta* chow mein and *Vesta* beef curry, the first time the aroma of a curry had found its way into a British kitchen. Other new delights were items like *Findus* crispy pancakes and dishes like spaghetti bolognaise and paella, items that would probably have been unthinkable just five or so years before. The prawn cocktail and *Cadbury's Smash* instant mashed potato had arrived. Some Luddites (or persons of taste and discrimination) blatantly refused to embrace the 'foreign muck', but the revolution was taking place. To add to the sophistication, more people could now actually afford to drink *real* coffee, not the hideous, liquid chicory *Camp* version. To be even more cultured people actually starting drinking wine; Blue Nun, Pomagne and Mateus Rosé was the order of the day. For those who couldn't afford that, a whole new generation of 'brew your own' came out. A number of houses had airing cupboards that contained *Boots* home wine making kits, bubbling demijohns of red liquid that made everything smell of yeast and occasionally exploded.

Television had moved on with the death of the 405 line screen and the arrival of the 625 line screen. BBC2 had expanded since the mid-Sixties with much more to watch. The first colour TV sets for the really wealthy started to appear at his time. The colour sometimes appeared crude with bright strawberry red and lime green fluorescent hues but it was revolutionary, and sport in colour was something few would have believed possible a decade earlier. Most people watched television now, and the times of listening to *Saturday Club*, *Worker's Playtime* and *Parade of the Pops* were probably over before the shows were finally axed. With much more music on television, even listening to Radio Luxembourg had more or less fallen by the wayside, the signal finally fading out for the last time for many with the arrival of Capital Radio in the early Seventies. The Home Service, Light Programme and Third Programme had all been replaced by Radios 1 to 4.

Many boys in their late teens had ceased collecting American comics and turned instead to the football magazines now being produced in abundance – *Goal*, *Shoot* and *Jimmy Hill's Football Weekly* – the increasing sales reflecting the resurgence of the English game. Soon there would be 'real-time' sport on the radio as well with the emergence of LBC (London Broadcasting Corporation) in the early Seventies. This was local radio, and all the London clubs were reported, from Chelsea to Leyton Orient, with up to the minute action as it happened – 'live updates'. For the away matches you couldn't get to or afford it was wonderful; no more 'not knowing', and often the LBC report was far ahead of the television equivalent.

The way of the community on the council estate was changing, and communal events were becoming fewer. The Salvation Army didn't oompah on the local green any more, fewer children attended Sunday School, and being a Boy Scout wasn't really cool any more. Only very few people went carol singing around the streets at Christmas time and even bonfire nights were now becoming a thing of the past. Fireworks were expensive and some were classified as dangerous, and events were now limited to one huge communal bash watched from behind a 'safe distance' cordon at a venue miles away from where you lived. Even attendances at the Bingo at the scouts' hut started to diminish. As Bob Dylan said, 'Times they really were a-changin.'

Summer and winter holidays on the estate in the early Seventies

For the footballing lads, times had changed drastically in the last five years. Those at the grammar schools were mostly still in education having probably passed GCEs and then dreaded 'A' levels. A couple had gone on to university, almost unheard of a decade previously. Those at university had grants – yes, free education! – and most of them made it last. Some others were still studying in other formats, day release or full-time at local colleges like Twickenham Tech or Brooklands College where new innovative courses were beginning to open up: journalism, tourism, catering, sociology, business studies, engineering and the first computer science (IT) courses. Many from the secondary modern schools had started apprenticeships. Grammar schools and secondary modern schools were being replaced by a new initiative, the comprehensive school, that did not select by academic ability, but rather from a wide range of backgrounds across a catchment area.

For most of the students, the luxuries of a summer holiday still existed to a degree even though many worked at some stage during the holidays for extra cash. For those who hadn't gone into further education there was a culture shock of a job. Forty-eight weeks a year, getting up early, putting on a suit, catching public transport, having to pay a shilling a day in fares, being somewhere by nine and not getting home until 6.30; it was a real eye opener. Still, for those there was the reward of a real pay packet every Friday, a beige envelope you could rip open with real money in it, less of course tax, NHI (National Health Insurance as it was then) and graduated pension, then giving a lot of it to your mum – but for the first time ever, cash in your pocket. These lads weren't around during the week, many finding work in the burgeoning air freight businesses proliferating at Heathrow.

So many things were legal now and the lads had a new found freedom. From crude fumblings many had discovered, and been waylaid by, the opposite sex, who were demanding time and attention from them. Football and girls, a real dilemma and the first major dichotomy in a young man's life. Then of course there was the pub. The delights of pale ale, Double Diamond, Watney's Red Barrel and a massive take-home Watney's Party Seven if you could carry it, a staple diet for all the parties.

After leaving school some lads played football in ex-school sides on a Sunday, whilst others, perhaps the more physically able, joined Sunday league sides. This was probably the roughest era in which to join such sides, although, to be fair, a number of men in their forties played, and played fairly, happy just to enjoy the run out. However, quite a few others didn't play that way. These were often pub sides that played in the afternoon after a lunchtime session in the local. It was not uncommon to see players being ill on the side of the pitch before the match had even started. Injuries were common and with some of these alehouse sides, violence was never far away.

For the few left that didn't work in the holidays, two or three would go out for a kick-about – they were all that was left. The playing field remained green and silent over the holidays waiting for the next wave of boys to hit puberty and chase that youthful dream of becoming a professional footballer.

Sometimes the lads' paths only crossed on a chance meeting, maybe to or from work. If a casual match was arranged on a Sunday morning, some of us lasted just a few minutes, eyes bulging and cheeks red, sweat falling everywhere, all of us embarrassed about our fitness levels, the extra pounds and lack of ball control. Most of us asked each other how on earth we had managed to keep it up for hours when we were fourteen! There was just casual running, short passing, aimless lobbing and shooting (punts at goal), but little dribbling or heading for fear of further embarrassment.

For those of us students on holiday, summer holidays were spent swimming, although we were softies now, relying instead on heated indoor swimming pools. With a few pounds in the pocket some lads still went fishing; we could afford better tackle, and despite the Thames starting to become polluted, a fair day's fishing was still there to be had. Some with the extra money joined angling societies and started serious carp and tench fishing.

We were still outside when we could be, but our footpaths were now often privately owned. Barbed wire abounded, fishing stretches for miles were now marked STRICTLY PRIVATE, and hedgerows had disappeared alongside all the fascinating species of insects and butterflies devastated by insecticides all in the name of 'progress'.

When we couldn't be outside, it had to be admitted that our leisure pursuits were now more sedentary. Snooker had begun to take off in a big way, re-marketed after a long absence. The show *Pot Black* (a one-frame show!) was broadcast on BBC2 the only channel to have colour at the time, Ray Reardon and John Spencer began to tour doing local exhibition matches in clubs and working men's clubs taking on the local 'champion'. Being able to see such stars fuelled the interest of our young men, many joining clubs and playing regularly. Many of the local lads went to the Lucania club in Hounslow.

There was also ten-pin bowling usually at the Airport Bowl or at Tolworth Towers; there were often professional players at Tolworth so it was good to watch them. At these venues, even when not playing ten-pin, there was always a great selection of pinball machines to while away the time on.

Some of the working lads had copied their fathers and developed a taste for horse racing. Many could be found with a pencil behind the ear studying form and wasting their hard earned cash on a Yankee bet for the following day.

Cultural revolutions

Fashion and music had rivalled and sometimes overtaken football in some ways, and in the last five years both these areas had exploded in a variety of directions. Many young men realised that for work and socially, looking and smelling good was important. Initially your father's *Old Spice* was the only aroma available, now there was 'splash it on all over' *Brut, Hai Karate* and exciting new fragrances like Christian Dior's *Eau Sauvage*!

The availability of music was blossoming, and although vinyl still ruled the roost, a new medium was available: cassette tapes came into being, and for the first time it was possible to take portable cassette players around and hear your favourite music on foot or in your car. Universities and colleges could, through the SU (Student Union) entice famous name bands and it was possible to experience all sorts of new sounds. It was also the start of the era of music festivals like Woodstock, Glastonbury and the Isle of Wight.

It is difficult to know where to start to explain the expansion of music, suffice to say that the 'Mersey sound', so much the mainstay of the Sixties, had perished along with the Chicago rhythm and blues (real R & B) influences. However some of the bands who had started the revolution, for example The Stones and The Who were still going strong, but The Beatles had been torn apart and the bright flame of Hendrix had both flared and then gone out. A number of vastly different musical directions were emerging all at once, each possessing a distinctive sound and fashion of their own. Music was all over the television and radio; whispering Bob Harris would soon be guiding in the first *Old Grey Whistle Test* programmes and he and the late, great, John Peel would be championing the *Sounds of the Seventies*. During its heyday in the early 1970s *Top of the Pops* was attracting fifteen million viewers each week to its regular Thursday evening slot.

Amongst the college and university fraternities was the emergence of the British 'Heavy Rock' culture, black, deep, serious and leather, long hair, long sideburns and thick moustaches. Deep Purple, Black Sabbath, Free, an emerging Thin Lizzy and the sublime Led Zeppelin. These were complemented by the first ever supergroups, Blind Faith and of course Cream.

Another college fraternity preferred the surreal, light show, drug-induced world of Pink Floyd closely followed by Caravan, David Bowie, Roxy Music and King Crimson. Almost linked to this faction were the academic scholars (especially the active musicians amongst the students) who witnessed the arrival of Robert Moog and the first commercial mini-moog synthesisers and Mellotrons. Progressive rock had arrived, intelligent bands like Focus, Emerson, Lake and Palmer, Yes and the fledgling Genesis were stunning audiences across the country with their interpretations, complex compositions and links with classical music. The academics would also see the emergence of early 'concept' albums like The Who's *Tommy*, Mike Oldfield's *Tubular Bells* and Rick Wakeman's *Six Wives of Henry the Eighth*.

Music was also arriving in droves from America, and the voices of protest, Joan Baez and Dylan, were lessening and a new order was created. Following on from Simon and Garfunkel came the finger-picking guitar and piano styles of James Taylor, Carole King, Joni Mitchell, Carly Simon, Crosby, Stills and Nash, Neil Young and The Eagles. America also had time to push through the clean-cut all-American pop images of artists like David Cassidy and The Osmonds.

Running alongside and also coming in from America was the further evolution of the progressive 'underground' music with its psychedelic rock: Frank Zappa and the Mothers of Invention, The Grateful Dead, The Doors, Jefferson Airplane, The Velvet Underground, Iron Butterfly and Moby Grape.

For most of the above student groups, it was the era of hippy culture; very long shoulder-length hair and beards were almost obligatory amongst students. It was the age of flower power, kaftans, beads, braids and headbands, flares and moccasins, smocks and cheesecloth, brushed denim jeans, jeans with embroidered inserts and woollen shoulder bags, Laura Ashley fashions and macramé. Also it was the time of the first tinted lenses and people also began to ditch old, bulky, black NHS glasses for the latest innovation–contact lenses! It was a time also of liquorice paper roll-up cigarettes for the not so wealthy, Gitanes cigarettes for those who could afford to buy proper fags and of course dope for the ones that could get it, which wasn't many because it was hard to get hold of and very expensive!

Long before Neil and *The Young Ones*, the Seventies saw an upsurge in vegetarianism: lentil roasts, nut cutlets, yoghurt, home made bread, oats and muesli were the order of the day!

The students (when not protesting) were all trying to tune their minds into mysticism, the meaning of life and cosmology. It was an era of Isaac Asimov, Arthur C Clarke, Ray Bradbury and Velikovsky. Of course UFO phenomena were also everyday talking points, with minds fuelled by the arrival of Erich Von Daniken and *The Chariots of the Gods?* and Keel's *UFO-Operation Trojan Horse*. Others were content with the 'unexplained', the works of Charles Fort and the Fortean Society, especially *The Book of the Damned. Star Trek* was already on its way to becoming a cult institution. Interest of course was magnified due to the several moon landings that were happening at the time (allegedly!).

The soul music front also pushed through to great effect, the British finally getting to hear and understand the quality of Sam Cooke, Otis Redding, James Brown, Marvin Gaye, The Isley Brothers, Sam and Dave, Wilson Pickett and Aretha Franklin. This of course was still separate to a degree from the American Tamla-Motown stable.

Another culture just emerging at the start of the Seventies was the West Indian reggae culture, following on from the Sixties influences of Ska or blue beat with Prince Buster and Desmond Dekker. Soon Bob Marley would also be on the scene. This culture was unfortunately closely associated with the skinhead sect now prevalent in England. Known for its aggression and involvement in early Seventies 'boot-boys' soccer violence, it was the era of Ben Sherman button-down collar shirts, Levis and braces, Doc Marten boots, Crombie coats and of course close-cropped hairstyles.

Other alternative dress cultures also attached themselves to this music, but were more aligned to the first dance culture. These lads were the next generation of 'mods' and wore pork-pie hats, again Ben Sherman or Jaytex shirts but with neat Levi sta-prest trousers, sleeveless jumpers and tassel or brogue shoes. These lads would occupy Reading Top Rank in the evening and Cheeky Pete's in Richmond and buy their clothes from the Ivy Shop.

Also opening were the first discotheques in England, light shows on the wall, pretty patterns and lava lamp style movements. It was just music to dance to and a cheap evening. All sorts of music would be played from Donna Summer to Brown Sugar! Many relationships were formed at these get-togethers.

Another offshoot was beginning to make its way in, filling the void in the currently bland chart Top Twenty – the emergence of 'glam rock'. Out of Tyrannosaurus Rex came Marc Bolan and T-Rex, soon to be followed by Alvin Stardust, Gary Glitter, Slade, Elton John and the Sweet. An era of platform shoes, flared trousers, patches, badges, stars, outrageous costumes, big glasses, make-up on guys for the first time, mirrors, glitter, and spangles. Anything went in the name of shock!

Finally, it was also the start of the musicals, *Hair* was followed by David Essex and *Godspell* and *Jesus Christ Superstar*.

As usual instead of the Teddy Boys and Greasers fighting it out over Easter in Margate in 1960, or the Mods and Rockers doing the same in Clacton in 1965, most idealist factions didn't have much time for the others in 1970 either. The hippies didn't like the leathers, and vice versa, and the skinheads didn't seem to like, well, anybody!

For those of us capable of actually playing music, the effect that all these different influences now hitting us from all sides had was amazing. With money in our pocket we could actually own half-decent musical equipment. Although we still yearned for a Gibson, Fender, Vox or Rickenbacker guitar and a Marshall amplifier, many had to stick with acoustic guitars, an Eko Ranger or an Ibanez guitar. Those who could afford an electric guitar of some kind might have a Burns guitar. Technology was changing on amplifiers too, with some valve amps now being replaced for the first time by integrated circuit (IC) transistor models. With this new thrust, many of us were already 'gigging': folk clubs, arts labs, colleges and then semi-professionally in clubs. Content with performing 'covers' originally, some young adults were composing music themselves and using 4-track studios (16-track if you could really afford it) and getting their own work out in the public domain.

Computers had really started to have an effect on people's lives for the first time. Payroll systems were probably the first, but software packages emerged, specialist consultancies or software houses began trading. ICT (International Computers and Tabulators) had now been renamed as ICL and was countered by the influence of American IBM (International Business Machines); also on the horizon were Univac, Honeywell and Burroughs. The sci-fi paper tape had virtually disappeared along with magnetic drums. Punched cards had arrived along with magnetic tape drives; Cobol and Fortran became household words for the initiated. IBM launched the first floppy disks. However, the first interactive (screen based) systems were still over five years away.

There was also a sexual revolution and these were new 'enlightened' times. Page three of the *Sun* became the norm and Vivien Neves appeared nude in the Times in 1971 causing outrage and delight in equal measure. Stockings and suspenders had disappeared (still, we men can dream, can't we!); tights were here to stay, and micro-skirts and hot pants arrived on the scene very quickly. Many young women were now confident enough to forsake dead end clerical jobs and opt instead for further education. Germaine Greer's *The Female Eunuch* had just been published and *Cosmopolitan* had arrived. The unstoppable rise of equality, feminism, the pill and women's liberation had arrived.

But following the hedonistic Sixties era of the hippies, of free love, of pure optimism and of Timothy Leary's *Turn on, Tune in, Drop out* generation, dark clouds were gathering on the horizon, and it was as if the sun had suddenly gone in. Ted Heath's shock arrival with a Tory Government in 1970 came at a time when most were trying to forget about the Arabs, oil, gas and coal. But it was hard to deny that unemployment was rising, that inflation was a word that seemed to be on everyone's lips and that wages were struggling to keep pace with shop prices.

The switch to decimal currency in February 1971 fuelled some British opinion that this was a massive cause of inflation as 'everything was being rounded up' and it was all 'a right con'. Pensioners looked lost and there were furrowed brows everywhere. The threepenny-bit, tanner, bob, half-crown and ten-bob note notation was consigned to the history books. The ten pence piece and the fifty pence piece were the new order. Ridiculous assumptions were heard: 'Where you could get twelve for two bob, you will now only be able to get ten for ten new pence' – as if quantities were being decimalised as well as currency!

For the lads from the council estate who had gone to university, there was no guarantee of a job of any sort. For the first time the word trade union would become as common as many other everyday used words, and though we didn't know it at the time a decade of industrial unrest and social upheaval was about to follow. In this optimistic 1970, it would never cross our young minds that words like strike, Green Goddesses, power cuts and three-day week would become everyday phrases in the very near future and that we would all be affected in one way or another. A longer term period where the dead couldn't be buried and rats roamed the streets tearing at putrefying food in rotting garbage bags couldn't have even been contemplated. In the end many winters of discontent became a horrifying reality. It was summed up later as a decade of decline, disillusionment and defiance. The troubles in Ulster were just beginning, and soon terms like terrorism, bombings, sectarian violence and Bloody Sunday would be firmly imprinted on our minds.

If you were depressed and really wanted to forget the troubles, you could always tune in to Spike Milligan's *Q* series or for the vastly popular and surreal *Monty Python's Flying Circus*. On mainstream TV you could tune in for a selection of programmes that included Adam Faith in *Budgie*, Reg Varney in *On the Buses*, Peter Wyngarde as *Jason King*, Kenneth Cope in *Randall and Hopkirk*, Syd James in *Bless This House*, Nerys Hughes in *The Liver Birds*, Nina Baden-Semper in *Love thy Neighbour* and Bill Oddie and co in *The Goodies*. Those more enlightened may have preferred Peter Gilmore or Jessica Benton in *The Onedin Line*.

Fulham Football Club

For those on grants and those with jobs there was now a great deal of independence. This meant seeing *all* Fulham home matches; we could now actually afford to pay the train fare, though often five youths bundled into a car instead, and for the first time experienced the pleasure of being permanently stuck in traffic in Barnes and Mortlake coming one way or in Hammersmith and the Fulham Palace Road if coming in by the other direction. There was also the juicy prospect for the first time of being able to afford to go and see significantly more Fulham away matches; new grounds, new areas of the country and new experiences to be gained. We could even go and have a drink before the game. Some things were still the same though and the *Evening Standard* was still sought out on a Saturday night. *Star Soccer* had now become *The Big Match* and was still on Sunday afternoon after lunch but now with some post-match analysis from Brian Moore and Jimmy Hill. *Match of the Day* was now on BBC1 having secured a prime Saturday evening slot with the highlights of two matches or occasionally three being shown. It was the one programme of the week you just never missed.

Season 1969–70

The Build-up

THE 1969–70 season saw no changes or additions to the Fulham board of directors, and director Jack Walsh who had sadly passed away during the previous season had not been replaced. The long-standing board still comprised the Dean Brothers, Eric Miller and Noël (Chappie) D'Amato (vice chairman), with Tommy Trinder as chairman. Graham Hortop now held the position of club secretary/general manager.

Fulham's league crowds had dropped massively due to the club's second successive relegation, down from 22,200 to an average of 14,200. This represented a huge drop of around 36%. It was rumoured that Fulham would need to pull in attendances of 18,000 during the forthcoming season just to break even. Only a very good run would see gates return to that level.

Trinder, in his pre-season address, admitted that Johnny Haynes' testimonial match had been 'one of the few occasions from last season that we will want to remember' but still remained upbeat. He pointed out that, despite relegation, Fulham had continued to improve the ground, and had spent over £20,000 in the close season replacing turnstiles, the doors on the Stevenage Road stand and the toilets beneath the main stand. He also lost no time reminding supporters that the club had obtained planning permission for the construction of a significant new stand on the riverside terrace. By this alone he reminded supporters that the club had not lost its ambition.

Trinder was rather more enigmatic when he discussed the cash available, saying: 'Maybe there will be other priorities for the cash [rather than the stand] we will have to wait awhile. We want the club management to do the managing. We will try and make the money available when they ask for it.' After joking that the retired Tosh Chamberlain had looked the answer to Fulham's playing problems, he robustly put his weight behind Dodgin's short-term answer to cash flow problems – young players. He said: 'Seriously though, we have decided to tackle the situation from the other extreme – youth. This was the wealth of the club, the discovery of stars such as Haynes, Mullery, Macedo and Cohen. There must be more where they came from, if our set up is right to find, and develop, them. A lot of thought is going into that aspect, and the announcement we hope to make next season [1969–70] of the man who will take charge of our youth policy, will, I believe, delight everybody.'

The start of the season

Following relegation, the club sensibly decided to freeze admission prices at the previous season's levels, so they remained at 5/- (25p) for the terrace and 6/- (30p) for the enclosure. Prices for the Stevenage Road seating were 8/- (40p), 10/- (50p) and 15/- (75p).

The club had also pegged the season ticket prices at the previous level of 8 guineas, 10 guineas and 15 guineas: (£8.40p, £10.50p and £15.75p). It was rumoured rather ominously that the demand for season tickets had dropped by almost 75% compared with the figure of three seasons before!

Playing staff

For the second successive season, Fulham, this time under Bill Dodgin, started purging the playing staff, and, as last season, there were a number of casualties. Johnny Byrne had departed from the club immediately the Second Division fixtures had been concluded, moving to South Africa. Fulham reduced their goalkeepers down to two again when Irish international Jack McClelland joined then non-league Barnet on a free transfer. McClelland had been a hero in Fulham's 'great escape' season, but had found himself as second and often third choice due to lapses in concentration that had frequently cost Fulham goals and points. He had been, however, renowned for his bravery and loyalty. McClelland was with Barnet for more than six years, playing in an FA trophy final in 1972. Tragically the goalkeeper suffered ill health, and was diagnosed with a brain tumour. He sadly succumbed to the condition in 1976, aged just thirty-six.

Bobby Moss, the exciting young striker who had played under manager Buckingham, had never been given first-team action under Robson (in 1968–69), Haynes or Dodgin, and left to join Peterborough United on a free transfer. He remained there for three seasons where he made over 100 appearances. Eventually he dropped out of league football joining Wealdstone in 1973.

Midfield player and Irishman Ivan Murray was also given a free transfer and returned to Ireland to rejoin Coleraine. Reserve team players Dick Longstaff (a perfect name for the 'Carry On' team!) and Irvine Cardie, neither of whom had appeared in the first team, also left the club on free transfers. Cardie joined Southern League Guildford City, but there is no recorded information as to where Longstaff went after leaving Fulham.

There were, however, four other significant departures. Brian Dear had looked impressive in front of goal during his brief spell and had been the previous season's top scorer with seven goals in just thirteen games. Millwall manager Benny Fenton had been keen to sign Dear in February, and made another enquiry to Fulham during the summer regarding his availability. Fulham were in dire need of an experienced right back due to George Cohen's retirement and Mike Pentecost's broken leg, and so the club agreed to a 'swap' arrangement, with Dear moving to Millwall in exchange for craggy, Scottish full back John Gilchrist. Gilchrist was an experienced player and knew plenty about the Third Division, and so should have proven a good purchase; both players were 'valued' at £20,000.

Dodgin commented enigmatically on Dear's departure, saying: 'We shall make up for Dear's absence by spreading the goalscoring responsibilities amongst the forwards'. This seemed strange with Byrne gone, and Large and Jones out of favour; the manager must have been pinning his hopes on a swift return to form from Steve Earle and Les Barrett. Dear did not fare that well due to his off-field excesses, and never scored another league goal, making just five league appearances for Millwall in a few months, before returning to Upton Park via non-league Woodford Town in 1970. He made just four further league appearances for the Hammers first team before drifting out of football altogether.

Another player who was involved in the swap arrangement was Irishman and 'Sunderland cup hero' Brendan Mullen who also departed to Millwall, with a Millwall youth/reserve team player Danny O'Leary making the reverse move to Craven Cottage. Mullen also fared badly at Millwall, becoming homesick for Ireland. He failed to make a single first-team league appearance for the Lions, and also returned to Ireland to be reunited with teammate Ivan Murray and Coleraine.

Flanked by Stan Horne and Reg Matthewson, the Maestro, Johnny Haynes, prepares for his eighteenth season as a first team player with Fulham. Right: No entry without a tie, sir! – a pose more doorman than defender from new signing John Gilchrist from neighbours Millwall.

The two major surprises were the departures of John Ryan and Malcolm Macdonald. John Ryan had originally looked a very competent player who had lost confidence in the relegation season. Harry Haslam, now at Luton, had been instrumental in Ryan's early career, and he alerted manager Alec Stock to the fact that Ryan was currently 'frozen out' of the first-team reckoning. A deal was quickly done, and Ryan joined Luton Town for a nominal sum.

It proved to be another of Fulham's big mistakes and although Ryan never 'hit the heights', he proved a loyal and versatile clubman serving Luton Town, Norwich City and Sheffield United, and also having a spell at Manchester City. Ryan played more than 500 games in a career that spanned eighteen years. Although utilised at Fulham primarily as a centre back, Ryan played the majority of his remaining career as a midfield player.

The same Luton connection was responsible for the transfer of Malcolm Macdonald. Haslam had been a major influence in bringing the young, raw Macdonald to Fulham from Tonbridge and, seeing that the young forward was also being frozen out of the Haynes/Dodgin regime, Stock and Haslam made a considerable bid of £17,500 for the young player which Fulham eagerly accepted.

Haslam had recommended that Stock watch Macdonald, which he did on the final game of the previous season in a 1–1 reserve team game against Luton. Stock was impressed; Macdonald was told that a club were interested in him, and that he should report to the ground at 2pm. When Macdonald found out it was Harry and Luton he was 'dead chuffed'.

Two hours later, when nobody had appeared, he thought that the move had gone sour, when suddenly Haslam turned up covered in engine oil after the car transporting Stock and him had broken down. The normally sartorially elegant Stock looked decidedly ruffled, and flung the papers at Macdonald after briefly covering the terms. He snapped: 'Take it or leave it, I'm in no mood to argue; I've had enough trouble with the car.' Macdonald happily signed the papers in 'seconds flat' and agreed to join Luton Town to escape his Craven Cottage nightmare; the wily Stock announcing that he 'would use Macdonald as a full back!'

The move proved to be another disastrous error of judgement by Fulham. After scoring forty-nine league goals in eighty-eight league games for Luton Town in just two seasons, Macdonald moved into the big time with big-money moves, firstly to Newcastle United for £180,000 and finally to Arsenal for a £333,333 – a third of a million pounds. Macdonald, now known as 'SuperMac', enjoyed cult status at both clubs. Macdonald scored a magnificent hat trick on his Newcastle home debut to defeat Liverpool 3–2. Macdonald finished each of his five seasons at Newcastle as top scorer, and scored in every round of the FA Cup when Newcastle reached the Cup Final in 1974.

The aggressive, hard-running Macdonald also won international recognition, winning fourteen caps for England in the 1970s. In one England game he scored all five of England's goals in a 5–0 victory over Cyprus. He became a virtual goal-machine and when a knee injury cruelly finished his career at just twenty-eight, he had already netted over 190 league goals alone in around 370 league appearances, better than a goal every other game – a record to rival many of the league's greatest ever goalscorers! Macdonald would return to Fulham in another capacity, and play an instrumental role in the club's fortunes during the 1980s.

In all, *ten* players had left the club, and apart from the two arriving in the 'swap' deal, Fulham, due to day-to-day cost constraints, signed *no* other players in the close season. There was still £100,000 in the bank, received as compensation for George Cohen's retirement, but Dodgin was adamant that he was not going to be 'stampeded' into buying. Like Robson before him, he stated: 'Any player coming to the club must be better than those already here'. The club commented in the programme: 'Our staff has been necessarily pruned, but we retain enough talent to make us the envy of our rivals'.

Looking at resources already inside the club, Dodgin stayed true to his word, and brought a number of youth team players, who had also played for the reserves on occasions, into the first-team pool as apprentice professionals. These included: Don Shanks, David Carlton, Dave Robertson, Brendan McKevitt, and a young John Fraser. The senior squad, including two goalkeepers, comprised just *twenty* players.

Despite the very real fears around at the end of the previous season, star players and internationals Jimmy Conway and Les Barrett were both thankfully still at the club. Steve Earle had received cortisone treatment for his back injury during the close season, and, after missing virtually a complete season due to the ailment, was now fighting fit, having been cured in just a couple of weeks by England doctor Alan Bass.

Bass had found an 'abnormal formation' at the base of the spine that had made Earle prone to back strain. But he had confirmed that as the player had been playing football since he was six, there was no reason why he couldn't continue! The club had also retained the services of veteran Johnny Haynes for the ensuing year. Haynes commented: 'It should be easier in division three.' Forward Frank Large was still at the club, but was looking to move. Haynes would not, however, be captain for the forthcoming season. Dodgin awarded the job to Stan Horne on the back of some sterling performances during the last couple of the months of the previous season.

The players remaining at the club had been given significant bonus payment incentives if they managed to return to the Second Division at the first time of asking. The Third Division was known as the 'rat race' because although only two clubs went up, four were automatically relegated – there was no 'coasting' in this division.

The squad at the beginning of the season. Back row: Wilf Tranter, Reg Matthewson, Vic Halom, Brian Williamson, Ian Seymour, Dave Roberts, John Gilchrist, Danny O'Leary; middle row: Steve Earle, Johnny Haynes, Stan Brown, Stan Horne, Jimmy Conway, Cliff Jones, Frank Large; front row: Barry Lloyd, Mike Pentecost, Les Barrett, Fred Callaghan, Dave Moreline.

Other changes

In changes off the field, Fulham had appointed, from a long list of applicants, former Spurs star Terry Medwin to assist Billy Gray in the club coaching. Medwin was a friend and teammate of Cliff Jones, both having started their careers at Swansea Town. In an illustrious career, Medwin had won thirty Welsh caps, and had enjoyed numerous triumphs in the great Spurs sides of the early Sixties. He was a player who was, like Jones, a forward/winger, excellent in the air, who could also score goals regularly with either foot. His career had seen him score over 120 league goals but a broken leg meant that his first-class career finished prematurely. Medwin would join Dodgin in attending the first-team matches. This appointment allowed Ken Craggs to move up and maintain contact with the reserve side as well as the youth teams.

Fulham had again dug up the centre of the pitch to a depth of eighteen inches and done considerable re-seeding. Groundsman Fred Hall had been assisted by Bill Chapman, who, a month before the start of the season, was given the full-time job of looking after the pitch. The ground looked a picture, and Johnny Haynes remarked: 'The pitch is as good now as it has ever been in my time.'

The club's official programme remained similar in size, format and content. The green colour from the previous season was removed from the cover, which returned to being black and white. There was still an 'action' shot frame at the bottom of the cover, and, as an incentive, the Third Division championship trophy was given a prominent position. It was still priced at 1/- (5p).

As Fulham were now in Division Three with less chance of being 'televised', the brown/tan coloured football was still being used significantly rather than the white ball.

Again, perhaps due to the costs involved, Fulham decided, once again, *not* to make any changes to the playing kit. The club should probably have changed the kit to exorcise the bitter memories of successive relegations, but the strip remained exactly as it was: white shirts, black shorts with two vertical white stripes down the side and white socks with one black band.

Bill Dodgin himself started to unburden his heart and speak boldly about the forthcoming season. He passed no comment at all about the previous season's failures, but looked instead to the forthcoming season with the target in mind that everyone wanted – promotion. This was the first sign of Dodgin talking of his attacking ethos, backed up by competing physically. He said: 'We are not going to give up on our reputation of being a good footballing side. This is not because of any bigheaded belief that we are too good for the Third Division, but because safety-first football would not work for us. We have to play to our ability, and there is a lot of football in our side. It is no good trying to kick ourselves out of the Third Division; for one thing we would soon be kicked down again.

'For another, I do not believe that the Third Division is any more physically tough than the Second or the First. It is just that it is 'less obvious' in the higher division. I'm certainly not suggesting we should play fancy, purposeless football; certainly we have to match the opposition physically if we are to give ourselves the opportunity to show our class.'

Then he went on to self-belief, saying: 'We have to believe in ourselves again; we want people to be patient, we want people to realise that the players have been under pressure for years. We want them to appreciate that before we can start going forward, we have to stop going back. I have seen it happen before at Millwall and at Queens Park Rangers. If you believe in yourself, you can make the ball run your way.'

Dodgin signed off with the following plea: 'We do not need to be reminded how important it is to get back into the First Division. However, it will come a lot easier if we are not being reminded constantly that we HAVE to do it. We have the ability plus the ambition. These are all the elements we need as long as we have normal luck. Mixed together in the right proportions they are the right formula for what we all want – promotion.'

Club mascot 'Freddie Fulham' injected his own humour by saying: 'It wasn't all bad last season, us regulars who go every week saw a winning reserve team who should soon be doing their stuff in the big time!! Nobody can say we lack variety – three divisions in three seasons – but we didn't get much of a look at the Second Division. How about another glance next season on our way back to the top?'

Fulham also announced that George Cohen had been awarded a well-deserved testimonial match by the club that would take place sometime during the coming season. Cliff Jones, now sporting a long moustache that made him look like a Mexican bandit, had been awarded his sixty-first cap by Wales, playing against the rest of the United Kingdom at Ninian Park. He said: 'Still, that [my sixty-first cap] is not really prominent in my mind at the moment. My main concern is to do well at Fulham, and help them to do well. Nothing in football would please me more than a Third Division Championship medal. The biggest barrier to this I feel is psychological. I have been around long enough to be sure that we have the talent at Craven Cottage. What we need is for everybody to believe in themselves. Perhaps my own self-belief and the way it helped me back into the Wales team will help others.'

The annual cricket match with Putney Cricket Club went ahead as usual, with the proceeds going towards Johnny Haynes' testimonial fund. Haynes was the star of the Fulham show and demonstrated how he could have just as easily become a professional cricketer. Putney batted first and declared at 169-9. Fulham's response was 122 all out. Haynes was the top scorer for Fulham with a bristling thirty-seven that included five fours. Steve Earle was Fulham's best bowler with figures of four for twenty-three. The Fulham eleven taking part were: Haynes, Conway, John Clarke (Boxer), Denny Mancini, Earle, Halom, Matthewson, Lloyd, Large, Pentecost and Williamson.

New Arrivals

Once again, **Fulham** were the new arrivals in the lower division – playing Third Division football for the first time in 37 years – accompanied by **Bury**. The four teams arriving up from the Fourth Division were: **Doncaster Rovers (champions), Halifax Town, Rochdale and Bradford City**.

Pre-season

In pre-season, there was less to smile about. In their first friendly, Fulham were held to a **1–1** draw at **Aldershot** after leading at half time; John Gilchrist made his debut, and Cliff Jones scored the Fulham goal. The friendly was marred by significant crowd trouble and Fulham immediately announced a zero tolerance policy on the hooligans. General manager Hortop warned: 'There will be no second chances'.

On a Friday evening, in the only significant friendly that Fulham played at Craven Cottage, the team were beaten fairly easily **1–3** by Second Division **Norwich City**. In a strange line up, Barry Lloyd played on the right wing, with Stan Brown at inside right. Vic Halom took the centre forward's shirt. It was a match where both teams' defences were on top, with neither side showing much in the way of attacking flair. Albert Bennett, who had scored two controversial goals for Newcastle against Fulham the season before last, put Norwich ahead after twenty-five minutes.

Fulham received a lifeline when, following a foul on Cliff Jones, Jimmy Conway equalised from the penalty spot ten minutes after half time. Fulham held this position for just ten minutes when two goals in the space of three minutes from ex-WBA winger Ken Foggo clinched the match. The third was another misjudgement from goalkeeper Ian Seymour, who allowed a long-range shot from out on the wing to drift into the net. There did not seem to be too much pace in the Fulham forward line. Halom tried hard, but never really got the better of Norwich hard-man Duncan Forbes; Barry Lloyd looked out of position on the wing and Stan Brown had a match to forget. Dodgin had continued with young Dave Moreline at right back, but both he and Fred Callaghan struggled against the Norwich wingers.

Fulham's final friendly was against a much stronger opposition in **Charlton Athletic**. Fulham lost **1–2**, Vic Halom netting against his former club. The club admitted the defensive problems and said: 'At least we have time to put things right before league points are at issue'.

The reserves managed two draws, both times fielding a generally inexperienced side. In their first match they drew **2–2** with **Hillingdon Borough**, with new-boy Danny O'Leary scoring both goals. In the second game, they played out an entertaining **4–4** draw with now-defunct **Guildford City**. The Guildford City side included ex-Fulham player Irvine Cardie, the experienced former Portsmouth and Aldershot defender Ron Rafferty and Jackie Graham, later to star for Brentford. Fulham gave Large, Earle and Barrett a run-out in this match. Frank Large responded with two goals, and Steve Earle also got on the score-sheet, the fourth goal coming from amateur Alan Walker. Guildford were leading 2–1 at one stage and six of the eight goals were scored in the last twenty-five minutes. Such was the interest in the match that the ground – close to the A3 – hosted an attendance of almost 3,000.

FULHAM FOOTBALL CLUB

SEASON 1969-70
FOOTBALL LEAGUE DIV. III

SATURDAY, AUGUST 9th 1969
KICK OFF 3.00 p.m.

BRADFORD CITY

OFFICIAL PROGRAMME 1/-

The programme for the first home match of the season.

August 1969

In this month

* In Northern Ireland, the B-Specials were told to hand in their arms.
* Rupert Murdoch bid £250,000 to take over *The Sun* newspaper.
* Rocky Marciano, the only boxer never to have lost a professional fight, was killed in a plane crash.
* British troops sealed off the Bogside area of Londonderry with barbed wire after violence flared at the end of the Orangemen's parades.
* 150,000 watched Bob Dylan at the Isle of Wight rock festival.

'In The Year 2525' by Zager and Evans topped the charts.

The matches

FULHAM'S FIRST encounter against Third Division opposition was against newly promoted **Bradford City**. It was a beautiful August afternoon, and yet fewer than 10,000 arrived at the Cottage to see Fulham start their new campaign. The only surprise was the inclusion of Jimmy Conway as an orthodox right winger, a position alien to him. John Gilchrist made his debut at right back, whilst Vic Halom continued to hold the number nine shirt.

The Bradford team contained forwards Ham and Bannister. Bobby Ham had been a prolific goalscorer for Bradford Park Avenue alongside First Division star Kevin Hector, now at Derby. Bruce Bannister would, in later seasons, form a formidable striking partnership with Alan Warboys as part of the famous Bristol Rovers 'smash and grab' team. Warboys would play for Fulham in the mid-Seventies. Again it seemed remarkable that this was a league match; just eighteen months previously, Fulham were in the First Division and Bradford City in the Fourth!

Fulham almost shook Bradford with a first minute goal. Cliff Jones and Vic Halom worked an opening for Johnny Haynes whose twenty-yard shot was just wide. Halom then cleverly created an opportunity for the overlapping Fred Callaghan, but he shot just over. At this stage the attacking barrage was never-ending and Jimmy Conway, Halom and Haynes all went close with the City defence all over the place.

City retreated to almost an eleven-man defence, and relied on sheer grit and hard work to keep Fulham at bay. Near half time Halom harassed goalkeeper John Roberts into dropping the ball. He slid it in, but referee Dennis Turner instantly ruled out the effort. Halom was looking very able, linking well with Haynes and being at the centre of most of the good things that Fulham were creating, Bradford skipper Tom Hallett being unable to contain him.

Fulham carried on attacking after the interval. Halom sent an inch-perfect through ball to Jones, but he was too slow to capitalise on the opportunity. Conway seemed to be adapting well to his new-found wing role. Twice he came close to giving Fulham the lead: once forcing the keeper into a diving save, then heading just over the bar.

Little was seen of the Bradford danger men, with Dave Roberts and Reg Matthewson in control at the back. Halom was being used as a spearhead, working alone, but there were no other forwards present to pick up on his knockdowns. Frustrated at still being level on the hour due to weak finishing, Fulham started to become edgy; the team tried to relax to a casual pace, but the heat was beginning to wilt the team and their stranglehold lessened.

Barry Lloyd began to struggle with pace, and Stan Horne, looking slightly overweight and unfit, was getting caught out in defence. With Fulham not being able to hit the target, Bradford saw a chink of light and began to abandon their defensive shell. John Hall, the Bradford winger, began sending over some teasing centres and debutant Gilchrist was unusually nervous; fortunately Callaghan was on good form, clearing most of the trouble. Bobby Ham then streaked through the Fulham defence after a clever move to net an easy 'goal', only to see the effort chalked off by the linesman flagging furiously for offside; it was, however, very close.

At home to Bradford City on the opening day, defender Cooper prevents Vic Halom reaching goalkeeper Roberts. Such was the heat on the day that Cliff Jones (11) is seemingly enjoying a deserved siesta. A 0–0 draw was a predictable result on the day.

Stan Brown replaced the tired Lloyd, but the change made no difference. This increased Fulham's nerves, and minutes before the end the home side had another amazing let off. A defensive muddle let in City centre forward Norman Corner. He strode through, took the ball around goalkeeper Ian Seymour, and, with the open goal at his mercy, somehow put his effort into the side netting from just four yards! The Fulham supporters gasped with disbelief, and the Bradford team collapsed in dismay. It was an example of the finishing that was on show that afternoon; the match finished **0–0**, and was a fair result.

The opening match had been a tough baptism for Fulham, and again faced by a defensive workmanlike side they had struggled once more to find the net. The team's overall form had not looked too convincing either. Fulham had been given an instant reality check as to how difficult it was going to be to escape from this division.

If it had not been for that amazing late miss, Fulham would have still been searching for their first point. Halom had stood out with his hard work; Conway was dangerous on the wing and Callaghan tenacious at the back. However, apart from that, Fulham showed the same weaknesses as the previous season – a lack of quality and thought in midfield, and a lack of pace and agility in the box, with weak and hesitant finishing, never putting enough efforts on target to really test the Bradford keeper. Jones and Lloyd had been particularly disappointing.

For the second consecutive season Fulham had been drawn away at London neighbours **Orient** in the first round of the League Cup. The match was epitomised by expert goalkeeping by both Ray Goddard and Ian Seymour. Goddard made two superb saves, both from Fred Callaghan. The match typified Fulham's attacking problems as their best two efforts came from their left back. Fulham escaped without a repeat of the previous season's humiliating defeat. They might actually have won; Vic Halom unluckily missed when he picked up a rebound, and Jimmy Conway clipped the bar with a twenty-five yard shot ten minutes from time. The match finished **0–0** and Fulham were happy to earn the replay.

Fulham travelled to Lancashire for their first away match in the division to meet **Bury**, the side relegated with Fulham. Bury had lost their opening fixture 3–4 at Rotherham, but their centre forward George Jones had claimed a hat trick. Fulham played Stan Brown instead of Reg Matthewson at the back, whilst Frank Large was given another chance in place of the lethargic Barry Lloyd.

Fulham were given every opportunity to play football by Bury, but despite playing very neat and mobile football in midfield, the forwards again lacked any real punch up front. Bury, despite lacking the class, looked far more dangerous in the final third of the pitch, the Fulham defence giving them too much space. Ian Seymour was a very busy man, and centre forward George Jones was unlucky not to claim a hat trick for the second week in a row. Three times he tested Seymour with blistering drives, but fortunately the Fulham custodian was having one of his better days, and using sharp reflexes he kept everything out.

It was ironic that the goal that beat him, and Fulham, had looked well offside. In the seventh minute, Seymour conceded a corner following another fine reflex save, and from this the former Manchester City winger Paul Hince lobbed a pass through and Jones headed in unchallenged. Referee Maurice Fussey looked long and hard at the linesman, but no signal was forthcoming, and the goal stood. Dave Roberts was struggling woefully against the wily, experienced Jones and if it had not been for Seymour's reflexes, Fulham would have gone in at least four behind.

The early play in the second half reflected that of the first with Bury well on top. However, the game swung dramatically when Cliff Jones sustained an injury, and was replaced on the hour by Barry Lloyd. Suddenly Fulham looked a different side – sharp and eager. Stan Horne and Stan Brown began to control the midfield, supplying the ball to Johnny Haynes. Vic Halom ballooned Lloyd's centre wildly over the bar with twenty minutes remaining, and Haynes then did the same when presented with a similar opportunity. Then substitute Lloyd was twice unlucky, firstly having an excellent shot turned away by Bury goalkeeper Neil Ramsbottom, and then with a second effort just inches wide after a super run that took out three defenders. Fulham were by now controlling the game, but just couldn't finish. This scenario continued to the end, Fulham losing **0–1**.

Defeat was quite hard to accept; most of the media agreed that Fulham had played well in defence and midfield, but had looked very weak up front. One report stated: 'Football ability will not alone win matches for Fulham. They have had this message rammed home from the First Division to the Third – but still haven't taken it in.' The three opening games of the season had passed without a goal scored, and the Fulham fans were beginning to dread another goal drought similar to the one that the team had suffered in the corresponding period of the season last year.

The match proved to be the final game for misfit Frank Large. He had failed to produce any of the form expected of him, and both parties thought that a change of club would help matters. Rumours abounded that Luton manager Alec Stock was going to make his third swoop on Fulham in two months for Large, as he had cash available following the sale of the Rioch brothers to Aston Villa. This bid, however, never materialised, neither did a move from neighbours Brentford, also supposedly interested. The bid that did come in, however, was from Fourth Division Northampton Town. Personal terms were quickly agreed, and Large returned to Northampton for a *third* time for a transfer fee of £17,000. Fulham had lost £33,000 on this particular deal, a considerable sum, in the space of a year; Large's three goals for the club had cost £11,000 each!

The transfer was a relief, as Large had looked a very unhappy player towards the end of his stay in London, and the Fulham crowd were permanently on his back. Ironically, Large found his shooting boots again immediately on rejoining the Cobblers, scoring forty-two league goals in just 133 league games. Large later joined Chesterfield, and finished a long career with almost 230 league goals. He died in Ireland from cancer aged just 63.

With Large now gone and Cliff Jones recovering from having stitches inserted in a thigh wound, it was difficult to see where Fulham's goals were going to come from. There were rumours at the time that Fulham would move for Charlton Athletic centre forward Matt Tees, but this came to nothing, and Tees ended up joining Malcolm Macdonald at Luton Town soon after.

Ironically, it was due to the above two factors that Fulham put together a line-up that would have a significant impact on their future. Steve Earle came back into the team at centre forward, and Les Barrett was restored to the left wing position, and for the first time the Conway–Earle–Barrett partnership was given the opportunity to prove itself.

Two days after the Bury defeat, Fulham played **Orient** in the second round League Cup **replay**. Both sides now had the incentive of a visit from League champions Leeds United in the next round. Fulham switched fit-again Mike Pentecost to the 'wrong' side left back position, forcing

Fred Callaghan to push forward into Stan Brown's position. Brown took Frank Large's place at inside forward. The fixture was quite a reunion, as Orient's Ray Goddard, full back Mike Jones and winger Terry Parmenter were all former Fulham players, whilst Vic Halom had been an Orient player in the corresponding fixture the previous season.

Orient centre-half Terry Mancini was Fulham born, and part of the Mancini boxing family. Tony and Len Mancini were staunch Fulham supporters, who had both been major contributors and workers in Johnny Haynes' testimonial year. The Orient side also contained Dennis Rofe at full back, later to play for both Leicester City and Chelsea in the First Division and centre back Tommy Taylor later to become a star at West Ham.

Both Orient and Fulham had been in the First Division in the early Sixties and both teams were looking to recapture that status. The match had been put forward to Monday to avoid a clash with the First Division Chelsea v West Ham league game. Orient had not conceded a goal in their opening three games, whilst Fulham had not scored one! What followed was a cracking Cup tie filled with thrills and excitement, and for the first time in well over two years, Fulham resembled something of a team to be respected and feared.

Fulham started well and Jimmy Conway slammed a shot against the Orient bar in the first few minutes. It took Fulham, in the driving seat, twenty-five minutes to break both of those goal sequences, when the hardworking Stan Brown sent in a dangerous, low cross from the right. Terry Mancini and Tommy Taylor should have cleared the ball, but along with goalkeeper Ray Goddard they failed, and Steve Earle darted in between the defenders to scramble the loose ball home. Earle rejoiced – and not surprisingly; the goal was his first in *sixteen* months.

It was a half full of running and adventure, with both teams competing furiously for the right to stage the tie with Leeds in the next round. Minutes after Earle's goal, Goddard had to rush out and plunge at Brown's feet to prevent a second Fulham goal. After this, though, Orient launched several bombardments on the Fulham goal and began to gain the upper hand. Fulham completed the half having made *eighteen* scoring attempts and forcing seven corners.

Orient started the second half in determined fashion, with both Peter Allen and Mickey Bullock going close. They were, however, having difficulty getting shots on target. Orient finally pulled level around the mid-point of the second half. Malcolm Slater's corner was flicked on at the near post

In the final minutes of the League Cup visit from Orient, Jimmy Conway smashes a penalty high into the roof of the net with ex-Fulham keeper Ray Goddard diving the wrong way. The fortuitous award finally broke Orient's brave resistance, giving Fulham a 3–1 victory and earning a visit from League champions Leeds United.

by Bullock, allowing winger Peter Brabrook to get in a shot. The effort thudded into Ian Seymour's chest, but he couldn't hold it and the ball rebounded to Orient half back Dave Harper standing on the edge of the Fulham box, and he drove home the equaliser. The goal seemed to give Orient the edge in a replay filled with tension and action, although Goddard had to be awake to push Les Barrett's shot onto a post. Fulham's cause seemed to be fading when leader Johnny Haynes limped off with a pulled thigh muscle with twenty minutes to go to be replaced by Barry Lloyd.

But, as in the Bury game, Lloyd seemed to add zest and ideas to the Fulham midfield, and just three minutes after coming onto the field he was involved in the goal that gave Fulham the lead. Lloyd slotted a twenty-yard free kick around Orient's defensive wall to Brown. Brown, back to goal, steered the ball left into the path of Conway, who strode in and squeezed a shot between Goddard and the near post from a narrow angle.

The game could have gone either way from that point, and Orient were very unlucky when Taylor had the ball in the net, only for the effort to be ruled out for offside – it looked an incorrect decision by the referee. However, Fulham finally settled the tie three minutes from time. Barrett, whose pace had troubled Orient all evening, made yet another strong run and tumbled down in the box when challenged by Tommy Taylor. The referee, Tony Oliver, saw his linesman flag and had no hesitation in awarding the penalty, and Conway stepped up to score his second goal of the night from the penalty spot. Again, the decision looked to be slightly fortuitous as the incident looked no more than a harmless tangle of legs. Fulham emerged triumphant **3–1** winners.

Leeds manager Don Revie had been in London to watch the game and said afterwards: 'Fulham impressed me in the first half; it's not going to be easy … Fulham moved the ball about well in the first half, and the second half was a cracker. No away Cup games are easy, and we expect Fulham to put up a fight.'

Orient manager Jimmy Bloomfield was frustrated after the match and said: 'If you don't get the breaks you don't win. It [Orient's disallowed goal] didn't look offside, and why the referee, standing only four yards away, had to rely on the linesman to make the penalty decision I cannot understand!'

The media put up the headline: 'Fulham prove it – they can score!' The match had been a credit to both teams. Ray Goddard had done well in the Orient goal, and both Taylor and Mancini had been outstanding in defence. Brabrook had also caused the Fulham defence numerous problems from the wing, but the Fulham defence had generally handled them well. Young Dave Roberts had been on sparkling form, ably supported by Fred Callaghan.

It was, however, in attack that Fulham had shone. The rejuvenated Conway and Barrett had been excellent on the wings, and Earle had looked a new player, very fit and pacy. Lloyd and Brown had also made significant contributions in the middle of the field. Finally things were starting to look rosy again. Most importantly, after Haynes' departure, it was a very young Fulham side, with only John Gilchrist being anywhere near thirty!

Fulham hoped to continue this form when they faced **Gillingham** at the Cottage five days later. The Gillingham squad, with John Bond as coach, possessed few stars, but their squad did contain David Peach, who later moved to Southampton. The visitors had made a poor start to the season losing both of their opening fixtures. Fulham made just one change from the side victorious on Monday bringing in Reg Matthewson, following a back strain, for Fred Callaghan. The Orient epic had failed to bring in the spectators, however, and a meagre crowd of just over 8,500 turned up.

Heavy rain before the match had made the green surface particularly slippery, and in the early stages there was precious little football played, as both sets of players tried to keep their feet. Jimmy Conway came closest with a shot that was inches wide. Fulham, showing more class, took the lead in the twenty-second minute. Stan Horne picked up a throw-in and fed Conway. Conway made a clever dart down the right wing, and from his centre Johnny Haynes controlled the ball with his right foot and shot low into the net with his left all in one movement.

Stan Brown missed a golden chance to put Fulham further ahead when, following a brilliant run down the left by Les Barrett and with virtually all the goal to aim at, he headed straight into the goalkeeper's hands. Fulham held onto the lead for just a quarter of an hour, when right half Mel Machin equalised with a fine volley following centre half Bill Williams' headed pass.

Ian Seymour lofts a clearance into the opposition half to try to put more pressure on the visiting Gillingham defence.

Fulham struggled for a while, as some young heads dropped. Haynes was at his vintage best on the fast pitch, supplying a conveyer belt of passes to Conway and Barrett, keeping the Gillingham defence at full stretch. Three times, close to the interval, Fulham should have retaken the lead, Haynes shooting over, Barrett having a shot deflected wide, and Conway hitting a post.

It was Gillingham, however, who almost took the lead two minutes after half time, when goalkeeper Ian Seymour slipped on the wet surface, causing him to slide out of the penalty area and handle the ball. From the resulting free kick from Gordon Riddick, Ken Pound headed inches over the bar with the defence beaten. Fulham came back and only a last gasp tackle from Mike Green prevented Steve Earle from getting in his shot with just goalkeeper John Simpson to beat.

Fulham regained the lead in the sixty-third minute with their second fortunate penalty of the week. Full back Green was adjudged to have handled the ball in the box following a searing goalbound shot from Brown, when really he was merely protecting his face. Fulham appealed, and referee Arthur Jones from Liverpool (president of the Referees' Association) awarded the penalty, indicating a deliberate offence. Green tried to contest the decision, saying that the ball had hit his forehead, and play was held up for a while as Gillingham protested vigorously. For the second time that week, Conway converted from the spot.

A half-time snapshot during the Gillingham match. The jackpot result board is being loaded with the winning numbers before being paraded around the ground. At left is the drum that now holds only the unsuccessful jackpot tickets. In the background is photographer Ken Coton's black bag with his spare camera and lenses – hardly a designer bag, but it travelled to many grounds throughout the land!

Welcome to the Third Division! Referee Jones lectures Gillingham's Machin following a clash with Jimmy Conway, a tackle which would today have merited a red card, but in 1969 only warranted a stern talking-to. Steve Earle tends to his stricken colleague. Fulham won a feisty encounter 2–1 to record their first League win of the campaign.

Fulham continued to be the more dominant side, but failed to turn possession into goals. Brian Yeo came on as a substitute for Pound, with Riddick and Machin pushing up, but the Fulham defence remained calm. In the end, Gillingham were let off lightly, Fulham winning **2–1** and recording their first league victory in Division Three.

Gillingham had been a poor side, but Fulham had failed to fully turn the screw in attack. The Fulham defence had been tidy throughout, with Dave Roberts and full backs John Gilchrist and Mike Pentecost both impressing. Although the match had lacked the passion of Monday's Cup tie, wingers Conway and Barrett had demonstrated that, at last, Fulham could have unearthed a winning combination.

Jimmy Conway had been the first to pipe up when Bill Dodgin had asked: 'Who likes taking penalties?' and was awarded the job. Dodgin was pleased with the victory and was also delighted that Fulham had conceded just three goals in the opening five games, but added cautiously: 'Against Gillingham we lost some of our urgency, but still managed to outplay them in the first half. We made things difficult for ourselves by not finishing as well as we can. Les Barrett in particular was unlucky, but one way or another, the ball did not go into the net as it should. We had half a dozen chances before half time. If we had taken three of them we would have made it easy for ourselves.'

With Frank Large departed, Fulham used some of the cash proceeds to make their first signing of the season when they paid £12,000 to Brentford for nineteen-year-old utility player John Richardson. Richardson could play either in defence, midfield or, in emergencies, at centre forward. Richardson was a nephew of Fulham coach Billy Gray and had also been at Millwall. Richardson had been in dispute with Brentford, wanting more than the basic £20 per week. There had been an impasse and Richardson had decided to take his case to arbitration. During that time he had been transfer-listed.

Four days after the Gillingham encounter, Fulham played their third home match in ten days when they entertained **Southport** at the Cottage. The match was Southport's first ever visit to Fulham for a league match. Fulham recalled Brian Williamson in goal and Fred Callaghan again

Against Southport flying winger Conway adopts a Superman pose as he flies through the air. Conway delivered a super performance on the night in his new-found role, scoring twice and providing the cross for the third goal.

swapped places with Reg Matthewson. Southport played in an attractive all-gold strip. Their side contained no stars, and Fulham should have been confident, as the visitors had lost all of their opening three fixtures. Despite the two previous victories, the midweek evening crowd was still a disappointing 9,000.

It took Fulham just thirteen minutes to take the lead. Johnny Haynes supplied the slide-rule pass and Jimmy Conway collected the ball and hit a left-foot shot wide of Southport's Scottish

From Conway's accurate cross, Stan Brown (in the goal) has leapt and nodded in Fulham's third goal against Southport. Barry Lloyd (No 12) salutes the goal, and the five defenders and goalkeeper look as if they just want to get off the pitch. The 3–2 League win was the second in four days.

goalkeeper John Armstrong. The goalkeeper was kept busy as the Fulham forwards, Conway especially, peppered the goal with shots. Fulham suffered bad luck when Steve Earle pulled a muscle after just twenty-five minutes and had to be replaced by Barry Lloyd.

Conway doubled the Fulham lead just short of the hour. The winger was tripped by former Everton defender Ambrose Clarke just inside the penalty area after he had beaten two defenders and weaved into the box; Conway recovered and got up to convert the penalty himself, blasting into the roof of the net. It was the third penalty award in successive games, and this one was certainly not disputed. Southport immediately substituted Clarke bringing on Roger Aindow.

Fulham were making heavy weather of the victory against another poor side, and substitute Lloyd had the fans frustrated by muffing several easy goalscoring chances. Southport had not troubled the home defence at all, venturing out with only sporadic breaks that soon fizzled out. Therefore it was a complete surprise when, with twelve minutes to go, inside right George Andrews glanced in a header from Roy McCarthy's cross to reduce the arrears.

This forced Fulham to up the tempo, and their pressure was rewarded when, with just three minutes to go, Stan Brown leapt high to head home Fulham's third from Haynes' pass and Conway's final cross. Still the game wasn't over, and Southport centre forward Colin Alty exposed Fulham's defensive frailties with a second goal in the final seconds of the game.

Despite these nerves, Fulham clung on to win **3–2** and record their third successive win and second successive league win. With his brace on the evening, Conway had scored five goals in his last three games, equalling his total for the whole of the previous season!

Despite the win, Fulham had looked hesitant at the back, which was rather ironic seeing that Bill Dodgin had been praising the rearguard in the club programme for conceding just three goals in their opening five games. Certainly Southport had looked Fourth Division material and defensively were very poor; a more clinical Fulham attack would have netted double figures.

The game had been so easy that the two Southport goals had been the result of poor concentration rather than anything else. Johnny Haynes had once more supplied most of the class, but Conway had been the star of the night, giving a five-star performance, terrorising the Southport defence whenever he had the ball. The media agreed that Conway's quality and finishing had sent a timely reminder to the Eire selectors.

Fulham travelled to **Barrow** on the Saturday feeling confident of a victory. Barrow were rock bottom of the table having lost all four of their opening league fixtures, scoring just one goal in the process. Fulham made two changes, with Stan Brown taking the injured Steve Earle's place at centre forward and John Richardson coming in for his league debut.

Fulham made all of the early running and Barrow full back Charlie Cooper blocked a shot from Stan Brown. John Richardson, with a slice of luck, could have also had a debut goal in the first five minutes. Jimmy Conway and Les Barrett were beating both full backs, and it appeared that a goal would come soon. Barrow goalkeeper George Heyes made many fine stops, and for twenty minutes the Barrow goalmouth enjoyed a charmed life.

Fulham's defence began to look shaky, however, and the team were rocked back when the lowly Barrow side took the lead in the twenty-third minute. Mike Pentecost committed a needless foul, and Barrow forced a corner. From the short corner taken by Eddie Garbett, Tony Morrin headed the ball on and winger Roy Ellison stole in to beat Brian Williamson with a well-placed header.

Fulham continued to play the more attractive and purposeful football, but were hit on the break again just ten minutes later. The defence let in Jim Mulvaney, and from the ensuing penalty area scrimmage, Garbett slammed a shot against the legs of Williamson, but the rebound fell kindly to the same player, and he slotted in. A shocked Fulham team tried hard to recover and home goalkeeper Heyes had to dive full length to keep out a shot from Barrett.

Fulham came out determined to reduce the arrears, and in the first minute of the second half, Johnny Haynes slipped through a fine pass and Brown slid the ball home – only for the effort to be ruled out for a marginal offside decision. Ten minutes later, however, Fulham were back in the match when debutant Richardson scored a richly deserved goal. Full back Fred Callaghan made one of his characteristic forays down the left wing, and from his cross Richardson rose to head home.

Now it was Barrow's turn to panic, and they fell back on defence. Fulham spent the rest of the rugged half swarming through the Barrow defence searching in vain for an equaliser, but they had no luck. The away side were finally finished when, nine minutes from the end, Man of the Match Tony Morrin floated in a chip shot over Williamson to wrap the game up. Fulham went down **1–3** in a disappointing fashion.

In some ways Fulham had had no luck on the day, and Barrow had been forced to fight all the way for their victory. However, it was Barrow, after all, and it was a game that an aspiring Fulham side should have won and won easily. Although Barrow had played well, there were major concerns that the Fulham defence had not been able to contain wingers David Storf and Garbett and the hard-working Mulvaney; Bill Dodgin was very displeased with the result.

The Barrow game proved to be the last in a Fulham shirt for goalkeeper Brian Williamson. There was some confusion as to whether Williamson had been dropped after the Barrow defeat or had sustained an injury. When Ian Seymour was recalled to the team the following week, Williamson was furious that he had lost his place again, and after remaining at the club for a short period asked for his cards. He immediately retired from football altogether to become a security guard! Williamson's departure was not even mentioned in the club programme. The departure was another £10,000 down the drain, and Williamson's 'dream move' had ended after just twelve first-team appearances.

After having had the luxury of three first-team goalkeepers up until recently, Fulham now had just one! Fulham did have thirty-year-old John Swannell, the Hendon and England amateur international goalkeeper, registered on their books, but he was strictly for dire emergencies, so Fulham were now down to seventeen first-team players and were now in crisis as they had no back-up first-team goalkeeper. In the short term, Fulham turned to non-league Hounslow Town and signed their highly rated goalkeeper, eighteen-year-old Mick Byrne, on amateur terms; Byrne was immediately drafted into Fulham's combination side.

Apart from Williamson's blow-up with the club, the Barrow defeat was the first real indication that there was still significant unrest at Craven Cottage. Cliff Jones, who had scored for the reserves at the weekend, spoke of being unhappy at not being in the team, and gave a warning: 'I am not satisfied playing in the reserves. If I am left in the reserves for more than a few weeks, I will be putting in for a transfer.' There was also trouble brewing with Vic Halom, who blasted the club, stating: 'I wish I had stayed at Orient, the sooner I get away, the better off I'll be; manager Bill Dodgin has put me on the transfer list. I don't fit into the kind of football being played by Fulham.' The talk of Halom leaving the club was rife, with rumours of a swap-deal involving the Queens Park Rangers forward Alan Wilks.

September 1969

In this month

* Rebel army officers led by subaltern Muammar Gaddafi seized power in a bloodless coup in Tripoli, setting up a Libyan republic.
* The ruthless president of North Vietnam, Ho Chi Minh, died of a sudden heart attack at the age of seventy-nine.
* Jackie Stewart won the Italian Grand Prix and the world championship.
* *BIBA* opened its first store in Kensington High Street.
* Lillian Board won gold in the 800 metres at the European Games.
* ITV made its first colour television transmissions.
* Rod Laver won the US open to achieve his second grand slam.
* There were now 7,000 British troops in Northern Ireland.
* The Open University was established in Milton Keynes.
* US President Nixon ordered the continued bombing of North Vietnam using the B-52s.

'Bad Moon Rising' by Credence Clearwater Revival topped the charts.
The film 'Bob and Carol and Ted and Alice' was released.

The matches

AT THE start of the month, Fulham faced the might of league champions **Leeds United** in the second round of the League Cup at Craven Cottage. Leeds' draw at Burnley the previous weekend had seen the Yorkshire side reach *thirty-four* matches without defeat. Although most consider that fielding weakened sides is a relatively recent phenomenon, this is exactly what Don Revie did.

Opinions in the press varied; some castigated Revie for showing little respect to Fulham, whilst others thought that it was a very sensible move bearing in mind Leeds' European commitments. Revie rested Gary Sprake, Billy Bremner, Norman Hunter, Johnny Giles and Allan Clarke, insisting that all five were 'injured'. So there would sadly be no fairytale reunion between Clarke and his former Fulham playing colleagues. Clarke had joined Leeds during the close season for a British record £165,000 following Leicester City's relegation. Clarke had been looking forward to the game saying: 'It will be nice to meet the lads again – Les Barrett, Stevie Earle, Fred Callaghan, Johnny Haynes and the rest – they're a good crowd.'

However, although the Leeds team was termed as 'weakened' the replacements for the five stars would probably have walked into any First Division side. They were: David Harvey, Paul Madeley, Eddie Gray, Rod Belfitt and Terry Hibbitt. Even this weakened side contained Paul Reaney, Terry Cooper, Jack Charlton and Mick Jones. Also noteworthy is that the Leeds United senior squad comprised just seventeen players, two of which were goalkeepers. Leeds played in a very unusual strip of red shirts and white shorts. The occasion drew a crowd of over 20,000 to the Cottage.

Fulham made three changes: Reg Matthewson took over from the injured Fred Callaghan, Stan Brown took the place of cup-tied John Richardson, and Steve Earle returned from injury at centre forward. In a year of tough European competition, the match was clearly an irritation for Leeds, but they sought to make it through to the next round with as little effort as possible. All Fulham were praying for was an avoidance of a repeat of the previous visit made by Leeds to Craven Cottage in January 1968 when they won 5–0, with Mick Jones scoring three.

In the first half an hour Leeds were in total control and the replacements slotted in with impeccable style, the young Fulham side looking slightly overawed by the occasion. The Leeds team, clearly playing within themselves, were the usual well-oiled machine, contenting themselves by passing the ball around sweetly, keeping possession and waiting for a scoring chance, their customary efficiency and flair undiminished. Most of their opportunities came from set pieces.

Leeds had forced numerous corners. For four of these, Jack 'The Giraffe' Charlton had ambled up and taken his customary position beneath the crossbar, and on each occasion Fulham keeper

Frustration from Johnny Haynes during the League Cup defeat to Leeds. The goalpost takes a kick as another chance goes just wide.

Ian Seymour had managed to punch the ball away from his head. On the fifth occasion, from Belfitt's corner in the twenty-fifth minute, however, Seymour committed himself to a rash dive and punch at the ball, but Charlton managed to get in front of him, duck down and nod the ball deep into goal. Seymour was the busier keeper in the first half, saving courageously when called upon to keep Leeds at bay. The on-fire forward, Jimmy Conway, had no luck in the first half and his form seemed to desert him completely.

The second half continued in much the same vein, but Fulham, sticking to their task, began to come more into the game. Johnny Haynes was beginning to find his colleagues with accurate passes, and the Leeds team were, for the first time, looking stretched. Dodgin then sent on Barry Lloyd for the ineffective Stan Brown in an attempt to add more zest to the midfield. As the game ebbed towards its close, Revie and his star-studded team almost got the shock of their footballing lives as Fulham put on a final spurt in the last ten minutes.

David Harvey was now the busier of the two goalkeepers with Conway a constant menace. Haynes' pass reached Lloyd; Lloyd made a skilful burst down the left and centred accurately. Conway, for once free of the handcuffs of the Leeds defence, was presented with a virtually open goal. He beat David Harvey with his cross-shot, only to see the ball drift inches wide.

This, however, gave Fulham some encouragement, and just ninety seconds later, Conway was through again, and this time it took a world-class save from Harvey to dive and finger-tip the ball onto a post and out for another corner. Haynes, backing up, couldn't believe the luck, and kicked the post in sheer frustration. Fulham continued to press, but time was against them and they were unluckily edged out of the competition **0–1**.

The press were full of praise for the Fulham display saying: 'They [Fulham] are still rich in skills, and they often matched and, on occasions, out-matched one of the greatest football outfits in Britain'. It had been an exciting game and another paper added a postscript that: 'There should be a salute for both teams for playing a glowing brand of football in a game that was a credit to soccer.'

Fulham had played particularly well at the back, with Ian Seymour, Mike Pentecost and especially Dave Roberts magnificent in defence, limiting Leeds to very few clear-cut chances. Jimmy Conway and Les Barrett were showing clear, consistent form on the wings, and moreover had demonstrated it against the highest level of opposition. The statistics backed up this view. Fulham finished the match with twenty-six goal attempts compared with Leeds' fourteen.

World Cup winner Jack Charlton, never one to hand out cheap compliments, said: 'Fulham were twice as good a team as when we last played them in the First Division. Their work rate was much higher and I am still trying to think why all their moves were not better rewarded. Johnny Haynes is surely the best player ever seen in the Third Division. It is not only his class, but the fact that he is prepared to make the effort too.

'Those wingers must easily be the best pair in the division, but surely a place could be found for somebody like Cliff Jones. When I heard he was out of the team I thought that he must be injured.

'Fulham were fairly tight at the back, but seem to have the same trouble as my team. They dictate play for long periods, but fail to slot home the chances. We help to solve this by using me in attack from all the set positions, corners and free kicks.

'I hope that Fulham can find their own way to improve their goalscoring. They deserve to crash straight out of the Third Division at the first attempt. The way they played against us, it is ridiculous they should be down there.'

Fulham returned to league action on the Saturday with a visit from **Shrewsbury Town**, managed by former Manchester United goalkeeper Harry Gregg. He was taking over from retiring manager and former Fulham favourite and league record goalscorer Arthur Rowley. The match was Shrewsbury's first ever visit to Fulham for a league match. To add more to the attack, Fulham brought back Cliff Jones in place of Stan Brown, who dropped to substitute, Barry Lloyd standing down.

The Shrewsbury side contained no real stars, but included eighteen-year-old John Phillips in goal, later to star for Chelsea, and Alf Wood, later to play for Millwall. Also in the Shrews side was Gerry Bridgwood who had scored for Stoke at Fulham in the last home game of the 'Great Escape' epic in 1966.

Shrewsbury signalled their intent by playing full back Geoff Fellows on the left wing. Fulham's goalscoring start had still failed to entice more paying customers through the gates, and another very disappointing crowd of fewer than 9,000 turned up on the sunny, autumnal afternoon.

Fulham made an enterprising start, and were twice unlucky not to go ahead in the opening minutes, firstly when Jones headed fractionally wide from a Johnny Haynes free kick, and secondly when the same player dived to meet Les Barrett's centre only to see his effort skim just wide of a post. When no early goal arrived, the Fulham defence began to look jittery as they had done the previous week at Barrow. They seemed susceptible to long balls down the centre aimed at the gangling Wood playing number nine. From one flick, Denis Hawkins was through on goal and Ian Seymour had to rush out and dive at the forward's feet to prevent an opening goal.

A defensive Shrewsbury were catching Fulham, and in particular Jones, in a stifling offside trap, and the home side began to become frustrated. When they were presented with a chance after Phillips spilled a cross, Barrett completely missed his kick. Dave Roberts then moved upfield to miss another great chance for Fulham, but then he was in action at the other end of the field, clearing an effort from his namesake, ex-Villa man Dave Roberts, from the goal line.

Fulham finally made the breakthrough ten minutes before half time when Haynes, waltzing through defenders, was brought down unnecessarily in the penalty box by Shrewsbury full back

A Shrewsbury player tries to imitate the watching Barrett, taking on Fulham skipper Stan Horne. The defence allowed Shrewsbury just a consolation goal close to time.

Tony Loska – another penalty. The decision looked another 'soft' award, but for the fourth time in five home matches, Jimmy Conway made no mistake from the spot to give Fulham the lead, the kick giving Phillips no chance. There were further chances before the interval to wrap the game up totally.

Shrewsbury came out with slightly more attacking intent in the second half, and Bridgwood and Graham Clapham had the Fulham defence back-pedalling. They were awarded a dangerous free kick on the edge of the area, but Clapham's free kick travelled well over the bar. Fulham were still bunching up front, and the massed Shrewsbury defence was ably protecting young keeper Phillips. Conway began to show more of his current form and after one scintillating run where he beat two Shrewsbury defenders, he sent in an accurate cross, but Steve Earle's header smashed against the bar; Haynes also then hit a post.

The match was one-way traffic now and Barrett almost extended Fulham's lead with a brilliant flying header. The effort looked a certain goal, but somehow Phillips threw himself across goal to turn the ball around the post. Shrewsbury gave it another shot and should have equalised when Wood volleyed Roberts' cross against the bar. Shrewsbury finally began to tire; Fulham brought on Stan Brown for the exhausted Haynes and upped the tempo.

Fulham extended their lead fifteen minutes from time, when Barrett provided the cross for Conway to nonchalantly pull the ball down and slot it home through a cluster of Shrewsbury defenders. The visitors' heads went down and five minutes later, the match was sealed when Conway, too fast for the tiring defenders, returned the compliment with a slightly miscued cross-

The crowd appear to respond to Cliff Jones' 'Hands up!' request! In reality, Les Barrett has dived full length to meet Conway's cross to head Fulham's third goal against Shrewsbury. Another strong home performance produced a 3–1 victory.

cum-shot. The ball looked to be going wide, but Barrett popped up and intervened, and his diving header rocketed home. Shrewsbury sent on substitute Jimmy McLaughlin and four minutes from time the persevering Wood netted a consolation follow-up goal after Seymour had fluffed a routine save from Hawkins. The match finished **3–1**.

Shrewsbury had been decent opposition, and had kept going right to the end. Their main attributes had been grit, determination and hard work. Fulham had shown all the style, and with Conway and Barrett in their present form it was only going to be a matter of time until they broke through. Young Phillips in goal had completed an inspired game to keep the score down, and Alf Wood had toiled away all match for little reward. Fulham's defence, Reg Matthewson apart, had looked nervous and were fortunate that the skills of the five forwards had limited their exposure to counter-attacks. Fulham had accumulated almost 30% of the previous season's points total already.

The following week, Fulham made the trip to Eastville to contest the points with **Bristol Rovers**. The encounter was going to be a unique one, and would create history as the Bristol Rovers side were managed by Bill Dodgin senior, father of the Fulham manager. Bill senior had been appointed Rovers' manager at the beginning of the current season.

The week had been a difficult one for Fulham, as the club had been ravaged by a mysterious stomach bug. As the week wore on, some began to recover to some degree, but by the time of the match, Fulham were still without Mike Pentecost, Dave Roberts and Cliff Jones; some boarded the coach still not 100% fit, Stan Brown and John Gilchrist being the most affected.

Brown dropped back to replace Pentecost; John Richardson, replacing Roberts, came in to partner Reg Matthewson at the centre of the defence, and Barry Lloyd was recalled; new boy Danny O'Leary was named as substitute. Fulham had tried desperately, unsuccessfully in the end, to persuade the Football League to postpone the match in the wake of the epidemic. Dodgin had truly struggled to raise a team. Fulham changed to dark socks, to avoid confusion with Rovers' partly white socks.

Fulham controlled the first half, and it was a surprise that it took them twenty-three minutes to score. Jimmy Conway exchanged a wall-pass with Les Barrett and hammered the return under goalkeeper Dick Sheppard. The lead lasted just two minutes; Ian Seymour had to save bravely at the feet of Robin Stubbs, and then 'bug' victim Stan Brown chopped down veteran winger Harold Jarman in the box, and the same player rose to equalise from the penalty spot.

Then it was Rovers' turn to lose concentration straight after the equalising goal. A long ball from full back John Gilchrist split the Rovers defence, allowing Steve Earle to run on and beat three defenders in a magnificent solo run before lifting the ball over the advancing keeper's body

Jimmy Conway takes Barrett's return pass and drills a low shot under the advancing Bristol Rovers' goalkeeper Sheppard to score at Eastville. Despite taking the lead twice, a Fulham side struck down with a bug finally succumbed 2–3. The match pitched manager Bill Dodgin against his father.

as he came out to challenge; this was now three goals in five minutes. Fulham held the lead easily until half time, and could have increased it when firstly Stan Horne strode through and curled a thirty-yard shot just wide of a post, and secondly John Richardson headed just wide. The visitors looked to have the game completely sewn up. Johnny Haynes, not himself, was withdrawn at half time and replaced by O'Leary.

The second half belonged to Rovers, although Barrett could have increased the lead immediately after half time when he hit the bar. However, within two minutes of the restart Rovers were level. 'Bug' victim Gilchrist aimed a back pass to goalkeeper Seymour. It was a weary effort, and taking advantage of Seymour's failure to notice the danger, the alert Robin Stubbs anticipated the pass, and nipped in to beat the goalkeeper and score into an empty net from an oblique angle.

Just fifteen minutes later Fulham were behind to a lucky goal. Rovers' Wayne Jones hoisted a long, diagonal ball forward and, as it dropped, Ray Graydon raced in and spectacularly hit the ball on the volley; he mis-hit his shot but the ball flew low into the net off the inside a post and past Seymour.

The leg-weary and bug-ridden Cottagers never really looked like forcing their way back into the game, but Dodgin junior came down from the stands in the last ten minutes to demand a final flourish, as the home defence still appeared to be vulnerable. Fulham were very unlucky and twice almost netted the equaliser. Five minutes from the end, Conway sent in a rasping, angled shot that the home keeper Sheppard just held at the second attempt, and then the same player's shot was blocked by a posse of panicking defenders. Fulham's sickly side finally lost **2–3**.

Father and son agreed on a tactful summary of the game: 'Bad luck son ... the first half was Fulham's, but the second belonged to Rovers.' Dodgin senior said of Fulham: 'You are the best side we have faced this season, they are young, but have loads of know-how.' Privately, however, Dodgin junior was unhappy with the third poor display by the defence, despite the stomach bug. He muttered: 'After leading 2–1, we just threw it away.'

The result was the third consecutive away defeat in the league and already seven goals had been conceded. Dodgin let the team know of his frustrations in no uncertain terms. Danny O'Leary cannot have impressed the boss, as the forty-five minutes he took part in was his only ever first team contribution.

Fulham continued on their travels to Yorkshire just three days later to play **Halifax Town**, managed by Alan Ball (senior), father of the World Cup star. John Gilchrist was still unwell, and Stan Brown this time switched to right back, Fred Callaghan taking the place of the sick Mike Pentecost at left back. Dave Roberts had also not recovered from the illness, so Reg Matthewson continued at centre half; Fulham were effectively still without three of their starting back four.

With Fulham in vulnerable form away from home, a victory seemed unlikely particularly as Halifax had not conceded a home goal that season and were unbeaten at The Shay for nine months! Fulham photographer Ken Coton therefore considered it unnecessary to make the trip – but what a night he missed!

The first ten minutes were uneventful, but then things started to happen. A defensive blunder and a deflection off the referee let in Steve Earle for the first. Fulham plugged away, but were still only one up after half an hour, and Halifax missed one great chance to level the scores. Then the real fireworks started. Barry Lloyd lashed in the second, and just a minute later Earle beat three defenders in a great solo run to push in the third. A shell-shocked Halifax were unable to stem the tide, and before the interval Jimmy Conway made a marauding run into the penalty area. He was hauled down and rose to convert the penalty himself with typical aplomb; Fulham were four goals clear at the interval.

There was no rest for Halifax after the restart as Earle completed his hat trick within seconds of the resumption. There was a temporary respite for Halifax for a quarter of an hour, but then Conway took his second and Earle scored his fourth within a minute of each other. Stan Horne and Johnny Haynes were revelling in midfield, with Conway and Les Barrett untouchable on the wings. Halifax were now totally bewildered, and Earle netted his fifth and Fulham's eighth after just sixty-seven minutes.

All eight had been scored in the space of fifty-five minutes, the last *seven in the space of just thirty-seven minutes*. Halifax had made a decision, a few weeks earlier, to sell star player and centre-half Chris Nicholl to Luton Town. They must have regretted it bitterly on the night, as stand-in centre half John Pickering had no idea how to cope with balls down the middle or the goal-hungry Earle.

Fulham, with some compassion, took their foot off the gas at that point, and played out the last remaining twenty-five minutes at a much slower pace, although they still created a couple more clear chances. Halifax, whose side contained Freddie Hill, (who had scored for Bolton at Fulham just the previous season) and veteran striker Ian Lawther, were demoralised enough to miss the only two meagre chances that the watertight Fulham defence allowed them in the final twenty minutes. Fulham completed a record victory with an emphatic **8–0** rout.

Asked to comment on how it had happened, Bill Dodgin said simply: 'We had ten attempts at goal, and scored from eight of them! We had been threatening to do this all season. It was just tough luck on Halifax that they had to cop it.' Alan Ball senior was almost speechless, he stuttered: 'I still can't believe it, Fulham played as though they were still in the First Division.' Halifax had, on some occasions, contributed to their own downfall with some bad defensive errors especially at full back, but Fulham's performance had been sublime.

One reporter said: 'It was a night when everything the Londoners did was touched with magic.' It was almost as if it had been a joke match for chairman Trinder to include in his repertoire. It hadn't been, however – the events on the pitch were all very real. One paper commented: 'Above all it was a night when Fulham, after seasons of futility, sounded out a warning loud and clear – they have it in them to bounce back to the Second Division.'

The match broke records in profusion. For Fulham it was their biggest ever away win, and for Steve Earle, five goals in a game was the club's post-war highest ever, equalling feats held by club legends Beddy Jezzard at home to Hull City and Jimmy Hill away at Doncaster. The match was also Halifax's worst ever home defeat. It was the best ever away win by *any* club in the 'newly constituted' Third Division, (as opposed to Division Three north and south), and it also equalled, in margin, the highest ever post-war away win in the entire football league; matching the 9–1 away win set by Wolves against Cardiff in 1955.

Fulham had definitely carved out a couple of other scoring chances as well, and if these had been taken, the win would have surpassed the 9–0 away win by Barnsley at Accrington Stanley in 1934, the biggest that century, and equalled the all time league record of 10–0 set by Sheffield United at Burslem Port Vale as far back as 1892; it had been some night.

Jimmy Conway's brace, including his fifth penalty in eight games, made him the league's leading goalscorer with ten. Steve Earle took home the match ball, and Fulham asked the Halifax players to also sign it – perhaps understandably they refused!

The Fulham programme revelled in the result saying: 'It was always on the cards that someone would catch it from us. We have constantly outplayed our opposition, and outclassed some teams. We had not translated that superiority into goals until poor Halifax soaked it all up in one evening. When we went to Yorkshire, we were at the peak of our frustration. ... For us to lead 2–1 [at Bristol] and then drop the points was maddening. We wondered when it was all going to end, but we did not have long to wait.'

Fulham received further good news in the week inasmuch as Jimmy Conway had been recalled by the Eire selectors to play in the match against Scotland.

Fulham's conquering heroes returned home to a massive welcome when they entertained **Plymouth Argyle** five days later at the Cottage. The massive away win had obviously stirred something, as the game attracted a crowd of almost 13,000, an increase of well over 40% on the previous attendance.

Plymouth were just below Fulham on the same number of points. Irishman Billy Bingham then managed the Pilgrims, and their squad contained Pat Dunne, the former Manchester United goalkeeper, and Ritchie Reynolds, later to play for Portsmouth. Also in the squad were two young stars, full back Colin Sullivan and half back Norman Piper, who both later found fame with Norwich City and Portsmouth respectively.

The Fulham programme printed Plymouth's reserve team instead of the first team as the Plymouth secretary had inadvertently faxed the wrong details, so supporters keeping correct statistics had plenty of writing to do, as all eleven names changed! Fulham, unsurprisingly, named an unchanged side. Terry Medwin was in charge of the team, as Bill Dodgin was in Glasgow checking out a certain out-of-favour inside forward named Alex Ferguson playing for Glasgow Rangers reserves who had been highly recommended. Fulham failed to put in a bid, and Ferguson went on to be a club manager of some repute in Manchester!

Fulham, probably still high on the euphoria following Tuesday's massacre, started casually. Plymouth had decided that the best form of defence was attack, and twice in the first couple of minutes they could have taken the lead when long range drives by Ritchie Reynolds and Dave Bickle flashed just wide with Ian Seymour flat-footed and floundering. The home team then made the worst possible start inside five minutes. Following a throw, Stan Horne decided on a lob back to goalkeeper Seymour to relieve pressure. Under no pressure from any opponent, he lobbed back blindly, not looking where Seymour was, and the back pass looped high over Seymour into the top of the net; the 'oggy' was a candidate for the daftest own goal of the season.

Barry Lloyd collects an accurate cross from Conway (on ground) and volleys Fulham level against the Pilgrims. In a vibrant game, two profligate defences produced a thrilling match which Fulham edged 4–3.

Fulham fortunately didn't take long to equalise when Johnny Haynes' pass found Jimmy Conway, whose accurate centre found Barry Lloyd, and Lloyd shot Fulham level from close in. Fulham then began to assert their authority, and twice Pat Dunne had to make magnificent saves from Steve Earle and Conway to keep Argyle in the hunt. Ten minutes before half time, the mercurial Conway gave Fulham the lead after a magnificent solo goal, skipping through the entire mesmerised Plymouth defence before firing home.

In the second half it took just eight minutes for Fulham to extend that lead. A move ended with the ball bobbing about in the Plymouth penalty area, which was only half cleared to Haynes standing outside the box and he thundered in a beautiful low half-volley before the despairing Pat Dunne could move. Fulham became slightly arrogant thinking that Argyle would now fold, but just the opposite happened.

Driven on by the energetic Norman Piper, Plymouth pushed forward again, pinned Fulham back and reduced the arrears just after the hour when Ritchie Reynolds thundered in a thirty-yard volley that was in the net before Seymour moved. The home defence was now distinctly edgy, and they were thankful to goalkeeper Seymour for a number of dazzling full-length stops from Piper, Trevor Shepherd and Jim Hutchins to keep Fulham ahead.

Fulham seemed to hang on and broke out for Conway to score yet again, running in from the left and turning in Lloyd's accurate cross to score a 'picture' goal, and restore the two-goal cushion. That seemed to be it, but still Plymouth had other ideas and it was the turn of Mike Bickle to thrash in another super goal, a low drive from close in that Seymour never saw. The last ten minutes were total panic with the crowd having palpitations, but in a hectic finish Fulham just held on to record another victory, **4–3**.

There had been no doubt that this was a game of two skilful attacking sides against two poor defensive sides. Bill Dodgin could not have been fooled by Fulham's defensive performance. Apart from the superb Ian Seymour, who had his best game in a long while, and some headed clearances from new boy John Richardson, the defence had been a shambles throughout. Horne, Stan Brown, Fred Callaghan and Reg Matthewson had been cut open at will by the rampaging Argyle forwards.

This match was the third time that Fulham had conceded three goals in the last five league games, and fourteen goals had been conceded in just nine games, certainly not promotion winning form. On the other side of the coin, however, Fulham had already netted twenty-four, with Conway putting away exactly half of them, still the league's leading scorer.

One journalist described Conway's performance against Plymouth with a perfect ten marks out of ten, saying: 'Conway gave the first genuine ten-star performance I have seen this season, linking brilliantly with Earle and Lloyd he showed great skills and a match-winning flair.'

Plymouth goalkeeper Pat Dunne appears to be praying that it hasn't happened, but the ball in the net doesn't lie. Applauded by John Richardson, Johnny Haynes has volleyed in from outside the penalty area. The Plymouth defenders seem to be equally mesmerised by the Maestro's strike.

A delighted Conway spoke about his newfound role: 'Frankly I was a bit fed up with the way things went [last season]. We were going down again and I felt that I might be able to do more about stopping it if I was settled; this season everything changed. I had this talk with Bill Dodgin and it was agreed that I should start at wing half. Then I had to move to outside right, but the important thing was an assurance that I would be given an extended run there. Before long, things started to go really well for me, and now I am enjoying it all tremendously. I like going at the back and having a crack at goal. Les Barrett is going past his man too and we are getting behind the defences and really pulling them apart.'

Even at this early stage, there was intense interest from the First Division whose scouts were flying to the Cottage in abundance. Leeds United had watched Jimmy Conway against Plymouth, and it seemed that they would imminently lodge an £80,000 plus bid. Leeds saw Conway as the ideal replacement for transfer-seeking winger Mike O'Grady. Leeds had definitely made an initial contact with the club. If Leeds did not make a bid, then Derby County, Spurs and West Ham were all waiting in the wings. These scouts were joined by representatives from Chelsea, who were considering a bid for Steve Earle. Dodgin would say little other than he was obviously keen to keep the pair.

Fulham, in full flow, took a trip to Lancashire seven days later to face **Stockport County**. County were rooted firmly at the bottom of the table with just one win in ten matches. Fulham had to be confident of victory, and fielded virtually an unchanged side, the only change being Dave Roberts' return at centre half to replace Reg Matthewson.

Fulham were initially rocked as Stockport started aggressively, and Fulham had keeper Ian Seymour to thank for two excellent saves to keep the scoreline blank. Firstly he tipped a close-range shot from John Rowlands round the post, and then blocked a ten-yard volley from Fred Goodwin. After being forced onto the defensive for almost half an hour, Fulham eventually settled and thought they had taken the lead in the twenty-fifth minute. Barry Lloyd's shot was parried by Alan Ogley in the Stockport goal and the rebound found its way back to Lloyd, who squared the ball to Jimmy Conway to push in, but the goal was disallowed for offside.

Gradually Fulham began to get on top, and were rewarded with two goals shortly before half time. Steve Earle was fouled on the fringe of the penalty area, and Johnny Haynes touched in a beautiful swerving free kick that was met by Earle, whose spectacular glancing header gave Ogley no chance. Five minutes later, Fulham scored again when a move involving Haynes, Fred Callaghan and Les Barrett caused a catalogue of defensive errors in the Stockport goalmouth, which allowed Conway to run in from the right and score easily from an acute angle between the goalkeeper and post; this was the fifth consecutive match in which Conway had scored.

Fulham showed no mercy after the break, and it took Earle just eight minutes to notch his second and Fulham's third; again the jittery Stockport defence was to blame. Two defenders failed to clear from near the goal line, and a third, John Chapman, merely passed the ball straight to Earle, and he was in no mood to miss a chance like that. Earle was now running amok amongst the dispirited Stockport defenders, and no one was surprised when he bagged his hat trick. Earle had two shots charged down by the Stockport defence and keeper Ogley, but showed lightning reactions to score at the third attempt. The scoreline could have been even worse for County, and it took a number of fantastic saves from the ex-Manchester City keeper Ogley to deny Earle further goals; the striker could have easily equalled his feat at Halifax on the day.

Haynes took a knock and was replaced by Mike Pentecost. Fulham's dedication to attacking play left them exposed to the counter-attack, but they were rarely threatened until the last seven minutes when Seymour became embroiled in a mix-up with a defender; Goodwin collected the ball and set up Rowlands, who netted a late consolation goal; nevertheless Fulham coasted home **4–1** in the end.

The win had made it a spectacular sixteen goals in just three league games, thirteen alone coming from Earle and Conway. A stunned Stockport manager Walter Galbraith said: 'They're good enough to go straight back to the Second Division.' Fulham had been a class ahead in every department, but Conway, Earle and Haynes were playing as if Fulham were competing against First Division defences – totally unstoppable.

The Fulham supporters were convinced that the tide was finally turning. Fulham had to be cautious, however, as at this stage of the season, they had played just two of the top twelve clubs, but nine of the bottom twelve. The derby against Orient, currently lying joint second, would prove to be a much stronger test. **Note:** *At the time of this book's production, highlights of the match exist on the internet on YouTube.*

Fulham had already faced, and beaten, **Orient** in the League Cup, and so had no fears, but Orient were a good solid side, as the Cup tie had proved. Whether it was the result of an injury was not clear, but Dave Roberts was dropped down to substitute, with Stan Brown moving up to partner John Richardson in central defence. Mike Pentecost, substitute on Saturday, took Brown's place at full back. The encounter at Brisbane Road took place just forty-eight hours after the Stockport game. The good form of both clubs attracted a very large gate of just short of 19,000, Orient's best for three years.

The Fulham whirlwind continued just where it had left off on Saturday, and they were unlucky not to score in the first minute, when Johnny Haynes pushed a free kick to Fred Callaghan, who

Fulham keep on attacking! After sixteen goals in just three games, Fred Callaghan fires in a first-minute free kick which fizzes just wide at Brisbane Road. Despite an early Fulham lead, a strong Orient side finally overpowered the Cottagers 1–3. A crowd of 19,000 witnessed a game way above Third Division standard.

blasted fractionally wide. After just nine minutes, however, Fulham were ahead. The goal was a carbon copy of the first at Stockport. Haynes swept an accurate free kick from the touchline onto the head of Steve Earle, who darted in front of the Orient defenders and glanced a beautifully headed goal into the roof of the net. The goal was Earle's ninth in four games, and made him the league's second highest scorer – just behind teammate Conway.

This stirred Orient and just fifteen minutes later they were level. Former Fulham full back Mike Jones sent a free kick deep into the Fulham area. Centre half Terry Mancini muscled in and sent a powerful header over the entire Fulham defence. The ball looped over Ian Seymour and dropped behind him into the net, Stan Brown powerless on the line to keep it out.

Fulham were vulnerable to the swift counter-attacks coming at them from both flanks and were forced to defend almost incessantly; Orient were paying Fulham's attacking reputation little respect, and the Cottagers were glad to hear the half time whistle.

Fulham needed to slow the game down and consolidate, but were not given the opportunity. Just one minute into the second half, Orient took the lead. From yet another free kick, this time taken by Tommy Taylor, Mancini headed the ball down in the box, where centre forward Peter Allen turned smartly before hitting a piledriver into the roof of the net. The goal raised Orient's game further and just twelve minutes later Orient scored the killer third goal.

The unmarked Taylor was involved again, this time receiving a throw-in and lobbing in a centre. Eighteen-year-old Barrie Fairbrother threw himself forward, and his downward, glancing header found the corner of the net. Fulham could find no way back, and were further hampered when Haynes took a knock and had to be replaced by centre half Dave Roberts.

Fulham were being outnumbered and outfought in midfield and were fortunate not to concede at least three further goals. Winger Peter Brabrook continued to pull the Fulham defence out of position, providing ample ammunition for the Orient forwards; Fulham's spectacular three-match run was over, Orient winning comfortably **1–3**.

Although dedicated to attacking football, Fulham were criticised for paying scant attention to their defensive duties and taking Orient too lightly. The East End team had been superbly fit and had battled for the entire ninety minutes. They had gained ample revenge for the League Cup defeat a month earlier. There was no doubt that they had deserved to win.

The press thought that the match had been another superbly entertaining encounter that had been way above the standard of the Third Division, conceding that both sides looked likely promotion contenders.

Such was the quality of the game that reporter Peter Lorenzo wrote: 'This was a Third Division contest providing a much higher degree of satisfying entertainment than I have seen in many First Division matches this season. Perhaps some of the faults in technique and tactics would not be tolerated in the higher sphere. But the moral, as far as I am concerned, is to heck with the technique and tactics. Give the fans what they want – a high-speed, high-action match of incident and thrills!'

On a less happy note, Fulham had this week taken part in the London Challenge Cup once again, and a Fulham side containing John Gilchrist, Wilf Tranter, Don Shanks, Dave Roberts and Vic Halom were evicted from the competition in the first round, losing 0–5 away at ... Sutton United!

Bill Dodgin knew that with the team scoring so heavily they could be candidates for entry to the £80,000 sponsored Watney Cup next season. In true form he admitted candidly that the pre-season Cup was a competition they could do without. He said: 'Let's face it, it's a competition for clubs that do not win a European place or promotion; we'd rather settle for promotion. I'm not saying we'll go up, although I'm pretty hopeful. What I do say is that we should certainly finish in the top six. That in itself would be a turning of the tide after two successive relegation seasons.'

Bill Dodgin had also set Jim Conway and Steve Earle a target of fifty goals for the season between them. He said: 'It should be well within their capabilities. They have the pace to unsettle Third Division defences, and the ability to cash in on it; besides which we are not a physically strong side at the back. So obviously we must be a team that must go all out to score goals, not try and stop the opposition scoring them.'

Steve Earle responded by saying: 'We genuinely feel we are a cut above Division Three, and that's not said in a bigheaded way. We seem to play much more football on the floor than the opposition expects. There's a tremendous difference in the atmosphere at Fulham now, we are getting the breaks, and the ball just seems to be popping in for Jim Conway and myself. Bill expects fifty goals between us? I hope he's right for that would put us well in the promotion hunt.'

October 1969

In this month

* Concorde 001 broke the sound barrier for the first time.
* The first episode of *Monty Python's Flying Circus* was broadcast.
* The B-Specials were disbanded in Northern Ireland.
* The seven-sided 50 pence piece came into circulation.
* Rupert Murdoch bought *The Sun* newspaper.
* The Divorce Reform Bill was passed.
* Margaret Thatcher was appointed shadow education spokesman.
* Forty-seven were hurt in a riot at Parkhurst prison, where inmates protested at the early release of a soviet spy.
* Willi Brandt was appointed the new chancellor of West Germany.
* Millions across America protested at the USA's involvement in the Vietnam War, calling for a moratorium.
* British troops were ordered, for the first time, to shoot back at snipers and bombers after more trouble flared on the Shankill Road.
* The 'midi' and 'maxi' skirts appeared, as rivals to the 'mini'.

'I'll Never Fall In Love Again' by Bobbie Gentry topped the charts.
The film 'Butch Cassidy and the Sundance Kid' was released.

How the league was looking

Luton Town had stormed to the top with nineteen out of twenty-two points. They led the table by a clear three points, followed by Barnsley, Orient, Bradford City, Doncaster Rovers and Torquay United. Fulham were ninth, and Reading mid-table. A number of clubs were already struggling. Barrow were bottom with just three points out of a possible twenty-two; Stockport County were just a point better off, with Gillingham and Bournemouth in the other two relegation places. Rotherham United and Southport were just outside the zone, a point better off.

The matches

CHAIRMAN TOMMY Trinder was delighted with Fulham's start and warned off club managers sizing up the Fulham assets. He said: 'We must retain the players who are doing so well for us. Not only that, we are prepared to reinforce the staff in order to win back our place in the Second Division.' The efforts of the Fulham strikers were being recognised, and Steve Earle had been voted the *Evening Standard*'s player of the month for September. Chairman Trinder was pleased to present Earle with a silver salver.

Five days after the Orient game it was the turn of **Doncaster Rovers** to visit Fulham. The Yorkshire side were playing well and lying fifth, just a point behind second place. This was mainly due to their frugal defence, which had conceded just six league goals to date. Their side was managed by a young Lawrie McMenemy, and contained no real stars. In the team were former Liverpool reserve goalkeeper John Ogston, former Leeds United reserve striker Rodney Johnson and the former Sheffield Wednesday winger Brian Usher. Fulham omitted full back Mike Pentecost after Monday's defeat, moving Stan Brown back to full back and recalling the experienced Reg Matthewson. The crowd was up again to well over 13,000 and referee Clive Thomas officiated a brutal encounter.

Whilst Orient had attempted to stop Fulham winning by using skilful attacking play, Doncaster's approach was completely the opposite – kick anything that moves. The Doncaster side made no secret of their approach, and soon had the crowd on their feet, booing at the alehouse tactics. Doncaster had obviously marked out leading scorers Steve Earle and Jimmy Conway for special 'attention'.

Substitute Mike Pentecost (12) has already replaced the crocked Steve Earle. Johnny Haynes and Stan Brown remonstrate with Welsh international referee Clive Thomas. Doncaster's Johnson walks away after yet another assault on a Fulham player's thigh. The Yorkshire side's approach was described as 'an appalling exhibition of muscle'.

Doncaster could have scored first, but Ian Seymour pushed Stuart Robertson's fine header from John Haselden's diagonal free kick to safety via a post. Earle started in his current rampaging form, carving open the Doncaster defence at will and, following Barry Lloyd's astute pass, crashing one early shot against the crossbar. The effort beat John Ogston in goal, but full back John Haselden booted clear.

As soon as the massed Doncaster defence was in trouble, the tackles began to fly in; Earle was being hacked, punched and elbowed. The striker lasted just twenty-five minutes before being the victim of a crude late tackle from behind from Rovers centre half Robertson for which the Doncaster man was rightly booked. Earle attempted to return, but, minutes later, was helped from the pitch with a badly damaged knee. Pentecost was substitute and so he switched to full back, with Stan Brown pushing forward. Soon afterwards it was the turn of Rovers full back Stewart Gray to be booked; he was then severely warned over two further late tackles, but somehow stayed on the pitch.

Doncaster then turned their attention to Conway, who was the victim of shirt-pulling and further scything tackles. In the violent atmosphere, Fulham's attention was distracted from the job in hand, and from one isolated raid, against the run of play, six minutes before half time, Rovers full back Harold Wilcockson was allowed the freedom of Craven Cottage to race up and head the away side into the lead. Rod Johnson swung across a low thirty-yard centre, and Wilcockson, unmarked, powered home his effort past Seymour.

There was no change of style in the second half, and Johnson became the third Rovers player to be booked for a lunging tackle that saw his boots scrape down the leg of Fred Callaghan. There was worse to follow: Johnson had the whole Fulham team pointing to the dressing room when another late lunge left Conway writhing in agony in midfield.

At this stage Dodgin was probably considering removing Conway from the fray while he was still surviving. Stan Horne was the victim of a stamping tackle, but somehow survived. Referee Thomas was being incredibly lenient considering the assaults that were going on around him, and this frustrated the Fulham team even further. Doncaster could also have gone further ahead at this point, when Johnson hit the post from Usher's pass.

A superb Ken Coton photograph captures a picture goal. Following a match of thuggery, Conway (far right) escapes for once, and his cross is met by the diminutive Stan Brown (2) supporting the attack. Brown's salmon-like leap and perfect header bring Fulham level at 1–1 against Doncaster Rovers.

Spurred on by the crowd and showing remarkable self-control, Fulham finally rallied. John Richardson went close twice and had what looked like a good goal disallowed for offside. Conway was also very close with two shots blocked by a wall of red-shirted defenders. Finally, out of the chaos, the Cottagers contrived to produce an equaliser fifteen minutes from time. Conway for once escaped the illegal marking and floated in a perfect cross. The diminutive Stan Brown, pushing even further forward, rose above all of the towering Doncaster defenders to plant a crashing, downward header past Ogston and into the net.

Having failed with intimidation, Doncaster then proceeded to waste time, the crowd described by the press as being treated to 'all the sickening paraphernalia of gamesmanship'. With a point salvaged, Fulham continued to press, but concentrated on keeping away from the crunching tackles and the 'game' drifted to a **1–1** draw. The entire Doncaster team were roundly booed from the Craven Cottage pitch, and there was a noticeable lack of handshakes between the players at the end.

The press headline read: 'The toughs walk off to boos'. One reporter described Doncaster's approach as 'an appalling exhibition of muscle'. Another added: 'We wish [Brown's goal] could have been the winner!' A tactful Johnny Haynes said afterwards: 'No comment – it was that sort of game.' Another unnamed Fulham player defended the lack of handshakes saying: 'Why be two-faced after suffering that lot!'

The quality of Conway, Haynes and Brown had stood out; only Wilcockson in the Doncaster side had played *any* football. It was indeed a rarity in these times to have three opposition players booked in the same match. The ensuing Fulham programme stated that there was no truth in the rumour that the club were going to change their colours to black and blue!

Following his player of the month award, Earle talked about the contrast between the previous season and this: 'The [back] injury cleared up toward the end of last season, but by that time the confidence of the whole team had gone. When you are not playing well, you grasp at an excuse – like a persistent injury, and, if you find an excuse, this in turn destroys your confidence. The crowd did not know that I was not fully fit, and had a go at me. They still do – it's a hangover from those days. On the field we shout at each other what to do with the ball, and in home games the crowd intervene so that you get rid of the ball before you should. I prefer playing in away games, there is less tension, and you can play your natural style. I envy those clubs who shout their team on – even if they are playing badly.'

Earle's comments were reflected in the scoring statistics, he had scored ten goals away from home – and none at Craven Cottage!

Fulham had a chance to improve on Saturday's result when they entertained **Bury** at the Cottage the following Wednesday. Bury had been relegated with Fulham, and had beaten them in the second match of the season. The Shakers had made an average start to the season, but were

Jimmy Conway fires in another right-wing shot that is blocked by a Bury defender. Despite another goal from the Eire international, a lax Fulham lost their unbeaten home record to the Shakers with a 2–4 defeat.

weak away from home having secured just two draws from six away fixtures to date. Following Saturday's bruising, a number of players had not recovered. Stan Horne was hurt, and therefore Stan Brown was forced to move back to right half, with Mike Pentecost resuming at full back. Reg Matthewson had also been injured and Dave Roberts came in. Steve Earle was definitely out of the action following his knee injury, and Vic Halom deputised. The Bury side contained no stars, and defender Alec Lindsay had now joined Liverpool. Although it was a wet and cold evening, the match attracted a good crowd of over 11,500. Bury, like Doncaster, played in all red.

Fulham made a very sleepy start to the match, and were punished severely. Ian Towers, who had caused Fulham a great deal of damage the previous season, put the visitors ahead in just five minutes. Barely had Fulham settled when Towers rattled in another just three minutes later.

Fulham were stung into action and seven minutes later Jimmy Conway reduced the arrears. A cross came over from the left, and Conway scored with a very rare header, squeezing his effort between the goalkeeper and the post. Conway had disembarked from a delayed fogbound flight just an hour earlier after having played for Eire the night before! When Fulham were putting efforts on target, goalkeeper Neil Ramsbottom was handling very cleanly in the Bury goal.

In the second half, Fulham started poorly again, and, despite having more of the possession, shipped another goal in a breakaway, centre forward George Jones scoring. Fulham tried hard to come back, but two men were now marking Conway as Bury had a two-goal cushion. However, illegal tackles were still being required to stop Conway and as Bury began to adopt a 'Doncaster' approach, two players, Jimmy Kerr and Jones, were booked by referee Tom Reynolds either for fouls or for dissent.

Fulham were awarded numerous free kicks, but these came to nothing. As time ran out, Barry Lloyd did score for Fulham with ten minutes left, but as Fulham chased the game, they were caught on the break yet again and Bury winger Brian Grundy sealed the win five minutes later following more defensive mayhem in the Fulham penalty area; Fulham lost the game and their unbeaten home record **2–4**.

Fulham had now shipped eight goals in the last three games, and this match was the first sign that maybe the team were not as good as they thought they were. Despite the injuries and the reshuffle, the team should have been able to win this one, but in truth, Bury were worthy winners.

The defence had begun to resemble last season's rearguard. In the slippery conditions, Ian Seymour had been hesitant and loose in his handling. Full backs Mike Pentecost and Fred

Callaghan had been troubled by the pacy wingers of Bury all night. Dave Roberts and Stan Brown had also looked well below par in the centre of defence; only stout defending by John Richardson had prevented further goals. Barry Lloyd had a stinker and Vic Halom, with a rare first-team opportunity, had been anonymous. By this victory, Bury became the first team to do the double over Fulham that season. The only players to shine were, almost inevitably, Conway and Les Barrett. In a number of ways it was now back to the drawing board.

Now that Fulham had Terry Medwin on board, Billy Gray announced that he was retiring once again and returning to Nottingham. He had been at Fulham for almost a year, answering an emergency SOS from Bill Dodgin to help out. He returned to run his general store. Gray was later a groundsman at Nottingham Forest for several years.

Four days later, Fulham travelled to the south coast to play **Bournemouth and Boscombe Athletic**. The Cherries had made a poor start, lying fourth from bottom with only seven points from eleven games, and having won just one of six home matches. They had, however, obtained a creditable draw with table-toppers Luton during the week.

Bill Dodgin, angry at the defensive display on Wednesday, made changes. Mike Pentecost was dropped and replaced by the recalled John Gilchrist, Stan Brown taking the very unusual position of left back. Dave Roberts was dropped, and fit-again Reg Matthewson returned. Barry Lloyd was also dropped, giving Cliff Jones yet another chance. The biggest boost for Fulham was that Steve Earle, after lengthy treatment, had seemingly shrugged off the knee injury sustained against Doncaster.

Bournemouth took the lead as early as the thirteenth minute through Ted MacDougall, and the goal was a sloppy affair. David Stocks created the goal with a strong cross from the touchline. John Hold headed the ball down, and the casual Fulham defence presented MacDougall with a chance that he squeezed between goalkeeper Ian Seymour and the post that the keeper should have been guarding. The goal was Bournemouth's first in *seven* matches – 563 minutes!

Fulham, however, were level ten minutes before half time. Les Barrett gained possession near the corner flag, and was able to send in a well-flighted cross that Steve Earle leapt highest for, and buried with his head. The Bournemouth defence had virtually stopped, appealing that either Barrett's cross had gone out of play, or that Earle was offside; the referee had no sympathy for either case. Fulham were lucky to be level at half time, as the defence was again panicking under

Steve Earle times his run perfectly to get in front of Bournemouth defenders to head Fulham level from Les Barrett's cross. The home side appeals for offside, but the referee is unimpressed. Fulham fought back twice to secure a 2–2 draw at Dean Court.

pressure, clearing danger at just the last minute. Hold was only just over with a snapshot right on half time.

Fulham fell behind again just three minutes into the second half, when Hold finally scored. The goal had more than a touch of fortune about it: Hold stuck out an optimistic toe at Trevor Meredith's shot; he made contact, but the ball was deflected off Reg Matthewson, the deflection being enough to wrong-foot Seymour in the Fulham goal and bounce in.

Fulham, though, levelled things again within ten minutes when yet another fine piece of skill and cut-in by Barrett ended with another accurate centre that Jimmy Conway, with all the time in the world, ran onto and controlled before firing a stunning left foot volley over the advancing goalkeeper. Bournemouth had goalkeeper Roger Jones to thank for several other good stops from Conway. Considering their form and league position, Bournemouth belied their current placing and put in a fighting, spirited performance; the match finished **2–2**.

This was a match that Fulham should have won – and won easily. It was a travesty that Fulham had only scored two goals. In general play, they had outpointed Bournemouth in terms of control and passing. The forwards' finishing had been, on this occasion, much too casual. Earle, probably not fully fit, had missed two easy chances. Still, the statistics showed ten goals conceded in just four games, twenty-three overall and Bill Dodgin had plenty of reasons to be concerned.

With orders to tighten up, Fulham played their second consecutive away fixture this time in Yorkshire at **Rotherham United**. The Rotherham side contained ex-Fulham full back Barry Mealand. Cliff Jones was replaced by Barry Lloyd, this being the only change in the Fulham side. Rotherham, like Bournemouth, were struggling near the bottom of the table; with just one home victory in seven attempts, they had not scored at Millmoor since August.

Fans on a hot tin roof? Some Rotherham supporters get a free and bird's-eye view of the game. The picture is a lovely example of Seventies Yorkshire grounds. Photographed from behind the net, Barry Lloyd skips past a Rotherham defender, but the chance, like most on the day, came to nothing, with a 0–0 draw always looking a likely outcome.

In the very early exchanges, a save from Ian Seymour gave the home side a corner, and from this the Fulham keeper superbly took the ball from the head of the recently signed ex-Sheffield Wednesday star Johnny Fantham. Then, in the sixth minute, it was the turn of the ex-Arsenal keeper in the Rotherham goal, Jim Furnell, to save well, firstly rushing from his line to dive at the feet of Les Barrett, and then just two minutes later twice blocking point-blank shots from Steve Earle after Johnny Haynes had provided the openings. At this stage, a bright Fulham side were in control of the proceedings.

The Millers began to come more into the game, and the Fulham defence began to show some of its frailties, looking very ragged. Seymour had to dash from his line to foil United's Lee Brogden, then clearing from the same player with his feet. Haynes did provide Barrett with another chance with a perfect pass just before the interval, but once again Furnell showed great reflexes in advancing and saving.

Rotherham continued with their attacking intent, and early in the second half United's David Bentley had a great opportunity, but delayed his shot too long. Fulham were now hanging on and playing second fiddle to Rotherham's determination. Reg Matthewson had a rare fight on his hands against striker Steve Downes and little was seen of Haynes. His passes, when he was able to make them, were excellent, but he was being tightly marked.

Fulham were looking the better footballing side, but could put nothing on target. With defences in control, both teams were trying to play elegant football and walk the ball in, something the defenders would not permit. Long-range shots were rare, and those rare efforts finished nearer the corner flag than the goal! Fulham rarely looked like adding to their impressive goal tally thanks to poor finishing, and the stalemate finished **0–0**.

This had been a very dull and boring game; the press reckoned: 'If this lot had played until next Saturday, it could still be goalless.' The Cottagers welcomed the point gained; they were tighter in defence than the previous week and the clean sheet was just what Dodgin had ordered. However, the zero in the 'goals for' column was the first since mid-August.

The defence had been held together by Seymour, Stan Brown and Man-of-the-Match Matthewson, returning to his native Yorkshire. All five forwards, however, had experienced a rare off day; most being tightly controlled by centre half Dave Watson – later to star for Sunderland, Manchester City and England.

The following Saturday it was the turn of another Yorkshire side, **Barnsley**, to visit Craven Cottage. Barnsley were on impressive form, lying second in the table.

Barnsley had only lost once on their travels so far, and had already recorded three victories away from home. They had only conceded fourteen goals all season. Barnsley were managed by Johnny Steele, who had been with the club for thirty-two years as player, coach and manager.

The Barnsley side, like most in the Third Division, contained few household names. This Oakwell line-up contained former Blackpool and Burnley winger Jimmy Robson, and young star Pat Howard, later to play for Newcastle. Steve Earle must have sustained a recurrence of his knee injury, as Cliff Jones replaced him. Considering the opposition, the crowd was a slightly disappointing 10,500.

Fulham were on much better form on this day, and Barnsley had to defend desperately against the fast, fluent Fulham attacks. Cliff Jones had the home fans groaning following two early misses. One of the chances missed occurred when Jones failed completely to connect with a low cross across goal following a corner. There was little goalmouth action until the half-hour mark, when Barry Lloyd was just wide with a twenty-yard drive, and Brian Arblaster in the Barnsley goal then had to make a full-length save from Johnny Haynes.

Haynes was just wide again with a volley following a neat headed pass from Lloyd, and just on half time Haynes' third effort of the half, following yet another pass from Lloyd, was just inches over the bar. Haynes was at his vintage best, showing his shot-shy colleagues how to do it. Although dominated by defences, it had been an entertaining first half, packed with good moves and exciting individual runs.

The action continued in the second half. Lloyd made the miss of the match eight minutes after half time. A perfectly weighted cutback from Les Barrett, following a run down the wing, found Lloyd unmarked in the centre, but, with a panoramic view of the goal, he miscued with just the

He's still got it! Veteran Johnny Haynes in his midfield domain pulls away from Barnsley defenders to set up yet another Fulham attack. Haynes, at his best, was unlucky with three efforts against the Yorkshire side. Fulham failed to break the deadlock, and a dour encounter produced a second successive 0–0 stalemate.

goalkeeper to beat, side-footing the ball recklessly wide. Barrett was the next person to run out of luck; in a scintillating run he outpaced and beat three Barnsley defenders, but his final effort grazed the outside of the post.

Jimmy Conway was receiving little change from the polished Barnsley defender David Booth and getting little opportunity to shine. When Booth was left trailing, he also resorted to some strong-arm tactics. Following one nasty tackle he was lectured severely by referee Capey. Sensing this was not going to be their day, Fulham's play became less impressive in the last twenty minutes.

The experienced Eric Winstanley and Pat Howard in the Barnsley defence were covering expertly, and Fulham were given very few clear views of the target. Barrett was now being closed down, and he sent three efforts into the side netting. Sensing Fulham's frustration, Barnsley midfield players John Bettany and the tireless George Boardman pushed forward. Their swift counter-attacks were well timed, and Fulham got out of jail when, from one raid, Ian Seymour dropped a cross from full back Barrie Murphy. Fortunately he recovered to grab the ball at the second attempt just inches from the goal line. Finally, Barnsley forced two corners in the final minute that Fulham cleared with difficulty. Both sides were seemingly happy to accept the result – another **0–0** draw.

The result gave Fulham another clean sheet, but also a second consecutive zero in the 'goals for' column. The attack had been unlucky against another defensively obsessed side. Steve Earle had been badly missed in the centre, Jones looking a pale shadow in comparison. The media said of Jones: 'The thrust he used to show for Spurs and Wales is no longer there'.

The Fulham defence, with little to do on the day, still looked fairly uncertain. Although Reg Matthewson and John Richardson looked comfortable in the centre, full backs John Gilchrist and Fred Callaghan had struggled against the speedy Barnsley wingers, and Seymour's concentration in goal again looked brittle. Such was the poor play in the last twenty minutes that the slow handclap was heard for the first time at the Cottage that season. Ominously it was now six matches without a win – no victory at all in October.

November 1969

In this month

* Sixty-four died in a South African mine explosion.
* Barracuda Tankers, owners of the *Torrey Canyon*, paid the British and French a total of three million pounds compensation for the coastal oil pollution.
* The US manned lunar spacecraft *Apollo XII* was launched.
* Police battled with anti-apartheid demonstrators protesting against the South African Springboks' tour at Twickenham's rugby ground.
* US soldiers were accused of the massacre of 105 Vietnamese civilians at Mylai.
* The Ulster Defence Regiment (UDR) was formed to replace the B-Specials.
* Eighty-seven died when a Nigerian VC-10 aircraft crashed in a jungle.
* The Government authorised twelve new local radio stations.
* The Rolling Stones played at the Madison Square Gardens.
* Joe Kennedy, father of John, Robert and Edward, died aged eighty-one.
* *Apollo XII* splashed down safely in the Pacific Ocean after the second successful moon landing.
* 300,000 faced starvation in the Biafra/Nigeria War due to on-going problems with food aid and the Red Cross.

'Sugar, Sugar' by The Archies topped the charts.
The film 'They Shoot Horses Don't They?' was released.

How the league was looking

Luton Town still led the table, but now only by one point. Rochdale had put together a tremendous run to shoot up to second from tenth position. Barnsley were still close in third with Orient dropping to fourth. Torquay United had also put an impressive run together to take fifth place. Yorkshire sides Bradford City and Doncaster Rovers had both slipped. Fulham were a disappointing eleventh and Reading fifteenth. Barrow were in real trouble with just five points out of a possible thirty-four, and Gillingham were just two points better off. There was a three-point gap, but Stockport County and Bournemouth still held the other two relegation places, with Rotherham still lingering just outside.

The matches

IT WAS a trip to the south coast the following week to face **Brighton and Hove Albion**. Albion had made a similar start to Fulham, lying in mid-table, but were strong at the Goldstone ground. Fulham made one change, with Steve Earle returning to replace the ineffective Cliff Jones. Fulham played in dark socks to avoid a colour clash. A seaside crowd of 18,000 had turned up to watch.

As in the previous week, Fulham started strongly, but it was Brighton who twice came closest to scoring. Alan Gilliver, the Brighton centre forward, sent a scorching shot just wide of a post into the side netting, and minutes later Nobby Lawton deflected a shot from Kit Napier onto the Fulham post.

Fulham survived and broke away to take the lead in the nineteenth minute. Fulham produced a crisp left-wing move from Les Barrett, and from his centre Barry Lloyd touched a short pass across to Johnny Haynes. Positioned at the edge of the box, Haynes balanced himself beautifully and hammered the ball in. At this point, Fulham were well worthy of the lead and were playing composed football.

Unfortunately a poor lapse in concentration allowed Brighton an equaliser just ten minutes later. The goal was a simple one: Gilliver, rising high with little challenge, put a header from Napier's in-swinging corner straight into the net.

Fulham could have regained the lead moments after the interval. Following a smart move around the edge of penalty area, Jimmy Conway put in a shot that was brilliantly saved by Brighton keeper Geoff Sidebottom. Following this scare, Brighton upped their game and Ian Seymour did very well to turn a fierce twenty-five yard shot from Lawton over the crossbar. Brighton were looking very solid now, with Lawton and David Turner pressuring the midfield. Fulham were now reeling under the attacks. The defence looked as if it would crack again – and it did, just fifteen minutes from time.

Full back Stewart Henderson robbed Steve Earle, and sent the ball infield. He continued to support the move and when the ball was returned to him, he put in a fine cross for Napier to magnificently head the winner. Haynes then took a nasty crack on the ankle, and his influence on the match waned. Conway, Lloyd and Barrett worked hard to earn an equaliser, but the Brighton keeper showed first-class anticipation and held onto all their efforts.

The Fulham defence and midfield was not functioning, however, and John Richardson, Stan Brown and Fred Callaghan could assert little authority on the proceedings. Seymour was by far the busier keeper, and if it not been for a number of excellent saves, Fulham's margin of defeat would have been much heavier; Fulham were finally beaten **1–2**.

This had been another entertaining game but it was a disappointing display against mediocre opposition. Bill Dodgin was now saying little, either to the press or in the Fulham programme; privately he must have been a worried man. The match was memorable only for the fact that it produced Johnny Haynes' last competitive goal in a Fulham shirt.

Haynes had just celebrated his thirty-fifth birthday, but remarked: 'We don't talk about those things!' There were numerous press reports, including the club programme, that the goal scored by Haynes equalled Bedford Jezzard's record of 156 goals for Fulham. In most statistical publications, Jezzard's record is reported as being 154 goals. Even the Haynes count was inaccurate, most publications crediting the Brighton strike as being Haynes' 157th goal. Therefore, Haynes had beaten Jezzard's record with his first goal of the season against Gillingham, and plainly held the current record by a clear three goals. Whatever the rights and wrongs, Haynes said: 'I'm entitled to equal the record; I've been here long enough!'

Haynes received another award as he was nominated the 'Third Division's Sportsman of the Month' for his attitude to some rough tackling up at Halifax when the home side were 0–8 down.

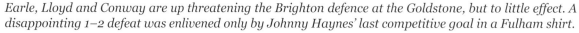

Earle, Lloyd and Conway are up threatening the Brighton defence at the Goldstone, but to little effect. A disappointing 1–2 defeat was enlivened only by Johnny Haynes' last competitive goal in a Fulham shirt.

Johnny Haynes receives an executive briefcase prior to the Torquay game. This was an award as the 'Third Division Sportsman of the Month', given for his attitude at Halifax in September.

Gillette sponsored the award and Haynes received a lovely executive briefcase – 'the best a man could get!'

A week later, Devon side **Torquay United** made the long trip to Craven Cottage. On a much earlier occasion Fulham, again in the Third Division, had beaten Torquay 10–2 at home; a result like that would have been welcomed on the day. Torquay were doing well, lying fifth in the table having lost only twice on their travels in eight matches. Their side included defender Bob Glozier on loan from West Ham, centre half Alan Young, formerly of Chelsea, and former Aston Villa forwards Tommy Mitchinson and Tony Scott. Also, at right half was a certain Jimmy Dunne who would join Fulham in the close season. Fulham pulled Fred Callaghan back to left back allowing a now fit Stan Horne to resume his place in the half back line. Stan Brown moved up from full back to replace Barry Lloyd.

Fulham proceeded to serve up their worst forty-five minutes of the season, and were a goal down in just six minutes. Eric Welsh found Jimmy Dunne with an accurate pass, and from his long, high centre, centre forward John Rudge leapt high to beat Ian Seymour with an easy header. The goal was an appalling lapse of concentration, as there were also two other unmarked Torquay forwards that could have netted if Rudge hadn't.

Fulham then seemed to pack their defence, as if petrified of repeating the mistake. They almost seemed reluctant to leave their half, and were pinned back for long periods. Despite the Fulham passes going astray and the home side surrendering possession and making little headway, Torquay did not seem to go for the jugular, and offered little in the way of attacking threat, content to sit on the one goal lead. Torquay finally woke up to this, and came at Fulham in the last ten minutes of the half. They were unlucky not to score on three occasions, the closest of these being a header from Dunne, desperately cleared off the line by John Gilchrist at the last moment.

Bill Dodgin must have been furious, and obviously plenty was said at half time, as Fulham emerged a totally different outfit. Johnny Haynes gave early intent with a stinger that Torquay goalkeeper Andy Donnelly brilliantly turned round the post. This seemed to be repeated time and again, and Fulham forced corner after corner. Stan Brown and Stan Horne were now pushing forward to support Jimmy Conway, Steve Earle and Les Barrett. Fred Callaghan was beginning

At last! After Fulham's twelfth corner of the half, Steve Earle rises highest and flicks Haynes' inswinging flag kick into the net with his head. The relief is almost tangible. Torquay have nine players in the six-yard box. Note the linesman almost in the penalty area himself. The goal, four minutes from time, gave Fulham a deserved 1–1 draw against the Devon side.

to show some real form, and his first-rate defending was backed up by some cavalier attacking moves, making him Fulham's sixth forward.

Fulham now laid siege to the Torquay goalmouth. The goal, however, proved elusive, and goalkeeper Donnelly was the hero with a string of breathtaking stops. Haynes produced a stream of left-wing corners, and Donnelly again excelled himself when one of these corners curved in towards the near post. Fulham had just one scare in the second half, when Mickey Cave clipped a fine shot just over the bar in a rare breakaway.

It looked as if it would all end in tears, but finally, from Fulham's twelfth corner of the half and just four minutes from time, Earle rose to rocket an inswinging Haynes corner into the roof of the net with his head, and a point was saved. Torquay were now worried, and Fulham could, and should, have won the game just a minute later. Hero Donnelly dropped the ball, and, with the goal gaping, Conway tried to dribble round the goalkeeper, collided with teammate Gilchrist – and the chance was gone; the match finished **1–1**.

Although the game saw another point dropped, it had been a far better second half; a complete forty-five minute onslaught on the Torquay goal. Certainly if it had not been for the brilliance of goalkeeper Donnelly and the defending of Dunne and Smyth, Fulham would have won comfortably.

Two days later, all thoughts of league action were swept aside and the Cottage had a carnival atmosphere for the second time in six months when the club celebrated **George Cohen's Testimonial Match**. George had been desperate to play, saying: 'I've been training a little recently to get in shape for this game, and I find that even after a short spell of work the old knee starts acting up. With luck, I may be able to play again perhaps once every three weeks. It would take that time for the knee to recover. There was also a danger that if I tried to play hard, competitive football that the knee would just crumble. I'm still trying to resign myself to it, but it's hard. Meanwhile it will be great just to pull on the jersey and trot out onto Craven Cottage again even if I limp a little – and it is for one night only.'

Even after picking the most appropriate day they could find, there were inevitably some absentees. Gordon Banks had broken a wrist, and had just had the plaster removed, but was optimistic. Club commitments initially forced the withdrawal of Liverpool's Roger Hunt, required for a Fairs Cup tie, and Leeds' Jackie Charlton, required for a European Cup tie. Everton had said that they were 'unable' to release Alan Ball and Ramon Wilson. A final late withdrawal was Bobby Charlton, required for a League Cup tie. Along with Cohen, these were the World Cup winning stars missing – the rest needed no second invitation.

Bobby Charlton was particularly upset at missing the game, and said: 'I really wanted to play, but it just wasn't on. Good luck anyway, I'll be thinking of you.' Nobby Stiles was still on crutches following a cartilage operation when the date was announced, but in true Stiles fashion, Nobby said: 'I'll be there – if I have to crawl.' Jimmy Greaves added: 'You'd think we had had enough football this season, but this was one we all wanted to play in.' Finally, an eager Gordon Banks said: 'Hold everything, don't fill my place – I'll be there.'

A crowd of almost 20,000 turned up to witness the host of stars on view. In a format similar to Johnny Haynes' testimonial, there were two matches on the evening.

The first was, like last time, a curtain raiser: a **Fulham Past XI** versus the **Fulham Present XI**.

The **Fulham Present XI** line-up, in all white, was:

Ian Seymour, John Gilchrist, Fred Callaghan. John Richardson, Reg Matthewson, Stan Horne, Tommy Steele (entertainer)–guest, Stan Brown, Steve Earle, Barry Lloyd, Les Barrett.

The Fulham Past XI line-up, in all blue, was:

Dave Underwood, Dave Sexton, Ken Collins, Bill Dodgin, Bernard Newcombe, Bobby Robson, Arthur Stevens, Graham Leggat, Beddy Jezzard, Roy Bentley, Trevor (Tosh) Chamberlain.

In a shortened match, the 'young-uns' finally beat the 'old-uns' 3–2. Although the 'senior side' could probably play more football, they lacked the necessary 'wind'. Graham Leggat still looked a useful player, and Fulham manager Bill Dodgin looked extremely fit. The biggest cheers were reserved for Tosh Chamberlain being urged by the crowd to 'shoot' each time he had the ball; the crowd were praying for one of his 'cannonball specials'. Both Roy Bentley and Beddy Jezzard showed delightful touches, with Jezzard going close with some fine shots. The Fulham Present XI won with goals by Steve Earle, Barry Lloyd and Les Barrett, with Roy Bentley and Graham Leggat replying for the Past XI.

John Richardson and Fred Callaghan walk off at the end of the Fulham Past v Fulham Present warm-up match. Also in the picture are Graham Leggat, Arthur Stevens and Beddy Jezzard. The young pups had finally won 3–2. Jezzard looks a little frustrated that he didn't score, but he went close on a number of occasions.

On the pitch, Fulham's vice-chairman Chappie D'Amato presents George Cohen with an inscribed silver tray prior to the match. Sir Alf looks on approvingly. Left: The stars sign up for George for the evening.

The main match of the evening featured a **World Cup XI** versus an **International XI**. The World Cup XI played in an all-red strip, actually Fulham's away kit (England had won the World Cup wearing red shirts), with the International XI in all white. In the end, George Cohen was not fit enough to take part and contented himself, fully clothed, with just kicking off the match. Sir Alf Ramsey led out the World Cup side, whilst Cohen led out the International XI. On the pitch, Fulham vice-chairman Chappie D'Amato presented Cohen with a silver tea service.

Old pals and England stalwarts Moore and Haynes chat their way on to the field prior to the start of George Cohen's testimonial match. George is sharing a joke with a smiling Alf Ramsey – this in itself a rarity! George's knee was not strong enough to allow him to pull a Fulham shirt on once again, but he did kick off the match. George's smiles hide the pain, as he was actually ill with pleurisy, and was rushed to hospital the following day!

Jimmy Greaves (Spurs) tucks away one of his three goals in George Cohen's 'main match'. The Chelsea trio of Dempsey, Harris and Bonetti and Fulham's Conway (2) are all powerless to prevent the strike. In a hugely entertaining kickabout the World Cup XI beat the International XI by 10 goals to 7. There were three hat-tricks and a penalty for goalkeeper Gordon Banks.

The **World Cup XI** was as follows:

Gordon Banks (Stoke City)***, John Hollins (Chelsea), Bob McNab (Arsenal), Alan Mullery (Tottenham)**, **Bobby Moore** (West Ham)***, **Nobby Stiles** (Manchester United)*, George Eastham (Stoke City)*, Jimmy Greaves (Tottenham)*, Peter Osgood (Chelsea)**, **Geoff Hurst** (West Ham)***, **Martin Peters** (West Ham)***.

The **International XI** was as follows:

Peter Bonetti (Chelsea and England)**, Jimmy Conway (Fulham and Eire), Ron Harris (Chelsea and England U-23), John Charles (Former Leeds and Wales), John Dempsey (Chelsea and Eire), Bobby Hope (West Bromwich Albion and Scotland), Keith Weller (Millwall and latterly Chelsea and England), John Radford (Arsenal and England), Jeff Astle (West Bromwich Albion and England)**, Johnny Haynes (Fulham and England), Cliff Jones (Fulham and Wales).

Bold Type *represents members of the 1966 World Cup winning team.*
* Members of England's 1966 World Cup squad.
** Members of England's 1970 World Cup squad.
*** Members of both squads.

As the game took place mid-season it was scarcely a contest, and very few real tackles were made. This inevitably gave rise to plenty of goal chances. In a knockabout game, the final score was the **World Cup XI 10 International XI 7**. The goalscorers were:

World Cup XI	International XI
Geoff Hurst 3	John Radford 3
Jimmy Greaves 3	Jeff Astle (penalty)
Nobby Stiles 2	Bobby Hope
Alan Mullery	Keith Weller
Gordon Banks (penalty)	John Charles

What was *not* realised until after the game was that George Cohen had been severely ill on the night; the following day he was rushed to hospital with pneumonia and pleurisy. Most thought that he didn't play because of the condition of the knee. Nobody at Fulham could have appreciated the tremendous effort that the sick George Cohen made just to be there. The hospital took X-rays and wanted to admit him until the danger was over. Cohen insisted on going home; a full recovery, however, was going to take some time.

Apart from the proceeds arising out of his testimonial night, Fulham gave Cohen a pay rise during his period of recovery, and also generously offered to donate to him £15,000 from the insurance compensation the club had received from the Football League for the loss of his services.

A special publication had been raised by journalist Peter Moss of the *Daily Mail*, called: *George Cohen – The man we'll miss in Mexico*. A number of the World Cup team had penned articles and paid tribute to the colleague who would tragically not be travelling with them to defend the World Cup.

Following on from the testimonial, Fulham travelled down to Fourth Division **Exeter City** to compete in the first round of the FA Cup. It was the first time in almost forty years that Fulham had been forced to endure the ignominy of taking part in the earlier rounds of the Cup. The trip down to Devon was a long one and Fulham knew that, despite Exeter being in the lower reaches of that division, it would be a difficult tie. Fulham were unchanged following the good second half performance against the other Devon side, Torquay.

After the testimonial, the match would have been an anti-climax, and so it proved. As the Cottagers were finding it hard to break even on their current league gates, a decent Cup run would have been critically important. The Exeter side contained David Pleat, later to become Spurs manager and subsequently a TV pundit.

The tie was a match in which nothing went right for Fulham. Early in the game full back John Gilchrist had to go off with a badly cut head that required three stitches and Wilf Tranter was forced to come on and play at full back. In the first twenty minutes Fulham swarmed all over Exeter, provided all the finesse and created chances galore. The main issue was that Fulham were trying to play neat, tight-passing football against a lower-division side on a lower-division pitch awash with cloying mud.

Fulham passed the ball around and across the Exeter goalmouth until the home defenders were dizzy. The shot-shy attack, however, did not put the final ball away, and Exeter must have counted themselves extremely fortunate to be level at the break. The Grecians goalkeeper Peter Shearing was forced to make a series of juggling saves, and full back Campbell Crawford was forced to kick the ball off the line.

In the second half Fulham continued to look the superior side, but the inevitable happened and on the hour former Arsenal youngster Johnny Corr put the home side ahead after an untidy goalmouth scramble. Pleat took a quick free kick, and following a scramble the ball was cleared to the experienced John Mitten, who found Alan Banks. Banks smashed the ball low and hard back into the Fulham six-yard box where Corr converted untidily from close range.

Fulham were suddenly given a lifeline, however. A shot was punched away from the line by the Exeter full back – a clear penalty. The Fulham players were furious that the penalty kick was needed at all, as the ball was *clearly* over the goal line when the back fisted it clear. The referee was a Mr Washer, and he certainly hosed down all Fulham's complaints. When order was restored, the inevitable happened and Jimmy Conway screwed his penalty kick wide of the post.

Minutes later, Fulham had a goal ruled out for no clear reason. Conway smashed in a superb shot but the referee ruled no goal. If it had been for offside, it was extremely harsh. Johnny Haynes was working like a Trojan to keep Fulham in it, and Stan Horne was backing him up with forceful play. In almost a farcical climax, Fulham put in a shot, and the goalkeeper stuck out a leg and succeeded in back-heeling the ball *over* his own crossbar.

With Fulham committed to finding an equaliser, Exeter sealed the win nine minutes from the end with a breakaway goal from Banks when Mitten slotted a long pass down the middle. Banks chased after the ball but looked second best. However, he somehow hassled the Fulham defender out of possession and scored with a brilliant opportunist shot. Fulham were dumped out of the illustrious competition at the first hurdle **0–2**.

This was probably the worst result of the season so far; Fulham should clearly have gone through. The result meant that it was the first time in *sixty-seven years* that Fulham had gone out of the FA Cup in the first round. The next-day headlines read: 'Poor old Fulham – what a flop!' A sorrowful Bill Dodgin sitting inside an unusually muted dressing room confirmed: 'We missed our chances in the first twenty minutes, we missed a penalty and had a goal disallowed.' The team had certainly been unlucky, and the Exeter manager was magnanimous enough to admit: 'It was one of those days where everything went right for my team.'

Fulham had now netted just two goals in the last five games, and the club programme commented starkly: 'This has been going on game after game. There are no points for style in soccer – only the scoring counts. We are stepping up our search for the type of player who will solve our problems.'

Certainly Steve Earle's form had dropped, which might have been down to the fact that he'd just become a father for the first time. It was ironic that in the last two reserve games Vic Halom had played in he had scored five goals, including a hat trick. Despite this, and Fulham's current goal drought, he seemed to be nowhere near getting a recall into first team action.

Following the Cup exit, Fulham next played another mid-table team, **Mansfield Town**. Despite their mid-table position, Mansfield had won four of their nine away games. The Mansfield squad contained some familiar faces: Dave Hollins in goal had been in the promoted Newcastle side of 1965, and John Quigley had appeared at the Cottage numerous times for Nottingham Forest. Also in the squad, but not playing on the day, were old Leicester City foes Jimmy Goodfellow and Nick Sharkey.

Mansfield also possessed some fine young players in eighteen-year-old Malcolm Partridge, later to play for Leicester City and twenty-year-old centre half Stuart Boam, who would later enjoy a long and distinguished career with both Middlesbrough and Newcastle United. Despite the Cup defeat, Dodgin decided to risk an unchanged side. Fulham's dip in form had seen the crowd slump dramatically to just over 8,000, the lowest that season.

Fulham put in a lot of work and effort against a workmanlike Stags side, but rarely looked like finding the goal spark to ignite the game. Johnny Haynes was, as usual, spraying a host of good passes around, but the 'powder puff' strikers were making little out of Haynes' creativity. In fact it was Mansfield who scored first in the twenty-second minute with a simple goal. John Stenson was quickest to react to a long goal kick down the middle, and the Fulham defence and Ian Seymour were too slow in sensing the danger, Stenson smartly slammed the ball home past Seymour from twenty-five yards. Fulham were getting nowhere in attack, where the extremely impressive Boam was blotting out Steve Earle.

Jimmy Conway was being asked to do a great deal of work in both attack and defence, and started to show his frustration at the recent events by being uncharacteristically booked after twenty-five minutes for a foul on Dudley Roberts. A minute later, Fulham produced their only worthwhile effort of the half, when Earle's header from Haynes' pass was well anticipated and safely gathered by Hollins. Fulham reached half time without offering another serious effort of note on goal. Stan Brown was having a stinker, looking distinctly unhappy with his inside forward's role, and Haynes had reluctantly pushed further up to assist as another striker.

The second half continued in a similar manner, with Mansfield appearing to be jogging along happily, prepared to sit on their one goal lead, very similar to the approach that Torquay had taken. Bill Dodgin then decided to swap over Stan Brown and John Richardson, and the change immediately had an effect: Richardson, showing good reactions, planted in two strong headers, both on target, but both saved well by Hollins just short of the goal-line.

Finally, Fulham's pressure paid off on the hour, when the home side equalised with a corking goal. Conway gathered a stray ball in the centre circle and worked his way out to the touchline. He looked to be running into a dead end, but suddenly found his direction, weaved his way inside past three defenders and slammed home an unstoppable, thirty-yard left-foot shot. The ball flew like a rocket into the top corner, dipping just underneath the bar at the last minute. Les Barrett then put in many good runs, but was usually crowded out by a mass of defenders. John Richardson almost won the game very near the end with a flashing header that was just wide. Although the Stags were groping for the draw in the last ten minutes, they managed to claw out a tame **1–1** result.

The press were unimpressed, saying that Fulham had played as if they still had an FA Cup hangover. Conway and Barrett had stood out, ably supported by the gangling Richardson, but that was it – another promotion point had gone down the drain. The lack of forward punch and 'zip' was now obvious, and the press said: 'Fulham must buy if they are to make up lost ground.' The media reported that the club were watching Spurs' Frank Saul in an attempt to boost the 'goals for' tally.

Three days later, Fulham made the short journey to a freezing Kenilworth Road to take on league leaders **Luton Town**. Luton were two points clear of the field and were managed by Alec Stock; they were also unbeaten at home. In the Luton side was Alan Slough who would later join Fulham, but more importantly the leaders had former Fulham defender John Ryan at full back, and former Fulham centre forward Malcolm Macdonald in attack.

Bill Dodgin made changes for this match. Wilf Tranter, who had been playing well in the reserves, was awarded his first league game of the season. Stan Brown dropped back again to his unusual number three position, allowing Fred Callaghan to push up again to the half back line. This released John Richardson to add punch to the forward line with height and muscle. An expectant crowd of nearly 16,500 turned up to witness the match. Fulham played in their change all-blue strip to avoid a colour clash.

The match turned out to be a total farce. On the high ground, snow soon started falling, which quickly became a blizzard. The captains tossed up in the centre circle, and the floodlights promptly went out; the teams were forced to leave the field before the match had even started. The teams returned after just three minutes, but within a few seconds of the kick-off the floodlights failed again and the players trooped off for a second time.

After a gap of five minutes, an appeal for an electrician was broadcast over the loudspeaker – greeted by hoots and jeers from the large crowd. After a gap of a further nine minutes, the lights staggered back into life, piercing what was now a snowstorm. Fifteen minutes later, the lights flickered out twice more – *four* failures in one half of a match, yet *still* the game was allowed to continue.

In the blinding snow flurries, Fulham appealed for a change of ball from the white to a coloured ball to aid vision, but the referee took no notice. To emphasise the point, during a hold-up in play, Johnny Haynes tried to hide the ball amongst the snow on the six-yard line, whilst other players built up a couple of 'snowcastles'. The referee eventually 'found' the ball, but even this display of open sarcasm had no effect! Eventually, the touchline markings also began to disappear. Fulham

Can you pick out the Luton goalkeeper at the far end? In this Lowry kind of picture, the pitch, players and supporters get whiter and whiter. Despite these worsening snowy conditions and four floodlight failures in the first half alone, the referee insisted on playing on, the game finishing at about 9.45 pm! For the record, Fulham slipped to a 0–1 defeat with a goal from Fulham 'old boy' Malcolm Macdonald. Luton's superb home record was rarely endangered.

began to become frustrated and Stan Horne was booked for a nasty foul on Luton winger Mike Harrison late in the first half.

For the record, and to document the formal statistics of whatever little football was played, Luton won with a goal scored just seconds after the restart. The goal came, almost inevitably, from Malcolm Macdonald, who emerged briefly from his fellow snow covered colleagues to haunt Fulham and score with a neat twist and volley, following a cross from the lively Luton winger Graham French, that gave Ian Seymour no chance.

Luton did have the Fulham defence at full stretch, playing the ball around beautifully at times, but there were few clear-cut chances created. The pitch deteriorated as the game progressed, and the majority of the ball-playing footballers like Haynes became bogged down in the morass. The blizzard continued for the majority of the match, and the farce ended **0−1** with Fulham, despite playing well, avalanching to yet another defeat.

Such incidents would never have occurred today. The referee, Harry Ellis from Goole, said afterwards: 'I never considered abandoning the match because of the snow, but I nearly called it off when the floodlights went out for the second time.' The home victory gave Luton the statistic of being unbeaten at home for forty-two matches!

Ken Coton's picture of the match in the following programme depicted the kind of night it was, with an 'L.S. Lowry'-style action shot that includes the Luton goalmouth. It is difficult to make out the Luton goalkeeper from the other spectators or the snowflakes falling around him! The débâcle proved to be Fulham's longest ever league match at the time, finishing at almost a quarter to ten! The programme lamented: 'If only the lights could have stayed out a little longer, the referee would have been forced to call it off. But this is becoming a season of 'if onlys'. It's time things started going our way.'

The poor weather continued for the rest of the week, and on the Saturday Fulham travelled to Lancashire to take on **Rochdale**. This away trip again proved to be frustrating and ultimately fruitless. The Spotland pitch was rock hard beneath a thin layer of snow, the media describing it as a 'sheet of ice, thinly disguised as a football pitch'. Despite the perilous conditions, both teams provided a commendably entertaining show. Jimmy Conway netted yet another penalty to put Fulham ahead in the seventeenth minute, when John Richardson was pulled down in rugby style by the sliding Rochdale goalkeeper Chris Harker as he was about to score, but Tony Buck equalised for Rochdale with a brilliant header from fifteen yards before half time.

Johnny Haynes then scored one the best goals of his career six minutes into the second half, a stunning thirty-yard shot into the top corner to restore Fulham's lead. But then Rochdale substitute Hugh Riley, on for the injured Buck, levelled just five minutes later with his first ever league goal, another headed goal. At this stage Fulham were in control and looking likely winners, with Les Barrett sparkling both in midfield and on the wing. The conditions, however, continued to deteriorate and after sixty-three minutes, almost three-quarters of the way into the match, the referee Ronnie Barker from Crewe (with no Arkwright to be seen!) decided to **abandon** the game.

As the darkness was descending, it looked like a compassionate decision – the pitch was beginning to resemble a skating rink. The match was expunged from the league statistics, and the two Fulham 'goals' removed from the records. The only statistic of note was that Dodgin was worried enough about the defence to make this match the last in the season for goalkeeper Ian Seymour. The teams were thankful for the abandonment, one Fulham player saying: 'We just couldn't go all out in those conditions.' Referee Barker said afterwards: 'It would have been dangerous to continue; I called the captains up, and they were in complete agreement.'

The club, resigned to the bad luck they were currently receiving, made little protest in the following match programme, but did contrast the inconsistency in the attitudes of the two referees in the Luton and Rochdale matches: one happy to carry on to a finish in a blinding snowstorm and multiple floodlight failures, the other happy to call a match off when conditions worsened underfoot.

December 1969

In this month

* Irishman Samuel Beckett won the Nobel Prize for Literature.
* The Supreme Court in the USA ordered four southern states to end segregation completely by February 1970.
* Almost 300 people died in one week in the UK from an outbreak of flu.
* It was announced that the first vasectomy clinic would open in Birmingham in January.
* Irish MP Bernadette Devlin was sentenced to six months' imprisonment for incitement to riot in the Bogside district.
* Charles Manson and three other members of a hippie commune were arrested and charged with first-degree murder, in connection with the deaths of actress Sharon Tate and six others.
* After an experimental period, the House of Lords voted to consign the death penalty to history.
* Deadly simultaneous bomb explosions in Milan and Rome killed twenty-seven and injured over 100.

'Yester-me, Yester-you, Yesterday' by Stevie Wonder topped the charts.
The film 'Hello Dolly!' was released.

How the league was looking

Luton Town still led the table, now by two points. Bradford City had recovered to re-take second place. Rochdale had continued their run to remain in third position, level on points with Bradford. Torquay United and Orient were still close in fourth and fifth place. Fulham were an embarrassing sixteenth, while Reading had moved up to eleventh. Barrow were still in real trouble with just eight points out of a possible forty, and Gillingham were just one point better off. There was a two-point gap, with Stockport County and now Southport anchored in the other two relegation places. Bournemouth had made a good recovery, with Plymouth Argyle now sailing perilously close to relegation waters.

The matches

WITH FULHAM out of the FA Cup, manager Bill Dodgin quickly arranged a **friendly** with **Southend United** at Roots Hall on the Friday night prior to the second round. Fulham had signed goalkeeper Malcolm Webster on a month's loan from First Division Arsenal. Webster, an England youth international, had already made three league appearances in the Arsenal first team, deputising for broken arm victim Bob Wilson. In a match against Manchester United shown on *The Big Match*, he had made an impression with a number of fine saves, despite one 'howler' when he mishandled giving away a goal. At last, after two months, Fulham now had a second senior goalkeeper on their books.

Webster immediately went into the team and played well on the night of the friendly, showing very safe handling. His 'decisive shouting' when calling for the ball had already earned him the nickname of 'sergeant-major'. Apart from Webster, Dodgin made little change to the side apart from positional ones. Cliff Jones was given another rare chance in the forward line. Despite a goalless first half, Fulham lost 1–2. Steve Earle netted the Fulham goal.

Despite the bad luck going their way, the latest run of poor results had seen seething anger build up amongst the Fulham supporters, and they began to vent their frustrations on the Fulham board. Statistics did not lie; the heady days of September now seemed just a distant memory. Fulham had now gone eleven games without a win, and had been dumped out of the FA Cup by a Fourth Division club in the first round. After scoring sixteen goals in three games in September, Fulham had managed just nine in the next eleven.

The team had gone through all of October and November without a victory. Without Steve Earle and Jimmy Conway banging the goals in, there seemed little firepower up front. Les Barrett had scored just once all season, and Barry Lloyd had managed just three; Cliff Jones and Vic Halom had not found the net at all. The team had also conceded thirty in just twenty games. There had been little sign of any personnel or tactical changes emerging.

The current loss of form had seen Fulham plummet down the table to an embarrassing sixteenth position. They now lay just two points ahead of Southport, who were holding down a relegation spot. It was frightening to think that, in fewer than three calendar years, Fulham had dropped down the equivalent of two complete divisions of the Football League, from fourteenth in the First Division at the end of December 1966, to sixteenth in the Third Division in early December 1969. The club appeared to be apathetic about the position, making no comments about recent poor results in the 'Voice of Fulham' section of the programme.

The **Bristol Rovers** home match the following week proved to be something of a catalyst. It was due to be an occasion where Bill Dodgin (senior) returned to his previous club to vie with his son's team, and it also marked the home debut of goalkeeper Malcolm Webster. Also, *The Big Match* had decided to make one of its rare forages into the Third Division to televise the match.

The Bristol Rovers squad included two Taylors and three Joneses, and apart from centre forward Robin Stubbs were a 'home-grown' team; Fulham were unchanged. Rovers came to Fulham on the back of a disappointing 1–3 second round FA Cup defeat by Aldershot. With Fulham's form attendances continued to plummet, and just 6,800 diehard fans turned up, the lowest for twenty years, beating the Blackpool attendance at the end of the previous season.

All this, however, was hi-jacked by a number of Fulham 'activists' who protested outside the ground before the game, handing out the famous leaflet *Fulham Football Club is Dying* at the turnstiles; 5,000 leaflets had been printed. The leaflets were handed out by businessman Richard Lawson from Maida Vale, John Stanley, who was a public relations officer from Chelsea, and eight other 'associates'.

Although the text included here is not verbatim, the principal paragraphs contained in the leaflet were as follows: 'This is the sad but spectacular story of a team that in eighteen tragic months has faded from the spotlight of the finest league in the world and is now diving headlong into obscurity. ... The time has come – perhaps belatedly – for something positive to be said and done to restore pride and position to Craven Cottage. Fulham Football Club urgently needs the kiss of life. ... Drastic measures are needed in this desperate situation. There must be wholesale changes at the top. The present board can no longer escape their responsibilities. ... Mr Trinder and his board have picked the managers who failed to stem the club's rapid decline. No doubt their

Defender Reg Matthewson, supporting the forwards, dives full length to hurl himself at the ball. With the goalkeeper well beaten, Bristol Rovers full back Parsons somehow blocks his effort close to the goalline.

intentions are good, but their record is bad. ... We publish this in the hope that someone somewhere cares enough to preserve the traditions, and to restore the glory to Fulham. We ourselves can do nothing. It will take a new board with money to back their vision. These men must be found soon – for there is little time remaining.'

Mr Stanley confirmed that the protestors were not seeking to take over Fulham themselves, and said: 'We are not trying to create trouble. We love this club and feel that this is the most effective way in which we can help.'

On the pitch, John Richardson had obviously been given orders to push up front, and in just the second minute he was fractionally wide with a header from Les Barrett's cross. A minute later Steve Earle just failed to connect with another waist-high cross from Barrett. Then it was Rovers' turn, and John Gilchrist had to be quick to concede a corner following a swerving shot from Bryn Jones.

The match was all Fulham, and both Johnny Haynes and Stan Horne also went close. Centre-half Reg Matthewson, supporting one attack, put in a diving header that was cleared off the line by Rovers full back Lindsay Parsons. After relentless pressure, Fulham finally took a deserved lead just four minutes before the interval. Barrett put in yet another fine cross after a solo run, and Jimmy Conway flipped the ball back into the box where Richardson was on hand to slam the ball home at the far post.

Fulham continued to push forward after half time, and their dominance was such that debutant goalkeeper Malcolm Webster was virtually a spectator. Haynes was the master architect feeding the forward line impeccably. On the hour, Fulham increased their lead when Conway zigzagged down the wing, then dribbled past two mesmerised defenders before putting through a perfect pass that allowed Earle to score. The effort was a fine low cross-shot on the turn from the corner of the penalty area that nestled into the back of the net just inside a post.

The impressive Earle twisted his ankle in scoring, and Cliff Jones was forced to come on as substitute, and he missed a golden chance a couple of minutes later through hesitation in front of goal. Bobby Jones came on as substitute for star Ray Graydon for Rovers. Rovers were making little headway against the biting tackles from the Fulham back line. The Rovers defence was looking leaden-footed and struggling to contain wingers Conway and Barrett, Conway giving full back Parsons an embarrassing runaround.

Fulham sealed the win five minutes from the end with the best goal of the match, and a candidate for goal of the season. Conway was once again the creator of the goal. He sped away down the right with a glorious run, and from his accurate cross Richardson threw himself forward to power home

John Richardson's diving header from Conway's cross has arced over the Bristol Rovers' goalkeeper for Fulham's third goal. Cliff Jones celebrates, the Rovers defenders look less happy. The televised 3–1 win hailed Richardson's goal as one of the best of the season.

a superb diving header that arced over the despairing goalkeeper. Veteran Harold Jarman finally managed to pull a consolation goal back for Rovers in the dying minutes with a low cross-shot from six yards that gave Webster no chance; Fulham at last returned to winning ways, **3–1**.

The win was the first home victory since the middle of September, and it had probably been Fulham's most determined display of the season. In patches they had reproduced form mirroring their former First Division status. The television replays praised Fulham for their play, and Richardson's second goal was recognised as one of the best seen on television so far that season. Conway had given a superb non-stop performance and had created all three goals. Les Barrett and Steve Earle had also looked to be back to their best.

Credit had also been given to John Richardson, who had worked hard all match and been a particular nuisance to the Rovers defence, fully deserving his two goals. Every Fulham player had contributed and at last the Cottagers looked a decent side. The result avenged the 2–3 defeat at Eastville. Bill Dodgin senior admitted: 'Fulham are by far the best team we have met all season, they have twice run us off our feet though we somehow managed to win the match at Eastville.'

The victory was slightly dampened with the news that goalkeeper Ian Seymour, who had been dropped for the Bristol Rovers game, had immediately asked for a transfer, thinking that he had been made the scapegoat for Fulham's recent poor run; recently the crowd had been quite harsh towards him. Fulham were disappointed in his reaction, but looked likely to accede to his request. ***Note:*** *at the time of this book's production, highlights of the game exist on YouTube.*

The previous season, Fulham had turned down a £40,000 offer for Seymour from West Bromwich Albion, but knew that they would be unlikely to receive that fee in light of the current circumstances. Recently both Nottingham Forest and Ipswich Town had shown an interest in Seymour. It was depressing, as alongside Jones, Halom and Roberts here was a fourth player 'wanting away'.

Tommy Trinder and the Fulham board had been concerned enough about the 'leaflet protest' to invite the two main organisers of the paper to a boardroom meeting at Craven Cottage. John Stanley said after the meeting with Trinder: 'After talking with Mr Trinder we realised that a lot of our criticisms were unjust. Points were explained to us, in confidence, which put a different light on the situation; it's only proper that we should apologise.' This was not totally in accord with what was printed in the next official Fulham programme, when the club, unwisely, tried to patronise and belittle the leaflet's originators and their terminology.

The club programme stated: 'We offered the signatories of that leaflet a platform for their further views. After talking together they said: 'We have absolutely nothing more to say'. This was after our chairman Tommy Trinder had taken the trouble to explain to them some of the things that were irking them.' Trinder rather sarcastically said: 'They were two very nice young men. It was simply a question of enlightening them. Now they see the other side of it, and we can only hope that the next time they feel strongly about something, they will come to see us before going into print.'

Whatever the rights and wrongs had been in the production and distribution of the leaflet and the subsequent meeting and responses, the barbed points had certainly hit home and stuck; the club were feeling pretty vulnerable at the time. The board were now acutely aware of the feelings of a significant number of their very loyal and long-suffering fans.

Seven days later, Fulham travelled with an unchanged side to **Shrewsbury Town**, who were lying alongside them in mid-table. Shrewsbury had won only three league games at home, but had lost only one, drawing the other seven. The Saturday was another cold day and snow was falling again.

Fulham started in good fashion and Steve Earle hit a post when Jimmy Conway drew keeper Bob Tooze out and whipped over an inviting cross. Later in the first half Earle was annoyed to see his twenty-eighth minute strike controversially ruled out by the referee by a marginal offside decision. Stan Horne touched the ball forward, and Johnny Haynes floated over a tempting cross, Earle then headed a fine goal but was disappointed to see the effort chalked off. The match was not one-way traffic, however, and Malcolm Webster was forced to make three great saves from home forwards Terry Harkin, George Andrews and Ricky Moir.

Town had a let off early in the second half when Tooze dropped an awkwardly bouncing Les Barrett cross, but fortunately Town's Tony Gregory booted the ball to safety. Surprisingly, Gerry Bridgwood gave Shrewsbury the lead seven minutes after half time, but the lead lasted less than a minute. Haynes speared through a pass into the Shrews defence and Earle, on the edge of the area, lunged in for the ball and managed to slot it past the advancing keeper.

This was now tough going for Fulham; Reg Matthewson gave a terrific performance at the back to secure Fulham's point, and Stan Brown was knocked unconscious near the end when heading away a late effort from Shrewsbury's Harkin. The match was drawn **1–1**.

Shrewsbury manager Harry Gregg paid tribute to Fulham, and in particular Johnny Haynes, saying: 'Fulham are a good footballing side, and Johnny is as skilful as he ever was. ... Haynes makes the ball do the work; he's a master, as good now as he was in his international days.'

Veteran Cliff Jones again came on as substitute for goalscorer Earle, but did little to impress. The game proved to be his final first-team appearance, and his last appearance in league football, bringing down the curtain on a distinguished career lasting over seventeen years that had given rise to over 500 league appearances and over 180 league goals. Fulham were beginning to realise that they had to turn to youth.

For the trip to the Priestfield stadium to play **Gillingham** on Boxing Day, Fulham were unchanged. The Cottagers, seemingly with a Christmas hangover, put in another very poor performance. Gillingham were lying just one place off the bottom of the table, and had won just two of their nine home games, but goals from Northants cricketer Ray Bailey and Ken Pound sent Fulham to defeat **0–2**. The first goal appeared to mirror Fulham's current misfortunes. A hefty Reg Matthewson clearance hit a Gillingham player and deflected straight to the feet of Bailey close to goal, and he couldn't miss. Johnny Haynes stood, hands on hips, disgusted at the lucky break.

Immediately after the goal, Jimmy Conway was clear through only to be cynically tripped just outside the area. Fulham created few chances, but from one swirling cross Les Barrett's diving header skimmed the wrong side of the post.

It was certainly a day when Fulham did not get the breaks. Although this appeared to be a terrible result at the time, just twenty-four hours later, Gillingham travelled to league leaders Luton Town, and promptly smashed their long-standing unbeaten home record!

The next day Fulham had the opportunity of putting this result right and try to avenge the 1–3 defeat at Holker Street earlier in the season, with a match against **Barrow**. The match was Barrow's first ever visit to Fulham for a league match. Barrow for some reason switched to an all-red kit instead of playing in all blue. Barrow were at the very foot of the table and struggling badly. Their team possessed no stars, and they had taken just two points (from two draws) from all their away

Not the Christmas present Fulham wanted. A freak deflection has given Gillingham's Bailey a simple goal to put the Whites behind. The goal and the game reflected Fulham's fortunes at the time. No wonder Johnny Haynes (10) adopts his trademark 'frustration pose'! A bleak Boxing Day saw Fulham suffer a 0–2 reverse at the Priestfield Stadium.

league matches that season. If Fulham could not win this match, then they didn't deserve to be anywhere near the promotion spots. As it was the Christmas period, the crowd, despite the lowly opposition, rose to 9,500.

Fulham took the lead as early as the seventh minute, John Richardson climbed high to meet a Johnny Haynes free kick and put a soaring header into net. The referee, Mike Kerkhof from Oxford, looked as if he was going to disallow the goal, putting his whistle to his lips to blow for an infringement on a Barrow defender, but he glanced at the linesman who made no signal and so awarded the goal; the award was hotly disputed by all of the Barrow defenders.

Then Fulham's luck was really in: Stan Brown kicked an effort from Barrow centre forward Bob Ledger off the goal line, and Eddie Garbett shook the Fulham crossbar with a real banger from outside the box. Fulham then had further bad luck when they lost goalscorer Richardson with a nasty ankle injury with Barry Lloyd substituting.

Substitute Lloyd then made the score sheet himself just five minutes after half time, heading home, unmarked, a high cross from Steve Earle who had drifted out to the wing to avoid the attentions of Barrow centre half Brian Arrowsmith. The two-goal lead lasted barely ten minutes: Barrow winger Roy Ellison, who often had the Fulham defence wrong-footed, scored a great opportunist goal after fifty-nine minutes, hooking a clever shot past Malcolm Webster. Minutes later the same player hit the Fulham bar.

The Fulham defence then began to look extremely jittery, with a number of last-ditch clearances. Webster was in trouble with many crosses, electing to punch instead of catch, and his uncertainty gave rise to several anxious moments in the Fulham defence. In the last quarter of an hour, the Fulham goal was leading a charmed life. Fulham tried to break away to seal the win in the final minutes, but both Haynes and Fred Callaghan muffed simple chances. Every one of the Fulham forward line had experienced an off day – it was that kind of match. Fulham hung on to scrape home **2–1**.

Despite the result, there was no getting away from the truth that Fulham had been extremely fortunate to take both points. The bottom side had often looked the better side and had deserved

An end of year view of Craven Cottage with sparse crowds and lacklustre football.

better fortune. Only defenders John Gilchrist, Fred Callaghan and Stan Brown emerged with any credit – the rest looking a very dispirited bunch indeed.

Fulham's end of year report looked like making sorry reading; after a bright start, the general trend had been downhill all the way. The current side lacked confidence and spirit, and there were very few encouraging signs that much would change. The main problems appeared to be in the goalscoring punch up front. Too much reliance had been placed on Steve Earle and Jimmy Conway; the pair were now very tightly marked (and kicked), and Fulham's goal supply had almost dried up completely. Jimmy Conway had scored just one goal in his last eleven appearances.

Despite some impressive wing play, Les Barrett had found the net just once so far. Barry Lloyd had been in and out of the side, and Fulham were now going to be without utility man John Richardson for some time. Cliff Jones and Frank Large were now both gone, and Johnny Haynes was beginning to look a tired player.

Vic Halom also appeared to have been frozen out. Although there was nothing written in the club programme to discuss transfer-listed Halom's absence, even from the reserve side, it was suspected that he had a worrying knee injury. The youth striker Danny O'Leary, signed from Millwall, did not seem to be featuring in Dodgin's plans at all.

The club must now have been bitterly rueing the sale of Malcolm Macdonald, level with Conway and Earle as the Third Division's leading goalscorer, and seemingly driving Luton Town to instant promotion. Fulham had made an approach to Birmingham City for the transfer of their reserve striker Mickey Darrell; the fee had been agreed at £10,000. Unfortunately, due to an on-going row over the percentage to be paid to Birmingham for any future transfer, the move foundered. Fulham then turned their attention to the diminutive Bradford City forward Bobby Ham, but this initiative also failed to materialise.

There had been little consistency at the back either, with goalkeeper Ian Seymour dropped after some good early form. Fulham could count themselves fortunate, however, inasmuch as Arsenal had now agreed to extend goalkeeper Malcolm Webster's loan until the end of the season.

New signing John Gilchrist had been in and out the side and Mike Pentecost was struggling with form. Former club skipper Stan Horne was having a very indifferent season, and David Roberts, after a bright start, had now dropped out of the first team reckoning altogether.

Fulham had essentially to be thankful to three senior players – 'Mr Play-Anywhere' Stan Brown, Fred Callaghan and centre half Reg Matthewson – for anything like consistent displays. Ironically, John Ryan, freed in the close season, was putting in quality performances at Luton. In terms of tightening up the defence, Fulham had made enquiries to Aston Villa regarding the transfer of experienced half back Lew Chatterley, but this move did not come to fruition either.

Certainly it was a shame that Fulham were not showing more consistency, as the league table at the turn of the year made very interesting reading. At the end of December, Fulham stood just six points above the relegation drop zone to Division Four, but on the other hand they were also just seven points behind the club in second place, second and twenty-first places being separated by just thirteen points!

The frustrating issue was that Fulham could not afford to buy expensive new players, and they also had precious little talent coming through from the reserves and junior teams. David Carlton and David Robertson had recently stepped up to become full-time professionals, but this was the sum total.

Fulham still had a number of players tied to First Division contracts, eight of the current senior squad having been with Fulham in the First Division. The only way the wage bill could be reduced (if a wage drop was not voluntarily offered), was to offer the player a free transfer instead. To aid Fulham's situation, Johnny Haynes, as loyal as ever, had offered to accept a reduction in his wages.

To make a comparison with the Premiership stars of today, it is interesting to consider some figures that were released in a newspaper article showing the poor wages senior Fulham players were earning at the time. For the very good week of the season when Fulham beat both Halifax and Plymouth Argyle, the players would have earned, before tax, a basic weekly wage of £40, plus two appearance fees of £20 each, plus match bonuses of £10 per point gained (4 points for 2 wins = £40); a total gross wage of £120 per week. This was *the best* the players could expect to earn; earnings could just as easily have been half that amount! Loyal First Division calibre players like Conway, Earle and Barrett could have been earning just £60 per week, the equivalent of £3,000 a year, during a poor run of results. A decent Premiership striker today could earn at least £50,000 *a week*.

The costs of running the club had stayed pretty consistent across the three divisions; the main issue now was that revenue had dropped dramatically by almost 60%, as gates had fallen from around 25,000 to 10,000.

George Cohen, who was helping at the club in his spare time, said: 'The supply [of young players] has dried up. If this club can't get youngsters, it can't exist – because they cannot afford to buy any [players]. They must find and groom their own. If the club want a helping hand they can rely on me.'

The lack of recent success was causing Fulham to fritter way any surplus money made from the transfers of Allan Clarke and John Dempsey and from George Cohen's insurance payout. The money was slipping away like sand through fingers in an attempt to bale out a club that was steadily losing money on a week-by-week basis.

A dejected Bill Dodgin, who had uttered little during the last two months, said: 'It's a vicious circle, and we are now paying for the failure of the youth policy of the past. We have not had recruits of quality coming up from below. We have been continually patching up, and when the bottom dropped out of our world, we had nothing to plug it with. For several years, Fulham bought players who were not really First Division standard. We were not even buying time because there was no genuine future.

'We should be rebuilding now, but we have nothing to rebuild on. Even when the youngsters are ready for promotion to the first team, we will have to pay for the experience they get – in league points. Aston Villa are in a similar plight; they have spent £230,000 this year to strengthen the staff, but are still anchored at the foot of the Second Division.

'About ten years ago, QPR plumped for youth and a vigorous recruiting campaign brought in the Morgan twins, Sibley, Hazell, Hunt, Springett (Peter), and Leach. League results suffered when they first went in the side, but under Alec Stock they finally came to the boil. ... Football demands quick results, and our case is urgent because of the financial structure; how patient can people be?'

January 1970

In this month

*   The age of majority, including voting rights, was reduced from twenty-one to eighteen.
*   The minimum London Underground fare was to be raised by 50% to one shilling (1/- or 5p) during 1970.
*   The FA suspended George Best for one month for 'disreputable conduct'.
*   4,000 died in the UK during the first week of January from the flu epidemic, now called the Hong Kong or Asian flu.
*   Biafra finally capitulated to Nigerian troops.
*   Colonel Gaddafi became the Libyan premier.
*   The grave of Karl Marx was daubed with swastikas and damaged in a bid to blow it up.
*   Mick Jagger was fined £200 for the possession of cannabis, but Marianne Faithfull was found not guilty of the same offence.
*   The First Pan-Am 'Jumbo' jet landed at Heathrow.

'Two Little Boys' by Rolf Harris topped the charts.
The film 'M*A*S*H' was released.

How the League was looking

Luton Town continued to show their resilience, still leading the table by two points with a game in hand. Orient now looked the danger side moving into second place. They were level on points with Bradford City in third. Just one point behind came both Rochdale and Barnsley. Torquay were sixth, just one point behind fifth. Fulham still languished in fourteenth position, with Reading now tenth. Barrow were still glued to the bottom, with Stockport just a point better off. Gillingham were a point above Stockport, but Southport in the other relegation spot were four points better off. Plymouth had made a recovery, and it was now Tranmere Rovers sliding down to just outside the relegation slots.

The matches

THE FIRST game of 1970 saw Fulham play their fourth game of the season against London rivals **Orient**. If the three previous encounters were any yardstick, the match promised to be a real cracker. The match had been brought forward twenty-four hours because of the FA Cup and was played on a Friday evening. The encounter brought a crowd of well over 12,000 into the Cottage, and the roaring crowd experienced another good match.

Fulham brought back Stan Horne for Wilf Tranter, with Barry Lloyd taking the injured John Richardson's place at inside right. The Orient side was virtually unchanged from the previous encounter at Brisbane Road, save that Barry Dyson was included at inside left.

In the first half both sides searched in vain for luck in front of goal. Tommy Taylor deflected one shot that flew straight to Jimmy Conway, but the Irishman's shot went high into the crowd. At the other end, Mickey Bullock released Mark Lazarus with a deft header, but he sliced well wide with a rash effort with the whole goal to aim at. Fulham came closest to taking the lead when Orient keeper Ray Goddard failed to hold a stinging shot from Steve Earle. The rebound fell to Barry Lloyd, whose clever bending shot beat Goddard but swerved just the wrong side of the post.

Orient had just about had the edge in the first half, and it took them just three minutes of the second half to take the lead. Peter Allen, superb in midfield, released Peter Brabrook, and from his cleverly flighted cross, Barrie Fairbrother put in a powerful header. The attempt looked a goal all the way until Malcolm Webster dived full length to keep the ball out with an outstretched hand. Unfortunately he couldn't hold it, and following a brief scramble at the far post, Lazarus somehow forced the ball home. A lucky Lazarus commented afterwards: 'I kneed the ball over the line.'

Fulham still looked too lightweight in attack, and Bill Dodgin waited just another ten minutes before withdrawing Lloyd and calling on Vic Halom as substitute against his previous club.

The game was Halom's first for some time, and his first since making a recovery from the serious knee injury he had received earlier in the season; effectively Fulham were now playing with four forwards. Orient were now forced to defend, and Fulham looked a much better outfit. Les Barrett had the beating of Mick Jones, the Orient full back, but the massed Orient defenders were blocking most of his crosses.

Fulham's pressure looked as if it would come to nothing, but just nine minutes before the end, Brabrook put a slack pass out to Dennis Rofe, which Halom collected. Halom provided a slick cross and, with Allen and Terry Mancini unable to clear, Jimmy Conway, Fulham's best forward, crashed home the equaliser; the exciting game finished **1–1**.

The four matches ended up honours even, one win each and two drawn. All four matches had looked a cut above Division Three standard. The loss of a point had prevented Orient from going level on points with leaders Luton Town. The Orient defence had looked impressive throughout, with Goddard and Taylor strong and centre half Mancini looking impregnable.

The Fulham forwards had kept them well on their toes, however, with Conway, Earle and Barrett all on top form. Fulham would have to maintain this improved form. Orient had looked a promotion chasing side, and Fulham had done well to hang onto their coat tails. Fulham's studied football had been in contrast to Orient's fast-moving style, but the teams had cancelled each other out.

The following week, Fulham made their second trip of the season to Devon to take on **Plymouth Argyle**. Plymouth were below Fulham in the table and Fulham had scored easily against them in September. The Cottagers had to be confident of earning a point. Fulham had John Richardson back, having made a swift recovery from his ankle injury.

Fulham had bad luck straight away. Reg Matthewson fell ill with flu on the day of the match. He travelled to the match with the squad, but manager Dodgin decided against risking him. This meant an immediate reshuffle with Richardson taking an emergency centre half role. Vic Halom therefore took Richardson's place at number eight. Fulham played in a change strip to avoid a clash with Plymouth's predominantly white shirts.

The match was only twenty minutes old when Fred Callaghan received a nasty kick on the heel and he was immediately withdrawn with Barry Lloyd making an early substitution. This forced yet another reshuffle with Halom dropping back virtually to defence and Lloyd playing at inside forward. This gave the team a very lop-sided look with Fulham virtually having seven forwards on the pitch! Fulham still produced the majority of the attacking football and managed to create three first-class chances to score in the first half, but none was taken, summing up Fulham's inconsistent last three months.

Fulham were foiled to some degree by Plymouth's reserve goalkeeper Martin Clamp, making a rare first-team appearance in Pat Dunne's absence. His anticipation kept out whatever shots Fulham were able to put on target. Fulham paid for these misses when, against the run of play, Norman Piper gave Plymouth the lead. Malcolm Webster punched out a low cross, but unfortunately the ball fell straight to Piper who was handily placed, and he calmly slotted the rebound back into the net from close in as two defenders converged on him.

The Plymouth defence was still erratic in the second half, but Fulham just could not find their way back into the game. Steve Earle and Jim Conway were both tightly marked and Johnny Haynes looked out of the game completely, producing next to nothing from midfield. Stan Horne was playing well and tried to drive Fulham on, but received little response from others. During a spell of Fulham pressure, Plymouth broke and scored again. Plymouth's Derek Rickard won a heading duel with Richardson on the halfway line, leaving Piper free to sprint half the length of the pitch to shoot home a scorching shot from over twenty yards. Fulham offered little after this point, and lost **0–2**.

Despite the enforced reshuffles, the match had been another poor Jekyll and Hyde performance from a team that had drawn with the highly-placed Orient side just the week before, and Fulham supporters were now just guessing at what sort of performance would follow next week. Many supporters considered the Plymouth game the worst Fulham performance of the season to date.

Fulham's season now had a very polarised look about it; despite having only lost just once at home in thirteen league games, the team, apart from the purple patch against Halifax and Stockport, had picked up just *three* other points away from home to date, with no other victories.

One very good piece of news emerged during the following week when the club announced that Jimmy Conway, who had recently come off the transfer list, had signed a new two-year contract. He had made it clear, however, that he expected Fulham to be out of the Third Division by then, or else he would definitely move on. The club commented: 'This is why the club needs to show extra urgency. Our intention must be in no doubt. Two years is no more than a breathing space.'

In change kit, makeshift defenders John Richardson and Vic Halom do battle with Norman Piper of Plymouth Argyle at Home Park. In another dismal Devon performance, Fulham went down 0-2.

Fulham had the perfect chance to show what they could do when **Stockport County** arrived at Craven Cottage the following week. Fulham had cruised past Stockport earlier in the season and should have been very confident. County were deep in relegation trouble, lying five points away from safety. They had lost eleven out of their fourteen away matches, gaining just four points so far on their travels.

The County side contained former Manchester City goalkeeper Alan Ogley, centre half John Coddington, who had played and scored against Fulham for Blackburn Rovers the previous season, and veteran former England player Peter Broadbent signed from Aston Villa a couple of months short of his thirty-seventh birthday!

To cover Fred Callaghan's injury, Fulham recalled centre half Dave Roberts for a rare game. The game was played under leaden January skies and the only thing that brightened the entire afternoon was Stockport's decision to play in a hideously garish all-orange strip. The kit was so bright that it looked almost luminous. The quality of the opposition and the poor weather kept the crowd down to a pitiful 7,500.

What the crowd saw in the ensuing minutes could not have cheered them one iota. Fulham started aggressively enough, and Stockport were only in the game thanks to a number of fine saves from goalkeeper Ogley. Two fine shots from Johnny Haynes were superbly blocked by Ogley and finally cleared.

Despite these saves, it took Fulham just seventeen minutes to break through with another goal from John Richardson. Malcolm Webster started the move with a long throw to Stan Brown. Brown passed the ball quickly forward to Les Barrett. Barrett ran forward, and lobbed through an intelligent pass for the unmarked Richardson to hit a shot that rocketed into the net off the goalkeeper's body.

Richardson almost had a second when a goalbound shot was deflected away by a defender on the line. Barrett also had a shot cleared off the line by Stockport's Barry Hartle. From then on the match was downhill all the way. Stockport possessed little skill, and made no pretence at dainty football. They tackled hard, belted the ball away and ran strongly whilst Fulham fussed and fiddled around on the muddy pitch.

Fulham had an early warning as to what could occur when winger John Price inadvertently diverted a goalbound Stockport effort away from goal and out for a goal kick. Inevitably Stockport

On a bleak and grey afternoon Fulham diehards witness a 1–1 draw against lowly Stockport County. A rare attack sees John Richardson head over the bar from close in. The match was instantly forgettable, remaining only in the memory as the final game in a Fulham shirt for the Maestro, Johnny Haynes (facing the camera).

levelled, with the last move of the first half, through Bobby Elgin. Price, following a fine run down the wing, made a good cross, John Rowland chipped the ball back in, and Elgin headed home via the inside of a post. The goal was only the fifth that Stockport had scored away from home all season!

The second half saw very little action, Stockport were content to take the draw, and Fulham showed few signs of being able to break them down; Steve Earle and Jimmy Conway were either fouled or closed down by an army of defenders.

Haynes' influence waned, and when he was the victim of a heavy tackle from Rowlands, frustration got the better of him and he reacted with a petulant verbal and physical response. Haynes was injured by the tackle, but played on. Ogley and the tall Stockport defenders Coddington and Bill Haydock, brother of Portsmouth's Frank, easily contained Fulham's aerial attempts.

Things became so bad that a sustained bout of slow handclapping eventually broke out. Incredibly, Stockport could have won the match when Price, on a breakaway, put through a lovely pass to Hugh Ryden whose delicate lob cannoned back off the Fulham crossbar with Malcolm Webster well beaten. The game became punctuated with needless free kicks, and there was very little flow; the crowd and the home team were close to boiling point. Fulham did not appear to have the heart to try and force a result, although the masterly Ogley did make two further fine saves near the end from Barrett and Reg Matthewson, and this excuse for a football match ended **1–1**.

The referee, Mr. D. Fieldsend from Sheffield, also had a poor game, disrupting what little football there was. He needed a police escort when leaving the pitch accompanied by a storm of booing. One frustrated Fulham youngster, who evaded the police and aimed a push at the back of the referee, was subdued, arrested and was later taken to the police station. The referee had police protection when he left the ground. The match had provided Stockport with their first point at Craven Cottage for over sixty-one years, following fourteen successive defeats!

The press didn't hold back with their post-match verdicts saying: 'Some of the players who showed little basic knowledge of soccer's arts would have needed protection [instead of the referee] if this shambles had been played on the Continent. It was beef, belt and hope for most of the way.' John Gilchrist and Stan Horne had done reasonably well, and Richardson had looked busy up front, but the rest of the Fulham side had looked decidedly poor. The team knew that they had controlled 90% of the game, but had failed to overcome a poor team. The match did not even merit a mention in the ensuing Fulham programme.

At this grey point in January the dispirited Fulham supporters were in despair, as it looked as if there was never going to be any end to this awful, downward spiral. Since beating Stockport in September this Fulham team had won just *two* out of seventeen league matches, scoring just seventeen goals, and keeping just two clean sheets. The team still lay in fourteenth position in the table and were still just six points above the Third Division relegation zone.

Due to the inconsistency of the other teams in the division, however, Fulham were still just eight points behind a promotion place! Nevertheless, the team were showing little consistency or cohesion that could form a platform for launching a promotion challenge. Fulham were also bracing themselves for an imminent £80,000 bid from Coventry City for flying winger Les Barrett, whilst Leeds United were still trailing Jimmy Conway closely.

The match would remain in the memory for just one reason: it proved to be the final game in a Fulham first-team shirt for the Maestro, Johnny Haynes; the last of 657 glorious games. Up to now, Haynes, even at his age, had been miraculously ever-present in the team (thirty-one appearances) that season. It had been a terrible shame to watch Haynes limp from the field with a thigh injury at the end of this farce with a chorus of boos directed at the team ringing in his ears. Haynes, the master, signed off in front of a small huddled crowd in the Third Division, under a grey, wintry sky, after experiencing an untalented orange-clad bunch of hoofers bustle their way to a most dismal draw.

The match had been a mile away from the silken skills and delicate passing that Haynes would have wanted to see. One thing was for certain – the Third Division would never see the likes of a player like Haynes again. Haynes' departure left Stan Brown as the sole surviving link from the Fulham team that had started the season just four years previously.

Fulham's game at **Walsall**, scheduled originally for the following Saturday, was postponed due to a waterlogged pitch, and moved to the following Tuesday. Fulham made changes: Mike Pentecost came in for John Gilchrist, John Richardson was again moved back to the centre of the defence in place of Dave Roberts, and Barry Lloyd returned this time wearing the inside left number ten jersey vacated by the injured Johnny Haynes. Vic Halom, now fully fit, returned at inside right. Walsall had lost five at home already, and were struggling below Fulham. Perhaps the tide could turn here? Fulham switched to their away kit for the Midlands fixture.

At long last the Fulham team began to click. On a muddy and heavy surface, they took the lead at Walsall as early as the eleventh minute with a well-worked goal. Les Barrett provided a well-flighted cross, Jimmy Conway headed the ball back cleverly across the six-yard line, where Barry Lloyd ghosted in amongst a hesitant defence and nodded the ball between the goalkeeper and the defender on the line.

A change of fortune at last, as Conway's cross is nodded home by Vic Halom at Fellows Park to restore Fulham's lead. The final 3–1 victory at Walsall was Fulham's first away from home since September. For Halom it was his first goal in over twelve months.

Walsall equalised with a headed goal through Ray Train after twenty-four minutes. A Fulham defender on the line appeared to have headed the ball away, but the linesman signalled that the ball had just about crossed the line and a goal was awarded.

However, Fulham took just four minutes to recapture the lead; a Conway cross came over from the other wing, and Vic Halom leapt between two defenders to head the ball neatly home with keeper Phil Parkes rooted to the goal line. The goal was the best tonic Halom could have had, as it was his first in over a year.

Fulham scored their third just twelve minutes into the second half, and it was a poacher's goal. A long ball down the middle seemed well covered by Walsall defender Stan Jones, who chased back with Steve Earle following up. But just as Jones looked as if he was going to pass back to the goalkeeper, Earle stuck out a long, determined leg, and crashed home a great shot from the edge of the penalty area into the roof of the net. Fulham never looked in trouble from that point, winning away from home for the first time in ten attempts **3–1**. At last it looked as if the club's luck had turned. The result had been a true one, and Walsall had been beaten by a polished and skilful team.

Four days later a rejuvenated Fulham were on their travels again this time to Yorkshire, hoping that this encounter with **Doncaster Rovers** was going to be less of a roughhouse than the match at the Cottage. Fulham unsurprisingly announced an unchanged side. Doncaster were now in the middle of a poor run, having slumped disastrously down the league since Christmas.

Early on, Steve Earle and Jimmy Conway tormented the Doncaster defence with their speed and aggression, and Halom was busy and workmanlike, but Fulham's finishing was way off target. In the first half Malcolm Webster had little to do except take goal kicks and free kicks.

In the second half Doncaster were well on top, but it was thanks to a faultless display by Webster that the Fulham goal remained intact. Doncaster was Webster's local club, having been born in nearby Rossington! Shots from Doncaster's Brian Usher and Stewart Gray were blocked. For long periods there was little to choose between the sides, and it looked as if the game would slide towards a goalless draw. Four minutes from time, however, Lady Luck shone on Fulham, and they took the lead.

A quick move out of defence set up a move down the left wing. The Doncaster defence was opened up, and goalkeeper John Ogston advanced to parry the shot from Barry Lloyd, but only succeeded in palming the ball straight to Conway, who gratefully cracked it back into an empty net. Fulham then immediately pulled all eleven men back behind the ball and in a frantic finish managed to hold on and record a **1–0** win.

Two away wins in five days had been just what the doctor ordered, and put Fulham in much better heart for February. There had been no repeat of the alehouse tactics at Doncaster, and Fulham emerged unscathed. In truth, the game had been pretty much a non-event from start to finish. Both sides had relied heavily on stifling defence, making the game a poor spectacle for those in attendance. However, for once, Fulham were not complaining, and the result had definitely been better than the performance.

The good news became even better when the club formally announced that George Cohen was returning to take charge of the club's neglected youth policy. A buoyant Cohen commented: 'A winning [first] team is the best possible news for me, especially to help me in my new job. There are so many clubs competing for the same youngsters; not only Arsenal, Spurs and West Ham, but also others like Leeds United and Manchester United! It's so easy for me to talk to boys and their parents about what Fulham have done in the past, started the careers of men like Mullery, Macedo and myself for instance or of others like Haynes, Callaghan and Earle in the present team. What I want to be able to add to this is a bright picture of the present day prospects. It would be good to stress that they would be associating with a club who are clearly on the way up. ... With our current smaller staff, youngsters have an opportunity to make the scene much earlier than at one of the clubs I have mentioned. Take John Fraser – signed on his sixteenth birthday and already he has made the reserve team.'

February 1970

In this month

* Police seized Andy Warhol's film *Flesh* from the Open Space Theatre.
* One person died and eleven others were injured in an Arab attack on a London bound El-Al airliner.
* The Government announced plans to decentralise the NHS under ninety new NHS authorities.
* Prince Charles took his seat in the House of Lords.
* Joe Frazier knocked out Jimmy Ellis to become the world heavyweight boxing champion.
* Buckingham Palace announced that Prince Charles would join the Navy.
* Rolls Royce asked the Government for fifty million pounds to develop the RB 211-50 airbus jet engine.
* Five further US marines were arrested and charged with murdering Vietnamese women and children.
* The philosopher and mathematician Bertrand Russell died aged ninety-seven.

'Love Grows' by Edison Lighthouse topped the charts.
The film 'Patton' was released.

How the League was looking

During a dramatic January it had been all change. Luton Town had finally cracked under the pressure, and it was Orient taking over at the top, although Luton still had a game in hand. The surprise packages were now Brighton and Reading, Brighton rocketing up from nowhere to take third position with Reading powering their way to fourth. Both these teams were just one point behind Luton. These four sides had pushed Bradford City into fifth, with Barnsley in sixth place. The runs of Torquay and Rochdale had both dramatically collapsed. Fulham had recovered to a mediocre eleventh position. Barrow were still stuck to the bottom and Gillingham were, once more, just a point above them. Stockport continued to languish, but Southport in the other relegation spot were three points better off. Tranmere Rovers were still in trouble with Bournemouth and now Walsall sliding back to just outside the relegation slots.

The matches

FULHAM'S FIRST game of the month was against **Bournemouth and Boscombe Athletic**. The game was brought forward to the Friday evening to avoid competing with the FA Cup fifth round tie between Chelsea and Crystal Palace. Struggling Bournemouth were below Fulham and should have been easy victims having lost nine away so far. The Bournemouth side contained few stars, but included Tony Powell later to star for Norwich City, former Tottenham youngster John Sainty and the prolific goalscorer Ted MacDougall, later to play for both Manchester United and West Ham. Fortunately for Fulham the first choice star keeper Kieron Baker was out injured, and the youngster Alec Bugg replaced him. Fulham omitted John Richardson as Fred Callaghan returned.

Fulham started the match very sluggishly indeed, and conceded a goal as early as the tenth minute, when MacDougall, inevitably, scored from a corner after Malcolm Webster had hesitated in coming for the cross. Bournemouth were the far more enterprising side, and much faster on the ball. The Fulham forwards were being held by a well-drilled defence and Jimmy Conway was being marked by two men. Fulham's attack became so blunted that you could count on the fingers of one hand the chances created.

There was a major surprise at half time when Bill Dodgin removed leading scorer Conway from the fray, and replaced him with full back John Gilchrist. This forced the Bournemouth defence to concentrate on marking someone else. The lacklustre game continued in the same way, with Vic Halom and Barry Lloyd not finding any space in the Bournemouth defence until Fulham finally managed to conjure up an equaliser with just twenty minutes to go.

Les Barrett, showing good reactions, robbed Athletic's Jimmy White near goal, and slid the ball through perfectly for Steve Earle to crack in his seventeenth of the season; that was as good as it got. Webster had to be alert as both Stan Brown and Stan Horne were off form; Fred Callaghan had been rushed back too quickly and did not look fully fit, but Fulham's substitute had already been used. Lloyd tried hard to win the game for Fulham, but found Bugg in the Bournemouth goal in fine form, gleefully accepting his rare first-team opportunity; the matched petered out as an uneventful **1−1** draw.

The most that could be said about the game was that it was now four games unbeaten. Certainly hard-working Bournemouth were no more than average, but as with so many other defensively minded teams that had come to the Cottage that season, Fulham had failed to effectively break them down; the Cottagers had been lucky to take a point.

Fulham travelled up to **Bradford City** a week later in an attempt to keep their run going at Valley Parade; it was their first visit to the ground in thirty-three years. Bradford City had faltered a little during the previous few weeks dropping down from second to eighth, losing their last three games. They did, however, possess a formidable home record having won ten and drawn four of their sixteen home fixtures played. The not fully fit Fred Callaghan was omitted and John Richardson resumed. The weather was still poor and the conditions had left the pitch frozen in some parts whilst being soft in others, not a recipe for flowing football.

Fulham went on the attack straight from the kick-off and Vic Halom tested goalkeeper John Roberts with a thirty-yard drive that the keeper handled capably. Three minutes later, it was the turn of Steve Earle to try his luck and his accurate twenty-yard volley looked worthy of a goal, but again Roberts just saved his shot; Barry Lloyd then shot just over as Fulham turned the screw. Fulham were in total control of the midfield with Stan Horne skilfully directing operations, having the Bradford defence at sixes and sevens.

Then, in a delightful three-man move, Fulham broke away with Halom beating the offside trap. Halom took the ball around the advancing keeper, but too wide. He therefore screwed a cross back into the middle, where the supporting Earle's shot hit the post. The ball rebounded into play, but Halom was just unable to convert the chance during an almighty goalmouth scramble.

How Fulham were not ahead at this stage was a mystery, and Jimmy Conway (twice) and Earle had efforts fractionally wide. Right on half time, it was Fulham's turn to be relieved when Bradford's right half Peter McConnell hit a shot from thirty yards that rattled the Fulham crossbar, with Malcolm Webster, blinded by the sun, helpless.

In the second half, Bradford started off the more aggressive side, but Fulham, with Reg Matthewson and Richardson impressive at the back, absorbed their best efforts, and were soon on the attack again. The visitors were desperately unlucky when, following a strong run and cross from Conway, Halom put in a powerful header that totally beat goalkeeper Roberts but was headed off the line by McConnell.

A few minutes later Halom had another super strike smothered by the home goalkeeper. Halom was having a fine game and was putting in a huge amount of graft both in attack and defence. In the end slightly slapdash finishing prevented the Cottagers from breaking through the unsteady Bradford defence, and the game finished for the second time that season **0−0**. Whereas Fulham had been lucky to secure one home point against Bournemouth, they had been very unfortunate not to secure two away points at Bradford.

The following week, Fulham travelled back again to Yorkshire, this time to vie with **Barnsley**. Fulham were again unchanged. It was going to be yet another very tough fixture, as Barnsley, like Bradford, had also won ten and drawn four of their sixteen home fixtures; Fulham once again switched kits.

Fulham took the lead in the first half with a spectacular goal. Barry Lloyd was clumsily brought down just outside the penalty area in a central position. The defenders lined up only to see Jimmy

Conway float the ball expertly over the wall and past the astonished goalkeeper into the top left-hand corner. Lloyd, Conway and Steve Earle were dominating the match, moving sweetly both in midfield and attack, but the team were just unable to increase their first-half goal tally.

Matters became even better when Earle added a second goal just three minutes into the second half. His first shot was blocked, but he followed up to hammer home the rebound. Fulham began to falter when Lloyd, in firm control of midfield, had to leave the pitch with a strained shoulder, full back John Gilchrist substituting. This was a signal for the Barnsley team to mount an astonishing fightback. The conditions were not too great, with a swirling wind that made playing difficult and caused crosses to hang in the air.

Barnsley coped far better than Fulham with these conditions, and this lead to Johnny Evans, the Barnsley winger, claiming a rapid second-half hat trick in just fourteen minutes between the sixty-fourth and seventy-seventh minutes to give the home side a very unlikely lead. He netted firstly with a ten-yard shot, then turned in his second from a cross, finally finishing off a great move with a searing drive. Whilst Evans had done very well, there was no doubt that the Fulham team had 'switched off' thinking that the game was already won. They gave the diminutive Evans far too much scope and paid dearly for it.

Maybe too many Oakwell Ales, as the Barnsley defence goes to sleep and allows substitute and full back John Gilchrist to hammer in a late equaliser. In a topsy-turvy game, Fulham drew 3–3 to keep their unbeaten run going.

Just when it looked as if Fulham's unbeaten run would end, substitute John Gilchrist thumped home an equaliser. In the dying minutes Barnsley's uncertain defence cracked, and three defenders stood and watched as Gilchrist took a pass and shot firmly low into the net under the advancing goalkeeper from close range; the goal was Gilchrist's only one for the club. The exciting encounter finished **3–3** and at least confirmed a newfound spirit within the team to battle back from behind to achieve a result. Ironically the match proved to be the last for full back Gilchrist, and his £20,000 transfer fee was repaid with just twenty league appearances.

An unchanged Fulham attempted to keep the momentum going the following week with a visit from **Rotherham United**. The United team were just two points ahead of Fulham. They had lost only five out of sixteen away from home, and so another tough fight was expected. Rotherham included former Arsenal veteran Jim Furnell in goal and towering centre half Dave Watson, who went on to Cup final glory with Sunderland and to win sixty-five England caps. On the wing was Neil Warnock, later to become a Premiership manager. Also in the team was the delightfully named Trevor Womble (who never did play for Wimbledon!).

A suspect Fulham defence allowed visitors Rotherham to come back from three goals down and kept the sparse crowd's interest firmly focussed on the pitch rather than on passing rowers – even during the lull in the action pictured above.

One face missing in the Rotherham side was that of former Fulham full back Barry Mealand, injured on the day. Fulham were unchanged, although Les Barrett had been doubtful right up to kick-off with stomach problems, Jimmy Conway had undergone a minor operation on his foot in the week, and Barry Lloyd had struggled like a Trojan to overcome the shoulder injury sustained at Barnsley the previous week. The crowds were not yet returning, however, and just over 8,000 saw this one.

Fulham's attack was in command from the start, and it took them just six minutes to score. Barry Lloyd cut in from the left and let fly with a cross-cum-shot from outside the penalty area. The goal was a little fortunate in that the ball threaded its way through a host of Rotherham defenders and appeared to have been deflected; but somehow it found its way into the net past the unsighted goalkeeper Furnell. This was the boost the home side wanted, and they produced a first half full of attacking enterprise. Les Barrett was back to his England under-23 form with a half full of runs, crosses and shots; with any luck he could have claimed a hat trick.

Lloyd, at last taking on Haynes' mantle, was superb in his distribution, nearly all his passes finding their mark. Vic Halom was also a constant nuisance to the United defence, chasing every ball and making life uncomfortable for the United goalkeeper.

Fittingly, it was Halom who scored the crucial second goal just three minutes before half time. Jimmy Conway, having one of his rare quiet afternoons, finally escaped the attentions of Rotherham full back Dennis Leigh, took off on a dazzling run through the middle and laid on a cross for Halom, who met the ball first time and calmly sidefooted it home from twelve yards.

Three minutes after half time, Fulham netted again. Steve Earle cheekily nutmegged Rotherham's Trevor Swift and passed to Lloyd. Lloyd chipped the ball in to Barrett. The pass was not ideal, but there was panic in the United goalmouth and the ball was not properly cleared, giving a half chance. Barrett steadied himself before crashing the ball in with a tremendous shot from fully twenty yards. Fulham now had the match in the bag, and were cruising to victory. With all eyes on Halom, Earle was now finding gaps, and giving the Rotherham defenders further headaches.

Fulham's dominance was continuing but then the usual defensive blunders let the team down. Eighteen minutes from time, Malcolm Webster somehow completely missed the ball following a

Some supporters are already celebrating, and there is good reason as Vic Halom connects with Conway's clever cross to sidefoot Fulham's second goal against Rotherham United just before half time, with goalkeeper Furnell powerless to intervene. Fulham's third consecutive game against Yorkshire opposition gave rise to a 3–2 win – and Fulham were unbeaten in February.

corner taken by Rotherham's David Bentley, and the ball trickled into the net off defender Watson's chest.

Sensing that they could still salvage something from the match, Rotherham attacked, and with five minutes left, Lee Brogden, substituting for centre forward Trevor Phillips, grabbed a second. The Fulham defence pushed up, and was static, anticipating the offside flag. The decision didn't come and Brogden tucked away United's second with an ungainly toe-poked shot. The last five minutes saw panic in the Fulham defence, but they managed to hang on to win **3–2**.

Although they had maintained their run, there was still much to put right. The forwards had all been superb, done their job, firing on all cylinders. Les Barrett had scored his first goal for almost six months; it had been heartening to see the team victorious without Earle and Conway scoring! The defence, however, had been very suspect. The game should have resulted in a 3–0 win – both the Rotherham goals had been absolute giveaways.

Webster had looked very vulnerable to the high ball, and both Reg Matthewson and John Richardson had experienced rare off-days in the middle. Stan Horne's form was still very patchy. The unstable defence had conceded five in the last two games, and this would have to improve if the team were to make any sustained challenge at the top.

March 1970

In this month

* The Greek Cypriot leader Archbishop Makarios survived a machine-gun assassination attempt.
* Eighteen children were awarded almost £370,000 for birth damages caused by the thalidomide drug.
* The quarantine period for dogs and cats was extended to one year, as an anti-rabies move.
* Henry Cooper beat Jack Bodell to regain the British heavyweight crown.
* The *New English Bible* sold one million copies on its first day of publication.
* The Catholic Bogside area of Londonderry was sealed off following violence from stone throwing protestors.
* Ian Smith declared Rhodesia a republic.
* The Nuclear Non-proliferation Treaty came into effect.
* An army coup ousted Prince Sihanouk in Cambodia.
* The leaders of East and West Germany, Brandt and Stoph, met for the first time since the country was divided.

'Wand'rin Star' by Lee Marvin topped the charts.
The film 'Women in Love' was released.

How the League was looking

During an even more dramatic February it had once again been all change. A fatigued Luton Town had seemingly lost form completely, dropping right down to fifth place. Orient were still at the top but now just on goal average. They were level on points with the form team Brighton. The major surprise during the month had been the sudden emergence of Bristol Rovers, up from ninth to second, also level on points with Orient and Brighton. Orient, however, did have three games in hand on both teams; Reading were still holding onto fourth place. These five had pushed Bradford City into seventh, with Barnsley still stuck in sixth place. Fulham had dropped a place to twelfth position. Barrow had put an amazing spurt on, picking up twelve points and were now only just inside the bottom four. Stockport had slumped to the bottom of the table, with Gillingham still in real danger just a point better off. Tranmere Rovers had dropped alarmingly into the other relegation spot. Southport, Bournemouth and Walsall were just outside the relegation slots, none of them looking safe.

The matches

AWAY FROM the first team, the club had announced that Fulham were going to make their first venture into the International Youth Competition. A party of sixteen players would fly out on Good Friday morning to Düsseldorf and return the following Tuesday. George Cohen would be in charge of the party, assisted by Ken Craggs. There would be eight clubs competing: three local sides from the Düsseldorf area, two from other parts of West Germany and two other foreign sides.

The club stressed that it was the start of the club's policy to go all out to give the Fulham youth team experience that would help them towards a rapid maturity. If this tour were a success, then it would assist the club in its negotiations to enter a more difficult and prestigious tour in the forthcoming August in San Remo. This August tour would include opposition such as AC Milan, Barcelona and FC Austria.

As the league championship was hotting up, so were the fixtures. Fulham were scheduled to play *nine* matches in this month! The club's attempts to play these games were hindered by the weather, and a freak combination of snow, ice and mud saw the cancellation of three scheduled matches in the space of just six days.

The first match against **Reading** at the Cottage on the first Wednesday of the month, the second away against **Mansfield Town** on the following Saturday and the third on the following Monday night at Prenton Park against **Tranmere Rovers** were **all postponed**. The upshot of these postponements was that Fulham's league season now stretched to four days short of the beginning of May. The re-jigged league fixture list saw Fulham involved in six matches in the next *seventeen* days.

At last the club were beginning to sound upbeat: 'What the new arrangements do serve to emphasise is that the season is not only far from over, but that the issues are barely formed ... there is still time for us to make our mark. To meet this biggest challenge of the season, we are, at last, developing consistent form. Until the weather came to interrupt our flow, we had played seven matches without defeat – easily our best spell. If only we can keep it up. Six matches ago teams like Bristol Rovers and Reading held a mid-table position similar to the one we now occupy – now they are challenging for the top.'

The next match was **Rochdale's** first ever visit to Craven Cottage for a league match. The Rochdale team included lanky centre forward David Cross, who would go on to make a spectacular career for himself with Norwich City, Coventry City and West Ham, and the combative Bobby Downes, later to star in midfield for Watford; Rochdale played in blue.

The Lancashire side were still above Fulham in the table. They possessed a good away record with seven wins in eighteen away from home. They had, however, lost nine on the road. The Fulham side were again unchanged. Despite the team's recent good run, the crowd was the lowest of the season and now the lowest for over twenty years; just over 6,700 turned up, even fewer than the crowd that had attended the Bristol Rovers game in December.

Fulham were so much on top it was an embarrassment. Again, the forwards looked two classes above Rochdale, and in the early stages it looked as if Fulham would grind Rochdale into the mud. A slip by Rochdale's Derek Ryder inside two minutes allowed Steve Earle to nip in, but he missed a sitter. Vic Halom then missed another glaringly simple chance. As Rochdale's frustration grew, Jimmy Conway was already the victim of 'clogging', so Dodgin decided to protect his star asset and concentrate the attacking efforts down the left wing instead.

The move paid handsome dividends. After just twenty minutes, Barry Lloyd released Les Barrett down the left wing with a slide-rule pass. Barrett found Earle, who outpaced three bewildered Rochdale defenders before putting in an excellent cross to the near post, where Halom netted by flicking the ball between the keeper and the post. The Rochdale rough stuff continued and both half back Hugh Riley and left back Ryder were booked for nasty tackles.

Steve Earle (on the ground) outpaces three Rochdale defenders, and from his cross Halom classily flicks the ball home at the near post. The goal opened the scoring.

Vic Halom repeats the treatment just before half time after Rochdale keeper Harker parries his first shot. This concluded the scoring, and the 2–0 victory extended the unbeaten run for the Cottagers to nine games.

Two minutes before half time, Halom struck again when the Rochdale keeper Chris Harker blocked his first shot with a full-length dive, but he followed up to score from the rebound despite the close attention of two defenders. Halom was enjoying a new lease of life and was unlucky not to complete a first-half hat trick.

In the second half, Fulham switched to cruise control and complacency allowed Rochdale to come back into the game, even to dictate the midfield for a spell, Rochdale's midfielder Billy Rudd looking impressive. This improved further when Ron Blair was introduced as a substitute. This time the Fulham defence were a lot tighter. Reg Matthewson and John Richardson were solid at the back, with Stan Brown and Mike Pentecost not putting a foot wrong behind them. So dominant were the defence that, apart from one very good stop, Malcolm Webster had nothing to do all afternoon.

Fulham re-asserted themselves eventually with Lloyd, improving with every game, controlling the centre. He gave one opportunity to the hardworking but unlucky Earle that he hammered just over the bar. Fulham were slightly diffident in attack in the second half, obviously with one eye on the following week's game at Reading, and seeing the rough treatment that had been dished out to them in the first half played within themselves, happy to pass the ball around. Fulham strolled home, winners by **2–0**.

The small crowd had seen another significant step in Fulham's revival; it had not been spectacular, but it was effective. All the Fulham players played well, and they were at last looking like a cohesive unit. The Fulham side was also a young one, and it was gratifying that Fulham could still win without the likes of Seymour, Gilchrist, Callaghan, Haynes and Jones being in the side.

Vic Halom was obviously delighted with his brace, and talked about his relief following a nightmare six months. He had originally been injured with a knee condition, but on being able to restart was nowhere near his known form, having a 'barren spell' in front of goal. He had been having nightmares about boarded up and shrinking goals and giant goalkeepers, but found life little different when he was awake! He spoke in the club programme: 'Even that [poor form] was better than three months ago when this famous specialist gave his opinion about my knee. He said that I had a knee of an old man; you can imagine how I felt. Fortunately I had a word with Johnny Haynes which helped to change the picture. He has had his injury troubles and got over them, so I went to see another specialist. This time it was the doctor who operated on Colin Cowdrey, the England [cricket] captain, who is now knocking up his hundreds again on tour with the Duke of Norfolk's team in the West Indies.

'He said that footballers' knees all appear to be worse than they are. Naturally they are like an old man's joints because so much more stress is put on them than the ordinary man's. After seeing him I felt it was all a bit of a fallacy about my trouble. Anyway, he told me not to worry, and, after a lot of treatment and as much patience as I could manage, I came back.

'I had an example of Mike Pentecost fighting hard after breaking his leg and we worked together to get things going again. How different it all seems now that things are happening for me again.

'Against Rochdale I took my share of knocks. The trainer came on for me three times in five minutes. They had two players booked, one for fouls on me. Yet none of these bruises hurt half as much as lighter ones in previous matches because I had managed to knock a couple in. I'm twenty-one now, and looking forward to making up for the three months I have missed.'

Fulham had an immediate opportunity to continue the good form when they faced struggling **Walsall** at Craven Cottage on the following Wednesday. Walsall were now hovering just above the relegation zone. Their team contained few names of note, but did include veteran former West Bromwich Albion centre half Stan Jones, winger Colin Taylor in his third spell with the club having been re-signed from Crystal Palace, and former Aston Villa pair, forward John Woodward, who had scored against Fulham at Villa Park the previous season, and wing half Alan Deakin.

The most notable name was an up-and-coming nineteen-year-old goalkeeper by the name of Phil Parkes, later to find fame with QPR and West Ham, as well as representing England in a career of over 500 league games. Walsall were without young star Ray Train, who was injured. Fulham were again unchanged. Due to the colour clash – Walsall also playing in white shirts – the away side played in all red.

In this performance it was apparent that something was really stirring at the club. Fulham despatched Walsall with a clinical efficiency that suggested a huge gap between the sides. Fulham took just sixteen minutes to score, when Vic Halom, still on a scoring run, took a pass from Steve Earle and flashed a superb overhead kick past the startled Phil Parkes. Fulham continued to press, and five minutes before half time scored again through Earle, when he headed home a Barry Lloyd cross during a goalmouth scramble, after Halom had distracted the defence.

Walsall tried to salvage some pride in the first quarter of an hour of the second half, but midway through Earle grabbed his second after a magnificent solo run, shooting low past Parkes. Stan Brown put the seal on an excellent night's work with a cunning lob a quarter of an hour from the end that the hapless Parkes could only help into his own net. Fulham won at a canter **4–0**, completing the double over the Saddlers.

Steve Earle's two goals took him to twenty, one ahead of colleague Jimmy Conway; it was Fulham's biggest home win of the season. A happy Halom now had four in his last three games. Apart from the slightly slow Stan Horne, Fulham played with a panache and style that dismantled the Walsall defence.

Aside from a ten minute spell early in the second half, Walsall were never in it. If it had not been for the agile Parkes, Fulham could have doubled their score. Every player played his part, and the media said: 'Fulham were crisp and confident in almost everything they attempted.'

This Fulham team, with twelve goals in the last four games, were now truly on a roll, and had claimed their first double of the season. Walsall captain, the veteran Stan Jones, said afterwards: 'Without doubt Fulham are the best team we have met this season. They have three players up front in Jimmy Conway, Les Barrett and Steve Earle, who are all good enough for First Division football. All three possess respectable pace and the real ability to receive and control a ball under pressure from opponents.'

Steve Earle had scored two goals at home for the first time that season, and commented: 'I must admit I became a bit sensitive to some of the crowd last season – there seemed to be no understanding. It carried over a bit into this season. They seemed to want me to charge round knocking into people, but this is not what I am good at. I try and use my speed and positional sense and I think there is more appreciation now of the things we are doing off the ball to help others.

'Having big Vic Halom up there to take the weight off me has made a lot of difference. I am picking up the stuff that falls out from him. If only people would show more patience, I think we could really make things happen. Maybe it helps that I don't allow criticism to affect me now. As long as the management are satisfied, I know I am doing a good job.'

Fulham probably faced their stiffest challenge in this run on the following Saturday when they travelled to Berkshire to meet **Reading** at Elm Park. Reading were also on a very good run having lost just one of their last ten games. The Berkshire side had also disposed of Barrow 6–3 during the week. This run had seen Reading soar up the table to challenge the leaders in fifth place, just two points away from the second promotion place.

Fulham were brave enough to make a change, even on a good run. Stan Horne was dropped, and Stan Brown moved up to his preferred number four shirt. This brought in nineteen-year-old Dave Moreline for his first full game of the season at left back. The combined success of both clubs saw a crowd of almost 16,500 turn up to watch. As the Reading shirts contained some white, Fulham switched to an all-red kit.

Such was the spirit of the side that Jimmy Conway insisting on playing despite the need for several pain-killing injections to get him out on the pitch. There was a significant amount of tension before the game, and several fights broke out in the crowd in the quarter of an hour leading up to the start; police moved in, and several supporters were arrested.

For once it was the home side's turn to suffer from the jitters as Fulham forced the pace from the kick-off. Fulham's pressure was such that it only took the home side six minutes to crack. A mistake by Will Dixon, the Reading full back, presented the ball to the feet of Les Barrett in the middle of the penalty area. Les made a quick body swerve that wrong-footed defenders, and a low right-foot shot did the rest. Fulham were rampant, and Reading goalkeeper Steve Death somehow stopped Steve Earle's thunderbolt, while Dixon headed off the line from Vic Halom.

After twenty-three minutes another defensive calamity let Fulham in for a second. Another miscued clearance from Fred Sharpe found Jimmy Conway all on his own in the penalty area. Conway immediately swept the ball low across the penalty box, where Halom, unmarked, slotted the ball into an empty net. The Reading goalkeeper Death made a valiant attempt to scramble back and stop the shot entering the net, but it was to no avail. The match was all Fulham now, and the away side went further ahead with a third goal ten minutes before half time. Barrett made a scintillating run down the left wing, and from his hard, low cross Earle flicked the ball impudently across the goalkeeper and into the net; the home crowd were stunned into silence.

Stung by their poor first-half display, Reading came out strongly to reduce the deficit, but were handled competently by the tough-tackling Fulham defence. Despite their possession, Malcolm Webster in the Fulham goal was hardly needed. The fire was soon dampened, and Reading's defensive frailties once again had them in trouble.

Fulham's fourth arrived in the sixty-fourth minute when Halom burst through again and Death had to rush from his goal to smother the shot. The ball spun away to Conway lurking on the edge

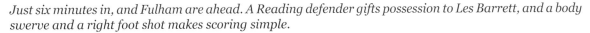

Just six minutes in, and Fulham are ahead. A Reading defender gifts possession to Les Barrett, and a body swerve and a right foot shot makes scoring simple.

In the second half at Elm Park, Barrett's corner is met with a corking header from Vic Halom from ten yards, with the Reading defenders out-muscled and out-thought. The was the final goal in a 4–0 win, a brilliant performance to which the home side had no answer.

of the penalty area. The Irishman fired in a goalbound rocket shot, with the goalkeeper helpless. Somehow a Reading defender had raced back, and he brilliantly headed the ball off the line for a corner. Barrett took the corner, and Halom headed the fourth. The goal was a corking header from ten yards; so powerful that the ball seemed to be still rising as it crossed the line. The goal was Halom's fifth in eight days.

Reading then improved considerably, and probably had the better of the last twenty minutes, but although Fulham conceded possession, their defence was rarely threatened, and the rampant London side ran out easy winners **4–0**.

Fulham were now a confident and classy outfit, and the victory made it ten matches unbeaten, four victories in a row, and sixteen goals in the last five games. Reading had contributed to their defeat, but Fulham had outclassed them from start to finish.

The Blueways coach driver chats to Malcolm Webster as they get ready for the long drive to the Good Friday fixture at Plainmoor, Torquay.

It is Good Friday at Torquay and Fulham keep the unbeaten run going. Les Barrett, now on top form, crashes Halom's cross first time past Torquay goalkeeper Donnelly, despite the close attentions of a defender. The 1–1 draw at Plainmoor was the least Fulham deserved, robbed of a second point by a late equaliser.

Seeing the number of matches they had to play against other teams at or near the top of the table, Fulham were becoming increasingly optimistic about their promotion chances – the situation was very much in their hands. The optimistic aspect of the victory for Bill Dodgin was the age of the side. With the inclusion of Dave Moreline, the average age of the team that had dismantled Reading was just *twenty-two*. Bill Dodgin commented: 'This was more like the old days. It shows we are getting our confidence back.'

On Good Friday, Fulham travelled to Devon for the third time to take on **Torquay United**. Fulham were again unchanged and played in a change strip, despite Torquay playing in all yellow.

Fulham took a first-half lead in the thirty-sixth minute. Steve Earle started the move and found Vic Halom. Halom crossed the ball into the Torquay goalmouth, where Les Barrett had made a late run from the halfway line. Barrett met the centre with a fast, scorching shot over the advancing goalkeeper Donnelly whilst in full flight.

Torquay made a great fight of it and John Rudge, who had scored in the league game at Fulham, netted Torquay's equaliser late in the second half. In the end, a **1–1** draw was a fair result. Due to Easter reporting in the press, there is little recorded information on the game, most suggesting that Torquay had been slightly lucky to salvage a point.

Just twenty-four hours later Fulham played **Tranmere Rovers** at the Cottage on Easter Saturday; Fulham were unchanged again. Tranmere were in the relegation zone with just two away victories to date, not having won away since November, so victory for the home side seemed a formality.

Tranmere contained few names of note, but included veteran Tony Knapp the former Southampton and Leicester half back. The other central defender was an appropriately named Dave Moorcroft, who was probably expected to do a great deal of running! Tranmere also possessed a goalkeeper named Frankie Lane, but he didn't appear to be singing any Western songs on the day! Despite Fulham's great run, and the holiday period, fewer than 10,500 turned up to watch, a big disappointment.

Fulham looked tired and jaded after the long trip to Devon, and made heavy weather of the match. The strange Easter conditions had thrown up a sunny day accompanied by a very strong swirling wind that made ball control and passing difficult. After shaking off the cobwebs and coming to terms with the conditions, Fulham started to find their feet. Jimmy Conway and Les Barrett began to take the full backs apart, and the chances started to arrive. Tranmere had offered little except a ten-man defence. However, this was holding up well, marshalled expertly by the experienced Knapp. Seconds before half time, Barrett thought he had given Fulham the lead when he netted, only to see the linesmen's flag rule the effort out for offside.

Tranmere's sporadic breaks out of defence, led by George Yardley and Jimmy Hinch, increased after the interval, but were handled competently by the defence where both full backs, Mike Pentecost and Dave Moreline, were having fine games. Fulham were dealt a blow on the hour when John Richardson sustained an injury and had to be replaced by Fred Callaghan. Fulham lost height and still had to contend with Tranmere's dangerous beanpole forward Hinch.

Fulham contained the Tranmere attacking verve and were soon in the ascendancy again. Vic Halom hit a post when it seemed easier to score, and then let fly with a twenty-yard drive against the Tranmere bar with keeper Frankie Lane beaten. Barry Lloyd then contrived to make the miss of the match. Halom chested down Stan Brown's centre straight onto Lloyd's boot, but somehow he managed to screw his shot wide.

Fulham's desperation to score was relieved when Barrett put Fulham ahead midway through the second half with a simple goal. Taking a clearance, he stepped forward and unleashed a ferocious, dipping twenty-five yard shot through a forest of Tranmere defenders and past the unsighted goalkeeper. This should have been the signal for Fulham to push on, but the opposite happened, and Tranmere, their own requirement for points desperate, came back at Fulham.

Fulham looked as if they would hold out, but four minutes from time Tranmere won a corner. Winger Frank Gill, Tranmere's best player on the day, took it. The ball was headed on and found experienced half back Alan King who, with the aid of some slack marking, somehow managed to curl a shot around Malcolm Webster and into the corner for a soft goal. Retrieving the ball from the net was the most Webster had had to do all afternoon. A point was lost, and the match finished **1–1**.

However, the result meant that it was now twelve unbeaten and Dodgin should have had reason to be pleased. He was, though, unduly pessimistic. He said: 'We had to win today to stay in with any hope, but after dropping this point – we're out of it. But we aim to have a big say in who goes up. Brighton, Luton and Reading all have to play here and we will be out to win.'

In truth, it had been a tired performance, and the home side had missed a number of chances, but Fulham should have had enough guile to have seen off the Prenton Park club.

Fulham had just forty-eight hours to recover before playing their sixth league match in just seventeen days on Eater Monday. The match against **Brighton and Hove Albion** was extremely important. Brighton, due mainly to an impressive home record, had taken over at the top of the table. Their away record, although not so impressive, had seen them concede just twenty goals away from home in twenty league games.

The game had been in doubt earlier in the day, due to several torrential downpours that had turned the Cottage pitch into a lake. Most of the water did soak in, but as the sun came out just half an hour before kick-off, the pitch glistened as the sun reflected off the still clearly visible puddles and streams. Fulham were struck with two blows. John Richardson had not recovered from his injury, and so Wilf Tranter was given only his third start of the season, ironically against his former club. Barry Lloyd had also picked up an injury and was unfit, and so Fred Callaghan, substitute the previous Saturday, was given a rare chance in the unfamiliar inside forward position.

Brighton, who switched from their blue shirts to an unfamiliar red, also had problems. The team were without captain and former Manchester United and Preston player Nobby Lawton, dropped by manager Freddie Goodwin, centre forward and top scorer Alan Gilliver and half back Brian Turner. Their team did include experienced former Leeds full back Willie Bell, plus winger and future England coach Howard Wilkinson, signed from Sheffield Wednesday. Also in Brighton's team was Alex Dawson, who had scored a hat trick for Manchester United against Fulham at Highbury in an FA Cup semi final replay in 1958. United had won 5–3 and Dawson was only a month past his 18th birthday. Fulham's form gave rise to a bumper Bank Holiday crowd of almost 18,000, by far the highest attendance for a league match that season.

Fulham, probably frustrated by Saturday's result, produced their performance of the season at home, with Jimmy Conway, Steve Earle and Les Barrett terrorising the slow-moving Brighton defenders on the fast and slippery pitch. Brighton hung on for twenty-two minutes, but were then

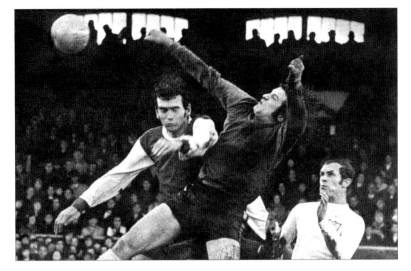

Under the watchful eye of Reg Matthewson, 'sergeant-major' Malcolm Webster dashes out to punch clear from the head of a Brighton forward.

hit by an avalanche of three Fulham goals in just twelve minutes. Vic Halom scored the first goal on twenty-two minutes. The Brighton defence gave Conway far too much room, and allowed him time to run to the by-line, beat Willie Bell and centre accurately for Halom to easily sidefoot home from six yards with a first-time effort.

Ten minutes later Fred Callaghan took advantage of another Willie Bell slip for the second. Bell flicked Conway's corner straight into the path of Callaghan and he shot in from fifteen yards; the goal was Callaghan's first for fifteen months. Before Brighton could draw breath, it was three. Earle dazzled the hapless Bell with a burst of speed that gave Halom the opportunity to knock the ball back to Barrett to powerfully drive in, shooting right-footed through a crowd of players low into the net.

Brighton substituted Kit Napier for Alex Dawson at half time, but the change made little difference. The second half was merely a continuation of the nightmare for Brighton, and Earle

I wonder if there are trout or salmon in here... The sun comes out on the Cottage lake, and reflections can clearly be seen. Several torrential downpours had put the Brighton game in doubt, and early on the entire middle of the pitch was under water.

The top of the table Seagulls had no answer to a rampaging Fulham side on Easter Monday. Here Fred Callaghan (10) takes advantage of another defender's mis-kick to drill home the second goal under the Brighton goalkeeper. Fulham won 4–1, further boosting their promotion credentials. Note the referee's pose in the six-yard box.

was unlucky with a fine header, early in the half, that struck a post. Then, just short of the hour, Earle made a determined burst down the right wing. He broke clear of the defence and had just the goalkeeper to beat. Defender Normal Gall, chasing back, brought down Earle from behind just inside the penalty area, and Conway converted efficiently from the penalty spot, low just inside a post.

Fulham lost a little concentration after that, which allowed Wilkinson to net a consolation goal for Brighton just three minutes later. Fulham soon regained their composure and coasted to the finish line winning easily **4–1**.

The Fulham showing had been superb, with every player excelling. Their performance was way above Third Division standard. Mike Pentecost, David Moreline and Reg Matthewson had offered Brighton few crumbs on which to feed, reading the Brighton attack very well. The marauding Fred Callaghan and effervescent Stan Brown, now playing as well as his First Division days, had sewn up the middle of the pitch totally.

The four forwards had led the Brighton defence a merry dance, and eventually run them ragged. The team had now scored twenty-two goals in the last eight games. The result made a mockery of the table; if Brighton were the best team in the division, then Fulham, on this display, were streets ahead. The match had been superbly officiated by the experienced Kevin Howley. The win had pushed Fulham up to eighth.

Brighton manager Freddie Goodwin was devastated, saying: 'That scoring burst really knocked us for six; we just hadn't the capacity to recover.' Bill Dodgin himself was for the first time wholly optimistic about the future saying: 'We can begin next season fearing nobody at all. ... If we could have just begun our run a few games earlier we could have been in the Second Division next season.'

April 1970

In this month

* *Gay Trip* won the Grand National.
* John Wayne won an Oscar for *True Grit*.
* Chelsea and Leeds United drew 2–2 in the FA Cup Final at Wembley, Chelsea winning the replay 2–1.
* Tax allowances were raised in the budget, exempting two million people from income tax.
* The Reverend Ian Paisley shocked the Irish Government by winning the Bannside by-election.
* British Leyland announced that the production of their longest-running car, the Morris Minor, would cease in 1971.
* Seven students were shot during rioting at the Ohio State University.
* The judge at the inquest of the Chappaquiddick river drowning stated that he doubted the truth of Senator Kennedy's testimony.
* US President Nixon sent US combat troops into Cambodia.
* Following a writ issued by Paul McCartney, the Beatles went to the High Court and formally dissolved the Beatles' partnership.
* An on-board explosion crippled the spacecraft *Apollo XIII*, the moon mission was aborted, and, after a very tense time, the astronauts were finally returned safely.

'Bridge Over Troubled Water' by Simon & Garfunkel topped the charts.
The film 'Woodstock' was released.

How the League was looking

During March, the table had stabilised somewhat. Orient remained at the top with a one-point lead. They were followed by Bristol Rovers, with Brighton just a point behind the leading two. Orient, however, still had three games in hand on both teams. Luton Town had recovered some pride, moving back to fourth place. Reading had lost form and had dropped down to sixth place. Fulham were now the team of the moment, pushing right up to eighth. Stockport had been unable to move off the bottom of the table and were now seven points adrift, and Barrow had been unable to consolidate their good run, dropping back into deep relegation difficulty. Gillingham had started to show some fight and were picking up points, and Southport were once again in the danger zone. Tranmere Rovers, Bournemouth and Walsall were all just outside the relegation slots, all far from comfortable.

The matches

FOR THE first game in April just four days after the Brighton win, Fulham travelled up to Lancashire on a Friday evening to play **Southport**, still lingering in the relegation zone. Fulham made two changes: a fit Barry Lloyd being recalled and Fred Callaghan replacing Wilf Tranter, who dropped down to substitute. Fulham again opted to play in their good luck all-red change strip, despite playing a team whose kit was all gold! The crowd was just over 3,400, the smallest to witness a Fulham game that season.

Fulham took a first-half lead in the seventeenth minute, when Barry Lloyd took an astute throw in. The ball found its way to Steve Earle, who put over an accurate cross to the far post, where Les Barrett met the ball with a well-timed downward header between the goalkeeper and the upright.

Fulham secured their win just thirty seconds into the second half when Jimmy Conway fired in a speculative shot from the corner of the six-yard area which found its way, with the aid of a huge deflection, through a packed penalty area, beating the goalkeeper and the defender on the line. Some reports credit the goal as an own goal by Southport player-manager Arthur Peat.

In front of a very sparse crowd of just over 3,400 on a Friday night, Jimmy Conway's shot is deflected and then touched in by a defender on the goalline. This was the second in Fulham's 2–0 win over Lancashire side Southport, which extended the unbeaten run to fourteen matches. Steve Earle seems to be a spectator for this one, watching from beside the goal net.

Fulham had a slice of luck later in the half when Southport were awarded a penalty. Play had moved away from the Fulham goal, but the linesman continued to flag furiously. Referee Harry Williams consulted with the linesman and awarded the penalty kick. However, Southport's Tony Field, making a comeback after a long injury lay-off, placed the penalty kick wide of the goal. Attractive Fulham eased home in fine style winning **2–0**.

Les Barrett, who had scored just once in six months, had now scored in the last *five* consecutive matches, and had six in his last nine! Fulham had now completed their second double of the season.

Fulham rested at the weekend but travelled back north on the following Monday evening for the rearranged match with **Mansfield Town** after the initial postponement. Mansfield were also in the thick of the promotion scramble with the same number of points as Fulham. Fulham were unchanged from Friday's game. A crowd of 10,000 turned up at Field Mill to see if it would be the Stags or Fulham that pushed on. The match was going to be tough, as Mansfield were unbeaten at home in the last thirteen games.

Fulham had a particularly rude awakening and were a goal down on sixty seconds. Mansfield's Dai Jones was fouled on the halfway line, Dudley Roberts touched on Sandy Pate's long free kick to Jones, who ran through a slack defence to score easily. Fulham could have equalised just two minutes later, but Mansfield were saved by an amazing reaction save from reserve goalkeeper Graham Brown. The goalkeeper was in trouble with the crosses raining in from Jimmy Conway and Les Barrett, but he was keeping Mansfield in the lead with a succession of reflex stops on the goal line.

Fulham were totally dominant, but were stunned by a second Mansfield goal on twenty-seven minutes. It was, however, a fine goal; Jones set up Malcolm Partridge, and his swerving shot, which entered the net via a post, gave Malcolm Webster no chance. An angry Fulham team went in at half time two goals down, thinking there was no justice.

There's hardly any light for the photographer at Mansfield, but Jimmy Conway gives Fulham a chink of light just after half time. Following a good move involving Halom and Earle, Conway slams in a right-footer to reduce the arrears. It proved to be a springboard, as Fulham quickly scored twice more to finally overcome the Stags 3–2, making their unbeaten run fifteen games.

Fired up by a pep talk from Bill Dodgin, Fulham came out with real determination, and in just two minutes their flair was rewarded. A lovely move between Steve Earle and Vic Halom created space for Conway to drive right-footed past goalkeeper Brown. Elated by the goal, Fulham struck again just four minutes later. Again the goal was a beauty; Barrett sped past Pate to connect with a beautiful long ball from Stan Brown. The winger produced another glorious cross, and it was met with a trademark bullet header from Halom that was so accurate and powerful that goalkeeper Brown could only punch the ball into the net.

In the sixty-ninth minute Fulham completed a magnificent comeback with a third and winning goal. The shot was a cannonball twenty-yard volley from Barry Lloyd that found the net and bounced out off the stanchion so quickly that the referee Mr Fallon had to check with the linesman before ruling that Fulham were ahead. It was now three Fulham goals in just over twenty minutes.

Now it was Mansfield's turn to be hurt, and they came at Fulham in the final twenty minutes and Webster made one superb save from Roberts. A few minutes later it was even closer, when an excellent header from Roberts struck the Fulham bar and dropped down onto the goal line. Despite loud appeals from the Mansfield players, referee Fallon remained unmoved and waved play on. Fulham held on nervously to win **3–2**.

The win had been reminiscent of Fulham's three-goal fight-back at Bramall Lane in 1968 after being two down. The match virtually finished Mansfield's promotion chances. The media headlined: 'Fulham, two down – triumph!' It had been an excellent forty-five minutes from the turbo-charged Cottagers that had left Mansfield standing. For Fulham, the run was now *fifteen* games unbeaten and they were now up to seventh, five points behind Bristol Rovers in second place but with two games in hand.

The fifteen-game unbeaten run had yielded thirty-three goals and twenty-four league points, virtually doubling the total that the club had prior to the start of the winning run. The atmosphere was heady with optimism, and there was just one word now on everyone's lips with just five games to play and that word was – promotion.

It would be interesting to see just how much had been taken out of Fulham with that scintillating performance when they played **Luton Town**, holding down fourth place but just two points ahead; the match was critical for both clubs. The clubs met at the Cottage just forty-eight hours after the emotional night at Mansfield, meaning that Fulham would now be taking part in their ninth league match in just twenty-five days – absurd! Again it seemed as if the 'fixtures god' had deliberately arranged this match for exactly this time – kismet.

Fulham were again unchanged, but many players were playing with cuts, strains and bruises. The Luton side had eighteen-year-old Alan Starling in goal in place of the injured Read, but apart from that was at full strength. The side contained two of Alec Stock's QPR men in critical positions; Mike Keen, the former QPR captain, at right half, and inside left John Collins, who later joined Fulham in a coaching capacity. Also in the side were Alan Slough at left half and Viv Busby at inside right, both players who would play a significant part in Fulham's future. Former Crystal Palace veteran Jack Bannister was at left back.

There were, of course, two other significant faces in the Luton side: John Ryan, the former Fulham centre half, was at right back, and the bulldozing, former Fulham striker Malcolm Macdonald was at centre forward. The crowd recognised the importance of the fixture, and the highest league crowd of the season – a fraction under 19,000 – arrived hoping to cheer the barnstorming Fulham side on to yet another victory. Luton had lost seven out of twenty away from home, so Fulham had to be in with a chance. Due to the colour clash, Luton wore blue shirts.

Eleven minutes only had passed when Fulham's promotion bubble was pricked. Young full back Dave Moreline, who had up to now not put a foot wrong, made the ghastly mistake that cost Fulham a giveaway goal, the match and possibly promotion. From a defensive throw-in, he attempted a casual back pass to goalkeeper Malcolm Webster that was not the best. Webster had advanced, but had not been expecting the pass, and, in a moment's confusion, Malcolm Macdonald seized possession, strode casually into the penalty box, waltzed round Webster, and planted the ball into an empty net; a soft, avoidable goal. The goal was eerily reminiscent of Macdonald's first ever goal for Fulham – same end of the ground, similar defensive mistake, same finish; the goal was all the incentive that Luton needed.

Tommy Trinder in the directors' box raised his trilby in apparent despair. He had seen many comical goals at Fulham, but few to rival this one. The Luton team fell back on defence almost immediately and fought an intense rearguard action. The goal seemed to completely knock the heart out of Fulham. Jimmy Conway was crowded out, Vic Halom was lost to sight and even Les Barrett's best efforts were dashed by one of the most committed teams to visit Fulham that season. The Luton team were just too experienced, with Slough, Bannister and centre half Terry Branston outstanding.

Stan Brown and Barry Lloyd worked hard in the middle of the field, but the approach play all fizzled out in and around the Luton penalty area. Indeed, Luton could have doubled their advantage before half time. Reg Matthewson, one of Fulham's better players on the night, gifted possession to Busby with yet another poor back pass. Busby was so amazed by the gift that he missed the easy opportunity.

The second half was very similar to the first, with neither side producing much quality football. When Luton did become rattled and started to commit fouls, they were aided and abetted by referee Clive Thomas who, as he had done in the Doncaster home game, failed to take one name and appeared happy to let the 'physical' stuff continue. All the Fulham forwards seemed to be having an 'off night', the only player really standing out was half back Fred Callaghan still determined to drive Fulham on. He lashed in one long-range shot, superbly saved by Starling in the Luton goal.

The only real skill from Luton came from winger Graham French, who fought a lone battle up front for most of the match, chasing lost causes. Webster was a spectator now, and Starling was by far the busier keeper, but most of his saves were routine rather than spectacular. Most of the danger to the Fulham goal seemed to come from over-hit back passes from the Fulham defenders that often had Webster sprawling in the mud.

There were so many blue shirts swarming around in the Luton box, it almost appeared as if they had fifteen defenders! Luton seemed content to boot the ball anywhere away from their own

Just two days after the Mansfield victory, Fulham faced promotion rivals Luton Town at the Cottage. Here dangerman Steve Earle is held and crowded out by four defenders. An exhausted Fulham side playing their ninth match in under three weeks failed to break down the Hatters' blanket defence and lost 0–1 to a gift goal scored by old boy Malcolm Macdonald. It was the game that cost Fulham promotion.

box with little purpose or direction. It was one of those games when you knew that it was just not going to be Fulham's night; the crowd began to thin out and desert the game, and the match finally slipped untidily away **0–1**, Fulham sadly being booed off the pitch.

The result was a devastating blow, and Fulham knew that they now faced a strong uphill fight to make it home. The team were still five points behind the promotion places, but there were still eight points available, and in theory anything could still happen; any two from seven clubs could still gain promotion to the Second Division.

Certainly Fulham had been very flat on the night, lacking plan and inspiration, and had tamely surrendered their unbeaten run. There had to be some sympathy for the team, however, as the clogged fixture list seemed to have finally caught up with them. The press were unimpressed by the quality of the fare on offer, saying: 'Neither side looked capable of contributing skill or entertainment to the higher division'. Another added: 'This was not just Third Division stuff – it was third rate.'

The Fulhamish manner of the defeat had been very hard to take. The one critical match the club had needed to win – they had lost. It was difficult to watch, as John Ryan, dumped by Fulham because of his perceived defensive deficiencies, proved to be the backbone of a Luton defence that had kept clean sheets in both games against Fulham.

Also it had been tough to watch Malcolm Macdonald, released with indecent haste at Fulham as 'not good enough', score the winning goal against Fulham on both occasions that season; Alec Stock must have been laughing his head off. Certainly Fulham had fallen for Stock's line that he intended to use Macdonald 'as a full back', and as the season was drawing to a close Macdonald was hard on the heels of Steve Earle and Jimmy Conway as the division's leading goalscorer. Luton had succeeded in completing the double over Fulham.

Another sad note took place just twenty-four hours after the Luton loss. Johnny Haynes stepped onto the Cottage turf for a competitive game for the final time. Playing in a side that included Ian Seymour, John Fraser, John Gilchrist, Wilf Tranter, Dave Roberts and Stan Horne, Haynes, at number ten naturally, took part in a 2–1 victory for Fulham reserves against Norwich City reserves; Wilf Tranter scored both goals. At least the great man stepped off the Cottage pitch for the last time a winner, in this, his final game.

Following another blank Saturday due to the FA Cup Final, Fulham played **Halifax Town** at the Cottage the following Wednesday. It can only be wondered what was going through the minds of the Halifax players following the 8–0 win against them earlier in the season. Halifax were in a solid mid-table position with no relegation fears. The match was Halifax's first ever league visit to Craven Cottage.

They possessed few stars and played a fairly young side on the night without veterans Freddie Hill and Ian Lawther. Halifax did include winger David Chadwick who had played so well for Middlesbrough at the Cottage the previous season.

Fulham made only one change, the inclusion of Wilf Tranter at left back for the suspended Fred Callaghan. Callaghan had recently been booked in a reserve match against Arsenal, and – as a result of accumulating just three bookings *over the entire season* – he was suspended for *three weeks!* The Fulham supporters must have felt that promotion was now beyond them, as just 7,000 turned up to watch the match.

Fulham were very slow in the first half and Halifax, showing little respect or nerves despite the previous result, took the lead as early as the tenth minute with a first-class opportunist goal from winger Phil McCarthy, who scored with a very neat header. Halifax started to show some physical stuff, and conceded eleven free kicks in the first half, compared to Fulham's two, referee John Hunting from Leicester taking little firm action. There were also a number of uncharacteristically shaky moments in the Fulham penalty area. Despite their previous excellent run, the crowd began, rather unfairly, to get onto the backs of the Fulham players, and there were remarkably even sporadic bouts of slow handclapping. Halifax Town were obviously out to at least salvage a bit of pride.

In the second half Fulham continued to show considerable mental and physical fatigue, and it wasn't until the last quarter of the match that the team found anything like their real form. Once they did they netted twice in six minutes to win the game.

In the sixty-fifth minute, Jimmy Conway scored the equaliser, and in the seventy-first minute Vic Halom netted the winner with a clever, hooked lob on the turn from the edge of the penalty area, the ball floating over the heads of a number of Halifax defenders pushing up. There was a slight suspicion of offside against Steve Earle for the winning goal, but the referee allowed it, and Halifax made no complaints, Fulham winning **2–1**.

The match had had a kind of end of season ring to it, but had yielded a further two points, and Fulham were still just about in the promotion hunt. Half backs Dave Lennard and John Pickering had done well for Halifax, but their forward line had rarely stretched the Fulham defence. The

Vic Halom (out of picture) has lobbed a hook shot from outside the penalty area that has floated over the defence and stranded the goalkeeper. The five Halifax defenders can't believe it's gone in. This was the winning goal in a 2–1 victory. It meant that Fulham had scored ten against the Shaymen that season.

defence, with little to do, had for once looked slightly brittle, but the five forwards, who were all on song, gave them plenty of breathing space. Vic Halom's winning goal took him to ten in just sixteen games; a miraculous turnaround for a player who thought his career had been over just six months earlier.

Fulham were still five points outside the promotion spots with just three matches to play. One Halifax player commented after the match: 'I wish to blazes you would climb out of this division. You have no right to be down here – it's not fair on the rest of us!' Fulham would be doing their best to leave the division by the front entrance as soon as possible.

The match had been Fulham's tenth against Yorkshire opposition that season, and they were undefeated in all of them, winning four and drawing the other six. The match saw Fulham complete the double over Halifax with a 10–1 aggregate.

On the following Saturday, Fulham re-played the match against **Rochdale** at Spotland that had been abandoned in November mid-way through the second half due to an icy pitch with the scores level at 2–2; Fulham were unchanged. Rochdale held a safe mid-table position. Fulham, still trying for promotion, were also chasing the goals that would clinch a Watney Cup place. Reading and Bristol Rovers were the rivals for this Cup place.

A tired Fulham started nervously and Rochdale's Dennis Butler lifted a drive against the bar after just five minutes. This time Fulham won the match by a single first-half goal in the twenty-fifth minute. Les Barrett swung out a neat pass to Steve Earle on the left, and Vic Halom read his cross perfectly, to score with a diving header. Fulham were outclassing and perplexing the Rochdale team at this point.

In the second half, Rochdale reshaped their attack and engineered several good chances. The home side's luck was out again when Reg Jenkins took careful aim for the top corner. Malcolm Webster was as relieved as anyone to see the ball thud back into his chest off the inside of a post. Rochdale continued to press, but Webster, who had been impressive in his handling throughout, saved all their on-target efforts. Halom's effort was enough to secure a **1–0** win.

The goal was Halom's eleventh in seventeen games. Fulham were not going to give this promotion up without a fight and although the thread was very thin, it was still real, the gap now just four points with two to play. Fulham's victory secured their fourth double of the season.

When **Reading** arrived at the Cottage on the following Monday night their position was similar to Fulham's, but the Berkshire side had one fewer game to play, and so, for them, promotion was now gone. The match was the second of the rearranged postponed fixtures. Despite the tiredness, Fulham were yet again unchanged. The Reading side contained young and athletic goalkeeper Steve Death signed on loan from West Ham, two players both confusingly called Dennis Butler and two Wagstaffs (Barry and Tony), who were brothers and were both signed from Sheffield United – both pals of Reg Matthewson. Up front, Reading had scoring potential with former Rotherham striker Les Chappell and young centre forward Dick Habbin signed from then non-league Cambridge United. The crowd, sensing that promotion was almost lost, was down to below 10,000.

On the night, however, Reading put up no resistance whatsoever and almost treated the game as a practice match. This was wrong considering the importance of the game to Fulham. Fortunately, Fulham turned on a superb spectacle for their fans that evening, leaving supporters in no doubt as to what might occur the following season if the team stayed together. Their speed, rhythm and understanding left Reading trailing in their wake. The defence had very little to do, and were therefore prone to occasional lapses of concentration at the back.

The forwards were, however, superb, running the leaden-footed Reading defenders ragged. Just three minutes had elapsed when Fulham scored through Steve Earle. The goal was a brilliant five-man move started by Barry Lloyd in his own penalty area, culminating in a fine cross from Les Barrett that Earle headed in. The match was one-way traffic for the remainder of the half. Reading were deeply indebted to goalkeeper Death, as he was the one player standing between Fulham and an avalanche. Despite his bravery Fulham had been fairly profligate with their chances.

Just two minutes into the second half Earle swooped again to net his second. Jimmy Conway seared through the Reading defence single-handed before laying the ball on a plate for Earle to convert easily; the goals were Earle's first in nine games, his longest spell without a goal that season. Barrett was also ripping the defence to shreds, and was unlucky with both crosses and shooting. Reading opted for damage limitation, and on the hour brought on centre half substitute Stuart Morgan for the hapless Fred Sharpe, who was being tortured by Earle's pace.

The game became tighter from that point and Fulham relaxed. Lloyd continued to fight for the ball, spread it around well and was the mastermind behind all of Fulham's creative work; the job seemed to be done. The defence allowed Reading the luxury of a consolation goal four minutes from the end, when half back Barrie Wagstaff netted. Fulham played out time to win **2–1**. It was now another three wins in a row, and Reading were the fifth team to have lost both matches against Fulham.

Had the result been enough? Had there been any slip-ups elsewhere? The immediate post-match period was a tense one, but finally the news came through that nobody wanted to hear. Luton Town had somehow managed to scramble their way to a goalless draw at Mansfield on the same evening, so the gap was three points but with just one match to play – Luton couldn't now be caught. At the end of the penultimate league game, Fulham's promotion dream was finally over for another season.

Even though Fulham's chances had always been a 'long shot', there was still huge disappointment. The recent Luton home defeat was now looking like the difference between promotion and failure. Although the goals had come at a good time for Steve Earle, there was less good news for the club. Dave Sexton, the Chelsea coach, was watching the game from the stands and had already made an initial approach to the club about Earle's transfer.

Elated by the team's recent performances, the crowd remained behind requesting that the players and staff appear on the balcony of the Cottage. Most of the players obliged, but chairman Trinder and manager Dodgin did not. Dodgin, who was a man of few words even at a time like this, would only say: 'I'll go up when there's something for me to go for – when we've won something.'

Fulham had another week off before playing their final league game just four days short of May against **Tranmere Rovers** at Prenton Park. The match was the final rearranged fixture covering

And as the sun and the season sets at Tranmere, we say goodbye. Be of good cheer. Wilf Tranter fires in a shot on the Tranmere goal, but Fulham produced little in the Monday evening gloom. A jaded side lost 0–1 having to be content in the end with fourth place in the division.

the bad weather period. With little hanging on the game, it was obviously going to be an anti-climax. Tranmere were safe from relegation, thanks to an impressive run of thirteen games that had hauled them clear of the relegation pack; therefore there was little to play for except pride. Fulham were unchanged.

Defensively Fulham were sound, with Mike Pentecost and Reg Matthewson being singled out for praise, but the forward line was very subdued. The season had appeared to finally catch up with the flying forwards on the evening. Steve Earle was unlucky in the twenty-fifth minute with a fine shot that hit the base of an upright before the ball bounced away to safety.

In the second half Ken Beamish was very unlucky in the sixty-second minute with a hard shot that crashed against the inside of the Fulham post, the rebound bouncing straight into the arms of grateful goalkeeper Malcolm Webster.

Tranmere won the game with a second-half goal from centre forward George Yardley just twenty minutes from time. Tranmere's Ray Mathias put in a deep free kick into the penalty area, beanpole Jim Hinch headed the ball on, and Yardley headed home from point-blank range past Webster. The goal was Yardley's twentieth of the season. Jimmy Conway and Earle had few chances to shine, and the game petered out to a **0−1** defeat.

It was certainly a shame that Fulham could not have won here, as they would have been rewarded with third place in the table, and just a three-point gap between them and the promoted teams, Orient and Luton Town. In the end, Fulham had to be content to end the season in fourth place, five points off the promotion places.

Fulham Youth tour to Düsseldorf (April 1970)

Before the start of the Luton game in April, the Fulham youth squad paraded around the pitch with the trophies they had won in Düsseldorf. They had gone out to Germany for their first ever competition and swept the board.

They had won a silver trophy that they would be defending next year, and a silver cup to keep. There was also a large bronze plate awarded to the team with most style.

The odds had been stacked against Fulham at the start, as the club had been under the impression that the age limit in the tournament was nineteen. The tournament was, in fact, for players up to the age of twenty-one, and the Fulham squad had turned up with five fifteen-year-olds in the party!

Düsseldorf results:

Group matches:

Turu '80	1−1	Friend
B.V. '04	1−0	Friend
Munich '60	2−0	Friend, Dunn

(Fulham were group winners)

Semi-final:

| Schalke '04 | 1−0 | Phillips |

Final:

| Fortuna Düsseldorf | 1−0 | Phillips |

The matches had all been 'sprint' matches of twenty minutes each way, except for the final which had been an hour in total. The matches had been played on shale pitches with balls that were quite large and soft.

On tactics Cohen said: 'Physical strength counted a lot in these conditions, and we were giving away weight as well as age. We had to find the right tactics – and quickly. In matches as short as these, it was too much to expect we would have been given a second chance. Fortunately we were solid at the back, and this gave us the breathing space to check the style and strength of the opposing sides, and to develop our tactics.'

Prior to the Luton home game, the successful Fulham Youth squad parade the trophies they won in Düsseldorf. The team were unbeaten in their first trip abroad.

Cohen, recalling old foes West Germany, said: 'We played five matches in three days, and before the end of it we had developed a touch of the fervour and dedication I remember from the 1966 World Cup winning days.'

Coach Ken Craggs said: 'We started off playing for Fulham, but after George had got them going they must have felt they were playing for England! In a way we were, because the German coach and the coaches from the Swedish team (Stockholm) and the Austrian Team (FC Wacker of Innsbruck) all buttonholed us to ask about our methods.'

Fulham's success had seen them apply for entry into the San Remo youth tournament, which was to be played over ten days in August. The standard would be much higher, but the club were confident of acceptance.

Tour management: George Cohen, Ken Craggs and John Kelly.

The sixteen-man Youth squad: (alphabetically): Roger Bensley, John Brickell, Barry Cook, John Cooper, Jimmy Dunn, Alan Fox, John Fraser, Barry Friend, Johnny Graham, Mickey Heath, McAndrew Johnson, Brendan McKevitt, Ray Phillips, Dave Robertson, Barry Silkman, and Derek Wells.

Of those names taking part, John Fraser became a professional and played for several seasons in the Fulham first team. Barry Friend also made two appearances for Fulham. Of the remainder, Mickey Heath played one game as an amateur for Brentford, after signing from Walton and Hersham.

Barry Silkman had the most interesting career. After being released by Fulham, he joined Barnet, finally entering the league with Hereford United. This was the start of a career that saw him play well over 200 league games for eight different clubs, including Crystal Palace, Manchester City and Queens Park Rangers, spanning ten years. He subsequently became a players' agent. None of the other players in the youth squad broke through into League football.

May 1970

In this month

- * Four students were shot dead by the National Guard at Kent University, Ohio.
- * Czechoslovakia signed a twenty-year treaty of friendship with the USSR.
- * The IOC banned South Africa from the 1972 Olympic Games.
- * *M*A*S*H* won first prize at the Cannes film festival.
- * Labour Prime Minister Harold Wilson called a June general election.
- * Charles Haughey and Neil Blaney, two former Irish ministers, were in court on gun charges following a find at Dublin airport.
- * A bomb was found on an airliner at Heathrow airport following explosions at three other European airports.
- * After protracted deliberations, the MCC tour of South Africa was cancelled due to the on-going apartheid issues.
- * Bobby Moore was arrested in Bogotá whilst with the England World Cup squad in South America, accused of stealing a bracelet. He was later cleared.
- * The great racehorse *Arkle* died.

'Back Home' by The England World Cup Squad topped the charts.
The film 'Beneath the Planet of the Apes' was released.

How the League was *won*

Orient remained at the top to the end, and won the League championship by a two-point margin. Luton Town put together an amazing recovery at the end of the season and took the runners-up spot comfortably by four points. Both Bristol Rovers and Brighton had been unable to sustain their excellent runs, finishing in third and fifth places respectively. Reading faded dramatically at the end, finishing in eighth place. Fulham, with a magnificent late run, were the division's unlucky team finishing in a very creditable fourth position.

Stockport were unable to move off the bottom of the table and were relegated, finishing seven points adrift; Barrow joined them. Southport also remained in the relegation zone at the end. Gillingham continued to find fight and courage to the end and completed their fixtures safe – though only on goal average. Tranmere Rovers and Walsall both put together late runs and hauled themselves away from the bottom in impressive style, abandoning Bournemouth who were relegated at the very last minute instead of Gillingham.

The events

WITH THE league programme complete before May, Fulham made immediate renovations to the Cottage pitch. The repairs concerned a quarter of the pitch at the Hammersmith End by the riverside. The club had to fill in a 'dip' that had re-appeared there and had become more and more noticeable in recent months. There was an advantage in that Fulham had a longer close season than usual for the pitch to recover.

Chairman Trinder said: 'The trouble is where one of the bombs fell during the war. They [the Germans] were after historic monuments, but they missed the Cottage. The other bombs fell on the stand and in the centre of the pitch. I am not sure whether we claimed war damage – I'll have to check the records. The only bother now we'll get is from Les Barrett if we flatten the pitch. It was easier for him running downhill!'

Although work was being done on the pitch, the club had made no further formal announcement on the development of the proposed stand on the riverside terrace, although sources within the club considered that the project was still definitely in the pipeline.

1969–70 Season Summary

The Fulham supporters had rarely experienced such a topsy-turvy season: a mediocre start, followed by a purple patch in September, a desperately poor three-month spell, and then promotion winning form in the last three months of the season, only to fail gloriously at the final hurdle. In the second half of the season, Fulham lost just three out of twenty-three league fixtures. In terms of points, the first half of the season yielded twenty-two, the second half, thirty-three, a 50% increase. Under the 'modern' rules, Fulham would have easily made a play-off position.

Although it sounds a little like a broken record, Fulham's season had again hinged on just three fixtures. The first was the Bristol Rovers away match, where half of the Fulham team were badly affected by a stomach bug and a match that Fulham desperately wanted to have called off by the Football League. The second was the farcical snow-covered match at Luton where the floodlights had failed four times in the first half, and again Fulham had requested that the game be called off, if not for the poor floodlights, then for the snow that obscured some of the pitch markings. Finally, there was the Luton match at the Cottage where the worn-out Fulham team were being forced by the Football League to play their *ninth* league game (almost 20% of the entire season's fixtures) in a space of less than *three weeks*! Probably none of those events would be allowed to happen in Premiership football today!

If Fulham had been allowed to properly play those three fixtures and if they had won them, even by the smallest of margins, (say 1–0), promotion would have been theirs easily, and Luton would have stayed in Division Three. The table would then have looked as follows:

	P	W	D	L	F	A	Pts
Orient	46	25	12	9	67	36	62
Fulham	46	23	15	8	82	50	61
Luton Town	46	21	14	11	75	45	56
Bristol Rovers	46	19	16	11	77	58	54

If Fulham had won the Bristol Rovers match, and merely drawn both games against Luton, promotion would *still* have been achieved.

Also, as usual, Fulham had performed in their time-honoured way by beating the teams at and around the top of the table, whilst floundering against those either relegated or just outside the relegation zone. Fulham would wince when they realised that against the relegated clubs alone they had dropped five points (out of sixteen), *enough for promotion*. When the two clubs just above the relegation zone were included, Gillingham and Bury, Fulham had dropped eleven points in total (out of twenty-four) – almost half! This is probably a more realistic reason as to why Fulham just failed to achieve promotion.

Fulham did have a little consolation inasmuch as they finished the season as the second highest goalscorers in the Third Division with eighty-one, six goals behind Reading and just one ahead of Bristol Rovers. This gave the team an automatic entry into the experimental Watney Cup competition to be played at the start of the following season, where the two highest scoring clubs from each of the four divisions would compete against each other. (Promoted teams and those involved in the next season's UEFA competitions were not included. Derby County in fourth spot should have qualified for a UEFA spot, but were banned from Europe due to financial irregularities.)

The goalscoring had been a feature of the season. Goals scored were the highest since Fulham won promotion to the First Division over ten years previously. The total truly reflected Bill Dodgin's dedicated approach to attacking football. Fulham scored more goals away from home than any other club in the division. The Jimmy Conway, Steve Earle and Les Barrett trio, ably supported in the later stages by Vic Halom, had been a revelation. Conway had been transformed from a left-sided midfield player to a right-winger to be compared to most in the First Division, his total of twenty-three goals outstanding. Steve Earle had also had a marvellous year in individual goalscoring feats and in total. He had also weighed in with twenty-three goals.

The Earle-Conway partnership had realised just four short of Dodgin's requested fifty goals! All three main forwards could shoot with either foot and could head the ball to score as well.

Vic Halom had certainly been the catalyst for the revival, his work rate and bustling style helping the stylish Earle in the middle of the forward line; Halom had contributed eleven goals in just nineteen matches. In the last three months of the season, Les Barrett had been back to the form that had won him England Under-23 honours. After a sticky start in terms of form and goalscoring, Les had steadily improved to be one of the most feared players in the division. The five principal forwards – Conway, Halom, Earle, Lloyd and Barrett – had weighed in with *seventy-one* goals between them, almost 85% of the total.

Defensively things had not been so straightforward. Ian Seymour had lost his place after some shaky displays and John Gilchrist had not really fulfilled Bill Dodgin's faith in him, playing only twenty games. Goalkeeper Malcolm Webster had helped to steady the ship considerably, but he was still a loan player. The left back position had been swapped around and given to many – Dave Moreline, Stan Brown, Fred Callaghan, Wilf Tranter and John Richardson to name but five; only late on in the season was consistency found in that position. Stan Horne had also had a very disappointing season, which was strange as in a far worse side the previous season he had looked as if he was going to be one of the principal players to drive Fulham forward this season.

Fortunately Reg Matthewson had been very consistent, as Fulham's bright young hope for the future, centre half Dave Roberts, had disappeared seemingly without trace after half a dozen games; Dodgin needed to do more work in this area and bring in new blood for next season's push.

Despite the defence looking rather unstable at times, it was Fulham's best defensive record for over twenty years. In the fifty matches played, Fulham had conceded more than two goals on just six occasions. In truth, this was probably a reflection on the quality of the Third Division forwards rather than a pointer to Fulham's defensive excellence.

The careers of both Johnny Haynes and Cliff Jones, now consigned mainly to the reserves, appeared to be over. Cliff Jones had not been able to produce any form when given a rare first team chance. It was ironic to think that Fulham's form and unbeaten run had begun when Haynes was out of the side through injury. After sustaining yet another injury playing for the reserves, Haynes was eventually fit enough to return. By this time, however, Fulham were on a roll and Dodgin was unable to change a winning side playing so well – not even to accommodate the Maestro.

Haynes' contract was up at the end of the season, and it seemed unlikely that either Jones or Haynes would be at Fulham at the start of next season. Barry Lloyd, after an uncertain start in the shadow of the great man, had blossomed in the final stages of the season.

After the previous season when Bill Dodgin had experimented with over thirty players, he had used just twenty-two players this season, an amazing fact, as *fifty* first team games had been played. In truth, six of those twenty-two players had only featured peripherally: Roberts, Jones, Large, Williamson, O'Leary and Tranter. These players had played just twenty-four league games between them, so Fulham had really made it through the entire league and cup campaign using just sixteen players, two of whom were goalkeepers!

Jimmy Conway, the Irish sprite, despite his allegiance to playing for Eire, played in all fifty games. This was remarkable when you consider the number of 'clogging' tackles meted out to him in the Third Division. Stan Brown had missed only two matches, Les Barrett three and Steve Earle six. In all, thirteen players played in over half the league games.

What was very encouraging was that, with the departure of names such as Cohen, Haynes, Byrne, Large and Jones, the average age of the Fulham side was now dramatically reduced to around twenty-three. This was what had been needed for a long time, and Bill Dodgin and Tommy Trinder really were building on young players.

What was also encouraging was that Fulham had possessed an excellent disciplinary record all season. No player had been dismissed, and a booking had been a very rare event indeed. Fulham's had been the cleanest (disciplinary) and most attractive (goals scored) record in the League when the two factors were put together.

These official facts were released when the FA announced that the Ford Motor Company was going to be handing out sponsorship money to teams *next season* based on disciplinary records and goalscoring. Two points were awarded for a goal scored away from home, one point for a goal scored at home. Ten points were lost for a player sent off, and five points were lost for any player cautioned by the referee. If these factors had been applied during this season, Fulham would have been the league's runaway leaders. They would have found fame, as well as £50,000 – a considerable sum. Chairman Trinder said: 'That's just our luck this season, but wait till next.'

At least the rot within the club appeared to have been stopped, and from the dark days in January when the club had dropped to sixteenth in the table, a new, vibrant young Fulham side had emerged from the ashes. Bill Dodgin's task would now be to hold the team together, as many First Division managers and scouts were already starting to look at the club's playing 'assets'. The team looked happier, the management more confident and there was at least a strong feeling around the place that after so many years going backwards Fulham Football Club had at last taken its first steps back on the road to recovery.

League Division Three - Season 1969-70 - Final Table

		P	W	D	L	F	A	W	D	L	F	A	Pts
1	LEYTON ORIENT	46	16	5	2	43	15	9	7	7	24	21	62
2	LUTON TOWN	46	13	8	2	46	15	10	6	7	31	28	60
3	Bristol Rovers	46	15	5	3	51	26	5	11	7	29	33	56
4	**Fulham**	**46**	**12**	**9**	**2**	**43**	**26**	**8**	**6**	**9**	**38**	**29**	**55**
5	Brighton and Hove Albion	46	16	4	3	37	16	7	5	11	20	27	55
6	Mansfield Town	46	14	4	5	46	22	7	7	9	24	27	53
7	Barnsley	46	14	6	3	43	24	5	9	9	25	35	53
8	Reading	46	16	3	4	52	29	5	8	10	35	48	53
9	Rochdale	46	11	6	6	39	24	7	4	12	30	36	46
10	Bradford City	46	11	6	6	37	22	6	6	11	20	28	46
11	Doncaster Rovers	46	13	4	6	31	19	4	8	11	21	35	46
12	Walsall	46	11	4	8	33	31	6	8	9	21	36	46
13	Torquay United	46	9	9	5	36	22	5	8	10	26	37	45
14	Rotherham United	46	10	8	5	36	19	5	6	12	26	35	44
15	Shrewsbury Town	46	10	12	1	35	17	3	6	14	27	46	44
16	Tranmere Rovers	46	10	8	5	38	29	4	8	11	18	43	44
17	Plymouth Argyle	46	10	7	6	32	23	6	4	13	24	41	43
18	Halifax Town	46	10	9	4	31	25	4	6	13	16	38	43
19	Bury	46	13	4	6	47	29	2	7	14	28	51	41
20	Gillingham	46	7	6	10	28	33	6	7	10	24	31	39
21	BOURNEMOUTH	46	8	9	6	28	27	4	6	13	20	44	39
22	SOUTHPORT	46	11	5	7	31	22	3	5	15	17	44	38
23	BARROW	46	7	9	7	28	27	1	5	17	18	54	30
24	STOCKPORT COUNTY	46	4	7	12	17	30	2	4	17	10	41	23

I SAY . . . .

The Editor,
Fulham F.C. Programme

Dear Sir,

As a Fulham Statistician for the last five years, I would like to comment on a statement in the Brighton Programme concerning Steve Earle.

The programme stated that Steve scored two goals at home for the first time against Walsall a couple of weeks back, this is not true as Steve has scored twice in a Craven Cottage match on two previous occasions:—

(1) Against Liverpool on 26th February, 1966. Result 2-0. At the start of the "Great Escape" from relegation Steve playing at outside right scored the first with a header between Lawrence and the near post from a centre by Johnny Haynes in the 11th minute, and he scored the second 16 minutes from the end taking a pass from Les Barrett and despite handling the ball scored with a great cross-shot.

(2) Against Manchester City, League Cup 4th Round, November 1st, 1967, result 3-2. Playing at inside right Steve scored the first in the second minute with a low cross-shot after a dummy by Allan Clarke had foxed the goalkeeper and twelve minutes later scored a second when Allan Clarke headed down Les Barrett's centre and Steve shot in from close range. Fulham went on to win 3-2 thanks to a late Allan Clarke goal.

Yours faithfully,

Martin Plumb (18),
19 Booth Drive,
Laleham, Nr. Staines,
Middlesex.

This appeared in the programme for the Halifax match. It certainly appears that the young writer knew his facts. Whatever happened to him? Well, dear reader, si monumentum requiris circumspice.

1969–70 Season's Results

	Sat, August 9	H	Bradford City	D	0–0		9,943
FL Cup 1	*Wed, August 13*	*A*	*Orient*	*D*	*0–0*		*8,676*
	Sat, August 16	A	Bury	L	0–1		5,648
FL Cup 1R	*Mon, August 18*	*H*	*Orient*	*W*	*3–1*	*Conway 2 (1 pen), Earle*	*11,424*
	Sat, August 23	H	Gillingham	W	2–1	Haynes, Conway (pen)	8,648
	Wed, August 27	H	Southport	W	3–2	Conway 2 (1 pen), Brown	9,134
	Sat, August 30	A	Barrow	L	1–3	Richardson	5,665
FL Cup 2	*Wed, September 3*	*H*	*Leeds United*	*L*	*0–1*		*20,445*
	Sat, September 6	H	Shrewsbury Town	W	3–1	Conway 2 (1 pen), Barrett	8,990
	Sat, September 13	A	Bristol Rovers	L	2–3	Conway, Earle	10,663
	Tues, September 16	A	Halifax Town	W	8–0	Earle 5, Conway 2 (1 pen), Lloyd	5,809
	Sat, September 20	H	Plymouth Argyle	W	4–3	Conway 2, Lloyd, Haynes	12,843
	Sat, September 27	A	Stockport County	W	4–1	Earle 3, Conway	4,231
	Mon, September 29	A	Orient	L	1–3	Earle	18,861
	Sat, October 4	H	Doncaster Rovers	D	1–1	Brown	13,535
	Wed, October 8	H	Bury	L	2–4	Conway, Lloyd	11,724
	Sat, October 11	A	Bournemouth	D	2–2	Earle, Conway	8,429
	Sat, October 18	A	Rotherham United	D	0–0		7,669
	Sat, October 25	H	Barnsley	D	0–0		10,535
	Sat, November 1	A	Brighton and Hove Albion	L	1–2	Haynes	17,760
	Sat, November 8	H	Torquay United	D	1–1	Earle	10,000
FA Cup 1	*Sat, November 15*	*A*	*Exeter City*	*L*	*0–2*		*9,181*
	Sat, November 22	H	Mansfield Town	D	1–1	Conway	8,038
	Tues, November 25	A	Luton Town	L	0–1		16,485
	Sat, December 13	H	Bristol Rovers	W	3–1	Richardson 2, Earle	6,765
	Sat, December 20	A	Shrewsbury Town	D	1–1	Earle	3,847
	Fri, December 26	A	Gillingham	L	0–2		8,265
	Sat, December 27	H	Barrow	W	2–1	Richardson, Lloyd	9,559
	Fri, January 2	H	Orient	D	1–1	Conway	12,308
	Sat, January 10	A	Plymouth Argyle	L	0–2		9,661
	Sat, January 17	H	Stockport County	D	1–1	Richardson	7,435
	Tues, January 27	A	Walsall	W	3–1	Halom, Lloyd, Earle	6,251
	Sat, January 31	A	Doncaster Rovers	W	1–0	Conway	8,180
	Fri, February 6	H	Bournemouth	D	1–1	Earle	9,713
	Sat, February 14	A	Bradford City	D	0–0		9,615
	Sat, February 21	A	Barnsley	D	3–3	Conway, Earle, Gilchrist	9,676
	Sat, February 28	H	Rotherham United	W	3–2	Halom, Lloyd, Barrett	8,142
	Sat, March 14	H	Rochdale	W	2–0	Halom 2	6,708
	Wed, March 18	H	Walsall	W	4–0	Earle 2, Halom, Brown	7,301
	Sat, March 21	A	Reading	W	4–0	Halom 2, Earle, Barrett	16,431
	Fri, March 27	A	Torquay United	D	1–1	Barrett	7,934
	Sat, March 28	H	Tranmere Rovers	D	1–1	Barrett	10,310
	Mon, March 30	H	Brighton and Hove Albion	W	4–1	Barrett, Callaghan, Halom, Conway (pen)	17,933
	Fri, April 3	A	Southport	W	2–0	Barrett, Conway	3,432
	Mon, April 6	A	Mansfield Town	W	3–2	Conway, Halom, Lloyd	10,322
	Wed, April 8	H	Luton Town	L	0–1		18,987
	Wed, April 15	H	Halifax Town	W	2–1	Conway, Halom	7,072
	Sat, April 18	A	Rochdale	W	1–0	Halom	5,077
	Mon, April 20	H	Reading	W	2–1	Earle 2	9,713
	Mon, April 27	A	Tranmere Rovers	L	0–1		5,665

1969–70 Season

APPEARANCES (maximum 50):

Football League Division 3: Conway 46, Brown 44 (+2), Barrett 44, Earle 41, Matthewson 39, Richardson 31, Lloyd 30 (+4), Horne 29, Callaghan 28 (+1), Haynes 27, Webster 26, Penetecost 25 (+2), Halom 23 (+1), Gilchrist 20 (+3), Seymour 18, Moreline 11 (+1), Roberts 9 (+1), Tranter 7 (+1), Jones 5 (+2), Williamson 2, Large 1, O'Leary (1 sub).

FA Cup: Seymour 1, Gilchrist 1, Callaghan 1, Horne 1, Matthewson 1, Conway 1, Haynes 1, Brown 1, Earle 1, Barrett 1, Richardson 1, Tranter (1 sub).

FL Cup: Conway 3, Brown 3, Haynes 3, Horne 3, Gilchrist 3, Seymour 3, Roberts 3, Barrett 2, Earle 2, Callaghan 2, Pentecost 2, Matthewson 1, Halom 1, Jones 1, Large 1, Lloyd (2 sub).

TOTAL: Conway 50, Brown 48 (+2), Barrett 47, Earle 44, Matthewson 41, Horne 33, Richardson 32, Haynes 31, Callaghan 31 (+1), Lloyd 30 (+6), Pentecost 27 (+2), Webster 26, Halom 24 (+1), Gilchrist 24 (+3), Seymour 22, Roberts 12 (+1), Moreline 11 (+1), Tranter 7 (+2), Jones 6 (+2), Williamson 2, Large 2, O'Leary (1 sub).

GOALSCORERS (all competitions):

Conway 23, Earle 23, Halom 11, Barrett 7, Lloyd 7, Richardson 5, Haynes 3, Brown 3, Gilchrist 1, Callaghan 1. (Total: 84).

Steve Earle and Jimmy Conway were joint top goalscorers for the season. Conway played in every match – cup and league – a total of 50 games.

June 1970

At this time

* *Nijinsky*, ridden by Lester Piggott, won the Derby.
* The Who performed the rock opera *Tommy* at the Metropolitan Opera House in New York.
* England relinquished their hold on the World Cup, losing 3-2 to West Germany in the quarter-finals.
* Rover announced the new all-purpose four-wheel drive vehicle – the Range Rover.
* Russian cosmonauts in *Soyuz IX* landed safely after a record seventeen days in space.
* Caroline Thorpe, the wife of the Liberal leader, was killed in a car crash.
* Luxembourg, Britain, Ireland, Denmark and Norway opened talks on their entry into the Common Market.
* The Tories claimed a surprise general election victory, and Ted Heath was installed as Prime Minister.
* Laurence Olivier was awarded a life peerage for services to the theatre.
* Brazil, outclassing all others, won the World Cup beating Italy 4-1 in the final.
* Tony Jacklin became the first British golfer to win the US Open for fifty years.
* Postage stamps in decimal currency were issued in Britain for the first time.
* Women were able to become full ministers of the Methodist Church for the first time.
* The bodies of two children were found in a shallow grave at Waltham Abbey, Essex. The case was known as 'The Babes in the Wood'.
* The author E.M. Foster died.

'In the Summertime' by Mungo Jerry topped the charts.
The film 'Catch 22' was released.

July 1970

At this time

* Chancellor Ian McLeod died aged fifty-six after less than a month in office.
* Irish ex-minister Neil Blaney was cleared of gun charges.
* A British Comet airliner, carrying 112 holidaymakers and crew, crashed in Spain killing all on board.
* In France, David Broome became the first Briton ever to win the World showjumping championship.
* Prime minister Edward Heath declared a state of emergency as dockworkers staged their first national strike since 1926.
* Twenty-eight further thalidomide children were awarded £485,000 in compensation.
* Jack Nicklaus won the British Open golf championship.
* The uninhibited sex revue *Oh! Calcutta!*, devised by Kenneth Tynan, opened at the Round House.
* After a night of violence in Belfast, 1,500 British troops fought a fierce gun battle with IRA snipers; several bombs exploded in the city.
* The conductor Sir John Barbirolli died.

'All Right Now' by Free topped the charts.
The film 'Myra Breckinridge' was released.

Early August 1970

At this time

* The British Army used rubber bullets for the first time in Belfast.
* The police and black civilians clashed in Notting Hill.
* The British Army used CS gas in the Bogside district.
* Magazines *Harper's Bazaar* and *Queen* merged.
* Ninety-nine people died in an air crash in Peru.
* A US marine was jailed for five years for murdering fifteen Vietnamese civilians.
* The 1,000th episode of *Coronation Street* was broadcast.

'The Wonder of You' by Elvis Presley topped the charts.
The film 'Soldier Blue' was released.

The events

THE FULHAM board, management, team and supporters took a slightly longer rest during this particular close season to reflect on their close call with promotion. All parties concerned with the club were rejuvenated, and were all eagerly awaiting the following campaign, to see whether this season's final fling could, next season, be consolidated into a promotion celebration. It was the close season, and the current affairs are included here to retain the 'feel' of the 1970 period!

Season 1970–71

The Build-up

THE 1970–71 season again saw no changes or additions to the Fulham board of directors. The long-standing members of the board still comprised the Dean brothers, Eric Miller and Noël (Chappie) D'Amato (vice chairman), with Tommy Trinder as chairman. Graham Hortop continued to hold the position of club secretary/general manager. Terry Medwin continued to assist Bill Dodgin as trainer/coach, and George Cohen continued in charge of Fulham's youth policy.

Fulham's league crowds had dropped from 14,200 to an average of around 10,200 due to the club's presence in the Third Division. This drop equated to 28%. It was imperative that Fulham continued from where they had left off at the end of the previous season to try and improve attendances; significant gates were still required just to break even.

In this year's pre-season address, Tommy Trinder was much more upbeat and as usual he showed a strong awareness of the world of League football. He stated: 'What a change it is to be able to look at the fixture lists and wonder who will be going UP this season. This may seem a bit obscure at first glance, but the Fulham faithful will know what I mean. After all those years looking at the activity at the foot of the table, of facing more perils than Pauline, we can at least raise our sights.

'When I was lifting my glass at Orient's promotion celebration dinner, they asked if I felt envious of them. I said, 'Of course not, because next season we will be playing among the really famous, against clubs with unequalled traditions like Aston Villa and Preston North End.' When I was halfway through making that crack, I couldn't help thinking that it was a fair reminder that we still have a fight on our hands.

'However, we begin with an advantage. Those two clubs have dropped into the Third Division for the first time in their histories. From recent experience, we know they will take a little time to adjust. In our case we found the formula just two or three games too late to bounce straight back to the Second Division.'

The start of the season

Despite inflation, the club had bravely decided to peg admission prices at the previous season's levels wherever possible. The changes to admission prices were for standing on the terraces. These were increased from 5/- (25p) to 6/- (30p) for the terrace and from 6/- (30p) to 7/- (35p) for the enclosure. Prices for the Stevenage Road seating remained at 8/- (40p), 10/- (50p) and 15/- (75p).

The club had also contained the season ticket prices at the previous season's level of eight guineas, ten guineas and fifteen guineas: (£8.40p, £10.50p and £15.75p). This was the third consecutive season that the season ticket prices had been frozen, a brave move indeed given Fulham's circumstances. Thanks to the encouraging form in the second half of the previous season, demand for season tickets, kept at the previous season's costs, was fairly brisk.

Playing Staff

Although the changes to staffing were nowhere near as drastic as those in the previous two seasons, a prudent Fulham managed to reduce the wage bill still further. Full back John Gilchrist lasted just one season at Fulham and was transferred for a small fee to Colchester United. He played a further season of league football there before moving to Tooting and Mitcham, and finally to Tonbridge as player-manager before retiring. He was a member of the Colchester side that enjoyed a fine FA Cup run, including the memorable 3–2 victory over First Division Leeds United at Layer Road that season. Gilchrist died from a kidney related illness aged just 52.

Danny O'Leary, who had joined Fulham as part of the same deal that brought Gilchrist to the Cottage, had not made an impression at Fulham and was released. He failed to make the grade in league football, and his entire league career was limited to forty-five minutes at Bristol Rovers.

Two young players also left the club, Brendan McKevitt and Don Shanks. In the case of Don Shanks, it was another in the catalogue of Fulham transfer mistakes. The crafty Luton manager Alec Stock made his third 'steal' from the Cottage in less than twelve months when he signed Shanks who had not yet broken into the first team at Fulham. Shanks made the first team within a year of signing for Luton, and ultimately went on to enjoy a successful playing career of twelve years and over 300 league appearances with Luton Town, Queens Park Rangers and Brighton.

Two of Fulham's senior players also left the club. Cliff Jones, having been relegated to the reserves for half of the previous season, retired from league football. He had a number of careers after leaving the game, including that of butcher, but did not retain his involvement with football. Bill Dodgin had a great deal of sympathy for Cliff Jones saying: 'It's hard for [players like] them because they have grown used to accuracy and quick thinking. Cliff was used to getting the ball where he wanted it from players who had the skill and the perception to see where he was going. When he was at Fulham he would make a run, only to find that the ball had ended up elsewhere. I don't think it was a coincidence or because of any lack of application that he couldn't score goals for us when he had been a prolific goal-getter at Tottenham. He just couldn't tune into a lower standard.'

The most significant departure was that of Johnny Haynes. He had decided to hang up his playing boots and call it a day in this country. His decision ended a magnificent twenty-year relationship and involvement with Fulham Football Club. It was widely considered by many that Fulham's elder statesman would go into business in this country, so it was somewhat surprising when Haynes elected to go to South Africa and continue his playing career with Durban City, following in the footsteps of his friend Johnny Byrne.

Former Fulham goalkeeper Tony Macedo, having completed his career at Colchester, had also made the journey to South Africa and was reunited with Haynes, playing alongside him for Durban where they both won a championship medal. Johnny Haynes later returned to this country and owned a dry-cleaning business, living in comfortable retirement in Edinburgh with his third wife Avril. Johnny Haynes died tragically young following a car accident, after suffering a brain haemorrhage in October 2005. Tony Macedo remained in Johannesburg until recently, and is now believed to be in Australia.

Before leaving the country in 1970, Johnny Haynes said: 'I never had any regrets about staying at Fulham for nearly twenty years. They were a great club and very good to me. But there came a time when I knew that I would have to move when my playing days in the Football League were over. I received a couple of offers, but the best came from Durban City, so I decided to take it.

'I will play for them until the end of their season in October and then I shall be coming home again. If things go well, and I like it out there, it will be up to me whether I go back next March for the new season.

'I've only been to South Africa once before, on holiday. But I have been told that it is a great place to live, and playing for Durban will give me the chance to meet up with my old Fulham friends 'Budgie' Byrne, Tony Macedo and Bobby Keetch. This is really a test period, if I like it, I could go back.'

An approach from then aspiring Southern League club Wimbledon is the only documented bid for Haynes' services. Many were dumbfounded that an English league club had not come in for Haynes. He was still only thirty-five and skilful players, such as Stanley Matthews, had continued to play at a high level much longer than Haynes.

Matthews had successfully drawn in the crowds and transformed the fortunes of Stoke City. He had achieved this despite being ten years older than Haynes. Many in the game considered that the fit Haynes, who still trained like a teenager, would have been an invaluable asset to another club, but there were perhaps worries over his influence and personality. It certainly seemed a tragedy that the final chapter of Haynes' magnificent career would be played out in a foreign country.

Although a new age was dawning at Fulham, the club wrote nothing about Haynes' departure in the official club programme – perhaps they were trying to make a 'clean break'. However, chairman and personal friend Tommy Trinder made many references to the Maestro in that season's Fulham handbook. He said: 'It is my belief, as well as my hope, that this is going to be quite a season, but whatever happens it is going to be strange not having Johnny Haynes around. After twenty odd years here, he was as much a landmark as Craven Cottage itself.

'In all football there was never a better example of loyalty. He had so many offers to move – and we knew all about them because he would come and tell us about them. But after we had talked them out and we had explained how much we needed him, he always stayed. To give just one example of what this meant, going back about ten years, he could have collected £15,000 for joining A.C. Milan. How grateful we are, all of us. ...

'When you think of how many of his fifty odd caps were collected whilst he was in the Second Division, it makes you wonder about what those players are moaning about when they insist on a move just because their team has gone down.

'I gather Johnny will be going into business soon [written before Haynes' decision to go to South Africa]; if he is half as good in that field as he was with us, he'll finish up a tycoon! He will always be welcome at Fulham and we are sure his mother will be taking her usual seat in Craven Cottage. She is more than Johnny's mother – she is a Fulham fan.'

Fulham had, however, made two significant additions to the squad. Firstly, and much to the surprise of a number of soccer specialists, Arsenal had decided to release goalkeeper Malcolm Webster, and allow Fulham to sign him permanently for a fee of around £10,000. Webster had been on loan at Fulham since the turn of the year, and had been instrumental in turning around Fulham's fortunes at the back. He was courageous and flamboyant without being overly flashy and was most of all, young. Arsenal had signed goalkeeper Geoff Barnett from Everton as cover for Bob Wilson.

Secondly, Fulham signed Irishman Jimmy Dunne from Third Division Torquay United. Half back and Eire Under 23 international Dunne had played magnificently during both encounters against the Devon side the previous season and Dodgin considered that Dunne was one of the principal reasons why Fulham had failed to win those matches. Try as they might, it had seemed to be impossible to get past him on the day.

There was, however, some history behind the transfer. Five years previously Bill Dodgin, then scouting for Millwall, had crossed the Irish Sea and persuaded seventeen-year-old Dublin-born Dunne to move from his Irish club Shelbourne. Success did not come quickly for Dunne and Millwall dropped him after making just one appearance for the club. At the end of the season Millwall handed Dunne a free transfer and the disillusioned player returned to Ireland.

Frank O'Farrell (later to manage Manchester United) seemed to have been a shrewd judge of character, and had offered Dunne terms at Torquay following an impressive pre-season tour of West Germany where the player had excelled. At Plainmoor he had been regarded as one of the finest free-transfer bargains the club had ever had.

In three seasons Dunne had been almost 'ever present' in the Torquay side, weighing in with thirteen goals whilst making 125 league appearances. He had given a number of 'five-star' displays and Torquay had been extremely reluctant to agree when Dunne had requested a transfer towards the end of the 1969–70 season. He had no real dissatisfaction with the Devon club, but from such a remote outpost it was very difficult for him to return regularly to his native Ireland. Being in London would put him much closer to Heathrow Airport. Initially Torquay did not want Dunne to play for another Third Division club, but did not really want to keep an unsettled player. Fulham's initial offer of £10,000 was dismissed out of hand, but when Fulham returned quickly with a bid of £15,000, Torquay readily accepted it.

Dunne was certainly quite a hard player: his career had started at sixteen years old with a six-*month* ban after being sent off in a schoolboy match! This suspension had ruled him out of winning an Eire schoolboys cap. Dunne had become a painter and decorator after leaving school but had soon been lured away by full-time football.

Dunne had now re-joined the man who had given him his first opportunity in football, and he was anxious to repay the debt. At twenty-two, Dodgin had bought another bright, young player. Dodgin was very pleased with his capture, stating: 'He will tighten up the defence and help cut out our big weakness of last season – allowing the opposition to come back after we have scored.'

Like the previous season, Fulham started out with a senior squad, including two goalkeepers, which comprised just eighteen players. Fulham also started the season without John Richardson, who had missed most of the pre-season games with a thigh injury. Talented young professional David Carlton was also out for a considerable period, possibly months, following a serious knee operation in March. He was still on crutches at the start of this season.

In line with his philosophy of bringing on youngsters, Dodgin had signed Johnny Graham, John Brickell and goalkeeper McAndrew Johnson as apprentice professionals. These three apprentices were augmented by Tommy James signed from Chelsea on the recommendation of Barry Lloyd.

George Cohen had also been looking at older youth team players, targeting university players, probably in line with Dodgin's edict for 'intelligent' football! To this end, three players had been training with Fulham in the close season and all would appear in pre-season fixtures for the reserves. John Lacy was a nineteen-year-old centre back, who stood 6' 3" and had already played in the Cheshire League with Marine. He came from the north of England and was currently at the London School of Economics. Steve Edmundson was a midfield player and captain of the London University side; he was studying medicine. Michael Naan was a centre forward and very good in the air. Naan already held a civil engineering degree, and was taking a post-graduate course.

Although not widely publicised, Fulham had also made a loan signing. Alan Morton had originally been on the books of Crystal Palace, without making their league side. During part of the previous season, Morton had been on loan to Stockport County, making ten appearances and scoring one goal. He had been released by Palace and had trained with Nuneaton on a non-contract basis. He had joined Fulham initially on a two-month loan.

Stan Horne had been captain during the previous season, but Bill Dodgin made a brave decision over the summer by appointing twenty-one-year-old midfielder Barry Lloyd club captain for this season. This would make Lloyd the youngest captain currently playing in the Football League. Dodgin said: 'The best captains are not noticed that much, they must have ability to make decisions on the field. Barry is a quiet boy who believes in his own ability.'

Other changes

The club's official programme remained similar in size, and the format and content were again very similar to that of the previous season. The 'action' shot frame at the bottom of the cover was moved to the centre of the page. The Third Division championship trophy was still given a prominent position on the cover. The programme was still competitively priced at 1/- (5p). The programme price was indicated in dual currency for the first time in view of the United Kingdom's impending switch to decimalisation. There were, however, more snippets of information about events happening within the club with a page entitled 'Inside the Cottage'.

Perhaps with the thought in mind that a 'new' Fulham had been born, the club decided to change the playing kit for the first time in four seasons. In order to keep costs down, the basics were the same: white shirts, and black shorts with two vertical white stripes down the side. The change to the shirts was to have red numerals on the back instead of the usual black, and the socks were now to be all red, rather than white with the single black band. There may have been some history in this, as the Cottagers always seemed to enjoy better fortune when playing in a strip that contained some red in it.

The club had also changed the away strip to an unusual kit of dark blue and sky blue vertical striped shirts, white shorts and white-topped dark blue socks. The previously used two away kits of all red or all blue had apparently been relegated in favour of just the one change. According to some, graduates of Oxford and Cambridge Universities originally founded the Fulham club, and so the away colours were appropriate, especially for a club lying next to the Thames. Perhaps it was another factor in Dodgin's quest for 'intelligent' football!

The Ford car company's sponsorship deal came into effect this season with points awarded for goals scored and points deducted for disciplinary offences. The first prize at the end of the season would be £50,000, a significant sum, the only conditions being that the amount awarded must be spent on the ground. That would not prove to be a problem for the ambitious Cottagers who had plans to swallow up that cash – and more besides. As well as the end of season award, there were also monthly divisional awards.

Thanks to Fulham's continually successful pools scheme, the money raised by agents had already been put to use. New toilets had been installed at both the Putney and Hammersmith ends, and new ladies' toilets had been installed underneath the main Stevenage Road stand. The boundary railing around the pitch had been strengthened and was now set in concrete. This safeguarded supporters from stepping into mud and water around the pitch edge when it rained! Catering facilities had also been updated all around the ground.

Thanks to his efforts in the previous season, Fulham had awarded Bill Dodgin a three-year contract. In the club handbook, he spoke boldly about the forthcoming season. Under the clever title of 'Cheer up – and we can have a winning team', he said: 'It is my job to see the players have just the right amount of pressure. Too little is a mistake; too much is usually a disaster. So I am more conscious than most of the danger involved if everybody assumes we will go up this season as if by divine right.

'On the way we finished last season, we can, of course, finish at the top of the table, but it is a mistake to take it for granted. If that is the attitude around the place, it will be making unnecessary demands on a youngish team.

'What we achieved in that late run was, for the first time in years, to stop losing. Our confidence had been shaken; it took a long time to get it right. To win and keep winning needs a touch of arrogance and killer instinct, but it is so easy for cockiness to become over-confidence. Once teams start thinking they will win just by sending the shirts out, they are in trouble.

'Of course we have our expectations, but it must be remembered that we have had to re-build completely, and the job has yet to be finished. It is pointless going up unless you have a team who are able to stay there, and also have potential to go up again.'

Dodgin knew what was required of this Fulham side and said: 'What we know is that we have the basis for such a team. Every move we have made has been with the object of improving a [team] position, sometimes by only a few per cent. The difficulty is to keep the right blend while doing so, and this, I believe, we have achieved.

'In all ball games there must be a considerable element of luck. This tends to even itself out over a season and we also have the ability to make things happen for us.

'We are a side in the best Fulham tradition – a football playing side, not a physical side. There is no real point trying to bend ourselves to any other method. Our strength is going to the opposition. It takes courage to do this and it does not help if the crowd become impatient. What we need are cheers and for them to continue when things do not go right at the first attempt.'

Dodgin then paid tribute to those around him, saying: 'I get a lot of help from the people I work with and I appreciate it. Terry Medwin in particular is doing a great job and often does not get the appreciation he warrants. He has been given the responsibility of taking the team away on several occasions and has done well.

'Finally, it's good to know that the youth scheme will be more productive again now that George Cohen has taken it over with Ken Craggs to back him up.'

Dodgin, the hard taskmaster, had set his team a very difficult points target. He set out his philosophy very simply: 'I've told my players that I expect them to get either sixty-four or sixty-five points, which I reckon will be good enough to get us back to the Second Division. We already have the reputation, thanks to the way we finished last season, of being an attacking side.

'That's why things are going to be easier for us away from home when teams are prepared to come at us. At Craven Cottage they will all arrive intent on putting up the shutters. We should have more troubles at home than on our travels. My basic instruction to the team is get out and enjoy playing – attack and you'll enjoy it.'

It was a huge total; Dodgin was asking the team to obtain around 70% of the points available that season! Continuing with his passion for attacking flair, he said: 'There are things going on in the game which are discouraging to say the least. There are too many teams frightened to lose, and I find this most obvious in the Second Division.

'There are managers who will ruin the game unless they have a good look at themselves and where they are going. There are fewer good players about, and we seem to have become obsessed with the belief that middle-distance running is the strongest point in our football.

'We seem to have forgotten that we've always produced players who want to get out there and enjoy the bloody game!'

Dodgin's philosophy regarding attacking football was coupled with another basic word on his agenda – 'intelligence'. In a blunt way he disclosed his philosophy by saying: 'It's not a question of basic skills. Third and Fourth Division players, as well as senior amateurs, are generally as competent as the others in this direction, but there is a vast difference in the speed with which the skills are performed. Players in the lower divisions need time.

'In the First Division the simple thing is done quickly and accurately. The ball is played much earlier, and players get it when and where they expect it to come. ... But leading First Division players are not divided from the rest by good fortune or opportunity. They are where they are because there is more to their talent than the fundamentals. They have got it between the ears and that's what counts.

'You can't teach a player to think more quickly. You can impress upon him the need for it, and encourage it in practice, but you can't give someone something he had to be born with.

'When I was at Millwall as coach, I used to get frustrated by players who would try to elaborate, when all I wanted them to do was to play simple, accurate and intelligent football.'

Fulham also announced that loyal club servant Stan Brown had been awarded a well-deserved testimonial match by the club that would take place sometime during the coming season, with FA Cup holders Chelsea the likely opposition. The exact date would not be known until later in the year because of Chelsea's European commitments. This season would be the third in a row where a long-service testimonial match had been staged at the Cottage, an unlikely event nowadays.

Tommy Trinder said of Stan Brown: 'He has been with us man and boy, yet he remains a tremendous worker. When you think of Stan, you think of team spirit. This is what drove us on to our great run in the second half of last season, and it is team spirit which can take us all the way to the top this time.'

Prior to his departure, Johnny Haynes, commenting on Stan Brown's testimonial, used some honest but very apt words: 'You only notice him when you need him.' Haynes continued his tribute: 'Stan takes over from me as the Fulham player on the books with the most number of first-team appearances. Yet when you think back over the years, it is hard to remember him being involved with anything sensational.

'He lives further away from the ground than anybody else down in Sussex, but he is never late for training or matches. You never see him arrive; when you look for him he's there.

'All you can say about him is that he is a good professional. Come to think about it, what better could you say? On the field he gets on with the job without a lot of fuss.'

New Arrivals

For once, Fulham were not the new arrivals in the league; they were joined by two very famous clubs, **Aston Villa** and **Preston North End**, both of them surprisingly relegated from the Second Division the previous season. Joining them from the other direction were **Chesterfield** (champions), **Port Vale**, Swansea Town, now known as **Swansea City**, and **Wrexham**, all promoted from the Fourth Division. Dodgin saw Villa as Fulham's main rivals for promotion, saying: 'If they get off to a good start, they will quickly get over the depression of last season's relegation.'

Pre-season

The first matches of the Watney Cup, football's first sponsored competition (brewers Watney Mann), took place on the first day of August, quite early for a very competitive match. The Saturday was a boiling hot day, and the spectators were frying in the heat. Fulham used a specially prepared matchday programme, and there was a carnival atmosphere at the Cottage. The match advertising carried the slogan: 'What we want is GOALS', the word 'goals' replacing the normal word in the slogan, which, of course, was 'Watneys'.

Reading had drawn a plum tie with Manchester United, and Fulham were to play First Division **Derby County** – the two highest scoring teams from the First Division taking on the highest scorers from the Third Division clubs. The game was to be ninety minutes, and then thirty minutes extra time if the teams were level, followed, if necessary, by sudden death penalties.

Derby had been in impressive form in the First Division, finishing fourth the previous season, just four points behind the runners-up. Since their last visit to the Cottage eighteen months previously, the Derby team had been strengthened by the signings of Terry Hennessey from Nottingham Forest and John McGovern from Hartlepool United. As in the previous league match, Derby switched to an all-blue kit. Despite the match being staged during 'holiday time', an excellent crowd of 18,500 turned up for the match. Apart from the possibility of penalties, Watneys had shown some vision by allowing *five* substitutes to be named, of which any two could have been chosen. There were also proposals in the future of the competition to limit the offside rule to just within the penalty area.

Despite his previous reservations about the Watney Cup, Dodgin was in confident mood about the match: 'I think we can win the cup. We are at home, and the way that our lads were playing at the end of the season, I can't see Derby beating us. They are a good side, and, like us, like to go forward looking for goals.

'When they won promotion from the Second Division two seasons ago, we lost to them by a single goal [on both occasions], but we did well against them, despite the fact that we were in the process of re-building. For me this is a game to get the lads warmed up for the league battles ahead, and for our bid to win promotion after so narrowly missing out last season.'

The match produced an initial quarter of an hour that few would have believed. It took the First Division side just three minutes to score. From a classy, pinball move of ten passes, Kevin Hector made a strong run down the left and from his accurate, low cross John O'Hare stabbed the ball in from just a couple of feet. Derby had the ball in the net again just two minutes later, but the goal was disallowed. It then took Fulham just four minutes to get level.

Whilst the Derby team were arguing about the disallowed goal, Steve Earle took things into his own hands and dashed off on a magnificent solo run that was beautifully timed and ended the run with a rising drive. Derby goalkeeper Les Green could only fingertip the ball onto a post and watch as the rebound bobbed into the net.

Just five minutes later Fulham were ahead. There was confusion in the static Derby defence following an excellent move involving Earle, Barry Lloyd and Jimmy Conway, and a mix-up allowed Vic Halom to waltz around John Robson and beat the paralysed Green with a low drive. Incredibly, just two minutes later, a vibrant Fulham extended their lead.

A Fred Callaghan pass released Conway, who breezed down the left and his cross was only half-cleared by the Derby defence. With his back to goal, Halom executed a perfect and flamboyant overhead kick with great panache that fizzed past the startled Green. That was three Fulham goals in just *seven* minutes! Conway was in superb teasing form and was giving Derby full back Robson a gruelling time.

Fulham were in the driving seat, but Derby reduced the arrears after just twenty-three minutes. Hector, poorly marked, took a long-range pot shot at the Fulham goal. Malcolm Webster was caught off his line and could only watch as the ball scraped in just inside a post – a very soft goal, given away.

The match was entertaining and well balanced, but it was Webster who atoned for his previous error by making three excellent saves just before half time that preserved Fulham's lead. Firstly, he kept out a murderously swinging drive from Hector, then he had to dive full length to make a

Just three minutes on the clock, and John O'Hare stabs Derby ahead from close in during the Watney Cup encounter, with Stan Brown powerless. Fulham hit back with three goals in seven minutes to lead, but an experienced First Division Derby side finally edged through 3–5 after extra time in the boiling sunshine.

thrilling one-handed save from Roy McFarland and finally he punched out Alan Hinton's shot.

Webster had to continue where he had left off in the second half, with further thrilling saves. He made a point blank block from O'Hare, and then scrambled across his line to stop Hector's header. However, it was not all Derby; Earle and Les Barrett combined well, and only a last-ditch tackle by McFarland prevented Barrett getting in a shot near goal. Derby veteran Dave Mackay was struggling in the heat against Fulham's pace, resorting to shirt pulling to haul back the marauding Fulham forwards.

The action would just not let up, and Webster made two further saves from O'Hare. One shot was pushed for a corner and the other was blocked by a dive at the forward's feet. After a tangle with

Most are watching the Watney Cup action, but some of the crowd seem distracted and one photographer has spotted a good picture away from the field of play.

In full flight in the first half of the Watney Cup match against Derby County, Barry Lloyd fires in another shot in an attempt to extend Fulham's lead.

McFarland, Halom earned a rocket from the official Bob Matthewson. Halom, in one of his 'court jester' days, responded by hiding the match ball up the back of his shirt, much to the bemusement of the referee and the amusement of both sets of players and supporters.

With just over twenty minutes remaining, Brian Clough, concerned at his team's position, left his seat to go to the dugout and replaced Hinton with John McGovern; the move had an immediate effect. McGovern was involved in the move with Hector that opened up the Fulham defence and Alan Durban, sprinting through, fired in a low shot that gave Webster no chance.

Kevin Hector could have won the game for Derby in the final ten minutes, when he thumped a fierce drive against the post. The searing heat was beginning to tell on both teams now and the pace finally slowed down. The day was so hot that when the Derby trainer Jimmy Gordon came on to attend to a player, he was stripped to the waist. Neither side could make another opening, and the ninety minutes finished 3–3, with extra time required.

The Fulham fans booed Clough in a light-hearted way when he came on to the pitch at the end of ninety minutes to talk tactics to his team. He took the booing in good spirit, bowing several times to the crowd.

First Division class and experience told – in the end. The concentration of Fulham's brave and buoyant youngsters finally wilted in the sweltering conditions. Fulham made two substitutions with Mike Pentecost and Wilf Tranter replacing Stan Brown and Dave Moreline, both Fulham substitutes wearing the number twelve shirt! Hector finally shot Derby ahead in the 103rd minute, and then right at the start of the second period of extra time Durban scored again in the 106th minute. By this point, the lack of sophistication in the Fulham defence had rendered them inevitable victims.

The remaining half of extra time produced little else, with two sets of tired players settling for a **3–5** scoreline. Whatever the result, Fulham had done Bill Dodgin proud.

It had been a superb match, recognised by all as great entertainment. The purists would argue that a number of the goals had been down to defensive lapses and poor marking, but it had been a real spectacle. Goalkeeper Webster was made the Man-of-the-Match with several outstanding saves – something also recognised by the press. Derby's Terry Hennessey, not playing for the Derby team due to injury, regularly rose from the dugout to applaud Webster's saves. The media had enjoyed the format, handing out a loud 'Cheers' to Watneys for dreaming up the competition!

The cover for the programme accompanying the Watneys Cup match against Derby was provided by the sponsors. It was of a larger format than the regular Fulham programme and was printed in colour.

Fulham's class had definitely shown through, and the press were sure of their headline the next day: 'Fulham in title form.'

Reading unluckily lost 2–3 to Manchester United, but the other two ties were not nearly as close. Second Division Hull City were triumphant at Fourth Division Peterborough United 4–0, with Second Division Sheffield United in rampant form winning 6–0 at Fourth Division Aldershot.

Manchester United beat Hull City in the semi-final of the Cup. After a 1–1 draw at full time and again at extra time, the first ever use was made of the new 'settling' rule and United finally won through 4–3 on penalty kicks. In the other semi-final, Derby County beat Sheffield United 1–0.

In the end, Derby won the inaugural competition beating Manchester United 4–1 in the final. The competition was to run for three further seasons (up until 1973), but Fulham did not feature in it again.

It is interesting to note that the use of penalty kicks to decide drawn matches was used for the first time *ever* in this competition, and because of its success the method was later adopted by the European Fairs Cup committee and FIFA, to replace the outmoded method of tossing a coin to decide the winners of European matches when scores were level.

After the main pre-season match in the Watney Cup, the first team played the following friendlies, all away from home. At **St Albans**, without the injured Steve Earle, Fulham won **3–2** after leading 2–1 at half time. Barry Lloyd, Les Barrett and Vic Halom scored the goals; Fulham experimented and used four substitutes in the match. At **Peterborough United** Fulham lost **2–3** after being 1–2 down at half time. Vic Halom and Jimmy Dunne scored the goals. Finally, in the serious warm-up match at **Portsmouth,** a week before the start of the season, Fulham won **3–1** after being 1–0 up at half time. Vic Halom, Steve Earle and Les Barrett scored the goals. Including the Watney Cup, Vic Halom had made a fine start scoring in every match, five from four outings.

The reserves, with an average age of around nineteen, had the following results from pre-season friendlies, again all away from home. At **Carshalton Athletic**, Fulham lost **1–2** after being 1–1 at half time, the goal scored by junior Ray Phillips. This team contained six juniors and two amateurs. At **Hounslow Town**, Fulham drew **3–3** after leading 3–1 at half time; the goalscorers were Naan, Edmundson and Morton. This team contained seven junior players. At **Woking**, Fulham lost **2–3** after being 1–2 down at half time, goalscorers Morton and Naan.

These Fulham teams were fledgling sides in line with Dodgin's youth policy. Goalkeeper Ian Seymour and centre half Dave Roberts, who made one appearance each, were the only players with any league experience whatsoever to take part in these friendlies, with Fulham sometimes fielding up to five players who were on amateur terms.

The club photograph at the beginning of the season. Back row: Bill Dodgin (manager), Dave Robertson, Stan Horne, Jimmy Dunne, John Richardson, Ian Seymour, Malcolm Webster, Dave Moreline, Dave Roberts, Fred Callaghan, Wilf Tranter, George Cohen (youth trainer), Terry Medwin (coach); middle row: Reg Matthewson, Mike Pentecost, Jimmy Conway, Barry Lloyd, Steve Earle, Vic Halom, Les Barrett, Stan Brown; front: John Brickell, John Graham, McAndrew Johnson, Tommy James, John Fraser.

FULHAM
FOOTBALL CLUB

SEASON 1970-71

FOOTBALL LEAGUE CUP, FIRST ROUND

WEDNESDAY, AUGUST 19th, 1970

ORIENT

OFFICIAL PROGRAMME 1/- 5p

The first 'Fulham-produced' programme of the season was for a Football League cup tie.

August 1970

In this month

* Part of the Windscale nuclear power station was sealed off because of a radioactive leak.
* The second Isle of Wight pop festival was held.
* A new four-wheel drive Rover was announced with a V8 engine – it cost £2,000.
* Bobby Moore was found not guilty of stealing a bracelet in Bogotá.

'Tears of a Clown' by Smokey Robinson and the Miracles topped the charts.
The film 'Kelly's Heroes' was released.

The matches

FULHAM OPENED the season with a summery trip to Yorkshire. Competing against Yorkshire teams had been good news for Fulham during the previous season, the Cottagers able to record a ten-game unbeaten run against all the Yorkshire sides from the division. On the strength of pre-season displays, Dodgin decided to give the number two shirt to Dave Moreline. Jimmy Dunne came in for his league debut at number six. **Barnsley** would be tough opponents, as they had lost only three home games the previous season.

There was little goalmouth action to report in the first half, but Fulham were really fizzing and threatening to walk all over the home side. Fulham's nippy wingers Jimmy Conway and Les Barrett were beating the full backs for speed, and the home defence looked distinctly ill at ease.

Fulham carved out chances that were either missed or halted by the excellent Barnsley keeper, Brian Arblaster. Barry Lloyd had a shot saved, but the frustrations were mainly reserved for burly Vic Halom. He had a shot well saved by the keeper, then shot wide from just ten yards when an awkward bounce left him with just the goalkeeper to beat; finally he hit the post when it looked easier to score.

Arblaster was soon in action again in the second half, saving twice from the luckless Halom. Skipper Lloyd was the star of the Fulham midfield show, adding plenty of art and craft in a game where these commodities up to now had been in short supply. At this stage, both teams seemed to be settling for a goalless draw in the scorching sunshine.

Fulham's unexpected winner came in the sixty-fourth minute when Barnsley failed to clear a disputed free kick. The ball found its way to Stan Brown who guided in his cross perfectly, bisecting the Barnsley defence. The cross was met by Barrett, who glided in, stooped low and directed his header just inside a post into the corner of the net.

On the whole, Fulham's defence coped well with the weakened Barnsley attack. The previous season's hat trick hero for Barnsley, Johnny Evans, had not played due to injury and further injuries had ruled out two other Barnsley forwards. Fulham's only real scare came near the end, when giant defender Eric Winstanley went up with the attack and crashed a diving header against the Fulham crossbar five minutes from time. Fulham were off to a winning start with a **1–0** score.

On the day Fulham had been slightly lucky to take both points against a weakened Barnsley side and the match had certainly been no classic. Both sides had struggled in the energy-sapping heat and on the whole it had been a very sluggish encounter. Fulham had been the steadier side, but had also missed a number of chances; however, the Barnsley keeper had been on excellent form to keep the scoreline down to just one.

Bill Dodgin knew that Fulham would require a lot more 'pep' than this when the season was truly underway. The opening game had resulted in a win, however, and a clean sheet, so there were few complaints from within the Cottage.

The match had an unfortunate postscript when Fulham supporters were caught up in rare clashes on the M1 with the supporters of Derby County returning from a 2–1 defeat at Chelsea. The club did not try to apportion blame, but distanced itself from the troubles intimating that the coach involved was from 'The Thamesiders', who the club claimed were not an 'official' body.

The day after the match the Fulham youth squad, who had been successful in their bid to take part in the San Remo tournament, left for Italy. Fulham would play Atalanta of Bergamo and then Roma. The winners of three similar groups of three teams would then go forward to a semi-final on a knockout basis. The club knew that the standard would be higher than in the previous tour of Germany, but were confident that they could spring a surprise or two.

By a most unlikely combination of probabilities, Fulham had been drawn for the third consecutive season to play **Orient** in the first round of the League Cup. This was the first time that Fulham had actually been drawn at home. In the first encounter Orient had been in the Third Division whilst Fulham had been in the Second; the previous season both teams had been in the Third Division and this season Orient were in the Second Division whilst Fulham were in the Third.

The Orient team was virtually identical to the one that had come to the Cottage in January, and there were no new faces in the team. The match was refereed by one of the best, Derek Nippard from Bournemouth.

Fulham were on good form and out to prove a point. They had one early scare when Malcolm Webster had to be alert to smother a firm shot from Orient winger Peter Brabrook; other than that, there was little action in the first half. Orient, this time, were showing Fulham plenty of respect and were reliant on their defence to keep the score goalless. Brabrook's runs down the left wing were all Orient really had to offer as an attacking force.

In the second half, however, Fulham took charge, and the match belonged to ex-Fulham keeper Ray Goddard. He alone was standing between Fulham and a cricket score. He made one spectacular save just after half time when he hurled himself across the goal to fingertip a Barry Lloyd volley around the post, and then arched back to turn a neatly placed lob by Jimmy Dunne over the bar. These saves were complemented with two sizzling point-blank stops from Jimmy Conway piledrivers. Lloyd was again playing a captain's role, showing plenty of class, and putting in an immense amount of hard work.

Just when both sets of fans were making plans for the replay, Fulham struck. Steve Earle took a pass from Dave Moreline and put through a long defence-splitting ball that Orient centre half Terry Mancini misjudged. The slip enabled Conway to dispossess him, coolly go round him and finally beat the brave Goddard with a low, angled drive into the corner of the net; there were just eight minutes left.

Orient then sent on their substitute Barrie Fairbrother for Dave Harper in a frantic attempt at an equaliser, but it was too late; Fulham knocked their rivals out of the Cup for the second year running, victorious at **1−0**.

Although the scoreline had been close, Fulham had merited their victory all the way, and the victory over higher league opposition had given the team a huge confidence boost. Fulham had forced eleven corners compared to Orient's three. The game had been once again a furiously fought local derby, extremely exciting, full of attacking play and a credit to football.

Les Barrett and Conway had both looked dangerous on the night. The defence, with little to do, looked watertight with Fred Callaghan, Stan Brown and newcomer Jimmy Dunne, on his home debut, outstanding. Most of the limelight was reserved for skipper Barry Lloyd, maturing with every game. Dodgin said after the game: 'People are very cautious of our forward line, and [league] clubs will be coming here to play defensively looking for a single point.'

Four days later, Fulham played their first home league match of the new season as hosts to newly promoted **Swansea City**, who were managed by former Fulham favourite Roy Bentley. Swansea had few stars, but the side included former WBA and Crystal Palace goalkeeper Tony Millington, former Preston striker Gerry Ingram and their most expensive ever signing, Welshman Barrie Hole, signed after a fairly indifferent spell at Aston Villa. The Swansea side also included, as substitute, the renowned Welsh international Len Allchurch, now thirty-seven, as well as the young goalkeeper David Davies, later to play for Everton in the First Division.

The Welsh team's squad also included some names to ponder over as well, with Willie Screen and Terry Cotton further candidates for the 'Carry On' teams! Due to the colour clash, Swansea switched to all red, while Fulham were unchanged. The Swansea team was heavily weighted with

A model of concentration, Jimmy Dunne calmly clears a Swansea attack. Dunne, making his home debut following his £15,000 transfer from Torquay, found enough time away from his defensive duties to score Fulham's third goal.

defenders, with midfielders Len Hill and Willie Screen named as winger and inside forward respectively.

Fulham were well aware that the Orient team had played defensively against them the previous Wednesday, and that Barnsley had failed to take the initiative against them even when at home the week before; it was a stance that the Cottagers would have to get used to.

Fulham set about the Swans straight away and were rewarded with a goal in the fourth minute. Goalkeeper Tony Millington could only touch a Fred Callaghan free kick straight to the feet of Steve Earle and he promptly despatched the ball back into the net. Jimmy Conway was again on rampaging form, and in the thirty-fourth minute he produced a fine right-wing run that ended with a perfect cross on a plate that allowed Earle to convert effortlessly, giving him his second goal of the afternoon. Earle waited until the goalkeeper committed himself and then calmly chipped the ball over the prostrate custodian into the side of the net. Earle was a major thorn in the side of Swansea, cleverly setting up attacks from the middle and then switching to either wing.

Fulham, however, then eased up a little and received a wake-up call just two minutes later

From Jimmy Conway's cross, Steve Earle waits for the advancing goalkeeper and clips home his second goal of the half. A classy Fulham performance easily disposed of promoted Swansea by a 4–1 score.

when lax defending allowed Swansea teenager Terry Cotton to clip home Barry Evans' low centre after Screen had set up Evans. Swansea began to come back into the game, with Barrie Hole showing numerous erudite touches, and up to half time Swansea briefly suggested a comeback. Swansea were, however, playing with a lone striker in beanpole Cotton, which was not nearly enough to consistently unsettle the Fulham defence.

Swansea's mini-revival was snuffed out immediately after the restart. In the forty-ninth minute, Swansea full back Vic Gomersall mis-kicked and was able to only partially clear a Conway free kick. The ball fell nicely at the feet of the on-rushing Jimmy Dunne, who snapped in the gift chance for a goal on his home league debut. Then, just three minutes later, Fulham scored their fourth when, from Les Barrett's centre, Vic Halom bravely dived in low and headed home acrobatically amongst flying boots.

Fulham then relaxed a little knowing that the game was won. Swansea sent on veteran Allchurch, but the change made little difference, with Swansea settling for damage limitation. Even at a slower pace Fulham were unlucky not to have scored further goals. Swansea full back David Lawrence kicked a goalbound header from Halom off the line, and a cunning lob again from defender Dunne was just scrambled over the bar at the last minute by the back-pedalling Millington. Fulham finally settled for a **4–1** scoreline.

The match had produced another good team performance and everyone had played well. Swansea's attack had never truly been in it due to the splendid Reg Matthewson and the biting Dunne. The Fulham forwards had all sparkled, but in truth the win had been achieved against an untidy and disorganised Swansea defence that had been carved open all too easily. Although Dodgin was happy with the four goals, he must have also been concerned at the chances tossed away.

The hard-working Earle could, on a luckier day, have gone home with five goals. Fulham could, and should, have doubled their score. Still, three consecutive wins was the ideal start to the season.

Dodgin said after the match: 'I was quite happy with the final scoreline, if we score four goals every week, we won't go far wrong. What did concern me was the way we allowed Swansea to come back into the game a little in the first half. We gave them several opportunities to score through some slack play. ... Steve Earle ran hard and worked hard and deserved his two goals, but we have come now to expect that kind of game from him.'

Fulham next tried to consolidate this start with a trip to Fellows Park and **Walsall**. Fulham had completed an easy double over Walsall the previous season, and so should have been confident. The Cottagers were again unchanged. The new away kit was used for the first time.

Fulham were shocked to go behind to a goal in just the second minute when former Aston Villa forward John Woodward gave Walsall the lead. Walsall started at a furious pace and there appeared to be some early hesitancy in the Fulham defence. No Fulham player challenged as Walsall winger Willie Penman cut in, and he was able to put in an easy cross where Woodward volleyed the ball first time into the net.

Fulham responded in excellent fashion and were soon ahead with two goals in the space of six minutes. Barry Lloyd drove in the equaliser after twelve minutes; Steve Earle's excellent header was only parried by goalkeeper Bob Wesson, and the rebound fell to Lloyd, who cracked the ball in first time.

Vic Halom then put Fulham ahead with a really good goal after just eighteen minutes. Les Barrett made a great run and cross, and Halom almost whipped the ball out of the goalkeeper's hands to convert Barrett's centre from close range into an almost empty net.

It looked like Fulham were back on course, but Walsall were given a lifeline in the thirty-second minute when they were awarded a penalty when Reg Matthewson brought down veteran winger and former Crystal Palace player Colin Taylor in the area after he cut in from the left wing. There were few complaints from the Fulham players, and Taylor rose to convert the penalty himself.

In the second half, Fulham appeared to be in control and Halom wasted a golden opportunity to put Fulham ahead again when, well placed, he shot wide, apparently put off when the goalkeeper left his line to narrow the angle. The pace in the sun was relentless, and both Taylor and Woodward were still troubling the Fulham rearguard.

In away kit, Jimmy Conway outstrips two Walsall defenders to supply another accurate cross. Despite Fulham taking the lead, the Saddlers inflicted Fulham's first defeat of the season, the Cottagers losing 2–3. Note the position of the child on the touchline wall – a sight that would give palpitations to today's stewards!

Fulham were made to pay for Halom's miss when Taylor scored again with a fine shot midway through the half, leaving Fulham looking deflated. The Saddlers were awarded a free kick in a central position and Walsall's Alan Baker rolled the ball thoughtfully into the path of Taylor. Taylor then let rip with one of his infamous rocket shots from fully thirty-five yards, and the ball swerved late into the top corner of the net leaving Malcolm Webster looking on flabbergasted.

With their tails up, Walsall continued to attack, and the slow Fulham defence could have conceded further goals, centre half Stan Jones blasting just over the bar. Taylor was unlucky not to complete a fine hat trick when he blasted in another thundering drive, this time from nearly forty yards, which Webster saved with difficulty at the second attempt. His shot actually crept under Webster's body, but the goalkeeper was just able to frantically grab the ball before it crossed the line.

Sensing that time was against them, Fulham pushed up Stan Brown, and both he and Lloyd were creating chances. Walsall sent on defender Alan Deakin to counteract this and the change was enough to ensure that Walsall ran out **2–3** winners.

It had been a dismal day; Fulham had lost their 100% record, and conceded three goals in the process after having conceded just one in the previous three games. It was back to earth with a bump; the only positive point to come out of the match was that after just four matches this season, all five forwards had already opened their scoring accounts.

The defence had not played well and Webster had experienced probably his worst game in a Fulham shirt to date. Both Dave Moreline and Matthewson had looked off the pace. However, the forwards were all still playing well and creating chances aplenty.

Fulham's bad luck that weekend continued when John Richardson, who had recovered from his thigh injury, resumed training. In a training match, a teammate accidentally trod on his foot. The studs pierced his boot, and Richardson was now out again with a nasty foot injury!

The San Remo experience

Following their successful tour of Germany, the Fulham youth squad had high hopes of further glory when they took part in the famous San Remo youth tournament in north Italy. However, this turned out to be a controversial and unsatisfactory trip. George Cohen summed up the whole tournament: 'When you have played in a World Cup final, you think you know a little bit about the problems of interpreting the laws here and abroad. Yet some of the decisions in San Remo were outside my experience.'

Fulham left England a rather depleted squad, minus goalkeeper McAndrew Johnson, still unfit following knee trouble, and Roger Bensley, tied up with work commitments. David Robertson and Barry Silkman were also unavailable as they were required for the reserve team squad. The squad, some flying for the first time, were involved in a turbulent flight on an Air France Caravelle that finally lurched its way into Nice. Even a seasoned flyer like Cohen found the flight 'uncomfortable'.

The shocks started soon after the start of the opening fixture with **Atalanta** of Bergamo, when the Fulham players were penalised *for calling for the ball*! An enraged Cohen said: 'Apparently someone had decided that if we wanted to signal we would have to clap our hands! Imagine that, after we had been drilling into their heads for years the importance of calling clearly.

'Calling has become almost second nature to them, how could they possibly forget something as basic as that? We wouldn't really want them to try. It would be like going from Cinerama back to the silent movie days!'

Even once this obstacle had been overcome, the Fulham team were pulled up time and time again – for tackling. An exasperated Cohen explained: 'We guessed tackling from behind would be frowned on, but they objected to every type of tackle we made. Against Atalanta we had three players cautioned and one sent off. Poor John Cooper, he had done nothing wrong.

'There was a bit of a scramble and one of their players went down. Cooper went to step over him, just as the Italian lad got up, and naturally they collided. The Atalanta boy pleaded with the referee [to allow Cooper to stay on], and the commission afterwards said that it was a pure accident, but John Cooper was still suspended for the following game! We still played quite well but with that sort of handicap, things were always likely to go against us.'

Fulham lost this opening match **0–1**. The Fulham team for the Atalanta match was: Richard Teale, John Fraser, Jimmy Marum, Derek Wells, Jimmy Dunn, Tommy James, Leslie Strong, John Cooper, Alan Fox, Ray Phillips and Barry Friend.

In the second match, Atalanta drew their match with Roma, so Fulham could not qualify as group winners irrespective of the result of their match with Roma. By this time, however, half the Fulham squad had stomach trouble; even Cohen was laid low in bed for a day.

A depleted Fulham side took the field for the match with **AC Roma**, and there were problems from the start. The team were spat on by some spectators and coins and cushions were hurled at them. Cohen said: 'None of this prevented us wanting to go out on a winning note, but when we scored early on, it was disallowed for a very doubtful offside. And to put the tin hat on it we had another player sent off – Alan Fox.

'Two of their players sandwiched him. One tripped over, and Fox bundled into the other one. We couldn't believe it when he was told he had to go. We had spotted a weakness in the Roma set up. They were playing with a sweeper, but when we put [Barry] Friend on him, he ruined all their plans. Yet when one of their lads lost his temper and hacked [Ray] Phillips down from behind, the incident was completely ignored. How much of all this was prejudice and how much ignorance I couldn't be sure. In one of the other games, we saw the referee order a direct free kick in the penalty area – and that should not happen in any circumstances.'

The Fulham team for the AC Roma match was: Richard Teale, Jimmy Dunn, Jimmy Marum, John Lacy, Derek Wells, John Fraser, Tommy James, Alan Fox, Ray Phillips, Barry Friend, and Leslie Strong.

Cohen also thought that the refereeing had been extremely suspect, and claimed: 'The standard of refereeing in the early stages of the Düsseldorf tournament was not too hot, but at least when we complained they listened and tried to do something about it. In San Remo, they just shrugged and said: 'Non capisco – no understand'.'

A diplomatic Cohen closed his summary of this difficult time, saying: 'We will be defending our title in Germany and we will look forward to it. But as for San Remo, all I will add is – thanks for the experience.'

September 1970

In this month

* King Hussein of Jordan survived an assassination attempt.
* Racing driver Jochen Rindt was killed in a qualifying race before the Italian Grand Prix.
* Four airliners bound for New York were hijacked, and one was blown up.
* Leila Khaled, a terrorist with the Popular Front for the Liberation of Palestine, was arrested as one of the hijackers.
* A BOAC VC10 was forced to land in Jordan, and was also blown up.
* Egyptian statesman Nasser died of a heart attack.
* Pop and rock legend Jimi Hendrix died in London from a suspected drugs overdose.
* The first Glastonbury festival took place.

'Tears of a Clown' by Smokey Robinson and the Miracles *still* topped the charts.
The film 'The Music Lovers' was released.

The matches

STUNG BY the Walsall defeat, Fulham had an early opportunity to put things right against **Bradford City** on the following Wednesday night. The two encounters with Bradford the previous season had failed to produce a goal, so Fulham would be trying extra hard to put that right.

Sadly, the City side were now the sole representatives of the great Yorkshire wool city in the Football League. Their sister club Bradford Park Avenue had dropped out of the league during the close season. Fulham had played Park Avenue as recently as 1967 in a difficult FA Cup tie. It was going to be a tough match, as Bradford were already second in the table and unbeaten.

It was also going to be a nostalgic night for George Cohen as the Bradford City squad included Ramon (Ray) Wilson as defender/coach. Wilson was, of course, Cohen's full back partner in the 1966 World Cup winning side.

City, in attractive claret and amber striped shirts, fielded virtually the same side as the previous season, the only significant addition being Colin Hall, signed in the close season from Nottingham Forest. City were, however, without centre half Tom Hallett, one of their key players. Despite the defeat at the weekend, Fulham were unchanged.

On this particular night, with the evening dew glistening on the pitch under the misty floodlights, Fulham put on a performance that the few who witnessed it would forget. In the warm evening air, Fulham were absolutely irresistible and destroyed Bradford City with a display full of enterprising and attacking football to which City had no answer.

Fulham opened the scoring on just five minutes when Jimmy Conway put them ahead. Steve Earle put in a fine, teasing cross that goalkeeper John Roberts fumbled and could only palm out, leaving Conway with a simple open goal opportunity. Roberts atoned for the error by stopping two certainties immediately after the opening goal, but was helpless when Earle added the second ten minutes before half time. This time Conway returned the compliment with a cross that two Bradford defenders failed to clear, leaving Earle free to ram the ball home.

There was no respite for City after the break either, when Vic Halom, whose strength and determination had played a significant part in the first two goals, hooked in the third on fifty-two minutes. Again the goal followed a mistake from goalkeeper Roberts, who mishandled a fiery cross from Les Barrett, leaving Halom free to score from the six-yard line, slamming the ball joyfully into the roof of the net.

The home crowd had to wait just a further eight minutes for another goal, when captain Barry Lloyd sidefooted the fourth with a perfectly placed swerving shot from the edge of the area that entered the net via the underside of the crossbar.

City did not know where to turn or who was going to strike next, as the Cottagers skilfully zipped into the gaps in the Bradford defence, stretching them to breaking point. Keeper Roberts

Les Barrett finishes off a superb forty yard solo run with a shot under the diving Bradford City goalkeeper. It was the fifth goal in a nap 5–0 victory over previously unbeaten City. The match was most noteworthy inasmuch as all five forwards found the net.

had to be on his toes all of the time, and it was only his lightning reactions that were keeping the score down to just four.

Bradford were not a bad side themselves and continued to probe diligently whenever they had the ball, which was not often. Bobby Ham was always a danger and on one occasion combined well with Les O'Neill, but O'Neill placed his final effort against the Fulham post.

The game was now won and Fulham used the final half hour to put on a display of exhibition soccer that had the crowd gasping. Winger Barrett was now the only forward without a goal, and the last half hour was spent trying to set him up with one! He went close on two occasions, set up by his teammates, but finally, two minutes from time, Barrett decided to do the job himself.

He picked up the ball just inside his own half and set off on a run that covered forty-five yards through the middle, beating three Bradford defenders and leaving them all trailing in his wake. He ended the run by slamming the ball past the helpless Bradford keeper Roberts with a low shot from just inside the penalty area.

Fulham had won **5–0** at a canter and totally destroyed City's unbeaten start; this was a champion's performance if there ever was one. It proved to be a rare event inasmuch as all five Fulham forwards, numbered seven to eleven, found the net. The only other time this had happened in recent memory was against Grimsby in 1958, in a 6–0 win. City were shell-shocked as they had only conceded one goal in their previous three games. The result made it twelve league goals for Fulham in the opening four games. It certainly seemed as if the club were already chasing another Watney Cup place!

Captain Barry Lloyd had delivered a fine all-round performance combining graft in defence with clever and quick switching of the ball into attacking moves, justifying Bill Dodgin's faith in the young player. Dodgin said: 'Barry represents what I feel about the game, it is hard to put into words. He has football intelligence, and the emphasis of his game is on skill. He is not the most demonstrative of leaders, but he has a quiet authority; the others respect him. I had no doubt that he was the right choice to represent me on the field.'

The key to the early successes so far this season were early goals that had forced away sides to adopt a less rigid defensive policy and come out. The club added a note of caution, saying that it was unlikely to run that way all through the season, and the quality that the team and the supporters would ultimately require was – patience. The press joined in the next-day euphoria, one headline reading: 'The top nap – Fulham to snatch title.'

Fulham also announced another loan signing at this time. Roger Davidson was twenty-one, and had been a junior player with Arsenal appearing regularly in their reserve side. After being freed by Arsenal, where he had made just one substitute appearance in the first team, he had joined

Portsmouth but had little opportunity to shine there because the Fratton side had no reserve team. Davidson had played three league games for Portsmouth before joining Fulham.

Four days later, Fulham had a further opportunity to build on the Bradford win with another home fixture, this time against newly promoted and champions **Chesterfield**. Chesterfield had also started well and were lying third in the table. In the Chesterfield side were prolific scorers Kevin Randall and Ernie Moss, while in the half back line was former Sheffield United midfield player Tommy Fenoughty, who had scored against Fulham in Fulham's 3–2 win at Bramall Lane in 1968.

Chesterfield had a reputation for producing fine goalkeepers – Gordon Banks of Leicester and Stoke, and John Osborne of West Bromwich Albion to name just two. Arsenal's Bob Wilson had also been born in Chesterfield. On this day, Chesterfield had in goal Alan Stevenson, who ultimately had a long career, starring in the Burnley first team for many years. Playing at centre half was 6' 4" Charlie Bell. Fulham were again unchanged. The crowd was an improved 13,000.

It would have been unreasonable to expect another performance like the Bradford one immediately, and the Chesterfield defence was far tighter than Bradford's. As expected, the away side packed their defence and attempted a stubborn resistance with physical endeavour and very tight marking. Three players marked danger man Jimmy Conway at times.

Fulham were on the attack for most of the half, but there was no early goal this time. Chesterfield were dealt a blow in the twenty-fifth minute when full back Albert Holmes, already playing with a broken hand, suffered a twisted knee when trying to tackle Les Barrett and was substituted by Roy Hickton, brother of Middlesbrough's John, who was fortunately also a full back.

Fulham were finding the going tough, Steve Earle and Vic Halom were being well held by Charlie Bell and Albert Phelan, and Conway was well shackled by John Lumsden, who had played in the Workington team that had lost 6–2 at Fulham in 1967. The football was too neat and too tight, and was spoilt by a persistent wind that caused passes to go astray. Fulham were, however, missing chances, Barry Lloyd hitting the post with one shot.

Fulham finally took the lead just two minutes before half time. A splendid Conway cross was headed out by Bell, who was being challenged by Halom. The miscued clearance fell kindly to Earle, who was on hand to hook in his fourth goal of the season, a first time, left-foot shot over the advancing Alan Stevenson into the top of the net from the edge of the penalty area. Inspirational captain Barry Lloyd was injured in a tackle just before half time, but was able to carry on.

Fulham started the second half slowly and Malcolm Webster had to be alert to palm away a dangerous cross from winger David Pugh that looked goalbound. Fulham almost increased their lead when Lloyd had a shot charged down; the rebound bounced up to Halom, but he was just

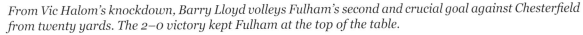

From Vic Halom's knockdown, Barry Lloyd volleys Fulham's second and crucial goal against Chesterfield from twenty yards. The 2–0 victory kept Fulham at the top of the table.

wide with his headed effort. Dodgin had ordered the Fulham players at half time to spray the ball about more, make Chesterfield do all the running, then go for the kill.

The Fulham pressure was unrelenting and Chesterfield started to creak. Lloyd's form was outstanding, and with Stan Brown tackling firmly the ball was rarely outside the Chesterfield half. The home side scored the clinching goal twenty minutes from the end. Conway again provided the perfect cross, the bustling Halom headed the ball down and skipper Lloyd controlled it with his chest before blasting home an angled twenty-yard shot across goalkeeper Stevenson and into the net.

Chesterfield, now forced to attack, came at Fulham and Tommy Fenoughty and Kevin Randall started to probe at the Fulham defence. Unfortunately for the Spirites, Reg Matthewson was again on great form, and anything not coped with by the centre half was swept up easily by the eager Jimmy Dunne. Fenoughty managed one long shot that Webster juggled with uncomfortably at the foot of a post, but that was it.

The Fulham team relaxed, and several further scoring opportunities were missed, but in the end the home side were happy with another victory, their 100% home record intact, and a **2–0** scoreline secured.

A worm's eye view at the end of the Chesterfield victory.

Barry Lloyd had typified the Fulham performance. He had again delivered a captain's performance, and his non-stop running and tenacious tackling had been a permanent feature of the game. His goal was his third in consecutive matches.

After the match he said: 'We were struggling against Chesterfield until Steve Earle volleyed a great goal. Then I tried for another, and someone raked his studs down my back. When I finally got up, the field was empty, and it took me a second or two before I realised it was half time! We were so on top in the second half we could have all scored, but I'm glad mine went in!' '

During the week, Fulham took on Chelsea in the first round of the London Challenge Cup at Craven Cottage. The side was, on the whole, an inexperienced one, but did contain Ian Seymour, Mike Pentecost, Dave Roberts and Stan Horne. Due to injuries, Fulham had both David Robertson and John Cooper, natural defenders, leading the attack. Fulham were a goal down at half time, but responded with an equaliser from defender Robertson. Three minutes from the end, however, Fulham should have wrapped up the game. They were awarded a penalty, and although Stan Horne's curling penalty kick beat the Chelsea keeper, the ball hit the post and was finally cleared, the match finishing as a 1–1 draw. The replay was not until three weeks later, when, despite two goals from Alan Morton, Fulham lost 2–3.

On the same night as the first London Challenge Cup match, Fulham's first team travelled 250 miles to play Fourth Division **Darlington** in the second round of the League Cup; this was Fulham's 'prize' for their enterprising victory over Orient. Fulham named an unchanged side. It would be a difficult tie, as Darlington were no pushovers and currently unbeaten.

Although the match was against Fourth Division opposition, the game produced another First Division performance from Fulham. The Cottagers looked likely to score right from the kick-off, but it took a penalty to get them on the road after twenty-six minutes. Vic Halom's drive, following Jimmy Conway's corner, was heading for the top of the net when the ball was fisted away by full back Billy Horner. Conway gave Fulham the lead from the resulting penalty kick without fuss.

Conway was the architect of the second goal five minutes before half time, releasing Steve Earle with a lovely pass. Earle's accurate cross was hammered in firmly by Les Barrett who had time to pick his spot before unleashing a low drive into the corner.

Just five minutes into the second half, it was three. The energetic Halom was the provider, sliding over a cross from the left for Barrett to run in and score again from a half-chance with a shot that glanced in off a post.

Darlington did come back at Fulham with the wind behind them in the second half, but the nearest the home side came was when Malcolm Webster had to be quick to turn over a clever inswinging corner from former Sunderland winger Alan Gauden.

Stan Brown had taken a knock, and was substituted midway through the half as a precaution, with Roger Davidson coming on for his Fulham debut. Halom looked fated not to score, but five minutes from time he grabbed his reward with Fulham's fourth. It was a delightful finish following a slick move, and it left Fulham running out easy **4–0** winners.

The only negative point of the evening was further trouble on the sparse terraces, where police moved in to eject a couple of dozen supporters after violence had flared.

The galloping style of the team had meant that the goal glut had now reached nineteen for the season already, and the Fulham fans were in dreamland. The result was important inasmuch as the win rewarded Fulham with a third round home tie against Second Division Queens Park Rangers, and a return to the Cottage for Rodney Marsh.

The Fulham performance must have been something special, as George Hardwick, the famous former England and Middlesbrough full back, had watched the tie and said: 'Over the years I have thrilled at the skill and flair of teams like Leeds, Everton, Liverpool and the two Manchester clubs, as well as the Londoners West Ham, Spurs and Chelsea. Yet it took my good friend Tommy Trinder to provide me with the thrill of them all.'

Fulham were posted away from home on the Saturday as well, travelling north to Lancashire to meet **Rochdale** at Spotland. Rochdale had not begun well, with just one win in their opening six league games, but must have been uplifted by the creditable draw they had gained midweek against First Division Crystal Palace at Selhurst Park in the League Cup. Stan Brown had recovered from his knock, and Fulham were once again unchanged.

Fulham got off to their usual ideal start, with an early goal after just nine minutes. A firm shot from Steve Earle was only partially stopped by the Rochdale defence and ex-Southampton keeper Tony Godfrey, and Les Barrett, forcing his way through and sliding in, was on hand to slam the deflected loose ball into the net.

From that point, however, Rochdale put up a tremendous fight and it was Fulham's turn to survive a sustained onslaught. The match was all-action football and Rochdale realised the reward they so richly deserved when Peter Gowans equalised in the seventeenth minute with a brilliant twenty-yard shot following a corner.

Despite the home side's pressure, the Fulham defence was again looking firm and resolute with Webster having little real work to do. However, on the balance of play Fulham were very fortunate to go in level at half time, despite having three speculative shots stopped, with difficulty, by the home keeper.

In the second half Rochdale started aggressively, but with virtually their *only* real attack of the half Fulham scored again with twenty minutes remaining. Again, it was a good move ending with a firm cross-field pass by Earle from the left that allowed Jimmy Conway, running in, time and

Steve Earle's early shot is only partially stopped by the Rochdale goalkeeper (not in picture). The ball squirms to the waiting Les Barrett (far left) to slide Fulham ahead.

space to shoot into the roof of the net from a difficult angle from the edge of the six-yard box; for once, the Rochdale defence was caught on the wrong foot.

Rochdale at last began to abandon their defensive formation and went looking for an equaliser. Norman Whitehead moved into midfield and was starting to cause havoc in the Fulham defence, unlucky not to score. Twice in the last twenty minutes Rochdale hit the post, but the ball just wouldn't go in; in another attack Jimmy Dunne headed one Rochdale effort onto his own crossbar. Rochdale's luck on the day was truly atrocious.

From Fulham's only raid of the second half, Jimmy Conway takes Steve Earle's raking pass to volley into the roof of the net from a very tight angle. It gave Fulham a 2–1 victory at Spotland.

Fulham fans celebrate the winning goal at Rochdale. The photo shows a diverse age range of Fulham supporters. The grimace on the face of the local 'Bobby' seems to imply that he doesn't share the fans' delight.

Fulham held on to win **2–1** somewhat fortuitously, but it was a truism that the ball usually ran with the team in form – and certainly it had done so on this particular day. The Fulham team, second best in everything during the second half, left the field to taunts of 'lucky' ringing in their ears from the home supporters.

The club admitted honestly that there had probably been a knock-on effect from the match at Darlington, and that they hadn't quite put together the flowing moves that had been wrecking defences recently, but that they were still happy with the team's overall form. The Lancashire press had been impressed with Fulham's all-round scoring power, and saw them as likely candidates for promotion even at this early stage.

Although it was very early in the season, there was also good news that Fulham were currently leading the way in the sponsored Ford sporting league. This was across the *whole* of the football league. They had amassed twenty-one points to date, one ahead of Oldham Athletic, and five ahead of the chasing pack.

Fulham's opponents the following week were **Doncaster Rovers** at the Cottage and everyone was praying that there would be no repeat of the previous season's tough-nut antics. Doncaster arrived at rock bottom in the league, with just one point from their opening six matches, whilst Fulham were perched loftily at the top. The game was an open invitation for an upset! The crowd was up to a healthy 13,500.

In goal for Doncaster this year was Glen Johnson, who would go on to play over 400 league games for Aldershot. At right half was a certain Ian Branfoot, later to manage Fulham. He had been signed by Doncaster from Sheffield Wednesday along with teammate Archie Irvine during the close season. Also given a mention in the Doncaster squad was a youth player named Peter Kitchen, who would become Fulham's record signing in several years' time.

Fulham were forced to make their first change of the season, as Malcolm Webster had picked up a thigh injury in training on the Friday, allowing Ian Seymour to deputise – his first game in nine months. As Fulham now played in red socks, Rovers switched their kit to white socks as opposed to the previous season's all red. The game took place on a glorious 'Indian Summer' September afternoon.

Fulham were quickly out of the blocks and two thundering volleys from Les Barrett and Barry Lloyd flew just wide with the goalkeeper beaten. Doncaster rallied and were unlucky not to score themselves in the fifteenth minute when the Fulham defence were asleep from a twenty-five yard free kick by Rod Johnson. Ian Seymour athletically beat the ball away and John Regan was just unable to convert the rebound.

It was Steve Earle's chance to miss a sitter from ten yards next. Vic Halom then upset the away supporters by lunging at the goalkeeper when he dived to make a low save. The anxious Fulham crowd were settled by a fine goal in the twenty-first minute. Fred Callaghan made a determined run and cross, Halom helped the ball on with his head, and Jimmy Conway moved in at lightning

Doncaster Rovers back in town. Here Fred Callaghan has to take evasive action to avoid a flying, dangerous, over-the-top tackle. The studs-up approach was much in evidence for the second season running, and the Yorkshire side again escaped with a 1–1 draw.

speed to control the ball neatly and steer it over the advancing, diving keeper into the net. Conway was the half's outstanding player again, with many darting runs and clever flicks that should have brought better reward.

The match suddenly became a case of *déjà vu*, and Doncaster, like the previous season, started to lose their cool, using spoiling tactics and halting most Fulham attacks by tripping or barging the players into touch. So many attacks were halted illegally that the ineffective referee Mr Lewis played an almost continuous solo on his whistle! Fulham were riled again minutes later when Halom was clearly brought down from behind in the penalty area; nothing was given, and the referee waved away Fulham's heated appeals.

The physical play of the Doncaster side was upsetting Fulham's rhythm. The home side failed to build on the slender lead and were beginning to look lethargic in the heat, and Halom especially seemed to be suffering, drawn repeatedly into the spoiling Doncaster offside trap. On the rare occasions that Fulham did break through, over-anxiety saw the final shots end up being wildly ballooned into the terraces. In one raid, however, Fulham were denied a clear second penalty.

Fulham eventually wilted and were punished twenty minutes from time. Experienced winger Brian Usher was put away by the tireless Rod Johnson, and from his cross John Regan helped the ball on and Doncaster's young centre forward Stephen Briggs scored with a low ground shot, the Fulham defence wide open following a real mix-up at the back. For once Seymour had no chance from point-blank range.

With a point salvaged, Doncaster were more than happy to return to a defensive, clogging formation. They were, however, lucky to escape with a draw after the Doncaster keeper Johnson left his line and aimed a petulant kick at Halom in the penalty area after the game had been halted. Despite observing the offence, the pressurised referee saw fit to award Fulham just an indirect free kick rather than a penalty; the free kick came to nothing. The Doncaster keeper, although lectured, was not even cautioned. The game finished, as the previous season, **1–1**.

True to Fulham style, this was the shock result of the day, but although intimidated by Doncaster's clogging tactics Fulham had been more than a little unlucky, showing all of the class that was on view.

Manager Bill Dodgin was philosophical: 'Naturally we were a bit disappointed at only winning one point, but with football being what it is, this sort of result is bound to happen from time to time. It was one of those days when things didn't go quite right for us. We had so much pressure that we were bound to leave ourselves a little open at the back. When you're so much on top you are bound to become slack. We're not too worried, though, about the result.'

The following club programme emphatically played down the loss of a point, saying: 'We dropped a point, but who dares say we lost form? How far away were we from another really rewarding ninety minutes? A repetition of our near misses and the hard luck stories would serve little purpose at this stage. The fact is that the way we played was again the envy of every other team in the division; more than that cannot be demanded.'

The club and team had an immediate opportunity to put this result behind them, when mid-table **Brighton and Hove Albion** were the Cottage visitors the following Wednesday. Although they had won only two matches, they had only lost two as well. Brighton were under the new management of Pat Saward, the former Millwall and Aston Villa player, Coventry City assistant manager and Irish international who had been appointed during the close season.

The Brighton line-up was, unsurprisingly, virtually the same as the one that had visited Fulham just five months previously, and there were no new faces. Included this year in the squad, however, was a young Peter O'Sullivan, who would have an impact in Malcolm Macdonald's Fulham promotion side over a decade later.

Fulham were also unchanged having turned down Eire's request to free Jimmy Conway on the night because of the importance of the match; Brighton again played in a red and white second strip. Fulham supporters were obviously hoping for a repeat of last season's Bank Holiday performance – and result. The referee was the portly Roger Kirkpatrick. The good news was that crowd numbers were up again, and despite being a midweek fixture, a healthy crowd of almost 14,000 turned out.

Brighton suffered some early bad luck when their full back John Templeman was injured and carried off in the tenth minute, his replacement being utility man but primarily inside forward Terry Stanley. Despite this advantage, Fulham looked strangely uncoordinated up front, with the star forwards not firing on all cylinders. As with the Doncaster game, Fulham frittered away a series of first-half chances. Barry Lloyd was the worst culprit, with two glaring misses that should have made it a comfortable second half. Vic Halom also shot straight at the goalkeeper with the entire goal to shoot at.

Fortunately Lloyd had the opportunity to redeem himself early in the second half and this time he took the chance. Ten minutes into the half a bobbing ball came across the face of the penalty area, and Brighton crucially hesitated in clearing it. There didn't appear to be time or room enough for the shot, but somehow Lloyd put in a twenty-yard volley, which fizzed low and hard just inside goalkeeper Geoff Sidebottom's post, giving him no chance to save. It was a real cannonball drive that would have dented a tank.

Fulham chugged away, seemingly in second gear, and only Les Barrett lived up to his reputation as a quality player, although even he was struggling to breathe life into the tepid attack. There was too much stop-start football, and showman referee Kirkpatrick appeared to be having one of his 'fussy' nights. Brighton laboured away in a solid and sometimes promising way, and pressed on with the idea of at least equalising. Indeed, Fulham were a little fortunate to hang onto both points when Ian Seymour, who had been little used on the night, was fortunately alert enough to save Brighton striker Kit Napier's late 'unstoppable' header. Fulham hung on to a **1−0** win, with the home crowd frantically whistling for the end of the match.

The press commented that Fulham had now opened up a gap at the top of the table, but were blunt with their appraisal saying: 'They will have to sharpen up their shooting if they want to stay there.' Dodgin knew this was true; it had not been a great showing, but in some ways the result had been more important than the display. Some of the players, although desperate to play, had been carrying niggling injuries. Skipper Lloyd summed up the morale, saying: You don't have injuries when you're winning!' Most of the press considered, however, that once again dumpy referee Kirkpatrick was the real 'star' of the show. One said: 'He held the poor show together like some old-time variety master of ceremonies. The real performers missed their cues, but the ebullient Mr Kirkpatrick never missed his! ... He controlled the game with a voice of steel, bellowing at players, overruling linesmen and gesticulating like an overworked gendarme in a Parisian rush hour!'

Skipper Lloyd had been the best player on the field by far, always in the thick of the action, but the defence had also played well, Reg Matthewson and Jimmy Dunne ably protecting goalkeeper Seymour when required. The club correctly pointed out that whilst the team had not produced their best form in recent weeks, they were 'winning and drawing matches that last season we were drawing and losing'.

The ball is just a blur as Barry Lloyd's rocket from twenty yards keeps low and beats the Brighton goalkeeper just inside a post. The goal gave Fulham a 1–0 win. Note all five Fulham forwards on the edge of the area, a testament to Bill Dodgin's attacking ethos.

At the weekend, Fulham travelled to Deepdale to contest the points with **Preston North End**, relegated the previous season. Preston had made a strong start to the season and were lying eighth, but were so far unbeaten at home. Fulham made a change for this match bringing in fit-again John Richardson for injured winger Jimmy Conway, thus breaking a run of seventy consecutive appearances.

Preston, with a newfound confidence, had much the better of the first half and Fulham were indebted to fine positioning by Reg Matthewson and Dave Moreline early in the match for keeping the baying Preston forwards at arms' length. John Richardson was also impressive in his first match of the season, grafting well in defence, and helping to launch counter-attacks.

Preston were very unlucky when a beautiful cross by North End's Dave Wilson was hammered first time past Ian Seymour by Gerry Ingram. Fortunately, the athletic Moreline was able to clear the shot off the line, and Seymour saved the return follow-up shot from Dave Hughes.

Seymour was also on top form – and he needed to be. He made one spectacular mid-air diving catch to foil Ingram and all round his agility and anticipation were first class. Certainly the luck was with Fulham who had further let-offs when a shot by Wilson and a powerful header from Ricky Heppolette both smashed against the post. Fulham then had yet another escape on the stroke of half time when the referee turned down Preston's appeals for a penalty when it looked as if Fred Callaghan had handled. Somehow, a battered Fulham left the field still on level terms.

It looked as if Preston had blown their chances when Jimmy Dunne, supporting the forwards, gave Fulham the lead from a corner just seven minutes after half time. Callaghan seized possession and drilled a low cross into a pack of Preston defenders in the penalty area. The outward deflection fell nicely for Dunne, who rocketed the ball past Alan Kelly in the Preston goal. That was really the first real opportunity that the home defence had presented. Most of the press the following day mistakenly credited the goal to John Richardson. Although this goal meant that it was two goals in his first nine games for Fulham, Dunne never scored another Fulham goal.

However, within a minute of Fulham's goal the match was all square again when, following a right-wing move, Preston full back George Ross held off the challenges of four Fulham defenders and centred accurately for the other Preston full back Jim McNab to leap highest and put in a powerful goalbound header that was deflected past the helpless keeper Seymour.

From this point, Fulham took charge and it was only thanks to their goalkeeper Alan Kelly that Preston held onto their point. The home keeper made fine saves from Steve Earle, Vic Halom and from a Les Barrett piledriver bound for the top corner, whilst Barry Lloyd made the miss of the match near the end, blazing over when it seemed easier to score. It was Seymour, however, who had the final say, racing back to make a further split-second stop from Ingram. The vibrant match finished **1–1.**

Fulham could have been well satisfied with the point that they had fought for so tigerishly; this had easily been their sternest test to date. Also it was welcoming to see praise heaped on the defence for a change. The match proved that, apart from the attacking flair and silky skills, the Cottagers were prepared to roll their sleeves up and battle when the need arose. Ian Seymour made all the headlines the following day for his 'five star' display, giving Bill Dodgin a future selection headache. The press were impressed with Fulham's dogged display, one saying: 'Fulham give title hint.'

There was no let up in the density of fixtures, as the rearranged fixture with **Tranmere Rovers** at the Cottage was scheduled for just forty-eight hours later, forcing Fulham to play their eighth match of the month in a space of just twenty-seven days! This was also Fulham's sixth home match in the last eight games.

Tranmere arrived as the division's draw specialists, having drawn five of their opening seven league games. They had, however, been beaten only once. The away team was again virtually identical to the one that had visited the Cottage just six months previously. The only significant addition to their squad was that of tough full back Brian Joy, signed in the close season from Torquay. The Tranmere substitute on the night was named John Dempsey, although he was no relation to the Chelsea and former Fulham pivot! Tranmere played in a very unusual but patriotic change kit of red, white and blue. Fulham recalled Jimmy Conway to the wing with John Richardson dropping down to substitute. Conway pluckily opted to play, but could only do so after receiving a pain-killing injection.

Fulham were once again handed the impetus of an early goal when Vic Halom netted after just six minutes. A Les Barrett cross came over from the left and the crowd howled for handball – breaking the concentration of some Tranmere players. The ball ran loose from Tranmere defender Tony Knapp to Jimmy Conway whose slick pass found Halom, and he netted with a firm drive past the diving Kevin Thomas in the Tranmere goal that ended all arguments. The keeper managed to get his fingers to the shot, but could only succeed in deflecting the ball into goal. Fulham then made hard work of adding to their score against a predictably defensive Tranmere. Conway and Barrett were both being tightly marked. Conway in particular essayed few solo attacks and appeared to be suffering with a leg injury.

Just after the half hour Fulham scored again. A curling Barrett corner was pushed behind for another by the Tranmere goalkeeper. Conway took the second corner and from it Stan Brown scored his first of the season with a bullet header from long range – an ideal sales pitch for his forthcoming testimonial year! The ball rocketed in just underneath the bar with the goalkeeper

Just six minutes in, and Fulham ahead again. Vic Halom takes Conway's pass and blasts in a firm shot which Tranmere goalkeeper Thomas can only deflect into the net with his arm. Although not on top form, Fulham secured another home win with a 2–0 scoreline.

a spectator in the middle of his goal. The effort had reporters reaching for superlatives. It was a cannonball header that few thought would go in; even club photographer Ken Coton was so surprised that he didn't 'snap' the vital moment. It was only Brown's second goal in the last twelve months. It would prove to be his final Fulham goal.

Even at two down, and not yet half time, Tranmere still shrank away into defence, often having nine men behind the ball, content with damage limitation and just hoping to snatch a goal on the break. There was usually a wall of red shirts waiting for any Fulham attack, and only George Yardley and Jimmy Hinch ventured anywhere near the Fulham goal.

Tranmere's efforts were restricted to two long-range shots from Yardley. He shot just wide when Ian Seymour was bundled whilst in the air and lost the ball, and then was close soon after when Barry Lloyd lost possession to him near goal.

There was controversy in the second half when the referee, Mr Ray Johnson, failed to halt the game and waved play on when Tranmere's Hinch stuck out an arm, clearly handling Seymour's throw-out. Fortunately for the referee, the Tranmere attack broke down and no harm was done.

Fulham had quite a significant 'flat' spell in the second half, playing at a much lower tempo in midfield and irritating the crowd by over-elaborating with their passing and then dithering near goal when clear opportunities arose. Fulham could have extended their lead further when hard-working livewire Steve Earle, watched by the West Ham manager Ron Greenwood, went close with a header that shaved a post; Halom also went close with a header minutes later and later missed two further presentable chances. In truth, Fulham barely had to extend themselves for the rest of the half and lost a lot of their early spark before cruising home easy **2−0** winners.

The Cottagers had produced an efficient and professional performance that had on occasions oozed class and confidence, but they had been faced with very mediocre opposition whom they had seen off easily. Fulham had now conceded just two goals at home after seven matches. Tranmere had been very disappointing and, apart from the experienced Tony Knapp holding the team together at the back and some attacking graft from centre forward George Yardley, had offered little at all.

Fulham's attack on the night had looked somewhat out of sorts, and it had been a case of Stan Brown, Reg Matthewson, whose reading of the game and interceptions were brilliant, and the untiring Jimmy Dunne getting on with things without fuss at the other end, ensuring that Tranmere never got a sniff of the Fulham goal.

At the end of this month, Fulham announced four new signings, although none of the players had cost the club a fee! Roger Davison's loan move from Portsmouth had been made permanent, as had that of the other loan player Alan Morton – both players signed on a year's contract. The club had also signed two young players. Firstly, eighteen–year-old Alan Collman, whom Dodgin had signed before as a fifteen-year-old at QPR, had switched to Fulham to join Dodgin for a second time as an apprentice professional. Secondly, another young player, Paul Shrubb, had been also been signed as an apprentice. Shrubb, although barely sixteen, had already appeared in the reserve side. The player had signed apprentice forms the day he had left his Guildford school.

To round off the unbeaten month perfectly, Johnny Haynes contacted the club to inform them that his Durban City side had won the South African League. Haynes quipped 'How about that – a medal at last!' Haynes was delighted at the club's current progress, and hoped to return and see the boys soon.

Without dwelling on the statistics, Fulham's position in the table at this stage may have been a slightly false one, as in the ten matches played to date the team had played just two sides occupying positions in the top half of the table, and eight sides in the bottom twelve, so it was very important to keep a true perspective on Fulham's progress! They had also played two more home matches than away matches. There was also yet another home fixture coming up the following week.

October 1970

In this month

* Nasser's successor was named as the moderate Anwar Saddat.
* Jochen Rindt became World motor racing champion posthumously.
* American rock singer Janis Joplin died of a drugs overdose.
* Fiji became independent from Britain.
* Canadian immigration minister Pierre Laporte was kidnapped and subsequently murdered by Canadian separatists serving the Quebec Liberation Front.
* Prime Minister Ted Heath created the Department of the Environment and the Department of Trade and Industry.
* Thirty-three died when the West Gate Bridge in Australia collapsed.
* Irish firebrand Bernadette Devlin was released from prison.
* 800 died after a typhoon in the Philippines.
* Racing driver Jack Brabham announced his retirement.
* Irish minister Charles Haughey and three others were cleared of illegally importing arms.
* 800 couples from Korea and other parts of the World, members of the controversial Unification Church, were married by leader Sun Myung Moon in a mass ceremony at the Changchung gymnasium in Seoul.

'Band of Gold' by Freda Payne topped the charts.
The film 'The Railway Children' was released.

How the league was looking

Fulham led the table, with Aston Villa just a point behind. The previous season's dark horses, Bristol Rovers, were third, and Rotherham United fourth, both two points behind Villa. A cluster of four teams that included Reading pursued these four sides on twelve points.

Rochdale had slumped to the bottom of the table with just four points, just ahead of Doncaster on goal average, and Bury and Gillingham held the other two relegation places. Three other clubs, Tranmere Rovers, Port Vale and Wrexham stood just one point outside the bottom four.

The matches

FULHAM PLAYED their seventh home match out of eleven when **Plymouth Argyle** visited Craven Cottage on the Saturday. Argyle were just above mid-table. The Pilgrims were now without the influence of midfield player Norman Piper who had joined Portsmouth in the close season, but the forward line had three new faces: former Luton and Portsmouth inside forward Keith Allen, winger Don Hutchins, signed for a nominal fee from Leicester City, and the vastly experienced Dave Burnside formerly of Wolves and Crystal Palace. Plymouth were now managed by the delightfully named Ellis Stuttard.

A change was forced on Fulham before the kick-off when Dave Moreline cried off with stomach trouble, leaving Stan Brown to fill the right back position. Jimmy Dunne switched to right half, and John Richardson came in to take the other half back role. Attendances were remaining pretty consistent, and 13,300 saw this game.

Fulham had problems early on when Stan Brown pulled a muscle, but signalled that he was just about able to continue. Plymouth, sensing that this might be their day, were proving lively opposition. They were tackling keenly, Vic Halom's legs bearing testimony to their no-nonsense approach. The Pilgrims seemed to want the ball more and were winning nearly all of the fifty-fifty tackles. Fulham had an amazing let-off early on when Trevor Shepherd was given an open goal to shoot at. Fortunately for Fulham, his unstoppable shot cannoned against the foot of the post and was cleared away.

Fulham were seemingly disjointed and their cause was made that much harder when Eire international Jimmy Conway collapsed in agony, the victim of yet another rugged Plymouth tackle. He tried gamely to continue but his withdrawal with a damaged ankle seven minutes before half time was inevitable.

Full back Mike Pentecost substituted for Conway, giving the Fulham team a further lop-sided look. In this enforced position Pentecost went to full back after half time, and Brown pushed into the half back line, allowing Jimmy Dunne to push forward to help the attackers – although he was no substitute for Conway.

Against the odds Fulham took the lead just five minutes after half time. Argyle's Burnside fouled Dunne and the Irishman played Fred Callaghan's free kick back across the edge of the area where it was met with a first-time shot from Steve Earle. Fortune favoured Fulham in this instance, as the ball appeared to be going just wide but was deflected nicely into the net by a Plymouth defender.

Fulham were now dominating, and it was only thanks to Argyle's former Manchester United goalkeeper Pat Dunne that the visitors were still in it. Dunne was excelling himself and had to make four blinding saves in as many minutes, one save from Les Barrett being particularly noteworthy. The home defence had little to do and the alert Ian Seymour ably stopped whatever Argyle threw at the home goal.

Fulham's fight, however, was not enough and they failed to build on their one goal lead. Halom, although always busy, looked slow on the turn, and a number of moves broke down because of this. The disjointed home team began to look susceptible to the counter-attack, and sensing this Argyle threw more men forward.

Midway through the half Plymouth equalised. Centre forward Shepherd was given far too much room on the right wing and he had time to measure an inch-perfect cross that evaded both John Richardson and Reg Matthewson. The gangling and hard-working Keith Allen dived cleverly at the far post to reach the ball and steer it home, his low header skidding just out of Seymour's frantic grasp. The goal was rough luck on Matthewson, as it was probably his only error in another impressive game.

Brown was now virtually a limping passenger and was totally isolated out on the wing. Fulham still tried to put in a spirited last fifteen minutes but no more goals were forthcoming. Despite a save from Dunne in the closing minutes to foil Earle the match finished as a **1–1** draw.

Big microphones, numerous leads and associated Seventies' technology are in evidence as ITV commentator Brian Moore and his co-host Jimmy Hill prepare to televise Fulham's home match with Plymouth Argyle. Fulham were not at their best in front of the 'Big Match' cameras but secured a 1–1 draw against the Pilgrims.

Another promotion point had been lost and what was worse, Moreline and Brown were both doubtful for the big clash with Queens Park Rangers, with Jimmy Conway definitely out. The loss of all three at once would be a big blow. The Plymouth match was featured on *The Big Match* the following day.

In a TV interview after the game skipper Lloyd spoke intelligently and candidly. He stated that he had been impressed by Plymouth and their determination, intimating that Fulham needed to work much harder in wrestling the ball away from their opponents if they were going to keep up their promotion challenge. Without doubt some of the early season 'fire' had gone out of the team, especially amongst the forwards, who were making very hard work of scoring.

Fulham had just three days to re-group before their west London neighbours **Queens Park Rangers** made the short trip to the Cottage to contest the third round of the Football League Cup. Fulham, by quirks of fate, had only met QPR in two seasons since the First World War, in 1948–49, and before that as long ago as 1931–32. The match had been switched from Wednesday to Tuesday to avoid clashing with other London ties.

The match was quite a reunion. Club manager Bill Dodgin was formerly boss at Loftus Road, whilst Gordon Jago, who had left Fulham in 1967 for America, was now Rangers coach. The main talking point of the evening was the first return to the Cottage of Rodney Marsh since his departure almost five years previously. Rodney would definitely be out to prove a point. The League Cup was seen as 'Marsh's competition', as it had been mainly through his magic that Rangers became the first Third Division side to win the League Cup at Wembley four years earlier.

QPR now had Phil Parkes in goal having signed him from Walsall during the close season. At left back was Dave Clement, who would later in the decade play for Fulham. Former Sheffield Wednesday pivot Vic Mobley was at centre half, and future England manager Terry Venables took the number eight shirt. Also in the Rangers squad, but not playing on the evening, was Frank Sibley, who would return to the Cottage in a coaching capacity almost thirty years later. Due to the colour clash, Rangers switched to their attractive red and black striped shirts.

Injury-hit Fulham had problems: Mike Pentecost took Dave Moreline's place, John Richardson replaced Stan Brown, and Bill Dodgin gambled by giving young Alan Morton his first-team debut on the right wing in place of the injured Jimmy Conway. Dodgin again named Roger Davidson as substitute. Fulham's evening got off to a good start when the press announced that Bill Dodgin had won the *Evening Standard*'s Third Division manager of the month award. The teetotal Dodgin won a gallon of Bell's whisky!

Dodgin was excited by the cup clash, but wasn't letting cup fever divert him from his main aim. He said: 'We want to get out of the Third Division – that aim supersedes everything; but having said that, this derby should be a cracker. The Rangers team has changed a lot since I left, and they play differently, but it should be a fascinating meeting.'

On a heady autumn evening, a massive crowd of over 31,700 flocked to the ground in eager anticipation of a cracking tie. The crowd was the highest at the Cottage since March 1968. The game also generated record receipts of £9,601 beating by £500 the previous record when Manchester United had visited the Cottage for a league match in 1967. All roads leading to the Cottage were congested and blocked two hours before the start.

Rangers, struggling in the Second Division, would as usual be an attacking threat, but Fulham's free-scoring forwards were looking forward to attacking a rather brittle defence. Rangers, however, would be no pushovers, having disposed of Second Division leaders Cardiff City 4–0 in the previous round. Torrential rain beforehand had greased the pitch and redoubled the promise of goals from a game between two sides totally committed to attack. The match was officiated by one of the best referees on the circuit, Ron Challis of Tonbridge.

Both defences looked uneasy on the wet surface, but Fulham quickly mastered the conditions and it took the home side just fourteen minutes to take the lead. Debutant Alan Morton released Steve Earle on the left with a superbly penetrative forty-yard pass, and from Earle's quick, intelligent cross Les Barrett joyfully flicked the ball first time wide of Phil Parkes into the corner of the net.

Fulham were unlucky not to go further ahead when Barrett almost scored again and Parkes struggled to save his cross shot. Sharper finishing would have seen Fulham comfortably ahead by the interval. Rangers had a chance just before the half time when Ian Morgan netted from Marsh's pass, but he was given offside. Apart from this effort, Rangers failed to put a shot on target in the first half.

Rangers made more of a fight of it in the first quarter of an hour of the second half but were offering little direct threat in front of goal. Their forwards looked particularly impotent, and most of the threats to the Fulham goal came from the Rangers full backs Ian Watson and Dave Clement, galloping upfield from the back. Rangers' one real opportunity came following a foul on Rodney Marsh. The free kick fell to Terry Venables, but Ian Seymour just managed to smother his shot at the foot of a post.

Rangers keeper Phil Parkes and defender Dave Clement can only stare as Fulham take the lead against QPR in front of 31,000 at the Cottage. Airborne scorer Les Barrett can scarcely conceal his delight, and others celebrate in the background. Fulham's deserved 2-0 victory eliminated Rangers from the Football League Cup.

Following this close shave, Fulham broke straight to the other end and doubled their lead. Once again Barrett was the tormentor. He accelerated away on a fine run following a throw in from Fred Callaghan, and Vic Halom, who had run into the penalty area, rather luckily deflected Barrett's cross-shot past Parkes into the opposite corner of the goal.

From that point, Rangers lost a great deal of confidence; a few heads were down and their attacking efforts had more than a hint of desperation. Marsh tried in vain to invigorate his team, but he could only draw life out of winger Mike Ferguson, who did at least look capable of unlocking the Fulham defence. In the end, the highly efficient Fred Callaghan and Jimmy Dunne crowded him out.

After one fair tackle, Marsh lashed out mulishly at Dunne and was lucky to escape a caution. In the end, Marsh was reduced to the role of a helpless onlooker, and although he was tightly marked some of his histrionics and protests to the referee made him unpopular with the home team's supporters.

Leaving future England manager Terry Venables as a static spectator, Les Barrett fires in a cross-shot which is deflected into the Rangers net by Vic Halom for Fulham's second goal.

Fulham just had to maintain possession and concentrate to hold out for an excellent **2–0** win. The revenge had certainly been sweet for Bill Dodgin, who had walked away from the Loftus Road maelstrom two years earlier.

In truth Rangers, a team expensively put together, had looked extremely disappointing on the night, showing little cohesion or team spirit. They had rarely looked like unhinging Dodgin's cavaliers, who had played well to a man and had truly merited this success; such a result could only have further boosted Fulham's confidence.

As a result of this victory Fulham secured yet another home tie in the fourth round to yet another Second Division club – Swindon Town. The draw was an interesting one, as Swindon were the other team to have won the League Cup as a Third Division side, defeating Arsenal 3–1 in a 1969 Wembley mudbath.

The press were highly complimentary about the home side's performance and said: 'For Fulham there seems nothing but optimism. It seems clear that they have developed not only into a Third Division championship side – but into an outfit that could well provide a few shocks in Cup football.'

Intoxicated with success, Fulham had rapidly to return to earth with a bread and butter league visit to Gay Meadow and **Shrewsbury Town**. Shrewsbury held a mid-table position after winning four and losing five of their opening eleven matches. The only piece of bad news emerging from the Cottage was that Jimmy Conway's injury looked to have been far worse than was originally envisaged, and he was likely to be out for some time. Stan Brown and Dave Moreline were also both still absent.

These circumstances prompted Bill Dodgin to give a debut appearance to Roger Davidson. It promised to be an interesting contest, as Shrewsbury had the division's most porous defence to date and Fulham had the highest scorers.

Fulham looked tired following their midweek exertions, but were at their best in the first thirty minutes. They battered the Shrewsbury defence with slick passing moves and skills, but their quality football brought no immediate return. Fulham forced four corners in the opening six minutes but the only real effort was a stabbed shot by Les Barrett that travelled weakly across the goalmouth. After Shrewsbury had seemingly weathered the early storm, Fulham took a surprise lead after twenty-four minutes with a gifted goal.

During an early spell of pressure at Shrewsbury, Fulham had a number of good chances. Here Fred Callaghan charges upfield but is just beaten to the ball by the home goalkeeper, with Barry Lloyd looking on. A slender 1–0 win was the result. Note just outside the ground a fine example of a GWR Brunel classic 'standard' signal box and semaphore signal on the gantry. Those were the days!

Shrewsbury full back Tony Gregory twice failed to control the ball and clear a Fulham attack and Vic Halom hustled him out of possession. The Shrewsbury goalkeeper Bob Tooze spotted the danger and ran out towards Halom, committing himself to leaving the goal. Halom intelligently punished these errors unmercifully when he crossed quickly leaving Barrett the simple opportunity of sliding in and side-footing the ball into an empty net.

Fulham's display was a competent one based on controlled defence and quickly mounted attacks. They appeared to be in third gear only and didn't suggest that they were able to score further goals. The Cottagers had a clear opportunity to extend the lead on the stroke of half time. Again goalkeeper Tooze committed himself, leaving Barry Lloyd with a clear sight of goal. Lloyd lobbed his shot over the stranded goalkeeper but unfortunately the ball bounced on top of the bar, finally landing on the roof of the net.

In the second half the Cottagers were far from their best and Shrewsbury were definitely the better side, hustling Fulham out of their composure. The Shrews created a number of chances but like Fulham seemed unable to finish off promising moves.

Fulham were fortunate that Ian Seymour was again at his alert and agile best, beating out and stopping all of Shrewsbury's efforts. Graham Clapham forced one great save, and then John Moore stung the goalkeeper's gloves with a vicious effort from almost forty yards. Time and again Seymour dived into a ruck of players always to emerge confidently with the ball. He punched away a Fred Callaghan skied mis-kick that was heading towards goal, and then dashed from his line to foil George Andrews. Shrewsbury's play was disrupted by an injury to Geoff Fellows ten minutes from time.

Fulham were lucky to hold on to both points, as in the final minute centre half Alf Wood, always a threat, unleashed a fine shot. Seymour was just able to get across and push the goalbound shot against a post and away. Fulham held out in the end to win **1–0**.

The result had certainly been better than the performance and Fulham had ground out a win, rather than using flair. Still, it was a very good sign indeed that the Cottagers could pull a win out of the fire whilst playing far below their best. Ian Seymour had performed heroically and was making the most of his opportunity. It would be tough if Dodgin dropped him when Malcolm Webster was fit again. Despite the win, Roger Davidson could not have impressed the boss as he never made another league start for Fulham.

League and Cup football were put to one side two days later when a host of stars turned out for **Stan Brown's testimonial match** at the Cottage.

Stan had joined the club after being recommended by former Fulham player Jim Langley. Stan wanted to join Fulham because Johnny Haynes played for them. Most thought that Stan would be too small for professional football, but through a mixture of dedication, thought and commitment he had established himself as a more than useful member of the side.

Stan had been given his chance in the first team when Johnny Haynes was away on international duty. When Johnny came back to claim his shirt, Stan had done well enough to keep his place in the team as he was switched to centre forward.

The match was against Everton, and despite being marked by England player Brian Labone Stan scored the only goal of the game, which came following a long throw by Jimmy Langley. That first goal against Everton put Stan on his way to a long career, but he did not remain in the team as a spearhead of the attack. Midfield was his best position and it was there that he had made most of his first team appearances.

Having said that, examining an analysis of his playing record showed that it was difficult to place Stan Brown into *any* strict category. Although Stan was definitely too small to be a goalkeeper, he had shown his flexibility and all round skill by appearing in *every* outfield position for Fulham, from right back to left wing and substitute! So he had worn every Fulham shirt from two to twelve in a league match. This unusual ability was recognised by George Cohen, who called Stan 'the player's player', a title that was adopted for Brown's testimonial brochure. Midfield was his favourite area and Brown said, 'I like to be in the game all the time'.

Stan was very grateful to Jimmy Hill for his assistance in organising the testimonial. Hill had been a significant influence on the young Brown's career when playing for Fulham reserves whilst coming back from injury. Stan always remembered the help and encouragement Jimmy had shown all the younger professionals.

An impressive crowd of 11,000 arrived at the Cottage, adding £3,500 to Stan's testimonial fund. The evening, as in the previous testimonials, was split into two matches, a **Past Fulham XI** versus the **Internationals Club**, followed by a **Fulham XI** versus a **Chelsea XI** match. Chelsea had been very sporting to fit this night in with their tough European programme and domestic fixtures, but they all wanted to take part.

The Internationals Club had been the brainchild of Jimmy Hill, who had done much organising for the actual match. Hill was unsure originally which side to play for in the opening match; he had hurt his back recently and had unfortunately been forced to sit out the early games for the Internationals Club! He did in the end declare himself fit for this one, opting to play for his club side – Fulham. Johnny Haynes was unfortunately absent, unable to return in time due to contractual obligations in South Africa. This year George Cohen made sure his knee was up to it!

The opening match didn't appear to have a strict duration and was played on a 'play until you run out of wind' basis! Tosh Chamberlain decided to make an immediate impact by entering the pitch wearing a white wig.

The Past Fulham XI

Dave Underwood
George Cohen
Jimmy Langley
Bobby Robson
Roy Bentley
Bill Dodgin
Arthur Stevens
Graham Leggat
Bedford Jezzard (sub. Alf Stokes)
Jimmy Hill
Trevor 'Tosh' Chamberlain

The Internationals Club

Jack Kelsey (ex-Arsenal and Wales)
Theo Foley (ex-Northampton and Eire)
Ken Shellito (ex-Chelsea and England)
Bill McGarry (ex-Huddersfield and England)
Sammy Chung (ex-Watford)
Pat Saward (ex-Aston Villa and Eire)
Tommy Steele (entertainer – guest)
Dave Sexton (ex-West Ham)
Eddie Firmani (ex-Charlton and Italy)
Alan Sealey (ex-West Ham)
Frank Blunstone (ex-Chelsea and England)

The Internationals Club were previously unbeaten, so it was fun to see a Fulham side demolish another record. After leading 3–2 at the interval, the Past Fulham side ran out 5–4 winners. Guided by a super and stylish display by Graham Leggat, backed up by the scheming Jimmy Hill, Fulham's goals were scored by sharp-shooting Tosh Chamberlain (2), Beddy Jezzard, Jimmy Hill and Arthur Stevens.

George Cohen kept it as tight as he could at the back with the tidy Bill Dodgin, but with passes from the probing Dave Sexton and the power up front of Eddie Firmani, Fulham conceded goals to Alan Sealey (2), Firmani and, delightfully, Tommy Steele – what a picture, a goal to stick in the family album!

Main match:

Fulham XI

Ian Seymour
Mike Pentecost
Fred Callaghan (sub. Roger Davidson)
Stan Brown
Reg Matthewson (sub. Dave Roberts)
Stan Horne
John Richardson
Alan Morton
Steve Earle
Barry Lloyd
Les Barrett

Chelsea XI

Peter Bonetti (sub. Alan Dovey)
Johnny Boyle (sub. Gary Locke)
Ron Harris
John Hollins
Marvin Hinton
Stewart Houston
Derek Smethurst
Charlie Cooke
Peter Osgood
Tommy Baldwin
Peter Houseman

STAN BROWN'S TESTIMONIAL NIGHT OCTOBER 12th 1970
OFFICIAL PROGRAMME 1/-

PAST FULHAM v THE INTERNATIONALS CLUB 7 pm
FULHAM v CHELSEA 8 pm

'The player's player' Stan Brown was rewarded for twelve years of loyal service to Fulham with an attractive testimonial match against neighbours Chelsea.

Stan Brown is presented with his inscribed silverware by vice-chairman Chappie D'Amato for his services to Fulham Football Club. Don't just say 'Brown', say 'Service'. Here he is warmly applauded by Peter Bonetti, Peter Houseman and other members of the Chelsea squad. The evening was a fitting occasion in front of 11,000 spectators, even though Chelsea managed to sneak a 2–0 win.

In the main match, the testimonial game was, for once, taken more seriously; local pride was at stake! Even though Chelsea fielded a very strong side, they could still afford to omit Paddy Mulligan, John Dempsey, Dave Webb, Keith Weller, Ian Hutchinson and Alan Hudson! Stan led out Fulham as captain, holding the FA Cup (Chelsea being holders) with his opposite captain Ron Harris. After the frolics of the opening match, the second would probably be a bit of an anti-climax.

Stan Brown was presented with an inscribed silver cigarette box and silver salver from Noël D'Amato as an appreciation from Tommy Trinder and the other Fulham directors for 'twelve years loyal and outstanding service to Fulham Football Club'.

In this second match, some tackles went in and the tempo was considerably higher than that of most testimonial matches. Chelsea eventually won the match 2–0 with a first-half goal from Derek Smethurst and a second-half headed goal from Peter Osgood. Barry Lloyd starred in the midfield as expected, showing Chelsea what they missed by selling him, and Steve Earle, still under the eye of Dave Sexton, kept Chelsea at full stretch at the back.

Fulham did all of the running and Chelsea did all the scoring. Chelsea had the edge in poise and control, although Fulham enjoyed the majority of the possession. Chelsea had players that could score at will, whereas it looked as if Fulham lacked a real marksman. ITV's Brian Moore provided the commentary for both matches, often having little sarcastic digs over the tannoy at the quality of the play coming from his *Big Match* co-commentator Jimmy Hill in the opening match!

On the Saturday it was back to the hurly-burly of league action with the return visit of **Barnsley**. It seemed quite strange for Fulham to be playing the team that they met on the opening day again so soon. Barnsley were in eighth place, but had only lost three out of twelve league matches, and only one in their last eleven overall. The Barnsley team now included John McPhee, the former Blackpool player, and Les Lea and Frank Sharp signed from Cardiff City in a £20,000 double deal. Winger Lea had caused Fulham trouble in the past with both Blackpool and Cardiff. Also in the Barnsley squad was a young Stewart Barrowclough, later to star for Newcastle United. The game was played on an unseasonably warm and sunny October afternoon.

Although Dave Moreline was now fit, the form of Mike Pentecost was keeping him out of the side. Fulham continued with John Richardson at right half, with Bill Dodgin experimenting by playing Stan Brown in Jimmy Conway's number seven shirt. Crowds were remaining at a consistent level and 13,000 turned up.

Barnsley were a no-nonsense side playing with strong emphasis on defence away from home. They had played that way in the goalless draw at the Cottage the previous season and their rationale this time around was no different.

Straight from the kick-off it was not unusual to see nine Barnsley players behind the ball trying to frustrate the home side. Fulham were still hell bent on going forward and goalkeeper Brian Arblaster was soon in action. Steve Earle and Les Barrett piled in shots that seemed certain goals, but Arblaster turned them both away. As the home pressure increased, a sloppy back pass by Barnsley's David Booth forced the goalkeeper to head the ball behind for a corner.

Just when it appeared that Fulham would score soon, Barnsley were presented with a gift goal on the half-hour, totally against the run of the play. Jimmy Dunne, under pressure, lobbed a back pass towards Ian Seymour. The pass was wild and drifted well wide of the Fulham keeper. The error presented Les Lea with a simple opportunity to intercept the pass and he slotted the ball into an empty net. The mistake was hard on Dunne, as it had been probably his only significant gaffe of the season so far. The goal threw Fulham out of their stride and they were lucky not to go further behind when Seymour saved brilliantly from the previous year's hat trick hero Johnny Evans. Barnsley manager Johnny Steele said afterwards, 'That was the turning point.'

A chaotic and slapdash match meandered along in the second half. When Fulham did threaten to break through, Barnsley were more than happy to pull the players down, with the referee Mr Judson doing little to prevent this happening. Although Fulham were awarded several dangerous free kicks around the edge of the area, they all came to nothing. Most of Fulham's danger was coming from the surging runs of full back Fred Callaghan.

The forwards, minus Jimmy Conway, looked right out of form, and the finishing was feeble. Bill Dodgin gambled by withdrawing the not fully fit Stan Brown with twenty minutes to go and

Just fifteen minutes left, and Barry Lloyd throws himself at Steve Earle's accurate cross to bullet home an unstoppable header. The goal salvaged a point for Fulham in an uninspiring 1–1 draw against Barnsley.

replacing him with Stan Horne, moving Earle out to the right wing in the process. Within five minutes Fulham had somehow contrived to get on level terms. Earle broke away and produced a pinpoint cross. Barry Lloyd, for once, escaped the tight marking and met Earle's cross to bullet a header from eight yards past the exposed goalkeeper.

From that point, apart from sporadic raids from the dangerous winger Lea, Barnsley shut up shop, with Booth and Eric Winstanley outstanding at the back. Fulham could find little impetus and this drab game finished **1–1.**

Fulham had now netted just eight goals in their last seven games, and it had only been thanks to some excellent defensive displays that Fulham were clinging onto the top spot. The Londoners were clearly missing the injured Jimmy Conway and were not showing their customary flair.

A disappointed Dodgin said afterwards: 'Despite our success, we're not playing really well – and the lads know it; we're waiting for the wet grounds.' With no experienced right-sided replacement easily identifiable, Bill Dodgin started to look seriously at making a significant signing. Somehow, though, Fulham were now unbeaten in ten matches.

Fulham had yet another midweek fixture on the Wednesday, when they travelled to Elm Park to play **Reading**. Reading were now eighth, but not setting the world alight and not scoring at the rate they had been the previous season. They were without regular keeper Steve Death, replaced by John Pratt. Fulham forsook their striped kit and played in their lucky red away strip from the previous season perhaps due to the fact that Reading played in blue. The Cottagers were unchanged and hoping for a repeat of the previous season's performance and scoreline. For a midweek game, the attendance was a respectable 14,000, Reading's biggest gate of the season.

Fulham as usual started briskly, eager for the early goal, but discovered that Reading's suspect defence had done their homework. Most of the Fulham forwards threatened individually, but keeper Pratt was having an easy night. It was Reading who carved out the first real chance when Dick Habbin and Williams set up a chance for Les Chappell. His shot beat Ian Seymour, but Fred Callaghan cleared the goalbound shot off the line.

Callaghan was upsetting the home crowd with some tough tackling but was looking a key player, driving the rather lethargic forwards on. The match then settled into a skilful midfield battle. Vic Halom was unlucky when he was just wide with a header from Steve Earle's centre, whilst at the other end Seymour fumbled Williams' shot and the ball was just about cleared from a goalmouth mêlée.

It took the home side just two minutes to forge ahead after the interval. A defence-splitting run by Stuart Morgan ended with Gordon Cumming carving an opening for Chappell. Seymour

Les Barrett (far left) has fired in a fierce shot that Reading goalkeeper Pratt cannot hold, and Vic Halom is handily placed to turn the rebound neatly into goal. It gave Fulham a point at Elm Park in a 1–1 draw.

could only parry Chappell's shot and Dick Habbin raced in to score from eight yards with the away defence caught cold and square.

Fulham could easily have conceded further goals, with Tony Wagstaff, Cumming and Chappell all missing further chances as Reading looked for the vital second goal. Fulham were now at sixes and sevens, and it appeared as if their unbeaten league run would come to an end.

Undaunted, however, the Cottagers kept pecking away, and finally equalised in the seventy-first minute courtesy of a Reading mistake. Scorer Habbin lost control of the ball with a loose pass and the ball ran on to Les Barrett to fire in a shot. As with Reading's goal, the goalkeeper could only parry the winger's effort, and Halom was nicely on hand to turn the rebound into the net.

The game produced a frantic final few minutes, with Reading's Williams missing an open goal. Fulham then took the game to Reading, searching for a late winner, and were unlucky not to get it in a nail-biting finish. The game finished **1–1**.

A few thought that Fulham had been slightly lucky to salvage a point, but many believed that the draw was a fair result. Certainly Fulham had never been allowed to settle and produce their known fluent football, but Reading had been too haphazard with their finishing to be fully deserving of the win. What was clear from this five-star clash was that both sides could be challenging for the honours come May.

On the Saturday Fulham took on **Halifax Town**, against whom they had scored ten goals the previous season, and Bill Dodgin decided to make changes. Fit-again Malcolm Webster was recalled in goal and Stan Brown, who had not enjoyed success on the right wing, was moved back to his customary number four shirt. John Richardson took the centre half shirt, with Reg Matthewson rested at substitute. Following Alan Morton's display against QPR, Dodgin brought him in for his league debut on the right wing.

Halifax were an improved side this season and were currently lying ninth. The Halifax team had changed little from the side that had visited the Cottage six months before. Halifax had in their ranks a goalkeeper called Barry White, and perhaps if the gargantuan 'walrus of love' had really been between the sticks, then Halifax may well have conceded fewer goals! One strange decision by Halifax was to play in a very peculiar strip of blue shirts and tangerine shorts. Fulham had a top class referee for this one, Tom Reynolds of Swansea.

As usual, Fulham searched for the early goal, and Les Barrett's low cross set up Steve Earle in the eighth minute, but he was just a little slow to convert. However, the team were in sparkling form and it didn't take Fulham long to score. In the seventeenth minute Earle gained possession, sold a smart dummy and centred. A harassed Halifax defender back-headed the ball and the confused Halifax goalkeeper Alex Smith fumbled it, leaving debutant Alan Morton with a simple chance that he converted with an angled shot.

Jimmy Dunne shields Malcolm Webster from a Halifax forward in a penalty-area tangle. The Yorkshire side gave the Fulham defence some scary second-half moments before the home side emerged as 3–1 winners.

Just ten minutes later Fulham doubled their lead: a good move between Barrett and Vic Halom allowed Earle to set up Barry Lloyd, and he scored with a crisp left-footed shot from eighteen yards that left keeper Smith standing. At this stage Halifax must have been feeling that they could concede another eight!

Sensing that this was going to be an easier afternoon, Fulham seemingly relaxed and were almost punished twice before half time. Firstly, Bill Atkins put centre forward Keith Brierley through the slack home defence and his shot scraped the outside of a post, and just three minutes later the same player was again just wide after winger Dave Chadwick had made a determined run beating three Fulham defenders. Fulham had been lucky; the scores could have easily been level by the interval.

Halifax made a determined start to the second half as well: Malcolm Webster saved Atkins' header, and a minute later winger Phil McCarthy curled a centre against the Fulham crossbar. This was the signal to wake up and Fulham broke away to increase their lead. In the fiftieth minute Halom's superb cross bypassed three Halifax defenders, leaving Earle with the simplest of chances to sidefoot the ball past the hapless goalkeeper.

Halifax still looked capable on the break and Lammie Robertson was twice unlucky, once with a shot just over the bar, and then with a shot that Webster pulled down with difficulty. Fulham had some further good fortune when Brierley finally beat the Fulham goalkeeper, but Mike Pentecost was well placed to clear off the line.

 Fulham had further bad luck on the injuries front, however, when debutant Morton badly injured an ankle and was carried off the pitch with suspected torn ligaments. Morton was replaced by Reg Matthewson, giving the attack an untidy imbalance. The adaptable Stan Brown was forced to return to his unfavoured right wing position.

Despite being well beaten, Halifax persisted with their attractive football. They continued to give the Fulham rearguard some scary moments. John Richardson looked uneasy at centre half and Mike Pentecost was having a difficult time against the tricky Halifax left-winger. Halifax finally gained some reward for their hard work when the dogged Robertson crossed and Brierley looped a classy headed goal over Webster for a deserved consolation a minute from time, but Fulham were ultimately comfortable **3–1** winners.

How Halifax must have hated Steve Earle! After the previous season's five-goal solo, he had once again inspired the Fulham forward line by scoring once and making the other two Fulham goals. The jittery Halifax defence had once again never really mastered him. However, Chadwick, Brierley and Robertson had all made the Fulham defence look cumbersome on occasions. The performance had been a lax and tired one in the last half-hour, and the team appeared to be conserving their energies for the League Cup tie looming the following week.

The injury to Alan Morton was unfortunate as he had seemed a decent prospect; however, due to other signings he was never again selected for a first team *league* match, joining a select band of Fulham players who played just one league game and scored in it.

Fulham were now twelve league games unbeaten – fourteen overall – and still progressing very well in the Ford Sporting League, a sponsored scheme covering the whole Football League designed to reward high-scoring teams. At this stage Fulham were ahead of *all* of the other ninety-one league clubs.

News for Fulham continued to improve when it was announced that defender Jimmy Dunne had been included in the Republic of Ireland squad for their European Nations Cup tie against Sweden. It was unfortunate for Dunne that Fulham felt that they could not release him for the match due to the forthcoming Swindon League Cup tie.

Fulham had just three days to recover before their massive fourth-round League Cup tie with **Swindon Town** at Craven Cottage. Swindon were a formidable side, having won the League Cup and gained promotion to the Second Division. A few months earlier they had become the first winners of the Anglo-Italian trophy with an incredible 3–0 success over Napoli in Italy in front of a 50,000 crowd. The doughty cup-fighting side could not be underestimated as two goals from winger Don Rogers had seen off the mighty Liverpool in the previous round.

The Swindon team contained Welsh international full back Rod Thomas, dangerous striker Peter Noble and mercurial match-winning winger Don Rogers. Also in the side was John Trollope, father of Paul, who would play for Fulham almost thirty years later. Absent from the side through injury was regular goalkeeper Peter Downsborough, replaced by Roy Jones. Swindon played in their usual red and white. Fulham were unchanged, Alan Morton seemingly recovered from the ankle injury. Referee Clive Thomas, a late replacement for Leo Callaghan, was given control of this tie. Another good crowd, of 22,500, turned up eagerly anticipating Fulham's next victims.

Fulham were given the best possible start – a goal inside the first three minutes. A flowing move, featuring half of the Fulham side, moved out of defence and progressed along the right wing. The ball found Alan Morton, and he created the goal with a fine cross along the edge of the box that found Steve Earle. Earle took aim and his shot from the edge of the area was deflected into the net off Frank Burrows and away from goalkeeper Jones.

From that moment the two sides, committed to attack, went at each other and most of the remaining match belonged to the visitors. Swindon forced seven corners in the first half, and Fulham three. The best Swindon chance fell to Rod Thomas who sprinted clear past Fulham's offside trap and ran twenty yards, only to slide his effort inches wide of the far post.

In the second half Swindon's dominance continued; again they forced seven corners, but with Fulham preoccupied with defence the home side failed to force a single one. Don Rogers was using every bit of his trickery to torment Mike Pentecost and, being ably supported by Thomas, looked like breaking Fulham.

In front of over 22,000, Fulham make an ideal start in their important League Cup tie against cup fighters Swindon. After just three minutes Steve Earle takes Alan Morton's centre and plants a right foot shot past Jones, the ball deflecting in. Swindon then produced eighty-seven minutes of relentless pressure, but somehow Fulham managed to hold out for a rather fortunate 1–0 victory. On the far left of the picture is John Trollope, father of Paul, later to play for Fulham.

However, Fulham stuck manfully to the task with Stan Brown, Barry Lloyd, John Richardson and Jimmy Dunne outstanding. They were also covering the inconsistent Malcolm Webster who, although making fine saves, was beginning to make a habit of rashly leaving his line for crosses that he failed to get. In this match he was fortunate to get away with his errors.

When Fulham broke, they broke quickly, and Earle was the pick of the forwards, fast and razor sharp, capable of running at the Swindon defence on his own in search of a second goal. With almost the entire Swindon side upfield, Earle caught the away side on the break and beat the keeper with a shot that was heading towards goal. Unfortunately the effort was just a little short, allowing a Swindon defender to dash back and stop the ball on the goal line and the goalkeeper to scamper back and retrieve.

Earle was doing a lot of work on his own. The other attackers just couldn't get going; passes were going astray, and the few shots that Fulham were able to muster were all off target. Earle sensed that the only way through was by 'going solo', running at the few Swindon defenders remaining at the back.

Swindon were now becoming desperate, with Rogers switching wings with John Smith. It was now Fred Callaghan's turn to receive a roasting from Rogers, but he just about held on. Richardson and Brown were becoming more confident in the middle and the threat from Arthur Horsfield and Peter Noble was finally diminishing.

Swindon launched one final foray, and in an hysterical goalmouth scramble the ball was finally edged untidily away, leaving Rogers shaking his head in disbelief that Swindon had not managed to touch the ball into the net. After what seemed an eternity the whistle finally blew and Fulham had edged home **1–0**.

After all the praise heaped on the goalscoring forwards, this match had been yet another triumph for the defence. The match was their tenth clean sheet of the season and the team had conceded just eleven goals in nineteen matches, three of those in one game. Swindon had become Fulham's third victims from a higher division and the Cottagers were now in the quarterfinal of the League Cup without having conceded a goal.

Although in truth Swindon had looked the better footballing side and had dominated the second half, they had also squandered a number of goalscoring chances that their impressive approach play had created, and had lost the tie for that reason. Fulham had again played well above their station; according to one reporter: 'Swindon were beaten by a Fulham side that made a laughing stock of their Third Division status.' Fulham's reward for this display was yet another tie at Craven Cottage and a fourth Second Division side in the shape of Bristol City. Bill Dodgin dwelt little on the detail of the match, just saying: 'It was a great result for us.' Fulham's proud record was now fourteen wins and just one defeat in the opening nineteen games.

The following day Bill Dodgin, now knowing that Jimmy Conway's recovery from injury was likely to take months rather than weeks, made his first foray into the transfer market by signing George Johnston from Birmingham City for a £7,000 fee.

Johnston, a Scotsman from Glasgow, had signed for Cardiff City upon leaving school in 1964. His goalscoring touch had developed him into a £30,000 player. Arsenal had paid that fee – a £25,000 deposit and a further £5,000 after he had played ten league games. In the season that he left Cardiff City, Johnston had scored twenty-seven goals in just twenty-nine appearances.

Johnston settled well at Highbury and put in many fine performances including scoring a late winner in a 4–3 victory over Leeds United. However, Arsenal thought they had better players and allowed him to leave. Birmingham City shelled out £20,000 for Johnston but his spell at St Andrews had not been a happy one, with just one goal in six appearances. He was, however, top scorer for their reserves with sixteen goals in just twenty-one games! It is possible that this is where Dodgin had seen Johnston, as Birmingham had visited the Cottage for a combination match a month previously. A loan spell at Walsall had also not been fruitful for George and he jumped at the chance to join Fulham.

Johnston's principal asset was his goalscoring; he was not tall, he was very stocky and pace was certainly not his main asset. However, he had experience, good skill and ball control, played using his brain, and above all had an eye for goal!

Jimmy Conway's injury had been worse than originally thought; he had been limping after many games and the tackle received during the Plymouth game had really made a mess of his knee. Conway had tried to continue training but collapsed after taking a shot in a training session, saying afterwards: 'It was as if the floor had collapsed underneath me.' Cartilage trouble was diagnosed and Conway had immediately undergone an operation; fortunately no significant damage was found. He was encased in plaster and likely to be out of the Fulham side for a minimum of five weeks.

A tired Fulham travelled all the way to Devon to play **Torquay United** on the Saturday, and Johnston was immediately given his debut, replacing Alan Morton in the number seven shirt. This was going to be a tough fixture; Jimmy Dunne would have to face his former colleagues and they would be out to prove that he had been wrong to leave them.

Torquay were also on very good form lying fourth in the table, with eight wins already and just four points behind the leaders. The home side were also fielding a debutant – Chris Barnard signed from Ipswich for £8,000 during the week. A juicy encounter was in prospect and the *Match of the Day* cameras made a rare drop into the Third Division to include the game as one of their televised matches. This was Fulham's eighth fixture in the month – in a space of just twenty-nine days.

Fulham possibly knew it was not going to be their day when their train was delayed by good ol' British Rail; in desperation, Bill Dodgin had to leave the train at Exeter and take a taxi to Torquay in order to hand the Fulham team sheet in on time, thus avoiding a mandatory £100 fine!

The matchday conditions were also very difficult, with a gale force wind blowing. It was a match that produced little good football, and the first half had little to commend it. Torquay goalkeeper Mike Mahoney put in one goal kick that was caught at the other end by Malcolm Webster before the ball had even bounced! Then, in an almost identical incident, Jimmy Dunne was forced in desperation to concede a corner on the first bounce from another enormous goal kick. Somehow Fulham went in level at half time with the match goalless.

In the second half the home team, the wind at their backs, upped the pressure and the visitors, for once, cracked. John Rudge, who had scored against Fulham in both league matches the previous season, was quickest to react, touching home Bill Kitchener's swirling, wind-assisted cross; Torquay were ahead.

Fulham did not heed the warning and former Villa star Tommy Mitchinson then got in on the act, scoring twice in the space of just two minutes. His first goal was a scrambled affair, and his second goal was a personal disaster for goalkeeper Webster; he jumped too late for a cross, allowing Mitchinson to push in front of him and head through his hands. Newcomer Barnard had had a hand in all three goals. At this point, the visitors' defence was definitely looking 'all at sea' on the coast.

For once, Fulham's small squad and tired legs had no answers. Torquay knew that the match was won and relaxed a little, allowing debutant Johnston to poach a consolation goal just five minutes from the end; at least this was a gem. Johnston collected the ball outside the box, turned quickly and shot into the corner of the net all in one movement. The goal had an element of luck about it inasmuch as former Villa man Richard Edwards, who was marking Johnston, still seemed dizzy following an earlier collision with Mike Pentecost. Johnston had obviously not yet settled into the team, and had been pretty anonymous throughout.

The match had been tough on skipper Barry Lloyd, who had put his heart and soul into whipping up a Fulham revival, but the Swindon Cup tie had taken its toll and Fulham slipped to a **1–3** defeat. It was hard to argue that Fulham had deserved anything from the game; Torquay had played well and Fulham had been too worn out to contain the energetic side.

Most neutrals agreed that the strong wind had ruined whatever chance there had been of making this a 'decent' flowing game. Certainly the conditions had not favoured Fulham's quick short-passing game. The forwards had looked anonymous nearly all match, with Vic Halom a pale shadow of the player he was just two months previously.

Without doubt it hadn't been a great Fulham show in front of the nation's cameras and, just like the previous season, Fulham's long unbeaten run had come to an end after fifteen matches! It was the first time that season that Fulham had played on a wet, difficult pitch, and Bill Dodgin's prediction that Fulham would prosper under such conditions had not come true on the day.

November 1970

In this month

* 146 died in a dance hall fire near Grenoble in France.
* Henry Cooper knocked out José Manuel Ibar to regain the European Heavyweight championship.
* The court martial began of Lt William Calley, accused of leading the Mylai massacre in Vietnam.
* Poland signed a treaty of reconciliation with West Germany.
* Missiles were thrown at the stage during the Miss World contest.
* A knife-wielding man was seized trying to attack Pope John Paul.
* A typhoon and subsequent tidal wave killed an estimated 150,000 people in East Pakistan.
* The Gay Liberation Front held its first demonstration in London.
* The number of days lost to industrial action and 'wildcat' strikes was the highest since 1926 – the year of the general strike.
* French statesman Charles de Gaulle died.

'Woodstock' by Matthews Southern Comfort topped the charts.
The film 'Ryan's Daughter' was released.

How the league was looking

Fulham still led the table, with Aston Villa ominously just a point behind. Bristol Rovers were still third, just a point behind Villa, and Torquay United held fourth spot, just two points behind Villa. Rotherham United had dropped to fifth, level on points with the rising Preston North End. These six clubs were seemingly just starting to edge away.

Gillingham had slumped to rock bottom with only eight points and Bury had fallen to one from bottom just two points better off. Doncaster were still in the bottom four, but Rochdale had put on a spurt and were now just on the fringes of the relegation spots. Tranmere Rovers, Port Vale and Wrexham had all made tremendous strides towards the middle and upper levels of the table, and it was now five 'new' clubs that had started to slide down the table – Swansea City with thirteen points, followed by four clubs on fourteen: Walsall, Barnsley, Brighton and Shrewsbury Town.

The matches

FULHAM HAD an opportunity to bounce back from the disappointing defeat at Plainmoor when they were visited by **Bury** for the first match in November. Bury were just one off the bottom place and their current form was poor. The Bury side, in red and white this year, contained a number of very experienced veterans including former Burnley and Blackpool wing-half Jimmy Robson, former Stoke City captain Tony Allen, former Manchester United, Burnley and England winger John Connelly, signed from Blackburn Rovers, and the former Crystal Palace and Aberdeen forward Tom White. Also in the Bury squad, but not playing on the day, was Manchester City's 'bad boy' Stan Bowles, loaned to Bury for three months in a hope that it would curb his 'wild' ways. Also coming through the Bury youth squad was a young player named Terry McDermott, described as 'versatile, with a good shot!' McDermott would go on to play a big part in several of Liverpool's triumphs over the next decade.

Fulham also made changes. Reg Matthewson returned at centre half and John Richardson took Jimmy Dunne's place in defence, after the defender claimed he was feeling unwell on the morning of the match. The match was the only one that Dunne would miss all season. New signing George Johnston was given a home debut, playing inside with Steve Earle switching to the wings. A miserable November afternoon brought a poor crowd of fewer than 9,500 to Craven Cottage; Norman Burtenshaw refereed the match.

The match was certainly not one to remember, and it took a fluke goal by Barry Lloyd after half an hour to put Fulham on their way. John Richardson sent Les Barrett away down the left and his quick cross targeted Lloyd in the box. Bury captain Tony Allen reached the ball first and volleyed the ball away low and hard. Unfortunately for him the ball hit Lloyd on the shins, and the rebound spun and floated into the roof of the net over the despairing fingertips of Bury goalkeeper Neil Ramsbottom.

The goal seemed very unfair as Bury at this stage appeared to have the upper hand, quicker in thought and deed and dominating the midfield with an outstanding performance from eighteen-year-old David Holt. There were large gaps appearing in the centre of the field where skipper Lloyd was being out-tackled.

Bury improved further after half time with winger Brian Grundy giving Mike Pentecost a difficult time and striker George Jones looking dangerous and Malcolm Webster was forced to make several saves to keep the home side ahead. Fulham's play was being dragged down to that of their opponents and Bury produced an unlikely equaliser from Tom White with just nineteen minutes left. In an isolated raid, Jones wriggled free on the left, a cross came over, Webster rashly committed himself to a catch, and veteran White climbed in front of and above him to head neatly home.

Fulham's play became even more disjointed when Jimmy Dunne's replacement Richardson suffered a thigh strain, needing to be replaced by full back Dave Moreline, who seemed unaccustomed to playing in the half back line. With Steve Earle isolated on the wings and Halom being bundled out of things in the middle, the game seemed to be petering out as a tame draw, with another valuable promotion point lost. Certainly, it looked as if Fulham's luck was going to be out when George Johnston cracked a first-time shot against the bar.

Finally, in stepped Les Barrett with just five minutes to go. Mike Pentecost produced a fine run down the wing and sent over a cross to Barrett on the left. Barrett, just outside the area, controlled the ball well, steadied himself and with all the time in the world sent a glorious shot into the top far corner of the net over the goalkeeper's head. A deflated Bury offered little response and a fortunate Fulham side ran out **2–1** winners.

Apart from the fact that the match had produced a win, there was little of positive note to report. The defence, with Reg Matthewson commanding and ably supported by Fred Callaghan and Stan Brown, had little to do, but the midfield and strike force had all been disappointing, Johnston having a very quiet match.

Bill Dodgin was obviously not happy with the general performance, stating: 'I was sure that we would improve further when the heavy grounds came, but there is no point in me hooting and complaining because we got two points. Nevertheless, it was a very disappointing display.'

Bury manager Colin Macdonald was obviously aggrieved at the result adding sourly: 'I don't think Fulham will go up, they are too unpredictable and their finishing is poor.'

The league's computer had forced another league fixture on Fulham just two days later when they travelled to the Potteries to meet promoted **Port Vale**. Port Vale held a spot just below mid table, but were seven games undefeated and had beaten high-fliers Aston Villa the previous week. Jimmy Dunne returned to the Fulham side.

It was immediately apparent how Vale had beaten Villa: they were quick out of the blocks and launched a number of aggressive raids. The Fulham defence was reeling and Reg Matthewson had to draw on every ounce of his experience to keep the sprightly Vale forwards at bay.

Malcolm Webster also had to be at his very best and he survived a hectic opening period, saving well from Vale forward Bobby Gough. Webster often came quickly off his line at the first sign of danger and seemed to be standing between Vale and a deserved opening goal.

After weathering the early Vale storm, Fulham broke out and stole a twenty-fifth minute lead. Vic Halom produced a fine right wing cross, and Barry Lloyd cleverly found space and met the ball squarely with his head from ten yards for a picture goal.

The second half was exactly the same, with Fulham hanging on against some furious and relentless attacking. Although Fulham were playing excellently in defence, the Vale forwards were not blameless, and they were guilty of not cashing in on the numerous chances they created. Malcolm Webster continued to make numerous saves, but was often helpless as Vale's efforts whistled just wide or fractionally over the bar. In the meantime Fulham could only muster two other goalscoring opportunities.

Vale in fact won ten corners in the second half, but Fulham were fortunate to have Matthewson and Jimmy Dunne in such fine form, and the defensive pair always appeared to be one step in front of the Vale forwards. Very little was going right for Vale in front of goal and late on, Mike Morris hit the outside of the post, half back John Green flashed a twenty-five yard shot inches over the bar, and Clint Boulton was just wide with another volley. In the end, a tired Fulham side held out bravely for a **1–0** win.

The win put Fulham four points clear at the top and the goal was Lloyd's eighth of the season. Without doubt, Fulham had been very fortunate to take both points and had on occasions been given the runaround, but it proved the point that this side could compete and battle it out physically, as well as playing attractive football. The game had been a keenly contested one, with Fulham receiving the rub of the green. Fulham had created just three goalscoring chances in the entire match, but had taken the one that mattered.

Five days later Fulham were on their travels again up to south Yorkshire to face **Rotherham United**. The northerners were on good form and were currently lying sixth in the table. On another cold day it promised to be a tough match. Sensing as much, Dodgin for once put out a more defensive formation with David Moreline taking the number eight shirt from Vic Halom, who was being rested in preparation for the League Cup quarter-final. Fulham switched to white socks.

In many ways the match mirrored the Monday game at Port Vale. The home side were immediately on the offensive. They were battling and running with the energy of a power station, stamping on any hopes Fulham had of an easy match. Early in the match goalkeeper Malcolm Webster sustained a knee injury and although badly impaired gamely carried on.

Although well in control, there was an element of luck about the Rotherham goal that gave the home side the lead in the eighteenth minute. John Fantham forced a corner from an attacking move. Jimmy Mullen took the inswinging kick and Webster was heavily challenged by a hefty combination of centre half Dave Watson and Trevor Phillips. The Fulham keeper was impeded and, as he was already injured, he could only manage to punch the ball into his own net.

Despite Rotherham's possession and physical play, they offered little threat in front of goal. However, Fulham were also making little impression up front. The Cottagers were putting neat moves together and zipping passes around, but were frustratingly not pulling the trigger when the chance arose. Finally Fulham began to flex their scoring muscles and Les Barrett smashed a shot against Rotherham goalkeeper Roy Tunks' post, the keeper well beaten.

The second half of the match was very similar to the first. Rotherham, with high energy, were increasing their stranglehold on the game without ever looking likely to extend their lead. Fulham were hanging in, but looking tired, and it appeared doubtful whether they would be able to raise their game further. Watson was still unfairly battering Webster, but the Fulham goalkeeper responded with some robust challenges of his own.

With just over twenty minutes to go, Rotherham started to relax, thinking that the one goal would be enough, and Bill Dodgin brought on Vic Halom for Stan Brown. Fulham immediately began to look more dangerous. It took just six minutes for Halom's presence to make a mark. Barrett accelerated along the right, outpaced Rotherham full back Dennis Leigh and crossed; Halom flicked the ball on, allowing George Johnston to steal in and cleverly roll the ball home from eight yards after a goalmouth scramble.

The match was not over and the injured Webster became the Fulham hero with just three minutes to go. Defender Watson, pushing forward, unleashed a surprise thirty yarder. Webster saw the ball late as it hurtled through a crowd of players, but somehow still managed a full-length dive to turn it away. This demoralised the home side, and Fulham clung to a **1–1** draw.

It had been a fighting performance with a lot of good football played, but Fulham were now beginning to look slightly jaded. The fixtures appeared to be catching up with them, and for a great deal of the match they had not looked leadership material.

The defence had once again proved to be the strong point, with both Reg Matthewson and Fred Callaghan again earning accolades for their fine performances. The highest mark was awarded

A never seen before Ken Coton picture sees George Johnston take Vic Halom's (12) deft flick from Barrett's cross and cleverly steer in Fulham's equaliser through a forest of Rotherham legs. This late goal secured a deserved point in a 1–1 draw at Millmoor.

to Dave Moreline who, despite playing in an unaccustomed position, stood out with fine tackling and hard running.

Things weren't so rosy up front. Steve Earle and Barry Lloyd had both looked badly out of touch and Johnston had clearly not settled in yet. Only Les Barrett was flying the forwards' flag consistently at this point. Fulham had scored more than one goal in just three out of the last thirteen league games.

Following the tough match in Yorkshire, Fulham had little time to recover before their important fifth-round League Cup tie with Second Division **Bristol City**. Fulham were hoping to exact some sort of revenge for the 0–6 mauling they had received at Ashton Gate two seasons previously. The Third Division was well represented in the competition, with both Aston Villa and Bristol Rovers also making the last eight.

Fulham, who were without Jimmy Conway, had a further problem in the right wing position, as George Johnston was cup-tied, having played for Birmingham in a previous round. With a small squad, Bill Dodgin decided to move full back Dave Moreline to the 'wing' position. Fulham were also hampered by the absence of first-choice goalkeeper Malcolm Webster who had not recovered from the knee injury sustained at Rotherham; Ian Seymour was therefore called upon to deputise.

The City side was much in line with the team that had played at the Cottage two seasons previously, the only major addition being centre half Dickie Rooks, signed from Middlesbrough. The Bristol side still contained the talented forward Chris Garland, coveted by many First Division clubs, who had done so much damage to Fulham in that 0–6 defeat. A certain Alan Dicks, who would become Fulham's manager two decades into the future, now managed Bristol City.

Fulham had to be confident, as City were again struggling in the Second Division and had not won away from home all season; they were sure to come with a draw in mind. The very poor weather conditions led to a very disappointing crowd of just over 16,000 at the Cottage. Fulham were able to hold the match on a 'lucky' Tuesday, a day that had seen them account for both QPR and Swindon Town. An ever-cautious Dodgin said: 'I don't want to forecast a result; I leave it to the lads, and let results speak for themselves. Promotion to division two is our number one target. We shall need some luck – as does any successful side – and the backing of our supporters. Already the buzz from the terraces has helped the lads, and there is plenty of confidence in our side.'

The match itself, played in a downpour lasting for almost the entire ninety minutes, was a very poor spectacle for a quarterfinal. The torrential rain quickly turned the pitch into a muddy quagmire that made good football difficult for both sides. There were numerous half-chances created by either side, but not a forward on view capable of converting them. Les Barrett was running his heart out on the flanks, but there was no one in the middle to convert his flow of crosses. Despite City's emphasis on defence, they looked the far more purposeful side in attack.

Fulham should have been behind in the eighth minute; City's Ken Wimshurst's clever pass put winger Gerry Sharpe clear on the left. Sharpe sprinted past Fulham's offside trap, and his curling shot beat Ian Seymour but left a muddy imprint on the base of the post.

It could have been worse; in the thirty-fourth minute Chris Garland spun and put in a ferocious left-foot volley from fifteen yards which Seymour dived spectacularly to reach and turn over between post and bar. For all their surging football, Fulham created just one worthwhile opportunity that Barrett wasted by stabbing weakly at Vic Halom's cross. City refused to buckle and rode out any first-half bombardments with a cool authority.

David Moreline's experimental run as a winger had failed badly and he had also suffered a muscle injury necessitating his withdrawal at half time. Fulham brought on fourth-choice winger Alan Morton, but this time the winger looked way out of his depth, contributing little to the second half. Fulham's continuing threat came from Barrett on the left flank, but even when he twice sped past City defender Alan Drysdale early in the half, Fulham's front two players were always heavily outnumbered.

The continuing inclement weather was making decent football impossible on a skidpan of a pitch and Fulham's lightweight forwards were struggling. Both teams were having to use the wings to get the ball moving at all. The mud suited the rugged, tough-tackling City defenders, and they definitely began to get the upper hand.

Having weathered what little Fulham could throw at them, City came forward and were desperately close to winning the game in the second half. Goalkeeper Ian Seymour had been roughed up, suffering kicks from City forwards John Galley and Ian Broomfield, and this had seemed to unsettle the goalkeeper in the second half, when he mis-handled several crosses and shots. However, he was still able to make match-winning saves when it really mattered.

City should have taken the lead ten minutes after half time when Garland climbed well to nod a centre from the left back across goal. However, with Fred Callaghan helpless, City's Broomfield slipped in the mud at the last minute in front of a wide-open goal and the chance was lost. Minutes later Stan Brown mis-cued a clearance straight to Galley, but fortunately his volley was just inches the wrong side of a post, with Seymour stranded. Finally, Reg Matthewson's frenzied thirty-yard back pass eluded Seymour, but luckily for Fulham landed on the roof of the net.

The League Cup tie against Bristol City has just finished 0–0. Rain has poured down throughout the entire match. Police and St John's finish up their duties. Fans with and without umbrellas look at each other and wonder why they bothered to turn up.

Fulham piled on the pressure in the final ten minutes with a late attacking surge, but with Rooks and David Rodgers outstanding in the Bristol defence, Fulham's floating crosses never looked enough to unhinge them. Fulham did have a chance to win the game just four minutes from the end when Halom headed downwards, but Matthewson's shot was placed straight at City goalkeeper Mike Gibson. A very unsatisfactory and untidy match finished **0−0**.

Fulham would have to hope that their fine away form would put additional pressure on the home defence in the replay. However, Fulham had done nowhere near enough on the night and none of the home forwards had looked on any real form. They had been very fortunate indeed to earn a second crack at the tie. Certainly City had made nearly all of the chances and received all of the misfortune.

The match created an interesting note as, including the Watney Cup match, it was the first time that Fulham had failed to score that season – a run of *twenty-five matches*. Fulham were the last team in the entire Football League to record a 'blank' ninety minutes that season! At least Fulham's record of not conceding a goal in the League Cup had still been maintained! Bill Dodgin, ever the realist, conceded: 'Obviously we are up against it now, and City will run themselves into the ground to try and beat us, but we haven't completely lost hope.'

After the first Bristol encounter, their counterparts **Bristol Rovers** arrived at the Cottage on the Saturday to contest the first round of the FA Cup. Rovers were still managed by Bill Dodgin's father, Bill senior. It was going to be another tough match as Rovers were on *very* impressive form, and they now lay in second spot, just one point behind Fulham in the Third Division table. In a coincidental first-round FA Cup draw, the divisions' third- and fourth-placed clubs, Aston Villa and Torquay United, had also been drawn against each other.

Fulham's only change was that of George Johnston, who was recalled to the right wing, as he was eligible to play in the FA Cup. The Rovers side was almost the same as the previous season, the only major addition being that of the former Sheffield Wednesday captain Don Megson at right half. The game drew a good attendance of almost 14,000. The pitch, after many successive days of rain, again looked in poor condition.

This time there was a significant improvement in the performance, especially amongst the forwards. Numerous chances were created but, as in the Tuesday game, all were frittered away. The first twenty minutes were dominated totally by Fulham and Rovers were seldom out of their own half. Fulham could and should have been three ahead by half time.

Star winger Les Barrett was creating all the opportunities, but they were being spurned with profligate finishing; Stan Brown, Vic Halom and George Johnston all missed convertible chances, and Dick Sheppard saved well from Steve Earle. The experienced Don Megson and the dynamic young Welsh pair, Bryn Jones and Frankie Prince, were holding Fulham back with grim determination.

Without a goal in the first half, the home side's confidence dropped, the off-the-ball running slowed and Rovers, beginning to sense a chance, went at Fulham, slowly turning the screw. On the heavy pitch Fulham persisted in short passing and were rapidly becoming bogged down. Rovers were making far better use of the ball using long passes, needing only one where Fulham were requiring two or three. Rovers also put an extra defender on Barrett, who was creating most of the chances for Fulham.

It wasn't long before their more direct methods paid off when, ten minutes after half time, Bryn Jones' searching pass put Carl Gilbert through. The burly, blond striker rode a tackle and calmly finished with a beautiful, angled twenty-yard ground shot into the far corner of the net over Ian Seymour's hands. Seymour did, however, appear to be rather slow in his reactions when going down.

Twenty minutes later, following a rebound, another arcing, pinpoint pass from Jones sent Ray Graydon away on the right. His cross landed perfectly for Gilbert at the far post, unmarked and finding space following an intelligent run, to grab his second, sliding the ball with power past Seymour.

Only in the final quarter of an hour did Fulham really threaten. The home side gained some consolation when Johnston dribbled through the Rovers defence and scrambled the ball home

A supporter has his hands on his head, as a Bristol Rovers defender heads yet another Fulham effort from the goal line with the keeper beaten; George Johnston is once again the unlucky victim. Despite a dominant first half, Fulham conceded two goals in twenty minutes in the second half, and Bill Dodgin (senior) was the victor in this particular Cup duel. Fulham lost 1-2, going out of the FA Cup in the first round for the second year in succession. Below is Ken Coton's picture of the same incident, apparently taken at precisely the same moment! At least Ken wasn't putting his hands on his head; instead he kept his finger firmly on his camera's button.

via the underside of the bar with just five minutes to go. Bill Dodgin senior couldn't bear to watch the last five minutes and left the dugout for the safety of the changing room! In a frantic last five minutes, with Fulham swarming around the Rovers goal, both Johnston and Earle had magnificent headed efforts brilliantly saved by Sheppard in the Rovers goal. However, the late surge wasn't enough and Fulham crashed out of the Cup **1–2**, losing their unbeaten home record in the process.

For the second successive season Fulham had been dumped out of the prestigious trophy at the first hurdle, something that displeased chairman Tommy Trinder, as once again the defeat denied Fulham the opportunity of cashing in with a 'big-name' draw.

Fulham had played the better, copybook football but their finishing had been woeful. Steve Earle and George Johnston both had undistinguished games, and only Les Barrett had shone, most of his crosses being totally wasted. Secretly, with a fifth round League Cup replay looming and a tough league fixture list, Dodgin junior was probably not too bothered. Most neutrals agreed that Rovers had been rather fortunate to win.

Bill Dodgin junior commented after the game to his father: 'What do you think of my lot letting you off like that; we should have been at least three up by half time.' Bill senior replied: 'Fulham gave us a lesson in the first twenty minutes and we were lucky to be alive by half time. But we went at them in the second half and got two great goals. Of course I feel sorry for young Bill, no two people in football are closer than we are, but if we were out there playing snakes and ladders, I'd still be all out to beat him!'

The match, however, had produced a stirring game that brought many comments from the press. One reporter said: 'This duel of the Dodgins lived up to all these two managers preach and practise. It was stirring, spectacular, clean and sporting.'

After this disappointment, Fulham had to prepare themselves mentally for the League Cup **replay** and a third consecutive fixture against a Bristol side. A crowd in excess of 23,000 was drawn to Ashton Gate for the game. The game was officiated by Jack Taylor. George Johnston was once again cup-tied, and so Bill Dodgin gambled with a more defensive formation, playing Stan Horne at right wing; defender Dave Roberts was named as substitute. To avoid a clash, Fulham switched to white socks.

Bristol City tried to attack at the start, and the first fifteen minutes belonged solely to the home side. The away side received a boost in this period when £100,000-rated City striker Chris Garland had to be carried off with a leg injury following a clash with Mike Pentecost as early as the eighth minute. It initially looked as if he had fractured his leg, but fortunately the injury turned out to be just heavy bruising.

Fulham weathered the early storm, and the game appeared evenly matched. But just when it looked as if Fulham might get on top, they conceded a needless penalty. There were no arguments about the decision; Stan Brown brought down winger Alan Skirton inside the box as he surged through the middle. Referee Taylor awarded the spot kick that Gerry Sharpe converted. It was his first penalty in seven years with City.

In the second half, Fulham were far the superior footballing side and City were defending desperately. According to the media, Fulham produced some of the finest attacking moves seen at Ashton Gate all season. The game was similar to Saturday's FA Cup tie, with Fulham playing neat football, creating the chances but not putting them away. Steve Earle, Les Barrett and Vic Halom were all desperately unlucky near goal. Time after time the away forwards scythed through the home defence but the final pass just wasn't there. Halom's miss was the worst, heading over from Earle's pinpoint centre when totally unmarked.

Fulham were showing more construction and polish in everything they did. They had to be wary of counter-attacks, but Ian Seymour made a super save from John Galley, diving full length to turn his drive away. City retreated into deep defence with no pretensions about tactics – content to hold onto their slender one-goal advantage. In fact, City were so poor that slow handclapping burst out from the home supporters.

As the clock ran down, Fulham forced one final surge. Jimmy Dunne, up with the forwards, connected with a low cross, only to see the ball hit the legs of goalkeeper Mike Gibson, who was

A sad end to a great run as Fulham are edged out 0–1 at Ashton Gate in the League Cup fifth round replay. Fulham were denied a clear penalty two minutes from time and the relief of the Bristol City players at the final whistle is almost palpable. Certainly the better side lost, and Fulham went out of their second cup competition in just four days.

diving the other way. Then, just sixty seconds from the end, Barrett was clearly brought down in the box by a clumsy tackle from City defender Geoff Merrick; the incident was a carbon copy of the one that had brought City their first-half penalty. However, referee Taylor controversially ruled 'no foul' and the last chance was gone; Fulham slid out of their second cup competition in just four days **0–1**, having conceded just one goal in the six matches of the competition.

The City players hugged their Fulham counterparts, such was their relief; they were almost embarrassed to have won. Even City manager Alan Dicks described the home side's win as 'disappointing and unsatisfactory'. Bill Dodgin was angry about the decision that had denied Fulham a money-spinning semi-final with Alan Mullery and London rivals Tottenham Hotspur. He said: 'We feel cheated ... we should have had a penalty for that [foul on Barrett] in the last two minutes. I've no quibble with the penalty that the referee gave Bristol in the first half, but this was an identical offence. What can you say? We missed our chances again, great chances in the second half, although not as many as we missed on Saturday against Rovers ... my only regret is that we gave City the chance of a replay ... we played the better football with nothing to show for it. At least we have not dropped any league points and we are now clear to carry on the drive for promotion. We are getting our rhythm and balance back.'

The press headlined: 'Poor Fulham let down by attack and referee.' Another said, 'There is no doubt that the better footballing side lost.' A third commented: 'City go into the records as probably the worst side ever to reach a League Cup semi-final.' Fulham had emerged with all the glory, but not the result. It was a great shame; if Fulham could have conquered City and then Tottenham, it would have been an all Third Division League Cup final, as Aston Villa defeated Bristol Rovers and then the mighty Manchester United en route to the final at Wembley. Fulham had been hustled out of both cup competitions by a club from Bristol.

On the subject of **Aston Villa**, the Midland side were the next visitors to the Cottage on the ensuing Saturday. Villa, now League Cup semi-finalists, were on good form and playing consistently well. They were lying in fourth place, but now just four points behind Fulham. The Villains contained some old faces but they had improved their strength in depth. Villa had signed the Luton Town pair Bruce and Neil Rioch, and in their forward line was veteran warhorse Andy Lochhead, formerly of Burnley. At inside left for Villa was Ian 'Chico' Hamilton who had been a colleague of Barry Lloyd in the Chelsea reserve side. Winger Jimmy McMahon was also a new face on the right wing, signed from Glasgow Celtic.

Predictably, the only Fulham change was the return of George Johnston as a replacement for Stan Horne, who was made substitute. The famous opposition brought the best league crowd of the season to date down to Fulham – over 16,000. In the space of just five seasons, Fulham had now played Aston Villa in *three* different divisions! The poor weather had not abated, and the pitch was again muddy and rutted, totally unsuited to Fulham's passing style of play.

Fulham had the edge in the early stages and Fred Callaghan was urging the team forward from full back. However, what little gloss there was in this encounter soon wore off and the match quickly degenerated into a dour and rugged midfield contest, devoid of almost any style.

Perhaps the teams had too much respect for each other, but both sides' cagey approach and chessboard marking left the spectators with little to write home about. For two sides with such a cavalier approach, both teams played as if they had a fear of losing. The pitch condition made good football a virtual impossibility and even passes on the best part of the pitch, along the flanks, were bobbling astray or going into touch. Ball control and touch for either side was proving to be a nightmare.

Villa were just about shading the encounter due to their harder running and better all-round understanding. On the day, the Midlanders looked the more likely team to score. The Fulham forwards seemed to be at their lowest ebb. Steve Earle, George Johnston and Vic Halom all seemed to have little appetite or fight for the encounter, and Barry Lloyd was losing out on most of the fifty-fifty balls. Fulham persisted in ploughing through the middle but this was finding no success at all. Les Barrett was the only player who looked hungry, but poor passing and pitch conditions were literally starving him of the ball.

The game continued along this way in the second half. It clearly looked as if the first goal would win it, and it was a case of which team would crack first; unfortunately that team was nervy Fulham. Villa winger Willie Anderson was now venturing out, running into different positions in the forward line and creating chances for others. Villa suddenly seemed to sense the opportunity to grab the extra point.

Just before the goal, the writing was on the wall when Stan Brown, with Ian Seymour beaten, headed away a Pat McMahon header from right underneath the bar. With just a quarter of an hour left, Ian Hamilton put the visitors ahead with a flashing, curling drive from an acute angle. The goal had a great deal of luck about it. Many thought that the attempt was an intended cross; the effort deceived Seymour, swerved onto the crossbar and dropped down, being unluckily deflected into the net by the luckless Brown running back.

Fulham had immediate chances to restore parity. The best of these occurred when Villa goalkeeper Dunn carelessly dropped a cross at Johnston's feet, but the forward skied the ball unhandsomely wide from just six yards. Fulham's heads immediately dropped and Villa bagged a second goal just seven minutes later.

The move began with a misplaced Fulham pass, again from Johnston, in the Villa penalty area. Hamilton again gained possession from Brian Godfrey in a swift counter-attack, and he pulled the ball nicely back from the goal line and across the goalmouth for McMahon to score with a totally mis-hit shot from twelve yards that bounced past Seymour's groping hands. Game over, a listless Fulham offered nothing in reply, losing **0–2**.

The result had a much more significant impact inasmuch as the defeat knocked Fulham from the top of the division. It had been a grim struggle full of misplaced passes and tackles; the abject performance was Fulham's worst of the season.

It was difficult to find anything positive to say about either team. Most of the class had come from the experienced players on the field, Fulham's Reg Matthewson and Villa's Willie Anderson. Certainly Fulham's tired play and woeful finishing had carried an air of dejection. To make matters worse, during the weekend snippets of the match were shown on television, certainly not presenting the Cottagers in their best light.

The press pulled no punches about Fulham's performance and were highly critical, one saying: 'The confident style visible earlier in the season was gone, and by comparison, this display was a shambles.' Another asked the question: 'Has Fulham's promotion burst burnt out?' After three defeats in a row, the Cottage faithful were starting to become more than slightly nervous. The

The promotion pressure begins to tell and Fulham begin to show the strain. Referee Kenneth Sweet tells Vic Halom and Villa's Brian Tiler to make up and get on with it. On a gluepot pitch a tired Fulham lost their unbeaten home record 0–2 to close rivals Aston Villa. It was the start of a winless streak.

only piece of good news to come out of the Cottage was that Jimmy Conway would soon be back in training again.

A clearly angry and frustrated Les Barrett gave a rare press interview the following day. He talked frankly, and said: 'We played with little enthusiasm against Villa, and they won nearly every fifty-fifty ball. We needed a dressing down from the boss earlier in the season as we went into matches thinking our skill alone would see us through. Fortunately, we did well so there was no need for the boss to say anything.

'Now we have got into the habit of not producing 100% physical effort, and it is beginning to have a bad effect on our chances of going up. Our style of play is unsuited to heavy pitches. Barry Lloyd is great at slipping the ball along the gulleys for the wingers to chase, but these passes lose their accuracy on a muddy surface. That's all the more reason why we must show more determination.'

December 1970

In this month

* MPs rejected a move to keep British Summer Time in winter.
* The Industrial Relations Bill was published, and the Industrial Relations Court was set up with the power to fine trade unions.
* Six people died over two days as a result of rioting over escalating food prices in Gdansk in Poland.
* Paul McCartney formally issued a suit to Lennon, Starr and Harrison to dissolve 'The Beatles and Co'.
* The outstanding British runner Lillian Board died from cancer at the tragically early age of twenty-two.

'I Hear You Knocking' by Dave Edmunds topped the charts.
The film 'Love Story' was released.

How the league was looking

Fulham had now dropped off the top of the table and Bristol Rovers had taken over, a point clear. Aston Villa were in third place, just two points behind Fulham. Preston North End had sustained their great run to be tucked in at fourth place. Torquay United and Rotherham United still held the fifth and sixth places. These top six sides were looking to be the ones who would decide the promotion places.

Gillingham were still rock bottom with just eleven points, and Bury were still one from bottom, now level on points. Rochdale had dropped back into the relegation spots, joined for the first time by Walsall. Three clubs were just outside, level on points with Walsall: Barnsley, Doncaster Rovers and Brighton. Shrewsbury Town had improved considerably and were now in mid-table.

The matches

TO PEP up the attack Fulham announced a surprise loan signing at the beginning of the month, going back to Griffin Park to sign longhaired winger Alan Mansley for a month. Brentford's Mansley had flair and trickery and was capable of scoring goals. In the first match of the month, Fulham visited **Mansfield Town**, bringing in Dave Moreline for Mike Pentecost, who had had a stinker against Villa, and Stan Horne in a defensive number seven shirt; Mansfield held eighth place but were beatable.

Goalkeeper Ian Seymour had no chance with the goal in the sixteenth minute that decided the match. Dudley Roberts chased a long ball from ex-Birmingham keeper Jim Herriot from the halfway line, kept possession, and bent a shot around Reg Matthewson and Seymour as he advanced from goal.

Steve Earle was foraging on his own up front with very little support; he broke through once only for Stuart Boam to clear his goalbound effort off the line. Fulham were proving unpopular with their tough tackling and repeated use of the offside trap. In the end, the home crowd started to slow handclap Fulham for their negative and stifling play. Roberts was unlucky not to claim a hat trick, with two other superb efforts kept out only by the agility of Seymour.

Fulham only came into the match in the final quarter of an hour, when they replaced the ineffective Vic Halom with George Johnston, moving Fred Callaghan into midfield. Callaghan immediately brought some aggression to the area, but was booked soon afterwards for a late tackle. Johnston immediately added some life into the forward line as well and was very unlucky with an astute header that hit the Mansfield post and bounced back into play with the goalkeeper beaten.

Vic Halom's header beats Boam's boot, but the effort flashes just wide of the angle of post and bar with the goalkeeper beaten. This was a rare foray on the Mansfield goal. Fulham's patchy form was still much in evidence and they slumped to a 0–1 defeat at Field Mill.

This was as good as it got, and Mansfield were soon in the driving seat again. Fulham lost meekly **0–1**; their fourth consecutive defeat.

No one could argue that Fulham had been unlucky, despite the narrow margin of the defeat. If it had not been for goalkeeper Ian Seymour, fortunately in top form, the margin of defeat would undoubtedly have been higher.

With a small squad and twenty-eight matches already played, Bill Dodgin resisted the temptation to arrange a friendly for the following weekend, scheduled for the second round of the FA Cup, deciding instead to give the players a deserved rest. To try to remove some of the tension building up in the squad, the club decided to allow the players to take a short break in the Channel Islands with a trip to Jersey in order 'to try to forget our recent results'.

The captain Barry Lloyd spoke honestly as usual when he said: 'We will just relax, and when we return it will be like starting a new season. We are lacking confidence at the moment, and the good results of Aston Villa, Preston, Bristol Rovers and Torquay are not helping us to settle down. They are not good sides, I am sure that they will fall away.'

Whether it had been the Mansfield performance, resting players or dropping them, Fulham's team at **Swansea City** a week later showed numerous changes. Swansea had improved considerably in recent weeks and now held an almost mid-table position. Stan Brown was omitted, allowing Stan Horne to return to his normal right half position. Centre half Reg Matthewson was also omitted, giving a first game of the season to blond defender Dave Roberts. Les Barrett switched to the 'wrong' right wing, with George Johnston moving inside to replace the omitted Vic Halom. Loan signing Alan Mansley came in for his league debut on the left wing.

Swansea were on top from the start, with centre forward David Gwyther giving young Dave Roberts a torturous time both in the air and on the ground. It took Gwyther just fifteen minutes to score. A Len Allchurch corner was headed back unchallenged across the goalmouth by City's Brian Evans, Gwyther's first header hit the crossbar, but he reacted the quickest to barge and bundle the rebound into the net. Then, just seven minutes later, he scored again. He darted into a clever position away from his defender, took Evans' pass, strode impudently around Ian Seymour, and rolled the ball into an empty net.

After a half time roasting from Dodgin, Fulham reduced the arrears within two minutes of the restart. Barry Lloyd slipped in between Swansea defenders Geoff Thomas and Mel Nurse, took the ball to the dead ball line and put in a low, hard cross. It was too hot for home goalkeeper Tony Millington to hold, and it fell nicely for George Johnston to round off; Johnston had now bagged an impressive four goals in only eight matches.

However, Fulham's luck was really out, and just five minutes later the impressive Fred Callaghan sustained an injury and had to be replaced by Stan Brown. Brown ran everywhere trying to plug holes but it was no use; the Fulham side almost seemed to accept that a rout would occur.

Fulham fell further behind midway through the second half when the impressive Gwyther combined with Herbie Williams, enabling him to restore Swansea's two-goal cushion. Gwyther crossed accurately and Williams dived full length to head in. Just ten minutes later the drubbing was complete. Williams sprang Fulham's desperate offside trap, ran half the length of the field and drew Seymour from the goal line before executing the perfect chip over the stranded goalkeeper. Seymour was now often alone, making breathtaking saves to keep the score down. Both Gwyther and Williams were denied hat tricks by the agile custodian. The Cottagers were now a beaten side and a dejected Fulham team trudged off **1–4** losers.

The result had made it an unprecedented five consecutive defeats and no win in seven matches. Fulham had thrashed Swansea City easily in August by the same score and on Saturday had shipped four goals for the first time in sixteen months. Fulham hadn't lost by a three-goal margin since the disastrous Second Division season. Only skipper Lloyd, Brown and Dave Moreline performed to anywhere near their capabilities.

For once, the normally placid Dodgin was furious with Fulham's 'performance'. He stormed: 'We have no excuses. Swansea had all the determination. We played it like losers; there just wasn't enough effort. ... It was our worst display so far. We haven't played well for a bit, but nothing as bad as this. Too many of the lads were feeling sorry for themselves, were too slack and not determined enough, but what's the use of ranting and raving?'

This dismal showing finished the Fulham careers of no less than three players. In the case of goalkeeper Ian Seymour it was surprising. Seymour had played superbly over the previous month but despite his heroics didn't play for the first team again. Centre half Dave Roberts was also dropped back to the reserves, never to be seen again. Winger Alan Mansley could not have impressed either as his loan arrangement was not extended and he returned to Brentford at the end of the month. It would also be four months before Stan Horne would play another league game. In this season, three players – Alan Morton, Roger Davidson and Alan Mansley – would each play just one league match for the club before moving on.

The Christmas **Gillingham** encounter had been moved from the Saturday Boxing Day to avoid the big Chelsea versus Crystal Palace derby match. The programme notes mentioned nothing at all about the three previous defeats. Originally this match had been scheduled for the Monday evening, but had been brought forward, very late in the day, to the afternoon.

It was the first time in a number of years that Fulham had not played at all over the Christmas period for any reason other than postponements due to bad weather. However, the icy season had blown in, and there had been some snow over Christmas. The Fulham match had not been in serious doubt, but snow and ice had to be cleared from the pitch in order that the match could go ahead. At kick-off time, large piles of snow still sat on the cinder track surrounding the pitch. The pitch was still in a very poor and muddy condition. The game would almost certainly not have been played today.

Even on their poorest form of the season, this was a match that Fulham had to be confident of winning. Gillingham were rock bottom with just eleven points; the Kent team had won just three times all season. The Gillingham side was similar to the one that had faced Fulham the previous season; the only significant new face was that of a young half back Dick Tydeman later to play for Charlton Athletic. In the Gillingham forward line was Mickey Darrell, who had been a transfer

On a frozen pitch, the match gets the go-ahead after the lines are cleared of snow. This was a midweek match during the day and the attendance is sparse. In terrible conditions, Vic Halom's close range toe-poke slithers under Gillingham goalkeeper Simpson for the only goal in a 1–0 victory. On the day, the result was far more important than the performance. It was Fulham's first win in eight outings in three competitions.

target for Fulham the previous season whilst with Birmingham City. Gillingham set their stall out by naming full back David Peach as a left winger.

Fulham made significant changes from the side thrashed at the Vetch Field. Out went Seymour, Horne, Roberts, Johnston and Mansley and in came Webster, Pentecost, Brown, Matthewson and Halom. The late switching of the time of the match backfired badly, with many supporters confused about the kick-off time. It was *not* a public holiday and a mere fraction over 7,000 turned out, Fulham's lowest crowd of the season.

In footballing terms, the match was a non-event, both teams slithering around desperately trying to keep their feet. Neither side could master the conditions, which was hardly surprising. It would have taken skis or ice-skating boots to remain standing. Although at times much of the play resembled Christmas pantomime farce, with players falling on their faces or backsides in the mud, both teams tried hard to provide some sort of entertainment. In truth there was little for the spectators to become excited about; judgement of pace was nigh on impossible and the game was littered with misplaced passes.

The only real chance of the first twenty minutes came when Les Barrett seized upon a mis-kick from Jim McVeigh summoning the first of a number of good saves from Gillingham goalkeeper John Simpson.

Fulham took the lead with a goal by Vic Halom just two minutes before half time. Lloyd's shot ricocheted violently off Gillingham's defensive wall and landed right in Halom's path. Before the Gillingham defenders could regain their balance and the goalkeeper could unglue himself from the far post, Halom controlled the ball and slotted it low into the inviting net. It was Halom's first goal for almost three months.

Although the Cottagers were by far the better technical side, playing the better football, nearly all of the clear-cut chances were made, and somehow spurned, by Gillingham. Brian Yeo, standing just two yards from the Fulham goal, somehow contrived to hit the Fulham crossbar. Reg Matthewson's unbalanced headed clearance dropped like a stone outside the box, Tydeman chipped the ball over and Yeo, with Malcolm Webster slipping, failed to convert the gift chance.

Then Andy Smillie beat two faltering Fulham defenders before blasting his shot straight at Webster when it looked easier to score. Following this, the unmarked Mike Green also put his shot over the angle of post and bar when he had time to measure his shot. Finally, early in the second half, Yeo slipped on his back and managed to scoop the ball wide of a gaping goal.

It was not all one-way traffic, however, and the Kent team's goalkeeper Simpson made good stops from Steve Earle and Les Barrett, but in the main the Gillingham defence managed to keep the Fulham team at distance, and long shots from outside the penalty area from Fred Callaghan and Barry Lloyd were easily dealt with. Gillingham's McVeigh almost increased the home side's lead with a hasty clearance that would have been a spectacular own goal had Simpson not intervened.

Fulham began to realise that their pretty, short passing game was getting the team nowhere, so at least tried to change with long passes. After fifteen minutes without success from the long ball game, Fulham returned to their normal style. As the freezing darkness began to descend again Fulham were able, somehow, to record a **1–0** win.

It had been a very poor game but in the circumstances the result had been far more important than the performance. The run of five defeats had at least been halted. Although Fulham had arrested their poor run, few could have been fooled by the overall performance. Bottom of the table Gillingham had made the better chances overall, and had deserved at least a draw. One reporter wrote: 'The score [Halom's goal] brought a sane outcome to the farce which had gone before and continued after the interval. This was not a football match, it was a game of chance played on a pitch which resembled a Christmas cake after the rats had got at it, snow covered around the outside and increasingly muddy in the middle. ... it seems ridiculous that vital points for promotion or relegation should be at stake on such a pitch.'

All of Fulham's current failings were still very much in evidence. Fulham had lost most of the battles in midfield again, and hadn't seemed to want to keep hold of the ball – confidence badly lacking. Captain Barry Lloyd had the look of someone who wished that he was somewhere else. Steve Earle and Vic Halom had produced little and the fire and thrust even appeared to have deserted Les Barrett, who until recently had looked the only forward capable of igniting the front line.

The end of the year sounded a dismal note, described by the programme as a 'grey spell'. Fulham were not just out of the top position, but were now also out of the two promotion places as well. Bristol Rovers were still top and Aston Villa were now second. Fulham were now four points behind Rovers, who had lost just two league games to date, but were just one point behind Villa.

Was this season going to be a total opposite of the previous season, with an excellent start followed by a declining and faltering finish? There were reasons to be optimistic, however, as in the last *calendar* year Fulham had won twenty-four league matches, drawn fourteen and lost just eight of forty-six matches played.

It was very clear though that Bill Dodgin still had plenty of work to do in order to restore the morale of his fragile side and get them back into the two promotion places.

January 1971

In this month

* The new divorce law came into force making 'irretrievable breakdown of marriage' sole grounds.
* President Milton Obote of Uganda was overthrown by his Army commander Idi Amin.
* Charles Manson was found guilty of the Sharon Tate murders.
* The postal workers went on strike for the first time ever.
* Sixty-six died and over 200 were crushed when crowd barriers collapsed at Glasgow Rangers' Ibrox stadium during a match against Glasgow Celtic.
* Hundreds were feared dead after a cyclone in Mozambique.
* A modified rocket, *Apollo XIV,* took off with the next manned lunar mission.
* Fashion designer Gabrielle 'Coco' Chanel died aged eighty-seven.
* Boxer Sonny Liston died.

'Grandad' by Clive Dunn topped the charts.
The film 'Little Big Man' was released.

How the league was looking

Bristol Rovers still led the table, three points clear of Aston Villa in second place. Fulham were third, a point behind Villa, but the Cottagers were only ahead of consistent Preston North End on goal average. Torquay United and Rotherham United still held onto the fifth and sixth places. The top six sides were still looking to be the teams who would decide the promotion places.

Gillingham were still rock bottom with just eleven points and were beginning to lose touch, and Rochdale were now one from bottom but three points better off. Bury had picked up points and were on the rise, but Walsall were still stuck in the bottom four. Swansea and Barnsley had improved no end and were moving towards mid-table safety. Three clubs were just outside the trouble zone: Doncaster Rovers, Brighton and, for the first time, Bradford City. The bottom of the table was now beginning to spread out, and these looked to be the seven likely candidates for the drop.

The matches

THE FIRST match of the New Year saw Fulham travel to the Racecourse to take on **Wrexham**. Wrexham were climbing the table and were just over half way, but this was always a difficult place to visit. Fulham were unchanged.

It took Fulham just three minutes to score. Fred Callaghan and Steve Earle provided the opening that allowed Les Barrett to run through and score with a half-hit shot. It was a difficult pitch, hard underneath and soft on top, but Earle and Barrett were masters of the conditions, giving the Wrexham defenders a tough time. Barry Lloyd drove just over the bar and Barrett put another shot into the side netting. Albert Kinsey missed a great chance to put Wrexham level when he hooked wide before Fulham streaked two goals ahead on the half hour; for once it was Fulham's turn to receive a gift.

Under pressure, Wrexham full back Steve Ingle lobbed the ball back from thirty yards over the hands of the despairing ex-Manchester United goalkeeper Dave Gaskell for a classic own goal. Fulham's eager attacking had the home defence rocking, and Fulham were unfortunate not to add to their score before the interval.

A half-time substitution by Wrexham, who brought on former Blackpool winger Ian Moir for Brian Tinnion, totally transformed the game. His clever footwork and trickery had the Fulham defence up against it. Fulham's defence was beginning to panic and the away side resorted to playing the offside trap, much to the annoyance of the home crowd. Midway through the half, the home side pulled a goal back. Centre half Eddie May, up with the forwards, let fly with a tremendous shot from fully forty yards that whistled past Malcolm Webster, rooted in the mud.

Fulham looked as if they would hold out for a much needed away win but just three minutes from time Wrexham levelled. Moir was again the hero with a stunning run from the wing that beat three Fulham defenders. He flashed over a low cross that Kinsey converted at the far post. In the end Fulham were hanging on for the one point and the match finished **2—2**.

It was another promotion point squandered but it seemed a fair result. It was the first time that the Fulham side had scored more than one goal in a game since the beginning of November!

Encouraged by the result, Fulham travelled to Prenton Park on the following Friday night to tackle **Tranmere Rovers**. Tranmere played at home on a Friday, hoping to encourage Liverpool or Everton supporters in for an extra game at the weekend. Fulham switched to their second kit of light and dark blue stripes, Dodgin again naming an unchanged side. Tranmere's form had slipped dramatically and they were now just two points above the bottom four. It therefore seemed a good opportunity for Fulham to press on. However, Tranmere had lost just two home games all season.

Anybody missing the first five minutes of the match would have missed Fulham's lightning start and opening two goals. In this match, it took Fulham just sixty seconds to score. In a quick raid they forced a corner that Steve Earle took. Vic Halom running in made good contact with

On a Friday evening at Prenton Park, Fulham score twice in the first five minutes. In the very first minute, Halom's header from Earle's corner is subtly deflected by Les Barrett's head and beats the goalkeeper just inside the post. Barrett is at the far right in the picture. A back to form Fulham won comfortably 3–0.

the ball and his header was goalbound but seemingly covered by the goalkeeper. However, on its way to goal Les Barrett intervened with his head and deflected the ball inexorably away from the goalkeeper and into the net.

Just four minutes later Fulham scored again. Jimmy Dunne won the ball and fed Barrett who, with a scintillating run, cut inside and laid a hard, low cross across the goalmouth. Halom, rushing in, made a first time contact from five yards and the unstoppable shot flew low into the goal.

Barrett was unstoppable on the night, performing one of his old tricks just after the half hour. Again he sped down the right and cut in, and with the defence and goalkeeper expecting another cross, he rammed a powerful curling shot between the crossbar and the far post from an acute angle that the despairing keeper Frankie Lane could only push into the roof of the net. Fulham were riding high and went in three goals up at half time.

Fulham were in cruise control in the second half, with Earle and Barrett on the wings ably supported by the energetic Stan Brown and Barry Lloyd, whilst the bustling Halom was keeping the home defence busy. Tranmere brought on tall striker Jimmy Hinch for Frank Gill in an attempt to add thrust to the attack, but Fulham's stonewall defence never looked likely to concede a goal.

Rovers tried hard to get on terms but in truth little fell right for them on the night. Tranmere looked jaded towards the end and Fulham were content to play out time and hold on to a **3—0** victory. This win earned Fulham the double over Tranmere; it had been a solid performance all round. Although beaten twice by Fulham, Tranmere that season set a record by drawing twenty-two of their league games, just short of 50% of all their matches!

The weekend news became even better when it was reported that Jimmy Conway had successfully come through a reserve game against Arsenal.

Fulham's first home fixture of the year brought **Reading** to Craven Cottage, who, after a fine start, had slipped dramatically down the league to below mid-table. The cold weather in the south of the country had continued, and the rain and ice had churned up the pitch that was now looking the worse for wear. This certainly would not help Fulham's cause.

Fulham experimented a little by playing Fred Callaghan in the injured Stan Brown's number four shirt, with George Johnston returning to the forward line. The Reading side was similar to that of the previous season. Considering the local opposition, the crowd, huddled together in the cold, was a disappointing one, just over 10,000.

After three decent performances, Fulham seemed to inexplicably fall away again. They started with a flurry but as the half progressed became very lethargic; most of their moves and ideas becoming stuck in the Cottage mud. Reading were the more direct and perky side, linking well between defence and attack, and doing the simple stuff. Steve Earle missed one opportunity, Halom another, whilst Reading winger Terry Bell headed just wide at the other end.

It took Reading just thirteen minutes to move ahead. Reading forced their second right-wing corner. Tony Wagstaff took it and his kick found Dick Habbin. Habbin played the ball back to eighteen-year-old Malcolm Swain and his firm, swerving left-foot drive gave Malcolm Webster no chance.

The goal frustrated Fulham and their first half play became scrappy and without any real shape; they were playing like individuals whilst Reading were playing some fluent team football. Reading were beginning to dominate the midfield and Barry Lloyd was forced into more of a defensive role, stifling his ability to set up attacks.

After another talking to from Bill Dodgin, Fulham emerged a sharper side. The football became more direct, and Reading found themselves under pressure. However, the direct route suited Reading's tall defenders Stuart Morgan and Barry Wagstaff, who remained firm and resolute. When Fulham did find a rare chink they were frustrated by Reading custodian keeper Steve Death, who was on superb form, making fine reflex saves whenever the need arose. In the meantime most of the Fulham finishing seemed particularly slow and hesitant.

Territorially it was now all Fulham but it looked as if it was going to be another of those frustrating afternoons. In desperation, Dodgin withdrew the ineffective George Johnston, giving John Richardson an opportunity as substitute to get amongst the tall Reading defenders. Fulham were then handed a slice of luck when Reading's Ray Flannigan and Stuart Morgan were injured after colliding with each other; both men were left feeling groggy.

Just as it appeared that Reading were going to hold out, Fulham equalised three minutes from the end. The Cottagers were awarded a free kick in a central position two yards outside the penalty area. Lloyd provided the decoy, but Fred Callaghan instead rolled the ball sideways to Earle, who powerfully blasted the ball wide of the wall of defenders into the left-hand corner of the net, past Death, who was slightly unsighted. The relief for Earle was almost palpable, as it was his first goal in fourteen games.

In the final five minutes Fulham went all out to win and could have scored a hatful with a number of hair's-breadth misses. The referee, Mr Castle, then added a significant amount of injury time. Right at the death Richardson received a pass on the right-hand side of the penalty area and, with two defenders converging, smashed a shot against the outside of a post with Death beaten. It was the last chance and Fulham had to be satisfied with a **1—1** draw.

In truth Fulham had again hardly looked like promotion candidates and hadn't deserved victory. The Cottage pitch had certainly done the home side no favours. It had really been a match of two solid defences. Callaghan, Reg Matthewson and Jimmy Dunne had been very solid at the back and goalkeeper Webster had little to do after the early goal, the Reading front five having little potency.

Just three minutes from time, Steve Earle takes Fred Callaghan's free kick and slams the ball wide of the Reading defensive wall and past the wrong-footed goalkeeper Steve Death. The late goal rescued an unlikely point for Fulham in a 1–1 draw at the Cottage.

But Fulham without Jimmy Conway were still having trouble breaking down defences and only the energetic Les Barrett had again really stood out. Bill Dodgin said afterwards: 'We have kept in touch by getting that point, we have badly missed Jimmy Conway who will be on test again with the reserves on Wednesday.'

The poor weather continued into the following week and the scheduled Friday evening match with **Bristol Rovers** at Fulham had to be **postponed**. This Bristol Rovers match had originally been brought forward from the Saturday to the Friday, to avoid Chelsea's fourth round FA Cup tie with Manchester City.

In the following week a rested Fulham travelled to the Midlands to meet **Aston Villa**. Villa, now top of the table, had appointed a young Arthur Cox to their backroom staff. Fulham again made team changes, with Wilf Tranter coming in for his first game of the season and Fred Callaghan returning to his customary left back position, with Dave Moreline moving up. The most welcome return was that of Jimmy Conway at number seven.

Aston Villa's Third Division attendances were amazing, not only better than *any* Second Division side, but superior to *nine* of the clubs in the First Division as well! Fulham would face a massive, vocal crowd of over 33,000 roaring Villa on. It had rained for most of the day and the conditions in Birmingham were poor; the Villa Park ground, like the Cottage, was very muddy with conditions extremely heavy.

Jimmy Conway looked in good form immediately but was the victim of a cruel tackle from full back Charlie Aitken as early as the nineteenth minute and this crippled his mobility and speed. It seemed a blatantly dangerous over-the-top tackle; the Villa man should have been sent off, yet he was not even cautioned – let off with just a wagging finger. Steve Earle had a glancing header cleared off the goal line and a snapshot by Vic Halom was well saved by the home goalkeeper.

Villa were being roared on by an incredibly partisan and hostile crowd that was almost worth a goal start. In the cauldron-like atmosphere it then started to become a bit unpleasant. Fulham had very good shouts for two first-half penalties greeted by silence and then jeers from the Villa crowd, both turned down by experienced, but alarmingly tolerant, referee Ken (not Rob) Styles.

For over an hour Fulham played the better football, showed the better control and had much more thrust in attack. Halom had another chance but tried to walk the ball in, which gave defender Fred Turnbull time to recover and hack it away. Les Barrett also had an opportunity, but over-anxious finishing let Fulham down.

Villa then finally came into the game. They began to play to Andy Lochhead's strength, and when they did it caused havoc as he appeared to have the beating of both Reg Matthewson and Jimmy Dunne in the air. As the heat in the stadium increased, skipper Barry Lloyd was booked

Steve Earle is dispossessed in front of a massive 33,000 crowd, who saw Fulham beaten 0–1 by promotion contenders Aston Villa at Villa Park. This was courtesy of a highly controversial penalty award. Fulham played well but were the victims of several crowd-induced refereeing decisions that went against them in a bad-tempered match.

for just a brush with Villa forward Brian Godfrey. The booking seemed trivial compared to other events that were going on in the game.

At the other end of the pitch there was a carbon copy incident of one of Fulham's first-half penalty claims, but predictably Villa *were* awarded the controversial penalty by Styles after Willie Anderson had fallen under a challenge by Dunne. Dunne was furious, as were most of the Fulham side, and the Fulham defender was booked for pushing and manhandling the referee, being fortunate to remain on the field. Despite the pandemonium Anderson remained cool and converted from the penalty spot.

John Richardson replaced an exhausted and injured Conway in the second half twenty minutes from time. Fulham were still matching and outplaying the home side in football skill, courage and chances created, but the enormous crowd and the referee were swaying the game in Villa's favour.

In the end a harassed Fulham, who were shown no protection by the referee and were kicked to death, failed to keep their heads and the last ten minutes was an ugly, untidy and shapeless ruck. It was a shame, as the Fulham side had promised so much in the early stages. Fulham were finally edged out **0–1** to one of their biggest promotion rivals and were now definitely slipping out of the promotion race. The undeserved victory gave Villa the double over Fulham. The enormous crowd was one of the largest *ever* to witness a Third Division match.

The match had been full of dumbfounding decisions by the referee. Fulham had been penalised virtually every time by the referee for strong but fair tackles. The booing by the home crowd seemed to indicate that Fulham were the only team competing physically, which was far from true. The away side, getting plenty of stick from the home supporters, received absolutely none of the breaks.

Dodgin remained optimistic and said afterwards: 'We played the better football, made the better chances and we have nothing to show for it. But there are nineteen games left, and if you know you are playing well you must be confident the results will come. No, there's still a long way to go. I would be a lot more worried if I thought that our football is not good enough to win us promotion.'

Despite the important defeat, a frustrated but defiant Jimmy Conway said later: 'Sometimes you get depressed when you lose, but it was hard to feel really bad after this one. We knew the team had played well, and that if we can keep it up we won't lose many more games.'

February 1971

In this month

* Rolls Royce declared itself bankrupt.
* *Apollo XIV* landed safely on the moon and two men walked on the surface.
* Britain recognised the Amin Government in Uganda.
* Enoch Powell predicted 'an explosion' unless there was a repatriation scheme for immigrants.
* Rupert Murdoch took control of London Weekend Television.
* Idi Amin declared himself President of Uganda and promoted himself to General.
* The first British soldier was killed in the troubles in Ulster.
* Britain switched to decimal currency (on the 15th).

'My Sweet Lord' by George Harrison topped the charts.
The film 'The Go Between' was released.

How the league was looking

It was dramatically 'all change' at the top of the table. Aston Villa's winning run had taken them storming to the top of the table. The rise of Preston North End was even more spectacular: unbeaten in thirteen games, they had soared up to take second place. Bristol Rovers, finding the pace too hot, had dropped to third, three points behind Aston Villa. Fulham were now a disappointing fourth, their worst position of the season, and a point behind Rovers.

There was also a new and unlikely challenger, Halifax Town, who had lost just two in the last twelve, sliding almost unnoticed into fifth place, level on points with Fulham. Torquay United still held sixth place, but Rotherham's challenge seemed to have gone. There was now a clear four-point gap between the top six sides and the rest.

Gillingham were still glued to the base of the table and losing touch; Rochdale remained one from bottom, but four points better off. Doncaster Rovers were the new team to slip into the danger zone and Bury had risen one position. Walsall had finally found some form and were at last clear of the bottom four, as were Bradford City. Three clubs were hovering just outside the trouble zone: Brighton, Tranmere Rovers and, suddenly again, Shrewsbury Town.

The matches

FULHAM'S FIRST match in February saw a visit from the Stags, **Mansfield Town**. Mansfield's challenge this year had never really taken off and they were perpetually hovering either side of ninth position; they also held the worst defensive record in the division. Fulham made one change, bringing in George Johnston for Vic Halom, who was substitute.

The Mansfield side showed no real changes to that of the previous season. An emergency goalkeeper, Rod Arnold, had been signed on loan from Wolverhampton Wanderers, due to injuries to first choice goalkeeper Graham Brown and young reserve Des Finch. On another freezing cold Saturday the crowds continued to desert Fulham, many now feeling that the 'promotion promise' had already been broken; fewer than 9,500 turned up at a bleak Craven Cottage.

Fulham's first-half performance was as bleak as the weather and the mood was not helped when Fulham lost centre half and mainstay Reg Matthewson with a cut forehead after half an hour, an injury that required numerous stitches. Vic Halom substituted, but the team looked lop-sided and unsteady. Like most away teams this season, Mansfield packed their defence and demonstrated very little attacking inclination. Jimmy Conway was showing some form on his return to the side but was being crowded out in a congested penalty area.

Fulham were attacking incessantly, and it should have been a 'shoot on sight' policy. The young stand-in Arnold looked nervy in the Mansfield goal, twice dropping the ball early on. Despite playing neat football, Fulham's laborious approach work produced only two worthwhile shots from Steve Earle and Les Barrett, both lacking power and both directed straight at the goalkeeper.

Malcolm Webster in the Fulham goal was a virtual onlooker and had no shot at all to save in the first half.

Skipper Barry Lloyd began to rally the Fulham troops after the interval and tried to add a little more guile to open up this packed defence. Pushing more men forward, Fulham began to start shooting, but young Arnold in the away goal was now in inspired form, handling the ball like a veteran and moving fluidly across the goal.

Mansfield began to gain a little confidence and pushed forward themselves, almost scoring twice. In two breakaway raids Wilf Tranter was forced to kick the ball off the line from Mansfield's John Stenson, with Webster stranded out of goal, and then Fred Callaghan made a goal-line clearance following a first-time shot from Dai Jones.

Finally raising their game to a decent level, Fulham themselves were unlucky. Lloyd, Fulham's best forward, put in one hot shot that Arnold saved with difficulty and then hit the foot of a post in another raid. George Johnston then made the miss of the match, shooting yards over the bar with an open goal facing him and the defence totally stranded. Barrett wasted another chance with a cross-cum-shot that hit the bar; goalkeeper Arnold injured himself crashing into a post keeping the centre from Barrett out.

The powder-puff home attack was getting nowhere and Vic Halom contented himself for most of the match by harassing the young goalkeeper when he was in possession of the ball, for which he was ultimately warned; this approach was counter-productive as it wasted valuable time.

This was as good as it got and despite a ninety-minute onslaught, a very disappointing match finished **0−0**. Fulham had done everything but score, but had dropped yet another valuable home point and had rarely looked like promotion contenders. Fulham had now won just two out of their last ten league games, and, on this dismal February afternoon, the promotion dream looked well and truly over; the season had gone completely down the drain.

Defensively Fulham had looked more than competent. Webster, Callaghan, Moreline and Dunne especially had been rarely troubled but the attack had once again looked very poor, with only Lloyd and Barrett showing anything like their form of three months ago. Despite having little skill in attack the Mansfield defence had played well all afternoon, Sandy Pate, John Saunders and the inspired, debutant loan goalkeeper Rod Arnold all outstanding.

Fulham had now picked up just thirteen points in the last sixteen matches. Key scorer Steve Earle had scored just once in this period, and Vic Halom and Barry Lloyd just twice. In the last sixteen games Fulham had scored a meagre fourteen goals, hardly promotion form. Fulham's only consolation on the dismal afternoon was that rivals Aston Villa and Preston North End had both lost.

The local press called the goalless match 'a bore from beginning to end', and added: 'On Fulham's showing, they may well miss out on promotion this year.' Barry Lloyd said: 'We were so on top it was ridiculous. Somebody is going to suffer, and it could be Bristol Rovers [next week].'

During the following week and despite having a small first-team squad, Fulham expedited another of their costly transfer mistakes. Centre half Dave Roberts had started well in Fulham's colours but a few poor performances during the early part of the 1969–70 season had seen him dropped. He had been given very little opportunity this season to show Bill Dodgin what he could do – just one match.

It was, however, quite a surprise when the news came out that Fulham had sold the young star for just £4,000 to a team in a *higher* division, Oxford United. The transfer proved to be a shrewd piece of business by the Oxford club. Dave Roberts went on to enjoy a career of over 300 games and gave excellent service to Oxford, Hull City and Cardiff City, winning eighteen international caps for Wales in the process. At the same time, Fulham allowed goalkeeper Ian Seymour to go out on a three-month loan to Brighton and Hove Albion. The Brighton goalkeeper, Geoff Sidebottom, had been forced to retire after suffering a head injury when colliding with a post; their second choice goalkeeper Brian Powney was also injured. This forced young McAndrew Johnson, just eighteen, to take over the spot as Fulham's number two goalkeeper.

To add to the misery there were now also administrative problems to contend with. The first signs of 'Seventies unrest' were beginning to unfold and the trade unions were beginning to flex

Steve Earle and Les Barrett alight from the team coach surrounded by waiting Fulham fans. The team are arriving at Eastville prior to the important fixture at Bristol Rovers.

their industrial muscles. The Post Office workers had gone on strike and this was playing havoc with the receipt and despatch of seat bookings for forthcoming matches.

The following week Fulham travelled to Eastville to vie with another of their serious promotion rivals, **Bristol Rovers**. Rovers were in third place in the table, so the match was a critical 'four-pointer'. Fulham made one change, with Stan Brown returning at full back for Wilf Tranter.

At least Fulham were playing a side that enjoyed playing attacking football, so the match promised to be entertaining, although it was also bound to be a nervy match with so much at stake. Skipper Barry Lloyd gambled after winning the toss and chose to play with the blustery wind behind him. The ruse worked and Rovers missed several first-half chances through poor control and shooting.

Fulham were playing a dubious offside trap that Rovers' Wayne Jones often cracked with some intelligent passes, but the home forwards spurned the opportunities in and around the penalty area. Winger Ken Stephens shot wide after rounding both Fred Callaghan and Malcolm Webster, Carl Gilbert shot over from just a few yards out, and finally Harold Jarman, with a clear view of goal, opted to pass instead of hammering the ball in and the chance went begging.

Rovers skipper Don Megson almost gave a goal away in the first half when Steve Earle dispossessed him on the halfway line. Megson tried vainly to recover, but Earle was left with a clear route to goal with just the keeper to beat. The striker went striding through the middle but held on to the ball for a fraction too long, allowing the goalkeeper to baulk him. The miss was Fulham's only real chance of the half and they were fortunate to go in at the interval on level terms.

Fulham came much more into the game in the second half, with Earle and George Johnston applying more pressure through the middle, and the only goal of the game came from Jimmy Conway just after the hour.

The experienced Megson again missed his tackle, which allowed Conway to run on and execute a curling shot from the edge of the area that bent at the last minute just inside a post – beyond the despairing dive of Dick Sheppard. The goal was tough luck on Sheppard, who had stopped everything else put to him in the earlier stages of the match. The goal was Conway's first since returning to the side following injury.

Robin Stubbs, the home side's centre forward, then missed the chance of the game on sixty-five minutes when he shot well wide from just a few yards out. Les Barrett put in one brave header,

Despite being surrounded by four Bristol Rovers defenders, Jimmy Conway still manages to get in a shot on the Rovers goal. Conway was on fine form in the match, scoring the only goal in an important 1–0 victory. The goal was Conway's first since September and returning from a serious injury. The defeat severely damaged Rovers' promotion hopes.

risking a punch on the nose from the goalkeeper, but the ball hit the crossbar and was eventually cleared. Barrett was now in a more confident mood and had Roberts struggling when he began to run at him.

Rovers were still attacking and created a number of chances, but very poor finishing coupled with excellent Fulham covering and defending, especially by Reg Matthewson, prevented the home side from scoring. Fulham might well have wilted if the Rovers side had taken an earlier lead, but the longer the game had progressed without a goal, the more confident Fulham had become.

Fulham won **1–0** and the result enabled the Cottagers to leapfrog Rovers back into third place, so the result had a huge psychological significance. Although Jimmy Conway was the hero with the match-winning goal, the defensive heroics and capabilities of Matthewson and Stan Brown at the back had once again seen Fulham through this particular stern test.

The following Saturday saw a visit from the Potteries side **Port Vale**. Vale had slipped down the table recently, mainly due to poor form away from home. They were now fifteenth and just four points ahead of the drop zone. Their side included Brian Horton, the future Brighton and Hove Albion manager, and John Green, who had played for many years in the First Division for Blackpool. Also worthy of a mention, although not in the Port Vale side that afternoon, was centre half Roy Sproson, who had played for Port Vale since 1950! He had made over 750 league appearances alone and was still playing on at the age of forty-one.

The weather had improved slightly and so had the crowd. A crowd of just under 10,500 turned up. Vale had only won once in sixteen attempts at Craven Cottage and skipper Barry Lloyd, sensing that the promotion dream was drifting, issued a rallying cry: 'We must get six points from these next three [home] games, nothing else will do.'

Fulham made the best possible start to this match with a goal in just seventy-five *seconds*. Les Barrett received the ball from Fred Callaghan on the left, accelerated past two startled defenders and, as the defence backed off, continued to run in on goal, finally placing the ball with a sidefoot shot into the net from the edge of the penalty area.

Just eight minutes later Barrett headed his and Fulham's second; Fulham forced a corner, Jimmy Dunne, unmarked, headed the ball on for Barrett to rise above two defenders and power home a header with the goalkeeper nowhere and two defenders rooted on the line. Port Vale goalkeeper Stuart Sharratt then made a wonder save from Barry Lloyd to prevent the score being three.

Vale were stung into action and, in honesty, Fulham took their foot off the gas. The home side recklessly allowed Vale back into the game and they reduced the arrears in the twenty-fifth minute,

From a Fulham corner defender Jimmy Dunne, up with the attack, flicks the ball on to Les Barrett (out of picture) who heads his and Fulham's second goal. In a fluent performance Fulham won an entertaining encounter with Port Vale 4–1.

when John Green scored. Mike Morris sent Green away in the middle and the midfielder forced his way through several half-hearted tackles to leave Malcolm Webster helpless.

Vale continued to press for the rest of the first half, with winger John James and centre forward Tommy MacLaren causing Fulham's defence a number of difficulties. Vale then hit the woodwork whilst another effort just shaved the post. However, despite their possession most of Vale's moves foundered around the edge of the penalty area due to the superb form of Dunne and the experienced Stan Brown and Fred Callaghan. At this stage Fulham were glad to hear the half-time whistle.

Despite Vale being in the driving seat at the interval, manager Bill Dodgin left the match at half time, handing the reins over to Terry Medwin whilst he travelled across the road to Stamford Bridge to observe a player turning out for Leicester reserves against Chelsea reserves!

Vale continued to press at the start of the second half but they were stopped in their tracks with a beautiful third goal ten minutes after half time. It was a goal carved out of speed, precision and clever thinking. Lloyd won the ball and sent Dave Moreline away on the right; Moreline put in a dangerous cross, George Johnston dummied it, allowing the ball to run on to Steve Earle. The chance was not an easy one but Earle cracked the ball first time, low past the goalkeeper.

This goal deflated Vale somewhat and Brian Horton was booked as Vale struggled to hold on. Earle then clinched the match with his second goal, thirteen minutes from the end, volleying home an excellent cross from Jimmy Conway. There was now no coming back for Vale and Fulham played out the last quarter of an hour to record an easy **4–1** win.

The win gave Fulham their second double of the season. Vale had not been a bad side, but this was a day when the Fulham forwards had started to look more like their old selves again. They had all looked sharp and Vale's overworked defence, none of whom had played particularly well on the day, had struggled. The Vale forwards had looked quite classy at times, but this was a match when Reg Matthewson and Malcolm Webster had kept things tight all afternoon and Vale had never seriously threatened the Fulham goal consistently after half time.

How did that get there? Torquay goalkeeper Donnelly looks resigned as he retrieves the ball from the back of the net inside the first fifteen minutes. Les Barrett has just thundered in the first Fulham goal in a comprehensive 4–0 victory and is duly congratulated. Fulham were on excellent form on the Friday evening, producing some of their best football of the season.

Fulham had a chance to improve on this performance with a Friday evening visit to the Cottage from **Torquay United**, Fulham eager to avenge the 1–3 defeat at Plainmoor earlier in the season. The Torquay match had been brought forward from the Saturday to avoid competition with the League Cup final. Fulham were, unsurprisingly, unchanged.

The Torquay line-up was similar to that of the previous season, the main additions being the captain, the experienced Mal Lucas, signed from Norwich City, at full back, and striker Bruce Stuckey, recently signed from Sunderland. Torquay had maintained their impressive form but they had failed to find that extra spark that would propel them into the promotion places.

However, the Devon side still remained in sixth position and just four points below Fulham so caution was definitely necessary. The Friday night switch and Fulham's improved form led to an encouraging crowd of just over 13,000 arriving at the Cottage.

This was a night when it was clear that things were on the move once again at Craven Cottage. Fulham were brilliant, delivering a performance that left their opponents dumbfounded and broken-spirited. Fulham took just fourteen minutes to open up and unlock the Torquay defence.

The goal was a beautifully crafted one involving a number of players. Barry Lloyd sent Steve Earle away down the left with an astute pass, Jimmy Conway dummied the accurate centre from Earle, and Les Barrett running in, crashed the ball first time past Torquay keeper Andy Donnelly without pausing in his run. Fulham still had to be wary, and the dangerous Torquay front man Mickey Cave hit a post in the twenty-sixth minute with Malcolm Webster beaten.

Four minutes before half time Fulham doubled their lead. Conway manoeuvred himself into a good position outside the penalty area and, spotting Donnelly off his line, curled a beautiful, spinning lob over the helpless goalkeeper and just underneath the bar.

In the second half Torquay appeared to run out of steam and on the hour it was three, with another well-thought-out goal. Conway and Lloyd started the move when they executed an intelligent one-two that beat Torquay's offside trap. Conway continued the run and, from his low centre, there was a rare visitor. Centre half Reg Matthewson, who had initiated the move, had continued to push forward and was perfectly placed in the box to blast Conway's centre past Donnelly from just a couple of yards out. The goal was his first for five years since his Sheffield United days and would also be his only Fulham goal.

Just sixty seconds later the rout was complete. George Johnston looked as if he was going to make a run down the wing but instead swivelled, turned inside and put in a vicious volley that Donnelly could only parry, Barrett following up to push the rebound home. The two goals realised Barrett's fourth 'brace' of the season.

Torquay, upset with the runaround that they were receiving, had Alan Welsh and Bill Kitchener booked by referee Clive Thomas. To make matters worse they lost their centre half Allan Young with a dislocated shoulder. Fulham, with hard games coming up, showed some mercy and eased up in the final half an hour, still finishing as easy winners at **4–0**.

This result made it three wins on the spin and eight goals in the last two games. With Aston Villa and Preston faltering slightly in recent weeks, the win had a double significance inasmuch as it returned Fulham, albeit temporarily, to the top of the table. The Villa team had been watching in the stands and were stunned by Fulham's improvement. The press added: 'Brilliant Fulham roar back to the top', saying: 'Torquay didn't know how to combat or contain them.'

In another five-star performance it was difficult to single out individual Fulham players. Jimmy Dunne was brilliant against his former club and the defence had hardly offered a chink of light all night. Lloyd had been excellent in midfield, having a hand in all four goals, with Barrett again in devastating form on the left wing. Conway was beginning to approach full fitness and he complemented Barrett excellently, drawing out the Torquay defenders and pulling them all out of position.

On the night Torquay had been undoubtedly poor, certainly lax in defence, and Fulham should have run up a cricket score, but it was questionable whether some clubs, even in the First Division, would have been able to hold Fulham on that showing. Certainly, with the Cottage pitch now dry and in better condition, Fulham looked capable of passing and tackling much more successfully.

The weekend proved to be a good one as Aston Villa subsequently lost on the Saturday and Preston were only able to force a draw, leaving Fulham still at the top, but just on goal average.

March 1971

In this month

* Two one-day strikes were held in protest against the Industrial Relations Bill.
* *The Daily Sketch* closed after sixty-two years.
* The postal workers strike finally ended.
* Boxer Henry Cooper retired after controversially losing his British, European and Commonwealth titles to Joe Bugner.
* Ulster Prime Minister James Chichester Clark resigned and was replaced by Brian Faulkner.
* Lord Olivier took his seat in the House of Lords.
* Charles Manson and three of his hippie 'family' were sentenced to death for the Sharon Tate murders.
* 4,000 women took part in a Women's Liberation demonstration from Hyde Park to Downing Street.
* Civil war erupted in Pakistan after the declaration of the independent state of Bangladesh.
* The Government planned Britain's first sixty commercial radio stations.
* Winnie Mandela was jailed for a year.
* Lt William Calley was found guilty of the Mylai massacre in Vietnam in 1968.
* It was announced that purchase tax would be abolished within two years, and that value added tax (VAT) would be introduced to bring Britain into line with the rest of the Common Market.
* US actor and comedian Harold Lloyd died.

'Another Day' by Paul McCartney topped the charts.
The film 'Get Carter' was released.

How the league was looking

It was dramatically 'all change' again at the top of the table, with Fulham's winning run taking them storming back to the top of the table. Preston North End's form was also very consistent and they were lying in second place on goal average. The new, unlikely challengers, Halifax Town, had pushed on admirably and were now tucked comfortably in third place and just one point behind Fulham and Preston.

Aston Villa had slumped dramatically into fourth spot, but incredibly they too were just one point behind Fulham and Preston. One point separated the top four clubs. Bristol Rovers, with only one win in seven matches, were still finding the pace a little too hot and had now dropped down to fifth, but even they were just four points behind Fulham and Preston. Torquay were clinging to sixth place, but were making no further inroads.

Gillingham were still at the base of the table and now six points adrift from safety. Brighton were now the team out of form, having plummeted disastrously to one from bottom, three points above Gillingham. Tranmere Rovers had also slipped into the bottom four for the first time, a point better off. Doncaster Rovers were still in the danger zone, but Bury had risen one position again, hauling themselves to just outside the bottom four. Rochdale's form had been the most impressive and they had sailed away towards a comfortable mid-table position. Above Bury the position was very tight and no fewer than five clubs, Port Vale, Shrewsbury Town, Walsall, Plymouth Argyle and Barnsley, were just two or three points above the trouble zone.

The matches

THE FOLLOWING Tuesday, Fulham had their third consecutive home match, which was the re-arranged fixture with **Bristol Rovers** following the initial postponement. It was an ideal time to play them, as Rovers were beginning to falter slightly and were dropping out of the promotion reckoning. They were, however, still only four points behind Fulham. The match was an opportunity to push another rival out of the promotion nest. There was, as usual, the added spice of the 'father versus son' clash, and Fulham would also be seeking revenge for the earlier first round FA Cup exit dished out by Rovers at the Cottage in November.

Fulham were again unchanged; Rovers were without the experienced Don Megson and forwards Harold Jarman and Ray Graydon. Fulham's best league crowd of the season, just under 16,000, piled into the Cottage eager to cheer Fulham on to another victory. The referee for this important encounter was the experienced Ray Tinkler from Boston.

Promotion pressure appeared to be eating into Fulham early in the match and their first-half efforts were far too frantic and impatient; indeed, Bristol Rovers had the edge. In one attack Sandy Allan hit a shot that was deflected off Reg Matthewson. The ball hit Malcolm Webster and somehow stayed out, with the keeper knowing little about it. Fulham pounded away at the Rovers goal, but with six-foot-four-inch centre half Stuart Taylor in commanding form alongside Frankie Prince, Fulham's clear-cut goalscoring opportunities were few.

Rovers' Ken Stephens then had the best opportunity of the half. Webster dashed rashly towards the corner flag in an attempt to dive at the feet of the forward to save but he failed to take the ball from the winger. The ball bounced around the untenanted goal for an agonizing number of seconds before it was finally cleared. Webster was injured as a result and never fully recovered, limping badly.

When Fulham did break through, goalkeeper Dick Sheppard rescued the away side with fine saves from Les Barrett and Steve Earle. Fulham forced a dozen first-half corners but Taylor, Sheppard and Co. dealt with them all admirably. A few Fulham supporters feared a repeat of the November FA Cup display and result. Certainly Rovers were winning the tactical battle in midfield and were defending with solid security.

Bill Dodgin jnr, unhappy at Rovers' midfield superiority, drafted another man into the centre and the change seemed to turn the tide. However, luck continued to go Fulham's way. Jimmy Dunne appeared to foul and bring down Allan en route to goal early in the second half, and the Fulham supporters were relieved to see the referee award nothing.

On the hour mark Fulham scored twice in the space of three fantastic minutes to swing the match their way. Rovers goalkeeper Sheppard, who so far this season had performed heroics in the Bristol goal, had an unhappy hand in both goals.

Rovers claim a foul in the build up, but Steve Earle doesn't wait and pushes the ball into an empty net with the keeper helpless on the ground. Fulham scored twice in three minutes to record a 2–1 win, virtually ending Bristol Rovers' promotion hopes.

Firstly, he was only able to palm out George Johnston's shot following Barry Lloyd's cross and Conway's knockdown straight to Earle in the middle of the goal, and Earle just casually pushed the ball back into the empty net from six yards. The goal was a real turning point; Rovers were furious with the award, claiming that Johnston had pushed Prince and Sheppard on his way to winning possession. Referee Tinkler would hear none of the complaints, and after a vociferous protest the goal was eventually awarded.

Then, just three minutes later, with Rovers still upset and rattled, the roles were reversed when Earle picked up Fred Callaghan's long pass and picked his way past two defenders on a twenty-yard run before unleashing a piledriver that was pushed away brilliantly by Sheppard. Unfortunately for Rovers the spinning ball fell to Johnston near goal and he somehow managed to squeeze his shot home from an impossibly acute angle; this time there was no contesting the goal.

The goal was Johnston's first for ten weeks and was made more ironic when it was discovered that Bill Dodgin had purchased Johnston partly on the strength of opinion and recommendation made by his father – Rovers' boss!

Rovers now looked a beaten side, but they raised their game and plugged away gamely. Fulham began to look nervous again, looking for the final whistle. With their concentration slightly off, the Fulham defence allowed Rovers' Prince to skip through virtually unchallenged to net a late consolation goal. Fortunately for Fulham the final whistle blew just seconds later, with the Cottagers stretching their current run to four wins on the trot with a **2−1** success.

The third win in ten days took Fulham two points clear at the top and virtually ended Rovers' promotion challenge. In the final 'Battle of the Dodgins' young Bill had ultimately come out on top; the win completed the double over Rovers. Most of the press agreed that it had been a very entertaining game and that on the pure quality of the football Fulham had deserved to win. Fulham on the night had certainly received the benefit of the majority of the refereeing decisions. On the down side both Steve Earle and Malcolm Webster had taken knocks and were doubtful for Saturday.

With the transfer deadline looming, the next day's papers reported that Fulham had agreed terms for the transfer of Bert Murray, the former Chelsea midfield/utility player. Murray was contracted to Second Division Birmingham City and had made eleven first-team appearances for the Blues that season. He was currently on loan at Brighton along with Fulham goalkeeper Ian Seymour. Despite negotiations being concluded, the transfer was never finalised. The clubs had agreed to a transfer fee of £12,000, but Murray could not agree personal terms and finally refused to sign. A disappointed general manager Graham Hortop was mystified, saying: 'I don't yet really know the reasons.'

Fulham did, however, sign twenty-year-old reserve Paul Gilchrist from Charlton Athletic on a month's loan. Gilchrist did not appear in the first team during his loan period and the arrangement was not extended. Gilchrist went on to have a decent league career, including a five-year spell in the First Division with Southampton.

Both injured Fulham players recovered sufficiently from their knocks and Fulham again took an unchanged side to the Shay to play **Halifax Town**. There was never going to be a repeat of the 8−0 scoreline of the previous season, but Fulham had beaten Halifax pretty easily in the last three encounters and so had to be confident. Underestimating Halifax would be dangerous, however, as they were on a magnificent run. The Yorkshire side had lost just two out of the last fifteen matches, a run that had included eight victories. This run had seen them soar into third place.

Fulham took the lead early in the first half. Jimmy Conway went on a scamper down the right and crossed beautifully, low and hard into the goalmouth. George Johnston rushed in surrounded by a posse of home defenders and the goalkeeper Alex Smith. Somehow the ball ricocheted around the six-yard box, finally being deflected in off Johnston and a Halifax defender. Johnston then had another chance to increase the lead; he successfully flicked the ball over the advancing keeper Smith, only to see the Halifax full back Andy Burgin race back and successfully hack the ball clear from the line. Later in the half Conway had a chance to give Fulham clear daylight. He was found by a cross just four yards out. With the open goal gaping and with Steve Earle even better placed, Conway recklessly and selfishly blasted over the bar when it looked far easier to score.

At the Shay in front of a sparse crowd, Steve Earle lets fly at the Halifax goal. Despite taking an early lead, a casual Fulham let the game with Halifax slip with two late goals. The 1–2 defeat was unnecessary and put extra pressure on the Whites. Note the local bus trundling past the ground at the top of the picture.

Despite not adding to their early advantage, the Cottagers had been in storming form and victory looked a formality. Conway and Les Barrett were ripping the home defence to shreds and Fulham were much the better-organised side, making excellent use of the open spaces. Fred Callaghan was relishing his rare midfield role, enthusiastically driving his team forward.

Although Fulham were playing with confidence in the second half, there was now a touch of arrogance in their play and they appeared to think they couldn't lose – but fate had other ideas. Fulham began to slow and allowed Halifax vital possession. Fulham couldn't raise the tempo again and were penned back in their own half for long periods.

Halifax totally dominated the last thirty minutes and in the end the pressure told. After holding the lead for over seventy minutes, Fulham conceded two goals in a sloppy five-minute spell right at the end of the match. Following a poor clearance, Wallace hit the first with a shot from twenty yards that seemed to swerve and beat the unsighted Malcolm Webster.

Then before the visitors could recover from the shock, the resurgent home side scored again. Dave Chadwick laid on the chance with a one-two move that split the Fulham defence, allowing Barry Holmes to head an unlikely winner. The late, late show meant that it was now pointless trying to attempt a meaningful recovery and Fulham went down to a needless **1–2** defeat.

The defeat was a very irritating one, as Halifax were a serious promotion rival and Fulham had lost because they had not given it everything. It was a reversal of the match played at the Cottage against Halifax in the previous season, where Halifax had taken the early lead and Fulham had scored two late goals to win. Halifax openly celebrated this win, and no wonder – they had wanted this revenge victory like nothing else and Fulham could have had few complaints. The match was important statistically, as it was the first time in seventeen matches that Fulham had lost to a Yorkshire side over the previous two seasons!

In midweek Fulham travelled down to the south coast for their fifth league game in just nineteen days, facing **Brighton and Hove Albion** at the Goldstone. Fulham's record at the ground was not that impressive, recording just one win in six visits. Brighton, having slumped badly recently, were in a similar need for points, but for the opposite reason; Fulham took an unchanged side and switched to their striped away kit. Fulham would face Bert Murray, who had turned down the chance of a move to the Cottage the week before. Apart from loan player Murray, Brighton also had another of Fulham's old foes on loan, former Burnley, Preston and Northern Ireland

The Brighton goalkeeper (on ground, right) has only been able to parry Steve Earle's powerful header and Jim Conway makes sure of the rebound with three defenders helpless. Fulham fought back bravely from two goals down to be on level terms, only to lose 2–3 to a deflected breakaway goal, heaping more stress on the team trying to remain in the top two places.

international centre forward Willie Irvine. Brighton's biggest crowd of the season, almost 15,000, arrived to watch the encounter.

In a hostile atmosphere, Brighton took the lead as early as the third minute with a goal from Peter O'Sullivan, later to join Fulham. Bert Murray wrong-footed the Fulham defence and gave Kit Napier the chance to cross accurately for O'Sullivan to smash the ball in. Before Fulham could settle, their old nemesis Willie Irvine added a sharp second just fifteen minutes later. He chased a long ball through a gap in the Fulham defence on the breakaway and managed to toe-poke his shot past the advancing Malcolm Webster.

Fulham had an immediate chance to pull a goal back but George Johnston's volley cannoned against the outside of the post and away to safety. Fulham then showed their mettle and managed to quickly get back on level terms. Firstly, Les Barrett produced a trademark accurate cross, but Johnston only managed a partial connection. After an almighty goalmouth scramble the ball was finally cleared back out to the wing. It was instantly pumped back in again where Steve Earle met it with a firm header; the keeper could only palm the powerful effort down into the box, where Jimmy Conway, lurking as ever, slammed it in. Johnston then produced a second goal soon after to level the match at half time.

In the second half, Brighton netted the winner with another smash and grab effort. From a Fulham attack, Napier won the ball near the halfway line and showed immaculate ball control, racing through the middle on a solo run. Fulham's luck was really out as Napier's final shot cannoned off defender Reg Matthewson and into the net, with Webster diving the other way.

The night had seemed to inspire the Seagulls; Fulham had played well but Brighton had scored three, *all* from breakaway moves. The Brighton supporters tried to console the away supporters by admitting that Fulham had been by far the best side to visit the Goldstone that season and that they had forced Brighton to produce form that even their own supporters didn't know they possessed; it was little consolation. The truth was another defeat, **2–3**.

Bert Murray had played well against the club he had rejected and signed a permanent contract for Brighton the following day. He and Irvine had formed an effective partnership up front, injecting skill and dash into the Seagulls' front line, giving Fulham's defence plenty of headaches in the process.

Fulham had performed their particular Fulhamish trick: having done all the hard work and having pushed themselves back into the top spot, they had thrown away four league points and handed back the initiative, once again, to their promotion rivals. This second consecutive defeat had once again removed Fulham from the top of the table, allowing Preston North End to claim the ascendancy.

At the weekend it was the turn of **Rotherham United** to visit the Cottage. The Rotherham side contained Ray Mielczarek in place of the departed Dave Watson at centre half. At inside forward was Rod Johnson, who had played his part in the 'thuggish' Doncaster team the previous season. Finally, the Rotherham substitute was Carl Gilbert who had scored the brace for Bristol Rovers that had knocked Fulham out of the FA Cup in November. Rotherham's promotion challenge had faded, although they held a place in the top seven for nearly all of the season.

Changes were also forced on Fulham; the unlucky Jimmy Conway had sustained an injury at Brighton, Dave Moreline took Stan Brown's place at full back, and Brown played right wing, John Richardson coming in for a rare game. Vic Halom was recalled to the squad and was named as substitute. Even at this late stage of the season and with Fulham needing a final push, a fickle crowd of fewer than 10,000 turned up.

Rotherham's attitude was clear from the start, a point at all costs. They lined up with only Neil Hague in an attacking position and for the majority of the half he was often the only Rotherham player in the Fulham half. Their Yorkshire 'grit' went over the top and a wild, crunching tackle from Dennis Leigh injured Stan Brown as early as the twenty-fifth minute, forcing an unanticipated reshuffle. The referee lectured Leigh at length, but he luckily remained on the pitch. The substitution was the right one: as Vic Halom came on to 'put himself about', Steve Earle took over the right wing position.

Rotherham's game plan remained unaltered, and the dour defensive tactics employed by the away side spilled over into provocative and violent play. The excesses were surprisingly allowed to continue, as the referee was Leo Callaghan, an experienced, international figure due to retire at the end of the season.

Tackles flew in all directions and players were bundled into touch, skipper Barry Lloyd being on the receiving end of several bad-tempered assaults. A prostrate Earle was then involved in a 'tangle' with Rotherham's Trevor Swift, who was marking him closely. Swift was also extremely lucky not to receive a caution. Fulham seemed mentally dejected by the two recent defeats and

George Johnston (behind the goalline) has beaten two Rotherham defenders in a mazy run, and pulled the ball back for Steve Earle (9). There are seven Rotherham defenders inside twelve yards, but Earle's volley evades them all and finds the roof of the net. The crucial strike gave Fulham a 1–0 win over the physical Yorkshire side.

seemed to have little answer to the 'clogging' tactics employed by the away side. The home side were lucky not to go in behind when Jimmy Mullen hit a post in a breakaway attack.

Fulham brightened up considerably in the second half and won the game thanks to a goal from Earle twenty minutes from time. George Johnston, playing one of his best games to date, won the ball and took it to the by-line, beating two defenders with a neat body swerve. He then centred accurately, allowing Earle to finish with a super, clipped left-foot shot from ten yards into the roof of the net, beating the diving goalkeeper and the inevitable defender on the line.

Rotherham then cautiously emerged from their destructive style, allowing the Fulham attack further half-chances, but none were taken. The best of these fell to Earle with another fine effort, but this time goalkeeper Roy Tunks made a fine point-blank save. In fact, Rotherham almost snatched an undeserved draw right at the death when Hague missed a great chance from close in. That would have been unjust, and Fulham held out for a slender but vital **1–0** win.

It had been a tired performance by the regular line-up, but at this stage of the season it was all about grinding out results. The win may not have been spectacular but the poached two points were the required outcome. So bad was the game that many supporters left before the end.

The defence in this game had, as usual this season, not let Fulham down. Veteran Reg Matthewson had shown immaculate timing both in the air and on the ground, and alongside Jimmy Dunne had sealed up the middle. Fred Callaghan had been the Man-of-the-Match, snuffing out the dangerous right wing whilst launching many effective counter-attacks of his own.

George Johnston appeared now to be settling in well. He had lost weight after Bill Dodgin forced him to put in extra training sessions. The crowd recognised his skills and were growing to respond to his neat footwork, perceptive passing and sharp shooting.

Apart from a few tricks from winger Mullen, Rotherham were a pale attacking force and only goalkeeper Tunks had prevented Fulham breaking through on further occasions.

With league fixtures coming thick and fast, Fulham were forced into action yet again on the following Wednesday when **Wrexham** were the visitors to the Cottage. Wrexham were mid-table and had little to play for. The Welsh side contained former Manchester United player Dave Gaskell in goal, former Crystal Palace player Tom Vansittart at full back, and former Aston Villa player Bobby Park at inside forward. The Wrexham substitute was Brian Tinnion, who had been a member of the Workington team that had given Fulham such a tough time in the League Cup in 1967.

Fulham had Jimmy Conway back on the wing and John Richardson reverted to substitute. The evening was another cold, wet, windy and thoroughly unpleasant one and this was reflected in yet another poor attendance – just under 9,000, the second lowest of the season.

The game appeared to have signs of the Luton 'snow encounter' from the previous season when the floodlights flickered after just two minutes. The lights failed completely after just five minutes and, with the ball at Steve Earle's feet in front of goal, plunged the entire ground into darkness. Referee Mr Lyden immediately whistled and ordered both teams to the dressing-room. After five minutes, the floodlights suddenly came on again and play was resumed.

Like the floodlights, Fulham stuttered through the first half and produced little, except a sharp shot from Earle that grazed the bar from just outside of the area. As in Saturday's Rotherham game, Fulham were soon the victims of heavy tackling. Earle was well shackled by Eddie May but one late tackle left the Fulham striker limping badly. Within minutes Jimmy Conway also took a nasty knock.

In the second half it was more of the same; Wrexham were no more than workmanlike, but Fulham were struggling to make an impression in front of goal. As Fulham strived to create an opening, the home side's supporters, who were beginning to tire of the ineffective attacking performances, started the slow handclap. In the past, this form of communication had usually deflated the Fulham side, but this time they seemed to get the message and upped the effort, the winning goal coming just a few minutes later.

In the sixty-fifth minute Conway swung over a high centre from the right, Earle challenged for the ball with goalkeeper Gaskell and both missed it, as did George Johnston. Fortunately, Les Barrett was coming in behind and he hooked home his sixteenth goal of the season on the run from ten yards. Barrett had done very well to accept the chance whilst being off balance.

A long centre evades almost everyone, but Les Barrett, arriving late and off balance, manages to keep his body over the ball and drill a low volley between the Wrexham keeper and a post. In a match punctuated by a floodlight failure, a tired Fulham managed to pull out yet another 1–0 home win to inch closer to promotion.

Fulham's cause of chasing further goals was hindered when George Johnston was also crocked by a Wrexham defender, forcing him to leave the field with John Richardson substituting. Wrexham then began to sense a chance and ventured from their defensive shell, launching dangerous raids down the middle.

Not for the first time, however, the Fulham defence would not be breached. Dave Moreline especially and Fred Callaghan kept both the wings very quiet, snuffing out the dangerous wingers Ian Moir and Andrew Provan. Cutting off the supply to the Wrexham front men Ray Smith and Albert Kinsey meant that Malcolm Webster had to face very few meaningful goalscoring attempts. If luck had run against them, Fulham may have conceded an equaliser – but they didn't. The Cottagers scraped home **1–0** and the win realised another two points and another clean sheet, pushing Fulham back to within one point of leaders Preston.

Fulham's regular line-up had certainly looked tired; it was the second time in four days that they had received 'a kicking' from the opposition on their own ground, with little intervention from either referee. Several of the squad were now walking wounded, but they had little prospect of enjoying a sustained rest.

Without doubt Fulham had looked nothing like promotion material on the squally night, a fact acknowledged by general manager Graham Hortop. He did, however, slam some of the supporters for the slow handclapping, stating: 'We deplore this; every team goes through a bad patch. What they [the team] need is encouragement; but it must be remembered that we have played two bad games and got four points and that is really what it's all about.'

Fred Callaghan also commented on the crowd's reaction, saying: 'It's awful when it [the slow handclap] happens. You're feeling terrible, because you know it's not a good game – you don't need anyone to remind you of that. You know that the harder you try, the worse it's likely to get, so you are striving to find a bit of poise which will help you to smooth things out. At this time, a bit of encouragement can work wonders – say when you win a corner. The crowd can set the game alight then, they can double the pressure on the opposition. ... If we had the backing Aston Villa have had, home and away all season, I think we would have the league wrapped up by now.'

The game had been fortunate to finish; it wasn't until the following morning that Fulham could arrange for a proper inspection of the floodlights! Hortop said: 'We tested the fuses and they were OK, I think one of the wires must have got wet and shorted. They came on again without us finding the fault, and we got through the match on a hope and a prayer!'

Although Fulham had played poorly, at least the players didn't have to read about their mediocre performance the following day. Further industrial action, as a protest against the Industrial Relations Bill, had now hit Fleet Street, and no national newspapers were printed on the Thursday.

The battle-weary troops took the long trip to Lancashire on the Saturday to play **Bury**. The Shakers had been struggling all season but were at last making a significant attempt to pull themselves clear of the relegation zone. On the day Bury were one of a cluster of clubs sitting nervously just outside the bottom four. For the Whites this was a potential banana skin and Bury were somewhat of a bogey side to Fulham at Gigg Lane. Somehow the injured Jimmy Conway, George Johnston and Steve Earle were all passed fit to play after intensive midweek treatment and Fulham once again announced an unchanged side.

It was a match when all the energy and fight finally drained out of Fulham, and the regular Fulham line-up had very little to offer. They put in another ineffective first-half performance and were lucky to be just one goal behind at the interval. Fulham tried to play defensively in a 4-4-2 formation, massing in midfield and relying on breakaways.

Bury should have taken the lead after just seven minutes when George Jones was put clean through by Terry McDermott, but he delayed his shot, allowing Malcolm Webster to make a spectacular save. Fulham rallied and Les Barrett, Fulham's only effective front player, put in a couple of excellent crosses that the Bury defence cleared only after difficulty.

Fulham should have gone ahead when Steve Earle put in a dangerous cross, but George Johnston skied the ball over when it looked much easier to score. Then Earle put in another cross that flew in front of the open goal with no forward handily placed to convert it. Just when Fulham looked like they were going to hold out until half time, they conceded a goal just two minutes before the break.

Lively ex-England winger John Connelly found a chink in the Fulham defence and broke through and his run was only halted when an illegal challenge by Fred Callaghan occurred in the penalty area, an uncontested penalty. The veteran Tom White converted from the spot to give the home side the advantage.

Once again the half-fit Johnston could not finish the match and was replaced by John Richardson. Fulham conceded a second goal in the second half on the hour when the defence panicked under pressure. They failed to clear Connelly's corner kick and the ball came out to the unmarked Jones, who calmly increased Bury's lead. Fulham, with confidence seemingly at rock bottom, offered nothing in response, especially in attack, allowing Bury to complete the match as easy winners **0–2**.

The defeat was the third in five games, and the performance could only have been described as dire. Club photographer Ken Coton summed up the dismal weekend with his review of the match by printing a totally blank picture in the club programme, saying: 'As to our match at Bury, well, no pictures, no comments – and that's being kind!' Only the consistent Reg Matthewson and tireless Barry Lloyd emerged from the match with any credit. Fulham had now lost seven out of the last thirteen away games in the league, certainly not promotion form. The only redeeming statistic about the result was that Fulham were the third consecutive promotion-seeking side to have lost at Gigg Lane.

At least Fulham had virtually a full week to overcome the cuts, bruises and strains, and they travelled on the Friday night to tackle **Chesterfield**. The Spirites were holding sixth place and were themselves only five points off a promotion spot, having come with a late surge, so the match would be a difficult one. However, Fulham normally performed well on Friday nights!

Some of the team had not recovered; Fulham were without both full backs, Dave Moreline and the influential Fred Callaghan, and George Johnston had also failed a fitness test. The game

Ken Coton's picture parade

Part of the centre spread in the subsequent programme following the last two matches. Photographer Ken got away with two non-pictures – at top left, a 'picture' taken when the floodlights failed against Wrexham, and at top right a blank 'picture' purporting to show the best moment of the dire display at Bury!

was the only one that Callaghan would miss all season. Wilf Tranter took Moreline's place, Mike Pentecost switched to his 'wrong' side, left back, to replace Callaghan and Vic Halom came in to replace Johnston.

After a dressing down from Dodgin following the Bury débâcle, at least the effort was there and the engine had returned to the team, although by now it was badly in need of a service.

Fulham emerged in search of two points but in the end had to settle for one. Chesterfield, surprisingly, played defensively at home, looking to contain the Fulham forwards. It was probably

In the dim floodlights of a Third Division game on a Friday evening at Saltergate our intrepid photographer captures the Chesterfield goalkeeper making a routine save. In a tight game, Fulham managed to eke out another point in a 0–0 draw which kept them on course for Division Two. (Photographer Ken Coton points out that, at many grounds at the beginning of the Seventies, floodlights were not very bright. High-speed films were not then available and it was almost impossible to achieve well exposed action pictures. However, computers now make it possible to get something from very 'thin' negatives.)

a sound judgement initially, as in the first half Fulham made all of the running and were quicker in both thought and action. They had none of the luck, with a shot from Jimmy Conway going very close. Despite their domination they were unable to prise open the tight Chesterfield defence. Les Barrett and Conway were splitting the defence but Steve Earle in the centre was unable to cash in. Fulham's best chance of the half fell to Vic Halom when he picked up a mis-hit back pass, but unfortunately his shot was scrambled off the line.

The second half was a different story and Chesterfield abandoned their cautious approach and launched a barrage of raids on the Fulham goal. Fortunately, Malcolm Webster was in fine form in the Fulham goal and repelled all of the home side's attacks; the defence, too, were extremely resolute and gave little away.

Chesterfield decided to launch a grandstand finish and John Archer had two good efforts on the Fulham goal, one blocked and one brilliantly tipped over by Webster. In the end the attacks began to abate, but Chesterfield had one final surprise. In an attack in the last minute, top scorer Ernie Moss got in a header that beat Webster but the ball crashed against the post and rebounded to safety. Both sides then settled for a **0–0** result.

At least the team had eked out a point from a very tight tussle, and at the moment points were all important. A piece of good fortune emerged after the game when news filtered through confirming that Aston Villa had gone down 1–2 at Doncaster Rovers, where a young Peter Kitchen had scored Rovers' winner. Fulham's promotion task, however, was made all the harder the following day, as Preston were victorious by a single goal at Port Vale.

Skipper Barry Lloyd commented: 'It looks as if Preston are strolling off with the championship, but I think we'll nick the other promotion place. We have set ourselves a target of sixty points which means taking twelve points from our remaining eight games.'

April 1971

In this month

* Lt William Calley was released while the Mylai conviction was 'reviewed'.
* President Nixon vowed to end the USA's involvement in Vietnam and said that 100,000 troops would be home by Christmas.
* In London, the City gave the go-ahead for the construction of the £17 million Barbican Centre.
* Unemployment in the UK was at its highest level for over thirty years.
* In South Africa, President Vorster said that his country would allow mixed-race sport at international level.
* Three Russian cosmonauts were put into orbit in *Soyuz X*.
* Plans were announced to redevelop London's declining Docklands area.
* Haiti dictator 'Papa Doc' Duvalier died.
* In Northern Ireland, the 'provisional' IRA split away from the 'official' IRA.
* Hot pants became the latest women's fashion item.
* The composer Igor Stravinsky died.

'Hot Love' by T-Rex topped the charts.
The film 'A Clockwork Orange' was released.

How the league was looking

The top of the table continued to swing erratically. Fulham's wobble had seen them relinquish top spot yet again in favour of Preston North End, whose form was still the most consistent; Fulham were now a clear *four* points behind Preston, who also had a game in hand. The unlikely lads, Halifax Town, had continued to push on strongly and were still tucked in, in third place. They were beginning to feel the pressure, however, and they were now three clear points behind Fulham. Aston Villa had failed to improve on their fourth spot, but they too were level on points with Halifax. Bristol Rovers were still in fifth and Chesterfield were now sixth. Torquay's challenge was over and they had slipped into mid-table.

Gillingham were still at the base of the table, but had found some form and were just four points adrift from safety. Doncaster Rovers were still in the danger zone, three points ahead of Gillingham. Just two points then separated the next *nine* teams. Walsall, due to a number of injuries, had slipped into the relegation zone and Brighton were just marginally better off on goal average. The clubs just outside the trouble zone were Reading, now faltering badly, Tranmere Rovers, Shrewsbury Town, Bury, Bradford City and Port Vale. Plymouth Argyle and Barnsley had both put on an impressive spurt and were heading towards mid-table safety.

The matches

FULHAM'S FIRST match in April saw them take on the Saddlers. Fulham had a 100% record against **Walsall** at Craven Cottage, so they were confident of winning this one. Walsall had slumped badly during the last three months and were now drifting towards relegation. They had lost young star goalkeeper Phil Parkes, now with QPR. The Saddlers had experienced severe financial problems, leading to a professional staff of just *fourteen* players! They had lost the services of Allan Baker, Frank Gregg and Willie Penman through injury. Fulham's George Johnston had been loaned to Walsall earlier in the season to help them out in their forward crisis. They were not a team to be underrated however, as they had recently taken three points out of four from local rivals Aston Villa.

Fulham were still without Dave Moreline and were now further hampered by the loss of Steve Earle, who missed his first league game of the season due to a groin injury. Mike Pentecost came

As in the Rotherham game, George Johnston (8) has danced through, and with Walsall expecting a shot, has instead cut the ball back for Les Barrett to fire home through a wall of Walsall defenders. A third consecutive tight home game finished 1–0, two more precious points in the bag.

in at right back and Vic Halom deputised for Earle. Despite being second in the table another very poor crowd of under 8,500 turned up to watch.

Walsall, like teams before them, dug into the trenches ready for a defensive battle. It was a day when the Fulham defenders would have to watch for breakaways, but they were admirably vigilant and Jimmy Dunne was again in inspired form, backed up by the ever reliable Reg Matthewson and Fred Callaghan. They gave Walsall virtually no opportunities to score.

However, it wasn't so bright at the other end. Apart from the effervescent Les Barrett, the forwards were again off form, Jimmy Conway and George Johnston especially, and the team were again making hard work of scoring. The effort and application were there, but individual opportunism and flair were once again sadly lacking. Despite dominating as usual, the first half was a no-score bore with neither side looking remotely like creating a goal.

It was fitting that Barrett should be the scorer of the winning goal on the day, as he had looked head and shoulders above anything else on the pitch. Five minutes after half time Matthewson found Johnston with a superb pass out to the wing inside the full back. Johnston made progress and then cut quickly into the penalty box. With some expecting a shot, Johnston pulled the ball back cleverly to Barrett racing in, who hit a thunderous right-foot shot first time through a line of Walsall defenders and into the far corner of the net.

Walsall now had to come out and they pushed Stan Bennett into the front line, but had very little to offer up front. Forward John Woodward came on for loan signing Jimmy Seal but the change made little difference. Conway went close on two more occasions, and Barrett forced the save of the match out of goalkeeper Bob Wesson. Fulham should have increased their lead five minutes from the end, but Conway's header, from a central position eight yards out, hit the bar and was cleared. Fulham played out the remainder of the game comfortably to record yet another slender **1–0** win.

Again the football hadn't been pretty, but it had been effective. The match certainly hadn't been a great one for spectators, but two more promotion points had been secured. The win marked the third consecutive occasion where a defensive team playing in a red and white strip had come to the Cottage, and all three had lost by the same 1–0 margin.

Although the attack was definitely off colour, the Walsall match was the fourth clean sheet in the last five matches, so Fulham were still remaining a difficult side to beat. It was comforting to know that Fulham could still pick up points whilst delivering an under par performance.

George Cohen commented: 'I still think Fulham's chances this season of going up are very, very good. I don't think we can catch Preston but barring injuries I still think we can go up.'

Bill Dodgin agreed when the same question was put to him, saying: 'Yes, we are getting the points, and others have to catch up.' Dodgin, though, did admit that the pressures of promotion were building: 'It's nearly a month since they had the luxury of playing with a lead of more than one goal. I keep telling them to relax, but it's easier said than done.'

Steve Earle and Les Barrett had not been on tip-top form for some time, but a strong rumour persisted that if Fulham failed to obtain the necessary points for promotion then both players would be transferred to Queens Park Rangers for a combined fee of £120,000.

Although the rumours appeared to have some solid foundation, Steve Earle still considered his future to be with Fulham. He acknowledged that he and the team had not been playing very well of late but believed things were beginning to improve again. Even Les Barrett was more optimistic, and the day the transfer rumours officially surfaced, Barrett withdrew his long-standing on-off transfer request.

With little respite, Fulham had another midweek fixture at the Cottage when **Rochdale** were the visitors. The match had been brought forward from Good Friday to relieve Fulham's load, with away trips to Gillingham and Plymouth Argyle both scheduled for Easter. Rochdale had consolidated just below mid-table, but were still just three points outside the bottom four, so had to be careful. The Rochdale team had no new faces on show and Steve Earle returned for Fulham with Vic Halom as substitute. A slightly better crowd, inching to just over 10,000, turned up.

Fulham were, as usual, on better form under the floodlights, but the Fulham faithful had to endure a torturous first half where the ball did everything but go in. Barry Lloyd, Les Barrett and Jimmy Conway all went within inches of scoring, and Rochdale goalkeeper Tony Godfrey had to plunge spectacularly to his left to keep out a goalbound header from George Johnston. Stan Brown had a volley blocked by Rochdale's Norman Whitehead and Johnston rattled the angle of post and bar with another shot. Rochdale did not appear to have the attacking prowess to win the game but suggested that they possessed enough of the defensive mechanics to avoid defeat.

Fulham needed to break the deadlock quickly and did so within six minutes of the restart. A flash of Johnston trickery on the wing set up Steve Earle with a neat one-two; the return pass to Earle took a deflection and sat up nicely for the Fulham striker to finish with a magnificent volley that found the corner of the net from fifteen yards. The Rochdale play then became tetchy and their centre forward David Cross was booked after successive fouls on Barrett and Fred Callaghan.

Fulham at last began to relax, but were gifted their second goal just a quarter of an hour from the end. Rochdale half back Joe Ashworth impetuously handled in the penalty area when under little pressure and Conway made no mistake from the penalty spot.

Fulham now just needed to keep possession. Defensively it had been another excellent performance with the experienced Reg Matthewson and player of the season Jimmy Dunne never allowing the Rochdale forwards a real sniff at goal. Malcolm Webster had one of his easiest evenings of the season, barely used. Fulham played out time to record a **2–0** win, their seventh successive home win, another clean sheet and the double over Rochdale.

The win had been a deserved one if not a handsome one. Fulham had looked rejuvenated up front and all of the forwards had been given or had made chances for themselves. The defence had been very sound as on Saturday and, if anything, were currently the main driving force behind Fulham's promotion bid. The result made it five clean sheets in the last six matches. Skipper Lloyd heaped praise on the back four, Reg Matthewson, the 'old man' of the side, especially, saying that he had been the most consistent player throughout the entire season.

A delighted Dodgin commented afterwards: 'I would sooner have points in the bag than the games in hand. It now gives Villa a target to chase. I thought we played some good stuff at times, and we're just happy to get the points at this stage. We should have no fears about going to Gillingham and Plymouth over Easter.'

The Easter Saturday match with **Gillingham** at the Priestfield stadium always looked likely to be a tricky fixture. The Cottagers' record there was not good; Fulham needed the win badly and at the other end of the table, Gillingham's need was equally desperate. The Kent side had picked

Straight after the restart, George Johnston converts Barrett's low centre, sliding the ball past the Gillingham goalkeeper for the visitors' first goal. The Gills are shell-shocked and the Fulham players prepare to celebrate with the delighted goalscorer.

up a few points recently and by doing so had given themselves a fighting chance of Third Division survival.

It was a day when the sunny and windy weather made playing Fulham's brand of football difficult. Fulham were still carrying injuries. Stan Brown was out, meaning a recall for Stan Horne, his first start in well over three months. Steve Earle's injury had flared up again and he too was missing; George Johnston would play, but was only half fit. The supporters knew this was a real four pointer, and eight official coaches and hundreds of private cars streamed towards the Medway.

With the away support roaring, Fulham took off like a steam train and Jimmy Conway forced home goalkeeper John Simpson to dive and save at the foot of a post in the first few minutes. Vic Halom then sent a powerful header inches over the crossbar, and Simpson then had to rush from goal to dive at winger Les Barrett's feet to prevent an opening goal.

A rare mistake by Reg Matthewson allowed winger Tom Watson in, but he blazed high over the bar. Normal service was soon resumed, however, when Halom powered in another brilliant header, pawed away by Simpson.

Just as it seemed a matter of time before Fulham scored, Gillingham broke away and scored completely against the run of play just five minutes before half time. David Peach lobbed a long ball forward that appeared to hang in the wind and centre forward Mike Green timed his run well to dash on and beat the advancing Malcolm Webster as he came out to narrow the angle, Green slotting the ball into an empty net. Several Fulham players queried the decision; most of the defenders had stopped expecting the offside flag that never came. A shell-shocked Fulham went in trailing at half time, feeling that there was no justice.

After a pep talk from Bill Dodgin, who forced home the message 'keep playing football and the goals will come', Fulham, spurred on by the sheer number of cheering away supporters, obtained immediate rewards. Just a minute after the restart George Johnston equalised from Barrett's low cross, sliding the ball past Simpson, and before Gillingham could recover from the shock, Les Barrett put Fulham ahead just two minutes later.

Conway's corner was knocked on and then controlled by Halom, whose headed pass sent Barrett in to score with a rasping shot from six yards. Gillingham were shattered and whilst they

Job done! From Les Barrett's assist, Jimmy Conway cracks in a shot off the goalkeeper's hands from close range and it was the third Fulham goal in a fiery eight-minute spell. The 3–1 victory at the Priestfield Stadium took Fulham to the brink of promotion.

were still on the floor, Fulham cemented victory with a third goal just five minutes later. Conway converted from close range following yet another assist from Barrett and, although the Gillingham goalkeeper got his hand to the shot, he couldn't keep the ball out. This made it three Fulham goals in a devastating *eight-minute* spell.

Apart from the persistent running of Brian Yeo, frequently outnumbered by defenders, Gillingham could raise no real reply. They were still pressed back, and although David Quirke defended stoutly Fulham always looked capable of adding further goals. Gillingham were truly rattled and the appropriately named Mike Kent, on loan from Wolves, was booked for lunging tackles on Conway and Barry Lloyd.

The match looked won, and Dodgin withdrew Johnston from the fray and sent on John Richardson to consolidate the win. From the hour mark, Fulham just played the ball around, reserving their strength for the long, tough Monday trip ahead; Fulham ran out easy **3–1** winners in the end.

Although Fulham's defence had looked comfortable for the majority of the match, it was a swing away from the recent form inasmuch as the forwards won this game. All looked on sparkling form and dangerous; Les Barrett who scored one goal and made the other two was on particularly good form again. George Johnston, with his clever approach play and intelligent footwork, had finally seemed to have won over the fans. The win gave Fulham the double over Gillingham and virtually ended the Kent side's battle to stay in the division.

The match was shown the following day as the main game on *The Big Match*, retaining every moment of its quality. Preston had also slipped up slightly with a draw, and Fulham took over at the top of the table once again on goal average. A delighted Dodgin said wryly afterwards: 'I don't know how all the other promotion-seeking teams have got on, as long as we are winning I don't really care.'

Now exhausted, it was time for the team to approach the final run-in, and the run-in couldn't have been much harder than a lengthy trip to Devon to face the Pilgrims, **Plymouth Argyle**. Responding to supporters' requests, the club chartered a special train that was sold out quickly. A tired Fulham again reported no changes. Plymouth were in the classic mid-table position with nothing to play for. They were, however, quite tough to beat at home, but had drawn over half of their home league matches that season. Their current home form was not particularly good, however, and they had won just one of their previous six home matches.

Fulham were not as classy on the day and their attacks were more sporadic, but they were assisted by a strong wind blowing down the ground. George Johnston was the first to test the home keeper, but he saved bravely. Despite being on the back foot, Fulham managed to break out and secure a lead after half an hour. Stan Horne and Johnston combined cleverly to set up Vic Halom standing by the penalty spot. Halom's initial control let him down, but he received a second opportunity, swivelled quickly and stabbed a fine shot past Jim Furnell giving the keeper no chance.

Fulham were again forced back and were lucky not to concede a penalty when Malcolm Webster brought down Plymouth winger Don Hutchins in the box whilst racing out to clear. The Plymouth players asked earnestly for the penalty, but referee Norman Burtenshaw, supposedly on a leisurely outing before officiating at the FA Cup Final, turned them down; minutes later former Chelsea full back Alan Harris missed a fine chance to equalise.

Fulham thought that they had secured a two-goal cushion when Johnston hammered the ball in but the goal was ruled out for a marginal offside or pushing decision; referee Burtenshaw's reason for disallowing the effort was not wholly clear.

Finally, with the gusting wind assisting them, Plymouth launched an all-out assault. Striker Jim Hinch also had the ball in the net but this too was disallowed following a spot of pushing. The decision was again contested, many home supporters seeing nothing wrong with the 'goal'. Although they were dominating territorially, Plymouth were creating few real scoring chances and Webster was having a relatively easy afternoon.

Credit had to be given to Plymouth for their persistence and they never gave up. The two lanky strikers, Keith Allen and Hinch, were consistently out-jumping and hassling the Fulham defence into mistakes and they finally earned their reward with a headed goal from Hinch, recently signed from Tranmere Rovers, just three minutes from the end. Both teams seemed to settle for a draw and another promotion point was added to Fulham's chest in a **1–1** draw.

Even though just a point had been achieved, loud cheers went up when news filtered through that Fulham's main rivals Preston had just been beaten 1–0 at Reading. Fulham's football had been more enterprising than that of the home side and had carried greater conviction; in the end it had been just sheer tiredness that had led to a momentary lapse of concentration. Certainly with five points achieved over the Easter period, Fulham could not have been too unhappy. The only worry was the injury to another striker, Vic Halom, who limped off near the end to be replaced by John Richardson.

The Saturday brought **Shrewsbury Town** to the Cottage. Fulham needed the points, but Shrewsbury were just three points outside the relegation zone. The Shrewsbury side were little changed from that of the previous season, although their side now contained the experienced goalkeeper Ken Mulhearn, bought from Manchester City to replace John Phillips, now with Aston Villa. Shrewsbury also had nippy left-winger Allan Groves, signed from Chester and previously with Southport, in the team; Fulham were unchanged. With a sense of promotion in the air, well over 12,500 attended the match.

Fulham's problems were not helped when the half-fit Vic Halom suffered another serious knock after just fifteen minutes and had to be replaced by John Richardson; Halom's leg injury was a nasty one, requiring twelve stitches. Richardson was quite rusty, not having played regular first-team football for some time and looked rather out of his depth in the centre forward role.

Fulham should have had at least three goals in the first half of the match; firstly George Johnston just failed to put his head on an inviting Les Barrett cross, and then Fred Callaghan's intelligent, floating chip beat the Shrewsbury offside trap and the ball fell invitingly for Stan Horne. Instead of controlling the ball, Horne hit it first time and the ball sailed harmlessly over the bar. Then it was Jimmy Conway's turn; he was picked out by an accurate cross from Barrett but tried too hard to direct his header, and again the ball ended up amongst the crowd instead.

In the second half Johnston again took possession; he swivelled on the penalty spot, but he had more time than he thought. Instead of looking up, he, like Horne, opted for a first-time shot and smashed the ball wide of a yawning goal. All the hard work done in midfield was being wasted by some terrible finishing.

Fulham tried to commit more men forward; Barry Lloyd joined in the attack, but both he and Johnston were being crowded out by tall defenders. The commitment to attack always looked likely to cause problems even for Fulham's resolute defence and, paradoxically, Malcolm Webster was

Watched by six Shrewsbury defenders, this headed effort from 'Wee Georgie' Johnston just clears the bar. All efforts on the day were high or wide, and a tired Fulham side, now running on empty, could only manage a 0–0 draw against a mediocre Shrewsbury side.

the busier keeper, dealing with speculative shots from the isolated raids. In fact, the result could so easily have been worse.

From a corner taken by Dave Roberts, Alf Woods' header was tipped over the bar with difficulty by Webster. Finally, in the last minute Shrewsbury's Groves, put through by Jim McLaughlin, advanced and hit a shot that looked bound for the bottom corner; Webster stayed on his line and it took an unorthodox outstretched leg to keep the score sheet blank. Fulham were certainly making life hard for themselves; the match finishing **0–0**.

The performance was a worn and jaded one from a very tired team, now almost 'running on empty'. The game had been a non-event, and although Fulham rarely looked like conceding a goal, they had rarely looked like scoring one either. Apart from the trickery of Allan Groves, Shrewsbury had offered little up front and had really been let off the hook by an off-colour Fulham. Although the display had been probably the poorest home performance of the season, the team had not merited the slow handclap that started in the second half. All Bill Dodgin would say was: 'We'll still make it.'

Fortunately, spirits were raised again soon after the match when news came through that Preston North End had also lost yet again, so it was 'as you were', and Fulham's prospects had actually improved! Aston Villa's challenge had also hit the buffers with a run of poor form that had seen the Midlands side tumble down to fifth. Chesterfield were up to fourth, but a clear seven points adrift. Fulham and Preston now looked to be favourites for promotion, with Halifax as the long-shot outsiders.

At long last, Fulham had the benefit of a full week off to treat the cuts and bruises, strains and stresses, ready for the final push before setting off to **Doncaster Rovers** and Belle Vue. The match was another against relegation-threatened opponents. Doncaster were just within the relegation zone and needed further points badly to pull away. Another special train carrying over 400 supporters departed for Doncaster.

Fulham had Steve Earle back, which allowed the half-fit Halom to remain as substitute. For some strange reason, Fulham forsook their 'normal' change kit of light blue and dark blue stripes to

Just four minutes from time, and a goal worth a fortune! Les Barrett has wriggled through and Steve Earle has converted his short cross at the near post. On a bleak day and in a sea of mud the 1–0 victory over Doncaster at Belle Vue was crucially important.

play in blue shirts, white shorts with blue socks. The day in Doncaster was dull and miserable, with persistent rain and a grey sky. The playing surface was in very poor condition, a sea of mud.

The encounter was certainly not a classic, but Fulham rolled their sleeves up and battled. Fulham played brilliantly in the first twenty minutes; they created four clear chances to score but none was taken, increasing Bill Dodgin's clear frustration. Steve Earle and Les Barrett were combining well and keeping goalkeeper Glenn Johnson busy.

After just ten minutes, Johnson had to dive full length to prevent Jimmy Conway from running the ball into the net. Then, just five minutes later, the home goalkeeper had to leap spectacularly to push a dipping shot from Barrett over the bar.

With no early success forthcoming, Fulham lost confidence and began to fall away badly. However, it was possible to sense that it might be their day when Doncaster had the ball in the net, only to see the effort chalked off for a very marginal offside decision.

In the second half, Doncaster still appeared to have the upper hand and were unfortunate when Graham Watson should have opened the scoring. He was presented with a clear chance just ten yards out but hooked his shot well wide with only Malcolm Webster to beat, much to the relief of the arguing Fulham defence.

Although Doncaster had the majority of the possession, they weren't really hurting Fulham at the back. Bob Gilfillan and Peter Kitchen were having unhappy afternoons up front and Reg Matthewson as usual was mopping up effectively, goalkeeper Webster being a virtual spectator. Winger Brian Usher was constantly switching wings and troubling full backs Mike Pentecost and Fred Callaghan, but he badly lacked support.

Both teams now appeared to be settling for the blank-score draw. John Haselden was outstanding at the back for Doncaster and was limiting Fulham's chances. As Fulham came under further late pressure, they replaced George Johnston with the bustling Vic Halom to add weight and to stop the ball coming out of the home defence so quickly.

The substitution was an inspired one and Halom quickly began to make his presence felt. From a Fulham attack, with just four minutes left, he helped the ball on to Barrett on the wing. A single piece of Barrett magic then ensued with a left wing run. Barrett took the ball to the dead ball line and crossed low where Earle moved towards the near post and, after a scramble, sidefooted the ball into the corner of the net between goalkeeper and post, and that was that; a goal that was worth a fortune.

Fulham hung on grimly in the last five minutes for a **1–0** win and another clean sheet – promotion was now just a heartbeat away. The result was an unfair and ultimately disastrous one for the Doncaster side from which they never recovered. It had been a case of *déjà vu* for Doncaster, as they had lost at home to Fulham the previous season by the same score, thanks to a goal inside the final ten minutes.

Just four days later, Fulham were back in Yorkshire for their final away match at Valley Parade and **Bradford City** on the Wednesday evening. It was a third consecutive fixture against a club deep in the relegation mire. Fulham were unchanged, and the game was officiated by a Mr Jolly and everyone was hoping that Fulham would be exactly that after the match.

With the prize in sight Fulham started anxiously, and nervy forwards Steve Earle, Jimmy Conway and Les Barrett all wasted good scoring chances when the home defence was really struggling. The nerves were finally settled just after the half hour by George Johnston who pounced on a loose ball in the Bradford penalty area and volleyed home from eight yards with two defenders closing in. Just as it looked as if Fulham would take this lead into the interval, they were stung when Bradford equalised just two minutes before half time when John Hall scored a snappy goal.

The second half saw Fulham regain the lead ten minutes after half time with a full-blooded volley from twenty yards by Barry Lloyd. The shot was hit so hard that the home goalkeeper Pat Liney was only able to palm the ball up and over his head, finally fumbling the ball into the goal. The goal was Lloyd's first for almost six months, and what a time to score it.

Again Bradford took the goal in their stride, bravely fighting back to level the scores yet again just three minutes later with a spectacular header from defender Norman Corner. The home side were making Fulham fight all the way and it was now a real thriller of a match that could swing either way. Fulham were having to call on every ounce of their superior class to suppress the fighting spirit of the Yorkshire side.

Then finally, just twelve minutes from the end, Johnston grabbed his second of the night and Fulham's third with a crashing header from ten yards into the top corner of the net, following a super run and cross from Barrett. It was appropriate that Johnston had scored the two goals on the night, as he had experienced a tough time winning over the paying customers at the Cottage.

The game continued for what seemed an eternity, until the final whistle blew and Fulham knew they had finally done it *and that promotion was theirs*. After four depressing years, the team had finally turned the first corner and they would be playing Second Division football the following season. A tired but happy Fulham trooped off the pitch following an historic **3–2** victory.

One final push is all that's required, and nerves are partially settled as George Johnston volleys Fulham's first goal from eight yards between two Bradford defenders. But there was still an hour to go.

Bradford City fought back twice to drag themselves level, their need for points equally desperate. With just over ten minutes left, the brilliant Barrett produced another great run and cross and Johnston's header crashes into the roof of the net. Fulham are home 3–2 and promotion is theirs!

A triumph for 'intelligent football'; a smiling Bill Dodgin celebrates Fulham's return to the Second Division. After many years of non-success, Dodgin had turned round Fulham's fortunes completely in the space of just two full seasons.

A delighted vice chairman Noël D'Amato shares a celebratory victory drink with beaming captain Barry Lloyd in the dressing room at Bradford City.

The result had been very tough on Bradford, and Fulham had completed another double. Eventually Bradford scrambled the other point they needed to preserve their Third Division status. In their two seasons in the Third Division, Fulham had played twenty games against Yorkshire opposition (home and away) and lost only once! The Bradford board of directors sportingly supplied the Fulham contingent with champagne and congratulated the team on their success.

In his first post-match interview Bill Dodgin said: 'I'm delighted. Everyone has worked hard for this. We have been under a lot of pressure. Because we have been favourites, it has been hard for us. Tonight's game was one of our hardest, and we just made it in the end.'

An emotional Tommy Trinder was a relieved and delighted man immediately after the game; he had waited years for a change of fortune. He said: 'Tony Dean [the Fulham director] and I were sitting together at Bradford, and when we scored he got out a stopwatch. The seconds ticked away so slowly – then when they equalised, I swear that watch speeded up. When we scored our second, out came that watch again, and we had to keep shaking it to find out if it had stopped. They made it 2–2, but at last our third went in, and after that it seemed as if the referee would never blow his whistle.

'What a match! Psychologically people fighting to stay up like Bradford City are even more determined to get stuck in – as we well know from experience.'

On getting his breath back, he commented: 'What a season, and how marvellous to do our struggling at the top of the table for a change. It would be tough trying to go all through this again, but I'd love it to happen – soon. We did so well against Second Division teams in Cup competitions that it is obvious we have a great chance to settle down. We are the only London club in the Third Division this season, and we are looking forward to those derby matches in the second next season.'

Captain Barry Lloyd's immediate reaction after the match was one of relief; he said: 'We were leaping about in the dressing room after the win at Bradford. Of course we hadn't dared to bring any champagne along because we thought it might jinx things for us. Then came a knock at the door from our supporters who were carrying three bottles of champagne and a bottle of whisky. They've supported us fabulously this season, not just at the death, but all the way through. We know there is a real hard core of Fulham fans and we'll try to keep them shouting home and away next season.

'This is my first season as captain and everybody has done his best to make it easy for me. This season we have stopped going backwards. Next season we could well keep rolling forward. I believe we can keep it up. We want the best, and we'll do our level best to get it.'

Barring a miracle, Les Barrett was going to finish the season as top scorer with a total of eighteen, impressive for a winger. Les added: 'It's not hit us properly yet that we've done something at last. I began to wonder if the day would ever come. Ever since I started with Fulham in the First Division, we have been fighting relegation and sometimes losing the battle.

'Now the pattern has changed. I thought my future was elsewhere, but I've done my best to make it happen here, and I'm glad people think that I've done my share.

'It's still only the Second Division next season, but the higher we go, the better chance we'll have to show what we can do as footballers. The spirit is better than it's ever been while I've been here. The bonus money is going straight into a building society; I'm not bothering about that. We're all looking forward to the holiday, but much more we're looking forward to the start of the new season.'

Bill Dodgin reserved special praise for the two-goal hero George Johnston, saying: 'He has proved a terrific bargain. He has scored ten goals in twenty-four matches, and I've lost count of the number that he has laid on for the rest of the players. Ask me to name one man who has helped our promotion push, and it would be wee Georgie.'

The match had been rewarding for Bill Dodgin; in just his second full season, he had added to the successes he had achieved with both Millwall and Queens Park Rangers by guiding Fulham to a similar promotion, all based on an attacking philosophy.

The fact that Fulham had achieved promotion by scoring three goals in a difficult away match was testament to Dodgin's commitment to attacking football. In the eighteen league games played in the last three months, Fulham had won eleven and drawn four, securing twenty-six points, a pace that had been too hot for others to handle.

Jimmy Hill would now have to keep his promise and hire another boat, possibly the Queen Mary this time, to float down the Thames once again, this time in a promotion celebration rather than a relegation wake. As a thank you from the directors, the first team squad would all share in a £25,000 payout, based on the number of first-team appearances made that season.

Fulham Youth in Düsseldorf (April 1971)

Fulham's youth side again left on Good Friday in an attempt to retain the trophy they had won abroad the previous year. As holders, the team were greeted with television cameras, and there were other 'celebrity' pressures to overcome. George Cohen commented: 'On the whole I don't think we did a bad job as ambassadors of English football.' The results were as follows:

Group matches

Versus:		
Bale (the Greek National side)	0–0
Bielefeld	0–0
Schalke '04	0–1
Admira Vienne	2–0

The results had just fallen short of what was necessary to put the club into the semi-finals, despite conceding just one goal in the four group matches. Once again, however, the team had done the club proud.

In Fulham's party were six fifteen-year-old players. The vast majority of the opponents had been far older and stronger as they had been the previous year, so the younger lads had done very well. Fulham had also lost promising defender John Fraser with a cartilage injury that required an operation.

The trophy was never actually awarded that season at all. The final between the Greek National side and the host side was abandoned. The Greeks had taken the lead, and the Germans had equalised seconds before the end. During the extra time period, the Germans were awarded a highly controversial penalty.

The hundreds of Greek supporters in the crowd swarmed onto the field – and remained there, steadfastly refusing to let the penalty kick be taken. The 'riotous assembly' led to the final ultimately being abandoned; some things never change!

May 1971

In this month

* *The Daily Mail* was published as a broadsheet for the last time.
* In the USA, the police expelled 30,000 anti-war protestors from the banks of the Potomac River.
* Eric Honecker became general secretary of the Communist party.
* Over 100 Labour MPs defied their party by signing a declaration supporting Britain's entry into the EEC.
* Mick Jagger married Bianca Perez Morena de Maclas in St Tropez.
* Labour made large gains in the local elections, and took control of the Greater London Council (GLC).
* The Government announced plans to charge an entry fee (between 10p and 20p) for museums and art galleries.
* Edward Heath and Georg Pompidou of France ended talks, saying 'the road is clear' for Britain's entry into the EEC.
* Jackie Stewart won the Monaco Grand Prix.
* In Belfast, a soldier was killed and several others were wounded by a bomb.
* British golfers won the Walker Cup for the first time since 1938.
* The *Mariner IX* spacecraft was launched in the direction of Mars.
* London Bridge was controversially sold to an American consortium, transported brick by brick and re-assembled in Havasu in Arizona.
* Anwar Saddat foiled an overthrow attempt in Egypt.
* The US poet Ogden Nash died.
* Arsenal won the domestic League and FA Cup double.
* Chelsea won the European Cup Winners Cup, beating Real Madrid 2–1 in the final in Athens.

'Knock Three Times' by Dawn topped the charts.
The film '10 Rillington Place' was released.

How the league was looking

Fulham's eight-match unbeaten run had taken them to promotion; Preston North End, whose form had been patchy of late, looked likely to win promotion as well. They lay three points behind Fulham but they had a game in hand. Unlikely heroes Halifax Town had kept going to the last, consolidating third place, but the men from the Shay needed to win both their remaining games and hope that Preston slipped up badly in order to move up from their third place.

Bristol Rovers were in fourth place and Aston Villa had failed to complete the course dropping down to fifth. Chesterfield were still in sixth place, level on points with both Bristol Rovers and Villa, all three teams being a clear six points off second place.

Gillingham had been relegated along with Doncaster Rovers. Bury had slumped again in the final furlong and looked unlikely to survive, their fate resting on the performances of others. Three teams were fighting over the final relegation spot: Walsall, Reading, and Bradford City, all on the same number of points. Brighton had been impressive in the last ten games and had hauled themselves well clear.

The matches

ONCE AGAIN the fixture 'god' had stirred up the mixture and reserved the Fulham against **Preston North End** match for the final Saturday of the season: one club already promoted, the other looking highly likely to join them. The match took place on May 1st – May Day; it was to

Happy days are at the Cottage again, and it's smiles all round. Skipper Lloyd leads out his promoted side, hoping to clinch the championship.

be hoped that this was not an omen. Fulham had lost their First Division lives on May Day three years previously, so the superstitious were praying for a different outcome.

Bill Dodgin, still emphasising his attacking philosophy, said: 'We only need a point for the Championship today, but we will not be playing for a draw. We wouldn't know how to play that way. Somebody asked me if we would change our tactics for division two, but we have no choice really. We can only play the way we have been playing.

'We try to play good football and you could argue it is sound policy. After all, what would be the use of going up with a crude style which would not live in the higher class? But, the truth is, we're not equipped to play any other way. This season we had to do what we did and hoped it would succeed; we'll try the same next season.'

The stark truth of the matter was that Fulham, the home side, with only one defeat at home all season in the league, needed just a home draw to secure the Third Division championship trophy. Preston had won six and lost seven away from home, so statistically a draw seemed the most likely outcome. Preston were three points adrift of Fulham, but had a game in hand, so their goal was simple; they had to win both their matches.

On a boiling hot afternoon, the expectant home crowd were in party mood, and balloons, champagne and all sorts of promotion paraphernalia littered the terraces at the Cottage. Many turned up in T-shirts emblazoned with the words 'Fulham – Third Division Champions 1970–71'. The team arrived to a tickertape welcome.

Fulham were yet again unchanged and a huge celebrating crowd of almost 26,000 waited to watch Fulham deliver the *coup de grace*. Unfortunately Preston, kitted out in aggressive red changed shirts, had other ideas. Preston were an experienced side that had been together for a long time. They had also made some useful late acquisitions, including ex-Doncaster hard-man John Bird, experienced goal machine Bobby Ham from Bradford City and former QPR and West Bromwich winger Clive Clark, who had given Fulham plenty of trouble on previous occasions.

Alan Ball senior, a tough and uncompromising manager, now managed Preston; he had an extra special reason for wanting to 'get one over' on Fulham, as he had been the manager of the Halifax team comprehensively thrashed 8–0 by Fulham the previous season.

The experienced and impeccable Graham Hawkins, along with the Preston back four, started cautiously and attempted to break up Fulham's rhythm. Fulham's early attempts to play considered football had little success against the determined Preston rearguard. The over-anxious forwards were being knocked out of their stride by quick and forceful tackling. Preston relied on quick breaks, forcing a corner from one. From this, the gallant Hawkins sent in a header that was inches wide of the post with the home defence beaten.

Fulham didn't heed that warning and they fell behind in the twenty-second minute. Stan Horne mis-kicked badly to donate Preston an unnecessary corner. Clive Clark switched wings to take the flag-kick, and his precise cross eluded several players in the Fulham goalmouth before the ball was met with a fine, diving header from Richard Heppolette at the far post that flew past Malcolm Webster into the Fulham goal. From that point the Fulham defence yielded virtually nothing.

A goal in front, Preston fell back to man-to-man marking: Jimmy Conway was being shackled by Jim McNab, and Steve Earle had two players marking him in the form of Hawkins and John Bird. Things looked more impressive when George Johnston freed Les Barrett down the left. His curling cross beat goalkeeper Alan Kelly but was headed out from underneath the bar by Heppolette before Earle and Barry Lloyd could react.

Fulham started to look edgy in defence and Preston began to look like the home side, attacking effectively. Webster made a point blank stop from Preston's Alan Spavin and Fred Callaghan did miraculously to speed back to head a shot from Bobby Ham off the goal line. The referee then lectured the normally mild-mannered Earle for lashing out at Preston's Alex Spark after being held back by the shirt. The half-time whistle came as a huge relief to the lethargic home side.

Even after a talking-to from the manager, Fulham's jitters continued into the second half as they persisted with the same type of play, and a rare mix-up between Reg Matthewson and Webster, following a Hawkins through ball, almost presented Preston with a second goal. Nippy forward Ham ghosted in between the two Fulham players and only just failed to turn the ball into an empty net.

Fulham then had their best spell. Earle hit one shot that brought a brilliant, diving save from Kelly, and Johnston hit another volley just wide with the keeper totally beaten. Barrett then broke away and put in a teasing centre that McNab cleared for a corner at the last minute.

The tired Fulham team were now clearly showing the effects of the searing, energy-sapping heat of the afternoon coupled with the draining emotion of the promotion match on the Wednesday. They were probing away but the attack carried little conviction or bite and the possibility of an equaliser looked distinctly remote.

In a final throw of the dice, Bill Dodgin sent on Vic Halom for Johnston with twenty minutes to go to add some height and weight to the attack. The change had an immediate effect and Preston were at long last forced to defend with some desperation.

Fulham's best chance of the match fell to substitute Halom just a few minutes from time. Barrett's cross from the left for once eluded the Preston defence and found Halom, on his own, ten yards out with the ball at his feet and just the goalkeeper to beat. In a deathly hush, Halom steadied himself and fired in a hard shot to the goalkeeper's right. The shot beat the goalkeeper

So now for the championship trophy…? Les Barrett, top scorer for the season, fires in a shot against Preston, but finds this, like most on the day, blocked by the solid and resolute defence of the visitors. In front of a 26,000 crowd a tired Fulham just couldn't find an extra gear on the day, and North End deservedly took the match 0–1 amid a great deal of west London disappointment.

but also beat the post, ending up in the side netting. It would have been unfair to blame Halom for the miss, as he had hardly warmed up.

Fulham knew that the game was up; Preston, sensing Fulham's unease, decided that it was going to be their day and remained steadfast to the end; their tough, uncompromising and watertight defence held on to record a **0–1** win.

At the final whistle, Preston players openly celebrated with their supporters on the pitch, whilst Fulham were seemingly the bridesmaids yet again. The victory, although not securing the Lancashire side the championship, had guaranteed Preston promotion.

This had been a season where so many of the young Fulham side had grown to be men, but on this particular day, the very experienced Preston team had made Fulham look like the boys. They had too much in the locker once they had extinguished Fulham's initial fire. The home defeat was hard to swallow but Preston had played very well on the day and had thoroughly deserved their victory.

Despite promotion there was an extremely muted and disappointed atmosphere on the terraces. The supporters were shattered in disbelief; champagne remained corked, torn-up programmes littered the terraces and many just sat on the terraces staring blankly, many weeping. This was Fulhamish in the extreme; after engineering themselves into a virtually unassailable position, Fulham had blown the one final match, even though just one point would have sufficed.

Despite the agonising defeat, several hundred Fulham supporters remained at the ground and converged on the Cottage for a glimpse of the Fulham team. So disappointed were the team that almost an hour elapsed before they came out to acknowledge the waiting throng.

One significant face, however, was missing from this balcony celebration – Bill Dodgin. He refused to come to the Cottage balcony for a personal appearance, reflecting just how upset he was and just how badly he personally had taken the defeat. Some time later he said: 'I have never lost my temper like it. At half time I really gave the team some stick. It was a real roasting, and why not? It was their big day and they threw it away. They were far too cocky and casual and were surprised when I tore into them. It was important to finish off just right. The championship would have been a big booster to start off next season. Now one or two will start worrying if we are really good enough. ... It was an anti-climax for us; they saved their worst performance for the biggest occasion.'

Dodgin's mood contrasted starkly with that of Preston boss Alan Ball, who kissed the Cottage pitch as he shared in a champagne celebration. He revealed that his wife had recently left him to stay with her mother because of the stresses of competing for the championship. He said: 'At least my wife can come back to me now. Two months ago she just had to go to her mother's because all this has made me a pig to live with. I've lost many friends as well.'

This victory took Preston to within one point of Fulham, so the Cottagers could still win the championship, but fate had now taken it out of Fulham's hands. Fulham had a far superior goal average, so Preston would *have to* win their final match to deny Fulham the title. On this display, however, few expected that Preston would slip up now.

Fulham's optimistic dream of snatching the championship finally went up in smoke just three days later. Preston won their final fixture with Rotherham United 3–0 at Deepdale and the first prize was theirs. It had been a very sad end to a very exciting season.

The champagne bottles remain unopened, and the camera lies still, the terracing now empty and quiet. A Fulham supporter with her heroes' names emblazoned on the scarf, is pensive and sad, the post-Preston mood hard to bear.

Dodgin's final words on the season were: 'This time last year I said that we would win promotion this season because we had re-established a winning attitude. We took twenty-nine points from nineteen games [in 1969–70], and we would have gone up if our run had begun earlier. So I had the basis and built on it.

'The team's average age was brought down a lot and I made Barry Lloyd captain at twenty-one. Why? I don't know; it just seemed like the right choice. In football you do more by sensing things than reasoning them. You buy a player like George Johnston when other people don't want to know, and it turns out right.

'My father being manager of Bristol Rovers has obviously helped. He's been a manager since I was fourteen, so I heard about all the political intrigue you have to cope with. But knowing about it and coping with it are different things so I have had to learn and I have made mistakes.

'I think we can do well in the Second Division. We don't want to go into the Second Division and struggle. We want to regain our rightful place in the First Division. I believe we have the right blend to go further, but I need several players to serve as first-team cover.

'I need some players, but everyone is looking to strengthen their sides, and you can spend £100,000 and find you've bought rubbish! You can't buy success; success in the league is just the icing on the cake. At the moment I have no specific players in mind. We shall follow up reports on players we have recently had checked by our scouts – it's pointless winning promotion unless we can stay up.

'We'll find it much tougher than the third [division]. Division Two football is faster and is also a bit more physical. Opposition players are quicker to get in close, you've got to think and act that bit faster. We're going into the Second Division to establish ourselves, and by that I mean finishing high in the table. Fulham are capable of doing this, and all things being equal, I'm sure we'll get established.'

Skipper Barry Lloyd pointing at the results against Second Division opposition reinforced the point: 'Look, these results speak for themselves. We played three Second Division sides in the League Cup, and beat all of them, scoring four goals and conceding none. True we lost to Bristol City in the fifth round after a replay, but surely we had made our point by then. We were capable of taking on and beating Second Division sides. I have no possible doubts that we can do more than survive. We shall be challenging for the top next season.

'It's a challenge I think I shall enjoy. I'm certain my own play has improved since Bill Dodgin appointed me captain at the start of last season. Bill obviously had faith in my qualities as a leader; I'm grateful to him. His confidence helped me to believe in myself.

'We must aim for twenty points from our first fifteen matches [next season] that will leave us well placed. We will be playing against a better class of player, and that will suit us fine. If the opposition allows us to play then we can really turn it on. In the Third Division we often had to play in front of crowds of just a few thousand, and it was not easy to find all of your enthusiasm. But when we played against Second Division clubs in the Cup, it was another world.'

After the dust had settled, Fulham were awarded a civic reception at Fulham Town Hall and over a hundred supporters arrived to greet the team. Most of the first-team squad and their partners attended the Sunday event. Tommy Trinder led Barry Lloyd and the squad up to greet and shake hands with the Mayor. As part of his speech, Trinder said: 'We promise you that if effort and hard work come into it, we will be back again to celebrate our rise back into the First Division.'

Earlier Cllr. Gordon Field had stated: 'Good teams don't just happen; they are built from a combination of circumstances: a strong board [of directors] with trust in their manager who in turn has the complete loyalty of his players who in turn have the ability to supply his methods. I hope that this celebration today is merely a rehearsal for next year where we hope you will attain promotion to the First Division, which, I am sure, is your rightful place.'

Alderman Bill Smith, leader of the council, although a Queens Park Rangers supporter, declared: 'There is no doubt that Fulham have proved that they have the talent, and we hope they get back to the First Division where they rightly belong. ... It was a tragedy when Fulham went down to division two from division one in 1968, and kept on going straight to division three, but now Fulham are on the way up again.'

To acknowledge promotion officially, the Mayor of Fulham held a reception at Fulham Town Hall, just down the road from Chelsea's ground. In the centre of the picture, highlighted by the spring sunshine, is chairman Tommy Trinder.

Barry Lloyd, intoxicated with optimism, confidently predicted: 'I am sure that we will finish in the top eight next season. The pressure will be off the side next term, and the bigger gates at the Cottage will spur us on. I was always confident that Fulham would win promotion, we were never lower than fourth, but we were lucky not to have many injuries.

'Steve Earle, Malcolm Webster and Jimmy Conway were the only ones out for spells. Four new players would strengthen the team squad, and protect us if we had a run of knocks like Chelsea did. I am shattered after playing in all fifty-three games, and looking forward to a long break before the training starts again in July.'

Stan Brown reckoned that team spirit had carried Fulham through, and this was mainly due to Bill Dodgin and Terry Medwin. He said: 'The trouble with Fulham in the past has been that we have never had a manager long enough. New managers bring with them new ideas, and we have to start all over again. But now we are all very settled.'

A final comment from Steve Earle cemented the evening. He stated that he was happy now that Fulham had won promotion and that he was happy to stay on at Craven Cottage, quashing any rumour of a move to either Chelsea or Queens Park Rangers, but then added impishly, 'Bill Dodgin told me the club was not going to sell me anyway!'

The long season would not finish for Bill Dodgin's number two Terry Medwin; he had been invited to accompany the Welsh squad as trainer/coach on a trip to New Zealand during the summer. After all his good work, it was good to see that his efforts for Fulham had been noticed and rewarded. Bill Dodgin paid tribute to his partner's work: 'No doubt I will get much of the credit for going up, but running a team is a two-man job. I think I helped a bit when Millwall and QPR went up, but I don't know what I would have done without Terry this season.'

The club's own celebrations took place at the Churchill Hotel, and after speeches, an excellent meal and some champagne, the serious business of dancing and checking fashion took place without a hint of embarrassment. Pictured in the foreground are George Cohen and Ian Seymour. It would be unkind to suggest that Ian was demonstrating how he fumbled the last shot...

June 1971

At this time

* A cholera epidemic was out of control in India.
* British Rail approved plans for the development of a high-speed Advanced Passenger Train (APT).
* Joe Gormley defeated Mick McGahey to become president of the National Union of Mineworkers (NUM).
* Terence Rattigan was awarded a knighthood.
* Local authorities protested at Education Secretary Margaret Thatcher's decision to end free school milk.
* Dom Mintoff won the general election in Malta and immediately scrapped the defence treaty with Britain.
* The Government announced that it would expand Britain's motorways by 1,000 miles by the 1980s.
* The Supreme Court cleared boxer Muhammed Ali of draft dodging.
* Three Russian cosmonauts were found dead in their capsule in *Soyuz XI* after an apparent normal re-entry and landing.
* The EEC agreed terms for Britain's entry.
* The broadcasting pioneer Lord Reith died.

'I Did What I Did For Maria' by Tony Christie topped the charts.
The film 'Carnal Knowledge' was released.

How the league was *won*

Preston North End's two late wins, including the victory at promoted Fulham, enabled the Lancashire side to leapfrog the Cottagers to snatch promotion and the championship. The season's unlikely heroes, Halifax Town, finished admirably, in third place, just four points off a promotion place. Aston Villa recovered slightly to take fourth spot, with Chesterfield in fifth place. Bristol Rovers finally finished in a slightly disappointing sixth place.

Along with the already relegated Gillingham and Doncaster Rovers were Bury. The final relegation spot was dramatically delivered to Reading, the team on the 'glass mountain', who had slipped alarmingly in the final two months of the season, having at one stage been eighth! Walsall luckily survived on goal average, along with Bradford City who were just one point clear of the drop zone.

The events

During the month Fulham Football Club formally announced the long-awaited news regarding the construction of what was known as the 'Riverside Stand' (It had no official name yet.) The scheme, originally mooted two seasons previously, was now going to become a reality.

The original cost two years ago had been estimated at around £150,000. Although no definite costs were publicly available, there were rumours circulating that these costs had already risen to around £250,000. There had been a sharp increase in the cost of building materials and labour and these costs were rising by an estimated 1% per month. Any further delays to this ambitious project were likely to prove fatal.

On a sentimental note, the new stand would see the removal of the famous white masts and flags that had flown alongside the riverside terrace for so long. The famous tower tea bar and the electronic half-time scoreboard would also disappear, but there were hopes that this popular facility could be retained and re-housed elsewhere within the ground, possibly within the Hammersmith end terrace.

General manager Graham Hortop said: 'This [new stand] could really be the making of Fulham. We are proving to our supporters that we are prepared to have all the facilities First Division clubs have. Today's public are looking for comfort, and are prepared to pay for it. We have to give them value for money. We have to educate people that football is not just a sport for men, but for all of the family.'

The stand would provide seated accommodation for 5,000 spectators, cutting Fulham's maximum capacity by 2,500 down to 42,500. It was hoped that the stand would be ready for opening sometime in November 1971. No decision had been made regarding admission prices to the new stand.

There were further rumours circulating that after this ambitious project had been completed, Fulham would look to the Putney end of the ground and construct a stand there as well, housing amongst other facilities dressing-rooms and a gymnasium.

Straight after the season ended, work began on the new riverside stand. It was a final goodbye to the flagpoles, still standing in this picture, and the half-time tea-bar. The electronic scoreboard which had stood atop the tea-bar would also disappear temporarily, but would emerge later, housed in the Hammersmith End terrace.

1970-71 Season Summary

Fulham fell short of Bill Dodgin's ambitious points total target by four points but despite this gained promotion to the Second Division. In the end, Fulham achieved just five more points than the previous season. The total of sixty was the highest ever achieved by the club, albeit this season over forty-six games. It was, however, disappointing to have been pipped at the post by Preston North End and statistics show that Fulham, as usual, squandered seven points out of twenty against the bottom five clubs. Just one point from those seven would have secured the championship.

With respect to goals scored, *five* players amazingly were able to get into double figures for the season, and one just short. Les Barrett top scored, his best season ever, with eighteen goals, Steve Earle notched fourteen, then three players, Jimmy Conway, Vic Halom and George Johnston, each scored ten. Barry Lloyd also netted nine. These six players netted seventy-one goals between them, well over 90% of the season's total.

Fulham actually scored *fewer* goals in their promotion season than they did the previous season, seventy-seven against eighty-four. This season the team failed to score in just ten of the fifty-three matches played, less than 20%. By scoring slightly fewer goals this time around, they were beaten by a whisker to a second successive place in the Watney Cup, Halifax Town and Wrexham receiving the honours this time around.

In truth, however, despite Bill Dodgin's attacking philosophy, Fulham's success this season had really been built around the defence. The defence had conceded just forty-four goals in fifty-three matches, five of those games against opposition from a higher division. This was an improvement on the previous season's exceptionally good defensive record by almost 30%.

Fulham conceded more than two goals in a match just *four* times in the space of fifty-three matches. If Fulham's 'worst' four defensive games of the season were taken into account (thirteen in four games) and removed from the figures, the results show that in the other forty-nine games Fulham conceded just thirty-one goals (0.63 per game). They had kept an incredible twenty-four clean sheets in the entire season (over 45% of the matches played). Fulham had won a number of fixtures by the slimmest one-goal margin.

In the league only Aston Villa had been able to register more than one goal at the Cottage, and in twenty-eight home games played that season in the league and both cup competitions, Fulham had conceded just *fourteen* goals, losing only twice. After the New Year, Fulham conceded a mere four goals at the Cottage.

Away from the Cottage, Fulham had been impressive at the start and the end of the season, but in the middle period had won just three and lost seven out of twelve matches played, a statistic that would have to improve in the Second Division.

Although the limelight had frequently tended to fall on the goalscoring forwards, often, particularly in the middle part of the season, the defence had been responsible for pulling Fulham out of trouble. Jimmy Dunne had performed brilliantly in his first season, tough and resolute; certainly he was the 'missing link' that Bill Dodgin had wanted. The wise Reg Matthewson had also been the kingpin of the defence, frequently lauded by the press for his experience, timing and overall organisation of the back four.

Despite his lack of height, Malcolm Webster, especially away from home, had had many fine games, winning many matches virtually on his own. He had been brave and commanding, settling his defensive colleagues when necessary. These three players had been readily backed up by the experienced Stan Brown and Fred Callaghan who had performed consistently well all season.

The line-up had been a very stable one – in fact, for the majority of the season, the team had revolved around just *thirteen* players: Webster, Moreline, Pentecost, Callaghan, Brown, Matthewson, Dunne, Conway, Johnston, Halom, Earle, Lloyd and Barrett. In all, twenty-one players were used, but the residual eight players mustered just thirty-five games between them.

The tired squad were very fortunate to scrape through without many serious injuries, running on empty for the latter parts of the season. In the three months from the beginning of December to the end of February, Fulham played just eleven league games. In the *two* months from the beginning of March to the beginning of May, Fulham played fifteen league matches, *a third of their fixture list!* Reading, Gillingham and Brighton had been the nearest away trips, and there had been many wearying journeys to the north and west; there had been *no* other London clubs at all in the Third Division that season! Next season, Fulham could look forward to derby matches against QPR, Charlton Athletic, Millwall and Orient, with Luton and Watford also on the doorstep.

Skipper Barry Lloyd and Les Barrett were 'ever present' during the season, playing in all fifty-three games; Jimmy Dunne and Fred Callaghan missed only one match each, and Reg Matthewson and Steve Earle missed just four matches. All the regular thirteen players had played in at least half of the matches.

Fulham now possessed a fine blend of youth and experience which could only become better. Fulham had to look forward pretty quickly, however, as Reg Matthewson was now thirty-two, and Stan Brown, who had made his 350th appearance during the season, was approaching thirty. Up front, the squad looked as if it needed one more forward with height and power, capable of scoring fifteen goals a season.

Fulham's disciplinary record had also been exemplary, with just three cautions registered against their name *all season*. This was the third successive season in which Fulham had not had a player dismissed. This had won the team a very high rating in the Ford sponsorship table, putting the team inside the top ten of all the league clubs. Unfortunately, with fewer goals being scored this year, the divisional award and prize money was awarded to Halifax Town.

A new Fulham had been born, but this team would have to be nurtured and progressed, as the Second Division would prove to be a much tougher proposition all round. The club had to realise that the tiny first team squad would need strengthening in terms of both quality and quantity. There was also a commitment to build the new stand. Serious money would almost certainly need to be spent on new players. Would the club be able to meet both of these obligations? Would they push on from this firm base and consolidate with new blood, or would they adopt a wait and see policy, hoping that the current squad augmented by a couple more youngsters plucked from the reserves and juniors would be sufficient – **only time would tell.**

League Division Three - Season 1970-71 - Final Table

		P	W	D	L	F	A	W	D	L	F	A	Pts
1	PRESTON NORTH END	46	15	8	0	42	16	7	9	7	21	23	61
2	**FULHAM**	**46**	**15**	**6**	**2**	**39**	**12**	**9**	**6**	**8**	**29**	**29**	**60**
3	Halifax Town	46	16	2	5	46	22	6	10	7	28	33	56
4	Aston Villa	46	13	7	3	27	13	6	8	9	27	33	53
5	Chesterfield	46	13	8	2	45	12	4	9	10	21	26	51
6	Bristol Rovers	46	11	5	7	38	24	8	8	7	31	26	51
7	Mansfield Town	46	13	7	3	44	28	5	8	10	20	34	51
8	Rotherham United	46	12	10	1	38	19	5	6	12	26	41	50
9	Wrexham	46	12	8	3	43	25	6	5	12	29	40	49
10	Torquay United	46	12	6	5	37	26	7	5	11	17	31	49
11	Swansea City	46	11	5	7	41	25	4	11	8	18	31	46
12	Barnsley	46	12	6	5	30	19	5	5	13	19	33	45
13	Shrewsbury Town	46	11	6	6	37	28	5	7	11	21	34	45
14	Brighton and Hove Albion	46	8	10	5	28	20	6	6	11	22	27	44
15	Plymouth Argyle	46	6	12	5	39	33	6	7	10	24	30	43
16	Rochdale	46	8	8	7	29	26	6	7	10	32	42	43
17	Port Vale	46	11	6	6	29	18	4	6	13	23	41	42
18	Tranmere Rovers	46	8	11	4	27	18	2	11	10	18	37	42
19	Bradford City	46	7	6	10	23	25	6	8	9	26	37	40
20	Walsall	46	10	1	12	30	27	4	10	9	21	30	39
21	READING	46	10	7	6	32	33	4	4	15	16	52	39
22	BURY	46	7	9	7	30	23	5	4	14	22	37	37
23	DONCASTER ROVERS	46	8	5	10	28	27	5	4	14	17	39	35
24	GILLINGHAM	46	6	9	8	22	29	4	4	15	20	38	33

1970–71 Season's Results

Watney Cup	*Sat, August 1*	*H*	*Derby County*	*L (aet)*	*3–5*	*Halom 2, Earle*	
	Sat, August 15	A	Barnsley	W	1–0	Barrett	8,805
FL Cup 1	*Wed, August 19*	*H*	*Orient*	*W*	*1–0*	*Conway*	*10,975*
	Sat, August 22	H	Swansea City	W	4–1	Earle 2, Halom, Dunne	10,384
	Sat, August 29	A	Walsall	L	2–3	Halom, Lloyd	6,176
	Wed, September 2	H	Bradford City	W	5–0	Conway, Earle, Halom, Lloyd, Barrett	10,328
	Sat, September 5	H	Chesterfield	W	2–0	Earle, Lloyd	13,175
FL Cup 2	*Wed, September 9*	*A*	*Darlington*	*W*	*4–0*	*Barrett 2, Halom, Conway (pen)*	*8,324*
	Sat, September 12	A	Rochdale	W	2–1	Barrett, Conway	4,791
	Sat, September 19	H	Doncaster Rovers	D	1–1	Conway	13,642
	Wed, September 23	H	Brighton and Hove Albion	W	1–0	Lloyd	13,856
	Sat, September 26	A	Preston North End	D	1–1	Dunne	12,105
	Mon, September 28	H	Tranmere Rovers	W	2–0	Halom, Brown	10,968
	Sat, October 3	H	Plymouth Argyle	D	1–1	Earle	13,334
FL Cup 3	*Tues, October 6*	*H*	*Queens Park Rangers*	*W*	*2–0*	*Barrett, Halom*	*31,729*
	Sat, October 10	A	Shrewsbury Town	W	1–0	Barrett	6,415
	Sat, October 17	H	Barnsley	D	1–1	Lloyd	12,952
	Wed, October 21	A	Reading	D	1–1	Halom	14,169
	Sat, October 24	H	Halifax Town	W	3–1	Lloyd, Morton, Earle	10,749
FL Cup 4	*Tues, October 27*	*H*	*Swindon Town*	*W*	*1–0*	*Earle*	*22,576*
	Sat, October 31	A	Torquay United	L	1–3	Johnston	7,598
	Sat, November 7	H	Bury	W	2–1	Lloyd, Barrett	9,390
	Mon, November 9	A	Port Vale	W	1–0	Lloyd	8,292
	Sat, November 14	A	Rotherham United	D	1–1	Johnston	9,398
FL Cup 5	*Tues, November 17*	*H*	*Bristol City*	*D*	*0–0*		*16,281*
FA Cup 1	*Sat, November 21*	*H*	*Bristol Rovers*	*L*	*1–2*	*Johnston*	*13,921*
FL Cup 5R	*Tues, November 24*	*A*	*Bristol City*	*L*	*0–1*		*23,249*
	Sat, November 28	H	Aston Villa	L	0–2		16,021
	Sat, December 5	A	Mansfield Town	L	0–1		8,051
	Sat, December 19	A	Swansea City	L	1–4	Johnston	10,625
	Mon, December 28	H	Gillingham	W	1–0	Halom	7,071
	Sat, January 2	A	Wrexham	D	2–2	Barrett, own goal	9,712
	Fri, January 8	A	Tranmere Rovers	W	3–0	Barrett 2, Halom	4,619
	Sat, January 16	H	Reading	D	1–1	Earle	10,141
	Sat, January 30	A	Aston Villa	L	0–1		33,343
	Sat, February 6	H	Mansfield Town	D	0–0		9,374
	Sat, February 13	A	Bristol Rovers	W	1–0	Conway	18,875
	Sat, February 20	H	Port Vale	W	4–1	Barrett 2, Earle 2	10,389
	Fri, February 26	H	Torquay United	W	4–0	Barrett 2, Conway, Matthewson	13,012
	Tues, March 2	H	Bristol Rovers	W	2–1	Earle, Johnston	15,871
	Sat, March 6	A	Halifax Town	L	1–2	Johnston	8,019
	Wed, March 10	A	Brighton and Hove Albion	L	2–3	Conway, Johnston	14,413
	Sat, March 13	H	Rotherham United	W	1–0	Earle	9,627
	Wed, March 17	H	Wrexham	W	1–0	Barrett	8,856
	Sat, March 20	A	Bury	L	0–2		4,121
	Fri, March 26	A	Chesterfield	D	0–0		13,370
	Sat, April 3	H	Walsall	W	1–0	Barrett	8,429
	Wed, April 7	H	Rochdale	W	2–0	Earle, Conway (pen)	10,054
	Sat, April 10	A	Gillingham	W	3–1	Barrett, Johnston, Conway	9,367
	Mon, April 12	A	Plymouth Argyle	D	1–1	Halom	11,712
	Sat, April 17	H	Shrewsbury Town	D	0–0		12,702
	Sat, April 24	A	Doncaster Rovers	W	1–0	Earle	4,399
	Wed, April 28	A	Bradford City	W	3–2	Johnston 2, Lloyd	6,430
	Sat, May 1	H	Preston North End	L	0–1		25,774

1970–71 Season

APPEARANCES (maximum 53):

Football League Division 3: Lloyd 46, Barrett 46, Dunne 45, Callaghan 45, Matthewson 43 (+1), Earle 42, Webster 35, Brown 35 (+1), Halom 30 (+5), Conway 29, Moreline 28 (+1), Johnston 25 (+1), Pentecost 22 (+1), Seymour 11, Richardson 9 (+7), Horne 8 (+1), Tranter 3, Davidson 1, Morton 1, Roberts 1, Mansley 1.

FA Cup: Lloyd 1, Barrett 1, Dunne 1, Callaghan 1, Matthewson 1, Earle 1, Brown 1, Halom 1, Seymour 1, Johnston 1, Pentecost 1.

FL Cup: Lloyd 6, Barrett 6, Dunne 6, Callaghan 6, Earle 6, Halom 6, Matthewson 5, Brown 5, Pentecost 4, Webster 3, Moreline 3, Seymour 3, Conway 2, Richardson 2, Morton 2 (+1), Horne 1, Davidson (1 Sub).

TOTAL: Lloyd 53, Barrett 53, Dunne 52, Callaghan 52, Matthewson 49 (+1), Earle 49, Brown 41 (+1), Webster 38, Halom 37 (+5), Conway 31, Moreline 31 (+1), Pentecost 27 (+1), Johnston 26 (+1), Seymour 15, Richardson 11 (+7), Horne 9 (+1), Tranter 3, Morton 3 (+1), Davidson 1 (+1), Roberts 1, Mansley 1.

GOALSCORERS (all competitions):

Barrett 18, Earle 14, Conway 10, Halom 10, Johnston 10, Lloyd 9, Dunne 2, Matthewson 1, Brown 1, Morton 1, own goals 1. (Total: 77.)

Note: Statistics exclude the Watney Cup match with Derby as it was designated an unofficial competition.

Captain Barry Lloyd was ever present during the season. Les Barrett was also ever present as well as top goalscorer.

July 1971

At this time

* John Newcombe beat Stan Smith in the men's singles final at Wimbledon.
* Evonne Goolagong was the surprise winner of the ladies' singles final.
* Crash helmets became compulsory for motorcyclists.
* A youth was killed in the worst rioting for two years in Londonderry.
* Lee Trevino won the British Open golf tournament.
* Seven explosions rocked Belfast City centre.
* *Apollo XV* was launched.
* In Yugoslavia, President Tito was elected for a further five years.
* 162 died in Japan in the worst-ever recorded plane crash.
* The first heart and lung transplant was carried out by Christian Barnard in South Africa.
* *Apollo XV* landed on the lunar surface, and two men, David Scott and James Irwin, drove on the moon in their moon buggy.
* Singer and trumpeter Louis Armstrong died.

'Chirpy, Chirpy, Cheep, Cheep' by Middle of the Road topped the charts.
The film 'Sunday Bloody Sunday' was released.

Early August 1971

At this time

* MPs approved the Industrial Relations Bill.
* *Apollo XV* returned to Earth safely.
* Edward Heath led Britain to victory in the Admiral's Cup.
* NATO pulled bases out of Malta.
* Harvey Smith won, but was disqualified from, the British Showjumping derby for giving a 'two-fingered gesture'.
* Riots flared in Ulster as internment was introduced.
* 7,000 homes of both Protestants and Catholics were burned down by gunmen.
* The provisional IRA threatened to start bombing the UK mainland.

'Get It On' by T-Rex topped the charts.

The events

THE FULHAM board, management, team and relieved supporters were for once able to relax and reflect on the season's success and the significant progress made. Already the optimism for next season was building, and there was an air of eager expectation all around. All parties concerned with the club were rejuvenated and eagerly awaited next season's 'step-up'. It was the summer, and the current affairs are included here to retain the 'feel' of the 1971 period!

ASHWATER
PRESS